Preface

This book is being published at a time when economic geography is expanding its primary focus from local and regional scales of analysis to national and global ones. When the writing of this book began, only a small amount of work on the international economy was being done by geographers or from a geographical point of view. Since that time, however, more geographers, and some economists for that matter, have been studying and writing on the international economy from a geographical perspective. This book, therefore, is being published at a time when economic geography is returning to its roots in international analysis. Increasing attention by geographers to the international scale is timely because it parallels growing popular and political interest, even in the United States, in the international economy. Not too long ago, items such as foreign trade balances and exchange rates were found only in specialized financial and economic publications. Now they often provide the substance of the front page in daily newspapers.

Geography's return to the international scale is timely not because it's fashionable but because geographical analysis of the international economy can produce insights that matter. The international economy consists of flows between countries, and although the international scale of analysis may have been neglected by geographers for a while, the study of flows, in the context of spatial interaction, was not. To no small degree, the purpose of this book is to illustrate the applicability of the theory and methods of economic geography to the international economy.

The book, then, is something of a hybrid. It draws on style of analysis and takes some substance from the geographical literature, but much of the material cited and discussed was first presented in scholarly literature primarily intended for students of economics and business. As a text, the book is designed to best serve students in advanced undergraduate and beginning graduate courses in economic geography. It should be useful not only for major coursework, but also in courses designed to contribute to the growing number of international studies programs, and in courses that serve to add an international dimension to business curricula. Ideally, students in courses using this book will be prepared with both introductory general geography courses and an introductory course in economic geography. The book provides sufficient background in these areas, however, so that such courses are suggested preparation rather than true prerequisites.

Many people have contributed, directly or indirectly, to the writing and publication of this book. Direct contributions were made by students in the Geography of Economic Development course at the University of Connecticut who used the book in manuscript form and gave me good advice on its content and style. External readers of all or part of the book included Rodney Erickson of The Pennsylvania State University, Gary Gaile of the University of Colorado, Gerald Karaska of Clark University, Edward Malecki of the University of Florida, Robert Mancell of Eastern Michigan University, James McConnell of the State University of New York at Buffalo, Simon Milne of McGill University, and William Muraco of the University of Toledo. They offered good ideas over a very wide range of opinions.

Other contributors include Richard "Gig" Giggey and Barry Harmon, both of John Wiley & Sons. Jimmy Houston, Roland Martin, and Dave Whitlock always provide good advice, as do Lee Wulff and Chester Tobin even after their deaths. The journal *Economic Geography* and The Ohio State University Press, publisher of *Geographical Analysis,* have granted permission to use some of my earlier work in this book.

The most important contributors to the whole enterprise were the members of my family. For their support throughout, I thank my parents Barbara and John. I am also thankful to the crowd that follows the Codfish Falls-Quimby circuit: Johanna, Sarah, Mary Caitlin, Emily, Ruby, Molly, and especially my wife Maureen, to whom the book is dedicated.

THE INTERNATIONAL ECONOMY:

A GEOGRAPHICAL PERSPECTIVE

. . .

Dean M. Hanink
University of Connecticut

JOHN WILEY & SONS, INC.
New York   Chichester   Brisbane   Toronto   Singapore

ACQUISITIONS EDITOR Barry Harmon
MARKETING MANAGER Catherine Faduska
PRODUCTION EDITOR Sandra Russell
MANUFACTURING MANAGER Andrea Price
ILLUSTRATION COORDINATOR Ed Starr

This book was set in 10/12 Sabon by TCSystems, Inc.

Library of Congress Cataloging in Publication Data:
Hanink, Dean M.
    The International economy : a geographical perspective / Dean M.
Hanink.
    Includes bibliographical references and indexes.

    1. International economic relations.   2. Economic development.
3. Economic geography.   I. Title.
HF 1359.H36   1993
337—dc20   93-6021
                                                                CIP

Printed in Singapore

10 9 8 7 6 5 4 3 2 1

Contents

CHAPTER 3   Models of Economic Growth and Development   57

CHAPTER 4   Spatial Interaction and Economic Development   79

CHAPTER 1

. . .

The International Economy from the Perspective of Economic Geography

. . .

1.1 INTRODUCTION

Different people can look at the same thing, a mountain for example, and see different characteristics. The differences in their perceptions can be attributed to a number of items, but it may be that the mountain is being viewed from different perspectives. The intent of this book is to examine selected aspects of the international economy from the special perspective of *economic geography*. As a field of intellectual inquiry, economic geography is primarily concerned with those economic relationships between places that can be generalized under the term *spatial interaction* (Wilson, 1989).

Systems of spatial interaction have two components: places that serve as origins and destinations of flows, and the flows themselves. With respect to the first component, any understanding of a system of spatial interaction requires consideration of the characteristics and conditions that lead to places generating and receiving particular flows. Analysis of current *locational patterns* and their determinants is an important step toward understanding spatial interaction in the economy. Frequently, this type of analysis leads to generalizations concerning the geography of multiple interrelated economic characteristics. Such generalizations, usually in the form of *economic regions,* are useful in both describing and analyzing systems of spatial interaction. With respect to the second component, any understanding of a system of spatial interaction requires consideration of the interconnections among places, called the system's *spatial structure.* Systems of spatial interaction are interesting and complex when considered in a static form. Such systems, however, are inherently dynamic because their flows can alter the places, and the subsequent changes in the places can alter the flows.

1.2 INTERNATIONAL ECONOMIC DEVELOPMENT, INTEGRATION, AND INTERACTION

Changes have thrust into prominence the reality of interdependence of all the members of the world community. Current events have brought into sharp focus the realization that the interests of the developed countries and the interests of the developing countries can no longer be isolated from each other; that there is close interrelationship between the prosperity of the developed countries and the growth and development of the developing countries, and that the prosperity of the international community as a whole depends upon the prosperity of its constituent parts.

This statement summarizes well the geographical perspective on economic development and the international economy. It effectively indicates that increased interaction between rich and poor countries is required not only in the interest of improving standards of living in the world's poorer countries, but also in the interest of maintaining the prosperity of the world's richer countries. International prosperity, or international economic development, is achieved by international economic integration, which can serve to diminish regional inequality at the global scale. The passage above, quoted by Fraser (1987, p. 533), is taken from the UN's Declaration and Program of Action on the Establishment of a New International Economic Order (NIEO), adopted by the General Assembly on May 1, 1974.

The NIEO was adopted as a resolution, but the evidence summarized here and provided in detail in the following chapters is that it has not been put into practice. Wide gaps in economic conduct and economic well-being still exist between the rich countries, or global economic Core, and the world's poorer countries, or global economic Periphery. While *globalization of the economy* is a commonly used phrase (Thrift, 1992), arguments have been made that *economic regionalization* is strengthening (Johnson, 1991; Nye, 1992), and true internationalization of economic activity is a selective prospect at best. Examples of the strength of regionalization are the growth of regional trading blocs, such as the European Community, and the growing prosperity of an East Asian regional economy centered on Japan (Funabashi, 1991). Ranking ten possible scenarios for a "new world order," O'Loughlin (1992) gave lower probabilities to those that were more integrative in nature and higher probabilities to those that had significant geographical segmentation of political and economic interests.

Certainly, regional problems and regional coalitions are important in international economic geography. The integration of regions within the broader international economy, however, can lead to improving standards of living that have the potential for ameliorating political and other regional conflicts. Currently, large-scale regional problems are many, and problems of integrating the parts of the former Soviet Union into the international economy have the potential to lead to a renewal of the Cold War (O'Loughlin, 1992). The most critical problem of regional integration within the international economy, however, remains Africa. The continent's low productivity in agriculture continues to drain its productive resources and limit its ability to develop a manufacturing sector that can compete internationally (Lemma and Malaska, 1989; Riddell, 1990). As described by Lewis (1977), low agricultural productivity limits the size of the domestic market and thereby limits a country's ability to trade. Africa's integration into the world economy is limited by its agricultural problems that have linked domestic and international implications.

In assessing the prospects for growth in the world's poorer countries, the World Bank (1991) described a worst-case scenario characterized by economic fragmentation. It includes, for example, a trade war among regional trading blocs and the collapse of the multilateral General Agreement on Tariffs and Trade (GATT). In addition, lack of macroeconomic coordination among Germany, Japan, and the United States creates high levels of uncertainty about inflation and exchange rates, and the concomitant rise in interest rates dries up the flow of financial capital from the Core to the Periphery. The World Bank's best-case scenario is characterized by increasing global economic interaction. A more integrated world financial system develops and capital flows from Core to Periphery are enhanced. The GATT evolves into a coordinating mechanism for trade among the emerging regional free-trade organizations. Again, increased interaction and integration are viewed as fundamental characteristics of global economic development.

Certainly, technological developments in communications and transportation systems that have helped make the world effectively smaller will continue to take place, and the spread of multinational corporations that serve to link places in the international economy will continue as well. These "enabling technologies," as Dicken (1986) termed them, continually improve the prospects for interaction in the international economy. They provide an infrastructure that supports international trade and investment as they lower transaction costs and improve the stock of knowledge of foreign markets. The pivotal question remains, however, whether interaction within the Core will continue to increase at a faster rate than interaction between Core and Periphery. As long as Core and Periphery have such limited interaction, segmentation of the global economy is maintained to the detriment of international economic development. The description and analysis of international economic spatial interaction is the purpose of this book.

1.3   THE SCALE OF ANALYSIS

The study of economic geography can take place at a number of scales, ranging from local to global. The scale of analysis emphasized in this book is national. That is, national states, or countries, are taken as the primary areal unit in the book's presentation of the spatial interactions that define the economic geography of the international economy. This scale is focused upon for two reasons. First, countries are the immediate building blocks of the international economy. The international economy is most easily observed as flows between national states. Second, and just as important, most national economic policies that affect and are affectd by international flows can be viewed realistically as having a uniform distribution across the space of the national states. In fact, political, legal, and economic systems are entities with sovereign countries as their primary geographical unit.

Two features of the international economy often blur the discrete characteristics of individual countries. One of these is the growth of multinational economic blocs, such as the European Community; the other is the widening spread of multinational corporations (MNCs). Despite their purpose of economic integration, regional blocs still consist of independent national units. The strength of a regional economic bloc is determined by its individual members. A regional bloc does not grant sovereignty to its members. To the contrary, the member countries grant powers to the bloc.

Inarguably, MNCs are prominent in the workings of the contemporary international economy. Flows that are internal to the multinational corporation account for a large share of international trade in goods, capital, and technology. Many MNCs effectively operate internal systems of spatial interaction over international markets for products, labor, capital, and knowledge. At the same time, many MNCs serve as types of conduits that facilitate and even direct other flows in the international economy.

Actions taken by MNCs drive the formation of national government policies. Such responses have been most visible in poorer countries concerned with domination by foreign interests in the form of multinational corporations. However, even the world's richest economies have concerns related to the taxation of MNCs and the employment and investment practices of these organizations. Indeed, MNCs frequently provide a very visible representation of the workings of the international economy because their local employment and investment decisions frequently are publicized as having been made in an international context.

It may be that MNCs and sovereign countries, ". . . play their locational games interactively . . ." (Berry, 1989, p. 1), but the countries have the home-field advantage. In fact, most of the interaction between multinational corporations and national governments actually is reaction by the former to the latters' exercise of fiscal, monetary, employment, and, occasionally, police power. It is true, however, that often the tables are turned.

The basic regional classification used in this book is that of rich North and poor South, or Core and Periphery, respectively. National income accounting figures, gross domestic product (GDP) and gross national product (GNP), are considered as the primary measures of national wealth. More precise classifications of rich and poor countries, the World Bank's four tiered income groups, are used throughout the book when illustrating the different characteristics of rich and poor countries and their differences as sources and destinations of flows in the international economy. Countries are classified within the income groups based on their per capita GNPs. Such measures of national income are not perfect correlates of economic development, but countries with higher per capita GDPs are considered to be better off than countries with lower values of per capita GDP.

1.4   THE ORDER OF TOPICS

One complexity of the international economy is the multilateral nature of its constituent flows. The flows between Canada and the United States, for example, have an effect on the flows between Canada and Japan. (Such multilateral flow effects can be characterized in a spatial interaction model over a matrix, as in the appendix.) Additional complexity is found in the international economy's spatial interaction because flows of goods between countries affect flows of capital which, in turn, affect flows of goods, and so on. Obviously, some partitioning of the full international economy is required if we are not to be overwhelmed. The approach taken in this book is, first, to consider the variable characteristics among countries that are important to generating international economic flows in general, and then to turn to the flows in particular.

Part I of the book, "Economic Growth and Development," provides a detailed yet selective view of national economies as a geographical set of discrete but interrelated markets. While disparity in national income separates rich countries from poor ones by definition, they are different in other important ways as well. They differ in human capital endowments, their sectoral shares of national income, demographic structure, and productivity. Productivity differences are marked particularly by low productivity of agriculture in poor countries and high productivity of services in rich countries. These and other differences among countries concern differences in economic development defined as a result, rather than as a process.

Economic development also can be analyzed as a process. Processes of economic growth and development are considered from a number of approaches. Longer-term views are considered in the contexts of environmental and cultural determinism, and as an economy's historical tendency toward modernization. Economic growth theories also are considered, from the crisis-ridden capitalism of Marx to the smoothly functioning neoclassical model. It is suggested that economic development is a process of integration: integration of the two sectors of the dual economy, integration of a country's social and income groups within the economy, and integration of a country's regions in a national economic space. Integration, like development, is both a process and a result.

In the context of the international economy, the economic growth and development of a country results from the successful integration of a mix of internal and external conditions. Trade, for example, has been called the "engine of growth," but a national economy cannot grow unless domestic institutions facilitate growth so that international exchange is used to broaden domestic resources as well as provide access to foreign markets. Spatial interaction models, such as the gravity model and the hierarchichal diffusion model, describe well the interdependence of internal and external conditions. Interregional growth multipliers indicate that large or rich economies are in better positions to benefit from external exchange than are small or poor ones. Drawn from pure economic theory, neoclassical models predict eventual balanced growth among the world's countries and the convergence of their national incomes. Pure spatial theory, which incorporates transfer and related costs of distance and tendencies toward economic agglomerations, predicts unbalanced growth as a result of market processes, with the rich getting richer and the poor getting poorer. Reality, of course, is somewhere in between.

Part II of the book concerns international financial flows. The neoclassical model of financial flows in a geographical economy is straightforward. Financial capital flows toward destinations of higher marginal return. The flow of financial capital, in turn, drives down those higher marginal rates until geographical equilibrium among rates of return is achieved. The neoclassical model is simple and elegant but does not appear to encompass the reality of international capital flows. Its failure to do so can be attributed largely to the relative immobility of financial capital in the international economy. Places of financial capital surplus do not interact fully with all places of financial capital deficit, so unequal rates of return are more persistent than expected.

Rates of return aside, the relative immobility of financial capital is surprising because the two dominant models of financial asset valuation, the portfolio model and the arbitrage model, indicate that gains are to be made by investing in international markets rather than just single, domestic ones. In the case of the portfolio model, portfolio risk reduction could be accomplished by diversifying assets internationally. In the case of the arbitrage model, the economic diversity of the international economy provides a geographical as well as sectoral basis for capital appreciation.

Both financial models and the general neoclassical model hold transaction costs as an implicit brake on the flow of financial capital. It does not matter if the transaction costs are current and known or anticipated and uncertain. They depress real rates of return on any single asset and thus can modify any portfolio's composition. The portfolio composition effects of transaction costs are typically more severe in international markets than in domestic ones. For example, domestic market transactions do not require currency exchange costs or raise uncertainty over exchange losses at the time of an asset's sale. Further, knowledge of foreign markets is usually more expensively obtained than knowledge of the domestic one.

Capital mobility is generally confined within the small set of the world's rich countries that comprise the Core. The Core provides the most opportunities for equity investment and is the greatest source of financial capital as well. Equity markets tend to be thin in the poorer countries on the Periphery, and their regulation by governments tends to be strict. Although segmentation is decreasing, Core financial markets are different than the financial markets on the Periphery, and the markets remain poorly integrated.

Debt markets as well as equity markets are segmented along the lines of Core and Periphery. Core debt finance is different than Periphery debt finance, with the private sector representing a much larger portion of Core borrowing and lending than on the Periphery. Debt finance in the Core that relies on the operations of money markets and corporate bond markets is not generally available on the Periphery. Peripheral debt finance more often revolves around transactions between multilateral lenders, such as the World Bank and the International Monetary Fund, and public sector borrowers.

Foreign direct investment, like other forms of financial capital, has its dominant source in the Core. Like equity investment, its destination is typically in the Core. Countries on the Periphery also are important destinations of foreign direct investment (FDI), but not to the same degree as the Core, and frequently FDI in the Periphery has different motives than FDI in the Core. One way to assess FDI's motives and resulting geography of destinations is in the context of least-cost location theory. The optimal location of foreign production can be determined by weighing the relative locational costs of a product's inputs and transportation and other costs of serving its market. Frequently, least-cost location theory seems able to account for FDI flowing from the Core to the Periphery, but intra-Core flows of FDI can conform to least-cost theory as well.

Least-cost location theory is most applicable to perfectly competitive product markets, but much of the international economy is characterized by less than perfect competition. Both monopolistic and oligopolistic competitive forms have been given as rationales for FDI as a means of maintaining market share on an international basis. Such FDI is most likely to be intra-Core, rather than flowing from Core to Periphery, and can frequently result in cross-investment by MNCs in each other's domestic market. MNCs exist, in fact, as conduits for international investment and exchange that integrate segmented national markets within a single enterprise.

Part III of the book concerns international flows of goods and services, or international trade. The flow of foreign investment of all types has been generally increasing, but the flow of goods and services in international trade is still the most important link among countries in the international economy. The dominant theory of international trade is based on international variations in comparative advantage of production resulting from international variations in factor endowments. This trade theory concerns differences among countries as the basis of trade. Its extensions concern the roles of differences in technology and economies of scale among countries. Recently, in response to factor endowment theory's inability to account for much of current real-world trade, an alternative trade theory has been developed. This new trade theory focuses on the similarities in demand structures among countries as the basis for trade. Rather than modifications, product differentiation, technological differences, and economies of scale are increasingly viewed as fundamental elements of international trade theory.

Despite differences in construction, all trade theories indicate that free trade is beneficial. In factor endowment theory, producers benefit from trade because production becomes more efficient and consumers benefit as prices decrease. In product differentiation models, free trade allows increased benefits for consumers who can buy greater and better varieties of products than those produced domestically. Unfortunately, the benefits of free trade that come about so quickly in theory are slow to be realized in practice. Due to different-sized economies, much of the competitive reaction of price equalization among countries is not the result of trade in goods. In addition, large differences in average incomes, factor endowments, scale economies, or technology among countries means that large quantities of noncompetitive goods enter into international trade.

Trade management practices are put into place by governments because existing trade patterns are taken to be unfair or simply not advantageous. The most common methods of trade management are the tariff and the quota, and many governments raise additional barriers to both imports and exports. The GATT has relied on international cooperation to facilitate free trade, but frequently regional coalitions are developed that do just the opposite. Cartels of commodity producers, such as the Organization of Petroleum Exporting Countries (OPEC), and regional trade blocs, such as the European Community, have resulted from special interests' promotion of particular product structures as well as geographical structures of trade. In addition, MNCs have developed internal systems of spatial interaction that manage trade toward their own special purposes.

Both the product structure and geographical structure of trade are considered as related characteristics that have a bearing on the effectiveness of trade in economic development. Currently, most international trade, like most capital flows, takes place within the set of rich countries that comprise the Core of the international economy. This pattern of trade is not surprising on the theoretical grounds of international trade in differentiated products, nor is it surprising in light of current practices of trade management. It seems that the best hope for poorer countries is to become more like those of the Core. Trade within the Periphery is growing, but major markets remain in the Core. Improving trade performance requires an integrated mix of domestic policy and economic adjustment that is focused on external relationships. This leads to the unhappy proposition that trade requires growth, but growth requires trade!

The book ends with an epilogue that reviews material presented earlier in the context of three critical events that illustrate the growing interdependence of the international economy. The events—the abandonment of the Bretton Woods currency system by the United States, the OPEC oil embargo, and the environmental summit held in Rio de Janeiro—are discussed briefly from the perspective of economic geography.

REFERENCES

Berry, B. 1989. "Comparative Geography of the Global Economy: Cultures, Corporations, and the Nation-State." *Economic Geography* 65: 1–18.

Dicken, P. 1986. *Global Shift: Industrial Change in a Turbulent World* (London: Harper & Row).

Fraser, R. 1987. *The World Financial System* (Burnt Mill, England: Longman).

Funabashi, Y. 1991. "Japan and the New World Order." *Foreign Affairs* 70/5: 58–74.

Johnson, H. 1991. *Dispelling the Myth of Globalization: The Case for Regionalization* (New York: Praeger).

Lemma, A., and P. Malaska, eds. 1989. *Africa Beyond Famine: A Report to the Club of Rome* (London: Tycooly Publishing).

Lewis, W. 1977. *The Evolution of the International Economic Order* (Princeton: Princeton University Press).

Nye, J. Jr. 1992. "What New World Order?" *Foreign Affairs* 71/2: 83–96.

O'Loughlin, J. 1992. "Ten Scenarios for a 'New World Order'." *The Professional Geographer* 44: 22–28.

Riddell, R., ed. 1990. *Manufacturing Africa* (London: James Currey).

Thrift, N. 1992. "Muddling Through: World Orders and Globalization." *The Professional Geographer* 44: 3–7.

Wilson, A. 1989. "Mathematical Models and Geographical Theory." In *Horizons in Human Geography,* edited by D. Gregory and R. Walford (Totawa, New Jersey: Barnes & Noble).

World Bank. 1991. *Global Economic Prospects and the Developing Countries* (Washington: World Bank).

ECONOMIC DEVELOPMENT AND NATIONAL WEALTH

PART I OF THIS BOOK CONSISTS OF THREE
chapters focusing on selected aspects of economic development, economic growth, and
national wealth and income. The discussion of economic development is presented first
so that level of national economic development can be used as a type of cause-and-effect
background for the international flows discussed in the remainder of the book. The view
taken here is that national economies provide a geographical matrix of discrete but
interrelated markets over which investment, production, and international trade take
place. As described later in the book, flows sometimes take place between countries
because they have similar markets, and sometimes because their markets are very
different. In turn, some international flows tend to induce similarities among national
markets; others tend to reduce similarities. Unfortunately, the international economy is
neither simple nor straightforward.

Chapter 2, "Measuring Economic Development and National Wealth," primarily
concerns quantitative assessments of a country's economy. This chapter explains some
of the different descriptive terms used in classifying the world's countries according to
their level of economic development. Measures of development and a country's national
income are described. The chapter ends with a description of the way that selected
economic and demographic characteristics vary among rich and poor countries.

Some perspectives on economic growth and development as an internal process are
described in Chapter 3, "Models of Economic Growth and Development." The potential
roles of the physical environment and culture are discussed first, followed by a description of models that treat economic development as an evolutionary process. Selected
theories of economic growth are briefly examined. The last part of the chapter concerns

various types of integration, both social and economic, as part of the process and condition of economic development.

The dynamic geography of economic growth and development is drawn out in Chapter 4, "Spatial Interaction and Economic Development." Processes of spatial inter-action are discussed in the context of the international economy, and the growth effects of exporting are described. The special problems of economic growth in a spatial econ-omy are considered. The chapter ends with a presentation of methods of measuring linkages and flows in the international economy.

CHAPTER 2

· · ·

Measuring Economic
Development and
National Wealth

· · ·

2.1   INTRODUCTION

The term *economic development* can be defined in two ways. One definition is that of
outcome, or state, and the other is that of process. The two definitions are linked,
however, because one's view of the appropriate outcome, or state of being developed,
determines one's view of the process. If the appropriate outcome is, for example,
socio-economic equity, then the salient processes toward that outcome may be
perceived as different than the salient processes toward, say, the achievement of a
particular level of national aggregate wealth. This chapter focuses on economic
development as outcome while the next two chapters focus on economic development
as process. As indicated in the use of the word "measuring" in the chapter's title, the
approach is one of quantifying a country's level of economic development and
wealth. The point of departure is a brief survey of the terms used to classify countries
according to their levels of economic development.

2.2   THE NOMENCLATURE OF RICH
AND POOR COUNTRIES

The World Bank (1992) currently divides the world's countries into four groups by
income: 1) low income, 2) lower middle income, 3) upper middle income, and 4) high
income. The distinctions are made on the basis of per capita gross national product,
or GNP (see Section 2.5). Low income countries are those with per capita GNP less

than U.S. $610; lower middle income, from $611 to $2465; upper middle income, from $2466 to $7619; and high income countries, per capita GNPs of $7620 or greater. Many similar types of global divisions by wealth have been made over time, and most have provided interesting descriptors in their categorizations. The poorer countries, in particular, have seen their descriptors evolve. Terms such as "backward" have given way to "lesser developed" and then to "developing" and "industrializing" (perhaps in the hope that wishing makes it so). A category with significant staying power, however, is *third world*.

The use of the term third world implies, of course, that there are at least two others. In fact, division of the globe into three worlds initially was a political categorization developed just after the end of World War II (Chilcote, 1984). The first world consisted of the industrial democracies that emerged victorious from the war, including the United States, the United Kingdom, and France. The phrase soon encompassed the newly created industrial democracies in western Europe, such as West Germany and Italy, and also Japan. The second world consisted of the centrally planned economies dominated politically, economically, and militarily by the Soviet Union, and the Soviet Union itself. The third world, in the original classification system, was a residual category containing those countries not encompassed in the first and second worlds. In the mid-1950s, the third world became closely identified with the nonaligned movement, led by the Yugoslavian leader Tito.

As the name implies, nonaligned countries were those following economic and political policy paths that were not fully consistent with those taken by either the first or second world countries. Yugoslavia, for example, was politically controlled by the Communist Party but relied on an economy based on a mix of central planning and market based allocations. In addition, it did not become a member of either the Warsaw Pact or NATO. The bulk of the nonaligned countries, unlike Yugoslavia, were recently independent colonies of European countries; like Yugoslavia, they were attempting a mix of political and economic policies that crossed ideological lines. Most of the nonaligned countries were, and are, poor, so the term third world soon took on a connotation of poverty.

In some respects, the evolution of the term third world coincided with the evolution of the United Nations. The initial role of the UN was basically that of a forum where political disputes could be settled peacefully rather than on the battlefield. The permanent members of the Security Council are the major powers on the winning side of World War II and were appointed permanently because they were considered to be the countries "that mattered" at the time. Since the UN's establishment, however, the number of countries that belong to the organization has grown dramatically, and the great majority of the newer members are those countries that once comprised the nonaligned movement, or third world. The common cause of the newer members is more relief of their poverty than peace, and much of the work in the UN's General Assembly has focused on economic development.

In 1974, the General Assembly passed a resolution calling for a New International Economic Order (NIEO). The NIEO, as designated, calls for a wholesale restructuring of the international economy in which the rich countries, regardless of their economic system, become active in contributing to the economic improvement

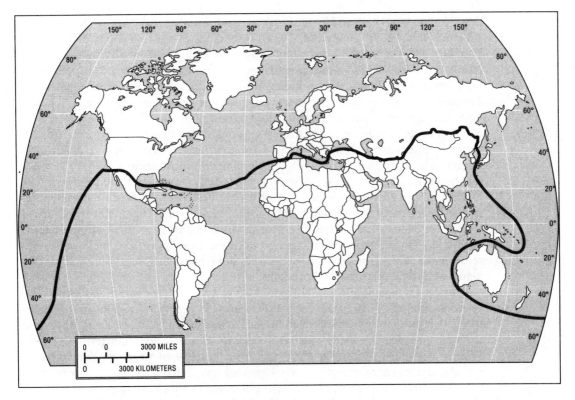

FIGURE 2.1   The "Brandt Map": North and South

of all poor countries (Bedjaoui, 1979). The baseline for the NIEO is a world divided simply into rich and poor, have and have-not, which indicated that the division between first and second worlds was considered meaningless in this context. From the NIEO we have a world divided into North and South (Brandt, 1980), not a wholly accurate geography, but a reasonably approximate geography of the rich North and poor South (Figure 2.1). The North-South division of the the globe is now the major one because the end of the Soviet Union has delivered the East-West, first world-second world distinction to history.

2.3   CORE, PERIPHERY, AND THE SINGLE WORLD ECONOMY

The UN's division of the world into North and South is not too different from an earlier conceptual division of the global economy into a rich *Core* and poor *Periphery*. The Core-Periphery categorization was initially described by Raul Prebisch, an

Argentinian economist, and by the German economist Andreas Predohl (Reitsma and Kleinpenning, 1985; Grotewold, 1979). In both cases, the categories of Core and Periphery were more than descriptive and were utilized for analyzing the role of international trade in economic development. The concepts of Core and Periphery are used here, as by Prebisch, at a global scale and are comprised of national units. Frequently, however, core-periphery relationships apply to subnational regional units that can cross national political boundaries.

A core region can be defined as an *agglomeration,* or spatial concentration, of vertically integrated industries and an associated service sector. In a vertically integrated system, producers sell goods largely to other producers in a chain of linkages that begins with raw materials, or roughly processed raw materials, and ends with the finished product for final demand. (Perhaps the best example of a completely integrated local production system is that of the Ford River Rouge plant in suburban Detroit, in which even the steel used for the plant's final product of automobiles is produced.) The existence of linkages between local producers and the local service sector make core regions virtually self-sufficient except in their need for nonlocal raw materials and markets for final products.

Peripheral regions also contain manufacturing, but not the sort that is locally and vertically integrated. The basis for manufacturing in peripheral regions may be local sources of raw materials, production for local consumer markets, or cheap labor used to make products for both local and external consumption (Grotewold, 1979). Peripheral regions produce a more specialized variety of products than do core regions, and in general peripheral economies are less diversified than core economies.

The different natures of core and peripheral economies have a profound effect on Core-Periphery trade. The Core can offer the Periphery a wide range of products and services for both its industrial and consumer sectors. In return, however, the Periphery can offer the Core only a limited range of low-cost consumer goods and raw materials either directly or in roughly processed form. While trade between core regions can be balanced, trade between Core and Periphery must always be unbalanced because of the disparity in production between the two regions. The unbalanced nature of trade between Core and Periphery was the primary concern of a number of Latin American economists, including Prebisch. In their view, the Periphery's terms of trade (the ratio of export to import unit values, or average prices) with the Core were not only expected to be poor, but to decline. Import penetration by the Core's products and services would eventually affect domestic producers' ability to compete with core producers even in the Periphery's domestic markets. The only reasonable policy response, in Prebisch's view, was that of protectionism, which would limit the Periphery's imports of core products and services and, combined with infrastructural improvements, encourage the growth of domestic production. (Trade protectionism is considered in detail in Chapter 10.)

The types of problems in Core-Periphery trade described by Prebisch and others are focused upon in a number of related *dependency* models of economic development that can be viewed as geographical analogs to Marx's work on economic class relations. The Marxist view is that capitalists, as a class, expropriate profit as surplus value from the working class (see Chapter 3). That is, the wealth of the capitalist derives from the efforts of the workers. The geographical analogy is easily made, that the wealth of the core economies is due largely to their ability to exploit peripheral economies. The Periphery is forced into an economic position that is wholly dependent upon its relationship to the Core. Historically, this dependency was formalized in the Core holding much of the Periphery in its colonial realm. While most of the former empires held by core countries have been dissipated, the dependency remains in the nature of international financial, trade, and political systems that underlie a neocolonial system.

Marx essentially ignored international relationships, but Lenin (1948) explored them intensively within a Marxist framework. He argued that the inevitable revolution caused by capitalist exploitation of workers could be delayed by imperialism, or the development of a colonial system. Capitalists in the colonizing countries could expropriate surplus value easily, but less visibly, from their colonies. Some of this colonial surplus value could offset less expropriation of domestic surplus value, and thereby be used as an ameliorating factor in the working class's ongoing interest in active class warfare. Frank (1979) has argued for the concept of "development of underdevelopment" in which economic growth takes place in the Core by appropriation of surplus from the Periphery. The appropriation of the Periphery's surplus is at such a rate that internal growth in peripheral economies is impossible. Frank's thesis on the relations between Core and Periphery are not too far removed from Prebisch's views, but Frank is less optimistic about the ability of the Periphery to develop as long as the Core exists. In opposition to the view that Core and Periphery represent two distinct types of economies, Amin (1974, 1977) and Wallerstein (1979) suggest that there is a single, capitalist world economy with a geographical division of labor. The regional distinctions between a single world economy and the more conventional Core and Periphery divisions are fairly subtle (Terlouw, 1989), and the world economy involves the same type of interregional exploitation that has been described in the context of the (other) dependency models.

2.4   CAN ECONOMIC DEVELOPMENT BE MEASURED?

Whether process is implied or not, terms such as Core-Periphery and North-South generally are used to distinguish the more economically developed from the less economically developed countries. In fact, economic development as a state is not easily defined in any precise way, so economic development as a state or condition of achievement probably never will be quantifiable in a single measure. If the distribution of wealth within the populations of all countries was consistent, then a measure such as per capita GNP would be more useful in describing differences and similarities in economic development among countries. However, income distributions vary widely across countries so per capita GNP reveals, at best, an incomplete picture of international differences in standards of living. Small differences in per capita GNP are effectively meaningless, but large differences accurately indicate real disparities in economic welfare.

Many efforts have been directed toward building measurements of economic development that can encompass a much wider variety of attributes than just national product alone. A study by Berry (1961) was a landmark of this type. Recently Berry's work was updated by Ginsburg, Osborn, and Blank (1986). Their analysis identified six complexes of variables for use in measuring economic development: 1) product and productivity, 2) technology and consumption, 3) population, 4) resource endowment, 5) accessibility and connectivity, and 6) external relations. Altogether, 75 individual variables were considered within the six complexes. In addition, two single-value indexes were defined for use in the geographical analysis of economic development. The first is a composite measure of national wealth; the second is a composite measure of growth potential.

The Ginsburg, Osborn, and Blank study focused on economic variables because it was designed to assess *economic* development. However, many related analyses take development as a concept that goes beyond the purely economic characteristics of a place. These consider a wider array of measures in quantifying development levels of countries. Tata and Schultz (1988) used this broad approach in a study that otherwise is similar to that by Ginsburg, Osborn, and Blank. Tata and Schultz considered 10 variables allocated over four systems: 1) physical, 2) economic, 3) social, and 4) political. Obviously, systems 1, 3, and 4 were meant to allow noneconomic characteristics to contribute to a country's measured development status.

Development, human welfare, quality of life, and similar constructs exhibit intranational geographical variation as well as international variation. Lloyd and Dicken (1972) examined regional differences in "economic health" over four countries; the United States, Canada, the United Kingdom, and France. They defined economic health in 11 variables allocated to one of five components: 1) personal income, 2) population, 3) employment changes, 4) unemployment, and 5) education. A temporal comparison (1970 and 1980) of interstate variation in American socioeconomic conditions was made by Berentsen, Brower, and Dinges (1987). Their study was fairly parsimonious in use of variables, with only five: 1) infant mortality, 2) per capita personal income, 3) unemployment, 4) adults with high school degree, and 5) households without telephone connection. They also derived a summary measure of well-being from the five original variables. Other intranational measurements of geographical disparities in human welfare include the work of Smith (1987), which is the most comprehensive study of this type in regard to scale. Using the variables and method similar to those used by Berentsen, Brower, and Dinges, Smith considered the geography of "inequality" within three countries; the United States, the Soviet Union, and the Republic of South Africa. In addition, he provided measurements of inequality at the scale of counties in the American South and at the local scale of census tracts within the city of Atlanta, Georgia.

Attempts at measuring development status at the international scale of analysis generally fall prey to some heavy criticism. For example, the Tata and Schultz study was attacked quite strongly by Yapa and Zelinsky (1989), who argued that development is too rich a concept to be measured in any meaningful way. In addition, they claimed that the variables chosen by Tata and Schultz for their measurements were the wrong ones. (This double criticism brings to mind the old Borscht Belt joke that the hotel's cuisine suffers in two ways; it tastes bad and the portions are too small.) Essentially, the entire development quantification problem is one of measurement without theory. Surely, development writ large or more narrowly defined in economic terms is a state that has many characteristics.

The concept of utility, as used in economic analysis, might provide a useful theoretical base for the contentious issue of measuring development. Briefly, utility in economic terms is a measure of satisfaction. The actions of households or individuals are explained by their attempts to maximize utility in the same way that the actions of firms are explained by their attempts to maximize profit. In the case of an individual tangible or intangible good, the total utility provided increases at a decreasing rate with its consumption. Total utility increases at a decreasing rate because successive increments of consumption provide successively lower increments of utility. This consumption-utility relation is called the *law of dimininishing marginal utility*. A trivial example is that of ice cream cone consumption. An individual's utility increment very likely will decrease as the number of cones consumed increases. The first ice cream cone provides more satisfaction than the second, the second more than the third, and so on. The marginal utilities of goods can be compared for the purpose of assessing value. If good X and good Y have the same price and provide equal levels of marginal utility, then X and Y have the same value. If good X provides one-half the marginal utility of good Y, then good X has one-half the value of good Y. Marginal contributions to utility provide a type of weighting system for making qualitative comparisons among goods or, for that matter, actions.

This type of utility analysis might be helpful in measuring development. For example, one of the variables used by Tata and Schultz (1988) to measure development was "radios/1000 population," which they employed as a surrogate measure of access to information. This variable contributes to development in a nondiminishing way in their study, so no distinction is made between the first and the nine hundred and ninety-first radio. There likely is some level of radio density, however, after which its contribution to development not only diminishes but vanishes. (Actually, their method is one of increasing marginal utility because they use standard deviation scores in their measuring system.) Another measure used by Tata and Schultz is infant mortality (infant deaths/1000 live births). The infant mortality and radio variables are not differentiated with respect to their relative contribution to development. However, the marginal contribution to improving human welfare by efforts to reduce infant mortality reasonably can be inferred to be greater than the marginal contribution from the same effort to increase the density of radios. Unless some type of utility theory context can be provided for defining and assessing development characteristics, international and even intranational measures of development should be viewed as exploratory rather than final.

The diminishing effect of per capita GNP on more general development characteristics is illustrated in an analysis conducted by Holloway and Pandit (1992). They measured the association between per capita GNP and a composite "physical quality of life index" (PQLI) comprised of three variables (Morris, 1979): infant mortality rate, literacy rate, and life expectancy at age one. The functional form of the association is PQLI = log (per capita GNP), so that PQLI increases rapidly with increases in per capita GNP at low levels, and then increases at a diminishing rate with increases in per capita GNP at high levels. Because of this sort of relationship, the UN limits the contribution of per capita GNP in its index of "human development" by capping its contribution at $5,000 (United Nations Development Program, 1990), which is defined as an adequate level of per capita national income. Other measures used to contribute to the index of human development were life expectancy, adult literacy rate, and purchasing power measured in American dollars. Purchasing power's influence on human development was limited by transforming its original value into logarithms, to capture the diminishing effect of material welfare on the more general summary measure.

Despite overall acceptance that measures of development must consider more than per capita GNP, the additional information has little bearing on most generalizations. For example, based on data taken from the World Bank (1992), the Spearman rank correlation of countries arrayed on per capita GNP and life expectancy is 0.886; per capita GNP and literacy, 0.828; and per capita GNP and purchasing power parity, 0.962 (see section 2.5). Given that perfect rank matches have a Spearman value of 1.000, any broad classification of countries based on per capita GNP alone would not differ in any fundamental way from a broad classification based on all four variables used by the UN. In fact, the relationships of average values of life expectancy, literacy, purchasing power, and per capita GDP (see Section 2.5) is systematic across the World Bank income groups (Table 2.1) as each increases from low income to high income in a fully consistent way.

TABLE 2.1   Mean Per Capita GDP, Life Expectancy, Literacy, and Purchasing Power by World Bank Income Group, 1990

Income Group	Mean Per Capita GDP[a]	Life Expectancy	Literacy	Purchasing Power[a]
All	5,132	63	68%	5,729
Low	301	52	47%	631
Low Middle	1,363	64	72%	3,815
High Middle	3,739	68	78%	6,171
High	19,005	76	94%	15,494

Source: World Bank, 1992. *World Development Report 1992* (New York: Oxford University Press).
[a] In $U.S.

2.5 THE STRUCTURE OF NATIONAL PRODUCT ACCOUNTS

Gross domestic product (GDP) is a measure of national income used in most *national accounts*. National accounting has a long history in the West where materialism has been a dominant cultural characteristic at least since the Renaissance. Early national accounts were developed in England and France in the seventeenth century. Contemporary national accounting procedures used by national governments with market-based economies, and by international agencies, owe much of their development on the theoretical side to John Maynard Keynes, and on the applications side to Simon Kuznets (Kendrick, 1972). The Keynesian view of national income is that it encompasses consumption, C, investment, I, and government spending, G, so that national product, NP, is defined as NP = C + I + G. Note the shift here between the terms "income" and "product." In fact, under standard national accounting procedures, the words effectively are synonyms. The national product can be measured in two ways. One is a flow-of-product measure in which the national income is taken as the money sum of the (annual) flow of final goods and services in an economy. The flow-of-product approach evaluates the national income at market prices. The other measure of national income relies on flow-of-earnings, which is the sum of factor earnings, such as wages and rents, that comprise the cost of producing final goods. Assuming accuracy in computation, flow-of-product and flow-of-earnings calculations yield the same figure because profits are treated as an earnings item. The accounting identity takes the form Price = Cost + Profit, with the price term taken from flow-of-product and the cost and profit values taken from flow-of-earnings.

The UN provides a standardized accounting system that facilitates comparison of national income on a country by country basis. The UN's system of product accounting is generalized in Table 2.2 and is used here to provide an outline for

TABLE 2.2   Structure of United Nations' National Income Accounts

A. + Consumption
B. + Gross Capital Formation
C. + Exports
D. − Imports
   = Gross Domestic Product (GDP)
E. + Net Factor Income from Abroad
   = Gross National Product (GNP)
F. − Consumption of Fixed Capital
   = National Income/Net National Product

Source: United Nations, 1986. *National Accounts Statistics: Analysis of Aggregates, 1983/1984* (New York: United Nations).

discussion of comprehensive national product accounting. National accounts are usually calculated both quarterly and annually, but annual values are more commonly used when international comparisons are made.

In Table 2.2, item A, Consumption, is the price-value of output of final goods and services consumed. Consumption includes payments to factors, such as wages, and profits. It also includes indirect taxes; a sales tax, for example, is considered an indirect tax. When a sales tax is paid, a portion of a product's or service's final price is paid to the government rather than to a producer. Direct taxes, on the other hand, are completely embedded in consumption prices. For example, an income tax is a direct tax on wages or company earnings. Payment of an income tax is simply a transfer payment to the government and not a separate contribution to national income. Other transfer payments, such as pensions, interest on long-term loans, or government subsidies to industry, are not considered to be additions to income, either. Additions to income must be payments to "currently" productive factors. Item B, Gross Capital Formation, is the measure of investment in the national income account. This definition of investment is more narrow than the one in common usage. In the context of national accounting, investment means only the production of goods in inventory or the formation of real capital assets such as plant and equipment. For example, buying a corporation's stock does not fit this definition of investment unless a direct link between the purchase of stock and real capital formation is shown. Otherwise, stock purchases are considered a form of saving, which is defined as income minus consumption. Items C (Exports) and D (Imports) define domestic production consumed abroad and foreign output consumed domestically. A net trade deficit, with exports less than imports, diminishes national income, while a net trade surplus increases national income.

Gross Domestic Product (GDP) is the sum of consumption, gross capital formation, and net trade. Most countries and the UN use GDP to define national income. The United States used Gross National Product to define its national income until 1991, when it switched to GDP. The two measures are similar. GNP is GDP plus item E, Net Factor Income from Abroad, which includes earnings of a country's firms and citizens from currently productive sources. GDP is a measure of a country's income as a place; GNP is a measure of a country's income as a population that owns factors of production. If GNP is greater than GDP then a country's net flow of international income is positive. If GDP is greater than GNP then a country's net flow of international income is negative. Most national income accounts use gross product to summarize income because Item G, Consumption of Fixed Capital, or the value of depreciation, is difficult to measure with accuracy and frequency. Fortunately, gross values and net values provide strongly related information.

Disaggregation of national product accounts is helpful in economic planning and monitoring. In addition, disaggregated product accounts can be linked to input-output accounts, which describe in detail the cross-sectoral flows in an economy (Miller and Blair, 1985). A generalized hypothetical GDP account is given in Table 2.3A and the disaggregated version is given in Table 2.3B. For this hypothetical account, the country's economy is disaggregated into four major sectors. The primary sector includes agriculture, forestry, mining, and fishing. This sector includes production that deals directly with natural resources. The secondary sector consists of

TABLE 2.3   Hypothetical Gross Domestic Product (GDP) Accounts

A. Summary Account

Consumption	+ 500
Gross capital formation	+ 100
Exports	+ 100
Imports	− 150
GDP	= 550

B. Sector Accounts by Flow-of-Product

Item	Primary	Secondary	Tertiary	Government	Total
+ Consumption	52	98	250	100	500
+ Gross capital formation	12	48	30	10	100
+ Exports	22	58	20	0	100
− Imports	42	78	20	10	150
= Share of GDP	44	126	280	100	550

manufacturing, but sometimes its definition is extended to include mining and construction. This sector contains production that modifies resources by application of capital, labor, and technology. The tertiary sector provides services rather than producing goods. These services include the distribution, via wholesale and retail operations, of goods produced in the primary and secondary sectors, and the distribution of services themselves, as in the so-called FIRE industries of finance, insurance, and real estate. Government is frequently considered to be part of the tertiary sector because, in an economic sense, its role is to provide services. However, in national product accounts it is always defined as a separate sector so that its place in the economy can be clearly examined. In the hypothetical account in Table 2.3B, the tertiary sector produces more than half of national income, and the primary sector contributes less than 10%. (The allocation of GDP across these sectors may provide additional information concerning a country's level of economic development. See Section 2.9.)

There is significant debate as to what does and what does not contribute to national income. Eisner (1988) raises five questions for national income accounting.

1. What activities can be considered to result in economic output?
2. What is the definition of primary incomes?
3. What differentiates final from intermediate output?
4. How are investment and consumption, the two ultimate uses of final output, defined?
5. What is the appropriate valuation of production?

The first two points raise the issue of defining the "production boundary" of a national economy. Determining productive activities also determines primary incomes because national income is essentially renumeration of the factors of production. By convention, or perhaps wishful thinking, illegal activities are considered outside the production boundary, as is nonmarket output. In the first case, national income can artificially increase or decrease by legislation. For example, during the years of national Prohibition in the United States, brewing beer and distilling liquor did not contribute to national income, while both before and after Prohibition, they did. Conceivably, rapid growth in GNP could be achieved in the American economy if libertarian thinking ever prevails and currently illegal drugs such as cocaine are legalized for production and use. The restriction to market output in national income designations is a serious measurement problem. In the case of poorer economies, Kuznets (1951) noted early on that national incomes are underestimated because of a relatively large share of nonmarket exchange in their economies. Grain exchanged for tools does not count, but grain exchanged for cash does. The market output restriction also affects richer countries; rides in personally owned autos do not count, but rides in taxis do, and so on.

The issue of differentiating final from intermediate output is a question that is largely answered by using value-added accounting to avoid double counting of production, and by defining final output as goods and services not resold. Value-added is the price of a product less its input costs, or the prices of intermediate (to the product) goods and services. However, definitions of "not resold" vary frequently between the government and other sectors of an economy. Police forces provide a final service, while private security guards provide an intermediate service. In the American product account, broadcast television does not contribute to GNP because it is considered to be resold advertising. Cable television, on the other hand, is considered to be final output.

Definitions of investment and consumption are usually made with regard to tangibility. Investment in human capital in the form of education is considered consumption because of the bias toward increases in tangible, physical assets in the investment definition. Investment in research and development, an intangible, is consumption under standard national accounting rules despite its potential to contribute to national output in the future.

The last question raised by Eisner concerns the appropriate valuation of production. A frequently encountered technical problem in national income accounting results from its constricted time frame. The purchase of a house or machine, the payment of tuition, a vaccination against disease, and so on, can be taken as one-time payments that have long-term benefits. When purchasing a house, for example, the owner makes a transfer from savings to consumption during one year thereby contributing to the national income. The owner then receives services from living in the house for many years, but the services are not paid for as market output. Estimates of imputed income to the owner of the house, as if the owner paid rent to herself, are made. Imputed values, like depreciation values, are difficult to compute accurately or to standardize from country to country.

All five of the national income accounting questions come to the fore when the use and abuse of the natural environment is placed in the context of national product. Under typical national income accounting, consumption of natural resources is considered income, and pollution or other environmental degradation is rarely considered a cost. Because of their limited time frame, national accounts are generally short-sighted, so the concept of *sustainable income,* which emphasizes the future instead of the present, is beyond the bounds of standard systems. Perhaps more important than the time limit to the account is the view of the environment held in most economic theory. In general, the environment is taken as an entity dominated by the economy. This view is held in two versions (Perrings, 1987). The first version is that the environment is not dominated fully by the economy, but is passive. The second version is that the environment is totally dominated; in effect, the environment does not exist. The first and much more common version holds that natural resources are a free gift, as in Marx, where ". . .man of his own accord starts, regulates and controls the material reactions between himself and Nature" (1954, p. 173). Items such as fish and timber are ". . .spontaneously provided by Nature" (1954, p. 174). Neoclassical theory—Perrings cites von Neumann (1945)—extends the free-gift notion to include free disposal of waste.

The free gift of natural resources, on the one hand, leads to the national income accounting principle that resource depletion yields income and is not a transfer or a depreciation reduction. On the other hand, free disposal of waste is not taken literally in national income accounts. Pollution abatement equipment, for example, is considered a productive asset. However, El Sarafy and Lutz (1989) note the argument that this type of equipment is an intermediate rather than a final good and should not be counted as contributing directly to primary income. Another argument is that this type of equipment is not truly productive at all and should be shown in a separate item, such as that of "regrettables" used for much of national defense expenditures by Nordhaus and Tobin (1972).

For better or worse, national product accounts are used to track economic growth over time and to make comparisons among countries. Temporal and international comparisons are problematic, however, because the product accounts are money measures. In the temporal case, inflation and deflation of monetary values require that some sort of indexation be used so that a decrease or increase in national income is a function of changing output and consumption rather than just an indicator of the value of a country's money. In the international case, comparisons require use of a single currency, or numeraire, to which all national currency denominated income accounts must be converted.

In the case of price indexation, price levels for a particular year are chosen to define a constant price level. Assume that wage levels in the base year are 100 and in the next year are 110. Using a price index, the wage level of 110 can be converted to the base year level by the fractional multiple of $100/110 = .91$ $(.91 \times 110 = 100)$. However, this holds only if the increase in wages was purely inflationary; that is, there was no concomitant increase in labor productivity, or output per worker. If labor productivity increased 10% at the same time wages increased 10%, then the increase in wages is due to actual growth and not inflation. The index value in this case would be 1.0 $(1.0 \times 110 = 110)$. When price measures are not controlled for inflation, they are referred to as *nominal prices* or *current prices*. When inflationary effects are considered in price calculations, then the prices are referred to as *real prices*. When national income increases at a rate exactly equal to the rate of inflation, then the nominal increase will be positive but there will be no real increase. If national income increases faster than inflation, then nominal and real income growth will be positive, with the nominal increase greater than the real increase. If national income increases at a slower rate than inflation, then nominal income growth will be positive but real income growth will be negative. Real income can grow faster than nominal income during periods of deflation.

The currency conversion required for international comparisons was more straightforward under Bretton Woods than under the current system of floating exchange rates. Under the present system, annual changes in currency valuation can alter a national income figure significantly. For example, let the currency of country Y, YC, be the numeraire. Real national income in country X increases by 10% during a one-year period, but its currency, XC, decreases in value against YC by 10%. The decline in XC offsets X's real growth and, measured in YC, the income of X did not grow at all. In the other direction, currency appreciation against the numeraire can mask low growth and even decline in a county's income as measured in its domestic currency.

In order to avoid currency conversion problems in international comparisons of income, efforts are being made to reckon national incomes in terms of *purchasing power parities (PPP)*. PPP is defined as the number of domestic currency units required to buy the same basket of goods and services in the domestic markets of various countries (International Comparison Program, 1986). Technical problems arise in calculating PPP because relative prices of goods and services are not the same in all countries. In many countries the price of food, for example, is significantly altered downward by government intervention so that its true relative price is unknown. In addition, countries that still have a command economy use prices not at all related to market value. PPP calculation for comparing market-price economies and command-price economies would require exhaustive baskets of goods and services in order to have any meaning. (On limited theoretical grounds it can be argued that PPP is revealed in exchange rates. See Chapter 5.)

For both temporal and international comparisons, national income totals frequently are divided by population to yield *per capita* values. The reason that per capita national incomes are used rather than aggregate national incomes is that, to some degree, national income is a positive function of population. Even when additional people consume at decreasing rates, aggregate GNP will increase. In a sense, per capita national incomes are a form of indexed aggregate national incomes. If either nominal or real national income increases at a faster rate than population increases, then per capita national income will increase. However, if national income increases at a slower rate than population increases, per capita national income will decrease.

Growth rates in national income, prices, and population during the years 1980 through 1985 are given for selected countries in Table 2.4. The amount of spread between nominal and real national income growth rates is a function of inflation rates. None of the countries listed experienced deflation during the period, so nominal

TABLE 2.4   Compound Growth Rates of Product, Prices, and Population in Selected Countries, 1980–1985

	United States[a]	United Kingdom	Nigeria	Hungary
Nominal GDP	7.98	9.08	10.96	7.47
Real GDP	2.56	2.06	−1.87	1.76
Nominal GDP in $U.S.	——	−2.96	−2.44	−1.48
Nominal per capita GDP	6.92	8.82	7.25	7.59
Real per capita GDP	1.55	1.82	−4.45	1.87
Nominal per capita GDP in $U.S.	——	−3.19	−5.01	−1.38
Prices	3.94	6.87	12.25	5.61
Population	0.99	0.24	3.40	−0.11

Source: International Financial Statistics Yearbook, 1988 (New York: International Monetary Fund).
[a] Indicates GNP.

growth rates were greater than real growth rates in all cases. Japan had the lowest average annual inflation rate and therefore had the smallest spread between rates of nominal and real growth during the first half of the 1980s. Nigeria experienced an average decrease in real national income of nearly 2%, however, because of its relatively high rate of inflation.

The numeraire used in most instances of national income comparison is the U.S. dollar; it is the most frequently used numeraire among international agencies such as the World Bank, the United Nations, and the International Monetary Fund. The American dollar appreciated against most currencies between 1980 and 1985, the time period used in Table 2.4. The general appreciation of the dollar deflates the rate of growth in national incomes when they are converted from national currencies to the numeraire. The Japanese yen experienced relatively low rates of depreciation against the dollar during the period, and the difference between its nominal income growth denominated in yen and its nominal income growth denominated in dollars is not that great. On the other hand, the weakness of the British, Nigerian, and Hungarian currencies during the first half of the 1980s turned their positive nominal rates of national income growth to negative rates after conversion to dollars.

Again, the rate of population growth in a country will determine that country's spread between its aggregate and per capita national income growth rates. Countries such as the United Kingdom, with essentially stable populations, have very narrow spreads between per capita and aggregate rates. Nigeria experienced a fairly high rate of population increase during the period, which led to a sizeable decrease in per capita growth rates as compared to aggregate growth rates. Hungary is an interesting case because its declining population yielded per capita national income increases that were greater than its increases in aggregate national income during the period.

2.6 THE GEOGRAPHY OF NATIONAL INCOME

According to data compiled and published by the World Bank (1992), mean GDP in 112 reporting countries with over one million in population was about U.S. $173.5 billion in 1990. Notably absent were the former Soviet Union and some other countries with recent military conflicts, including Lebanon, Iran, and Iraq. Median GDP, at about $17.3 billion, was much less than the mean, indicating a positively skewed distribution. In fact, only 21 of the world's reporting countries had a GDP greater than the mean value in 1990. The United States had the greatest GDP at just under $5.4 trillion, and Bhutan had the smallest at $280 million. The geographical distribution of extreme values of GDP is shown in Figure 2.2. With the exception of Bhutan, the Laotian People's Democratic Republic, and Honduras, the countries with the lowest GDPs are in Black Africa. The countries with the highest GDPs are mainly in North America, including Mexico, and Western Europe, and on the Pacific Rim. Essentially, countries with high GDPs are the industrialized countries of the world, the People's Republic of China, India, and Brazil.

The magnitude of GDP in the last three countries is heavily influenced by their large populations. The degree of this influence is revealed to some extent by an examination of the geographical distribution of countries with extreme values of per capita GDP (Figure 2.3). On the basis of per capita GDP, both the People's Republic of China and India were among the world's poorest countries in 1990. In addition, neither Brazil nor Mexico ranked among the 20 richest countries on a per capita basis although each had very large values for aggregate GDP. In general, however, the geographical pattern is the same whether using GDP or per capita GDP as a measure of national income. The industrial nations are rich and the greatest concentration of poor countries is in Black Africa. Like aggregate GDP, per capita GDP also is positively skewed. Mean per capita GDP was about $5130 in 1990 while the median was $1320. The poorest country was Mozambique with per capita GDP of $84. The richest was Switzerland, with per capita GDP of nearly $33,600.

An important empirical point concerning national income is that its level and rate of growth are not related systematically. Most growth rate models—for example, the logistic—allow high rates of growth from low levels and limit growth rates at high levels. However, these level-increase relationships work well only in closed systems that have no external inputs, no leakage, and fixed capacities. The international economy is not a closed system, and the geography of average real rates of growth in GDP from 1980 through 1990 is much less systematic than the geography of GDP (Figure 2.4). Regionally, Latin America experienced the weakest rates of average real growth during the period. The experience in Black Africa, the world's poorest region, was mixed. Some of Black Africa's incomes grew at rapid rates, some at slow rates, and some experienced declines in real GDP. In all, average real declines were experienced by 10 countries. The extreme case was Trinidad and Tobago with an average rate of decrease of −4.7%. Two small countries experienced average real growth rates in the double digits: Oman, 12.7%, and Botswana, 11.3%. The East Asian countries of the Republic of (South) Korea, at 9.7%, and the People's Republic of

China, at 9.6%, had the fastest national growth rates in the fastest growing region. Like GDP and per capita GDP, the numerical distribution of average real growth rates is positively skewed. The mean annual rate of growth was about 2.7%, and the median rate was 2.4%.

2.7   PRODUCTION FUNCTIONS

GDP is a measure of production, but it does not describe any of the production processes. Information on general production processes can be gathered in a number of ways. One method of measuring aggregate production processes is by way of a *production function*. A production function defines the mathematical relationship between the *factors of production* and output. Like all mathematical functions, production functions can be graphed, and their graphic form provides some insight into production theory at both microeconomic and macroeconomic levels of analysis. A typical production function is graphed in Figure 2.5. The factors of production are labeled K for capital and L for labor, and Q is the fixed level of output. Output has a negative slope from left to right, indicating that the factors have positive marginal productivities. The convexity of output with respect to the origin indicates that the marginal productivity of either of the factors diminishes toward zero as its use increases. The limits to marginal productivity are illustrated in Figure 2.5 by the invariance of output when capital is increased from K_2 to K_3 with labor fixed at L_1, and by the invariance of output when capital is fixed at K_1 and labor is increased from L_2 to L_3. Any combination of factors between K_2 and L_2—for example, K_* and L_*—retains positive marginal productivity in both factors.

Graphed production functions also are used to describe the way output increases. Figure 2.6 portrays three levels of output, Q_1-Q_3, which are achieved by applying increasing amounts of factors. Equal factor proportions in production are defined by the 45° ray from the origin. Doubling inputs of both factors doubles output in this example of a homogeneous production function. The constant increment between each output function describes a case of constant returns to factors. If the output functions had successively narrower gaps, returns to factors would be decreasing; if the gaps were successively wider, returns to factors would be increasing. In addition to the growth in output obtained by increased factor inputs, growth also can be attributed to technological progress. The effect of the neutral disembodied technology of the neoclassical model is illustrated in Figure 2.6 by comparison of output levels Q_1-Q_3 with output levels Q_1^T-Q_3^T, where Q^T indicates output at a higher level of technology. The effect of the higher rate of technology is a 50% increment over the output produced with the lower level of technology.

An explicit mathematical production function that is frequently used is the Cobb–Douglas function (Douglas, 1976):

$$Q = TK^{\alpha}L^{\beta} \tag{2.1}$$

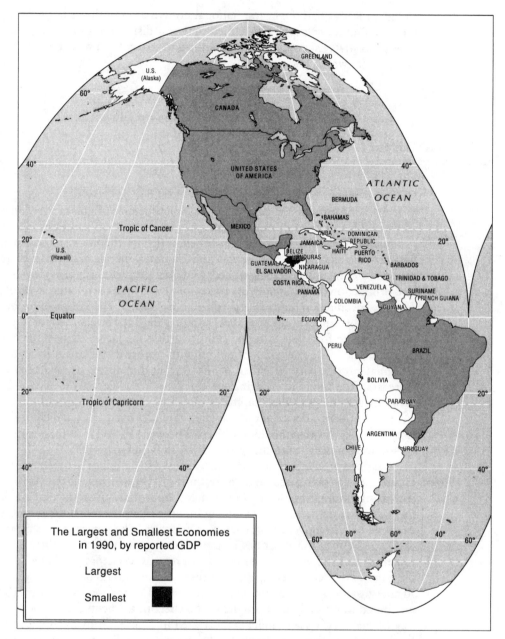

FIGURE 2.2   The Largest and Smallest Economies in 1990, by Reported GDP

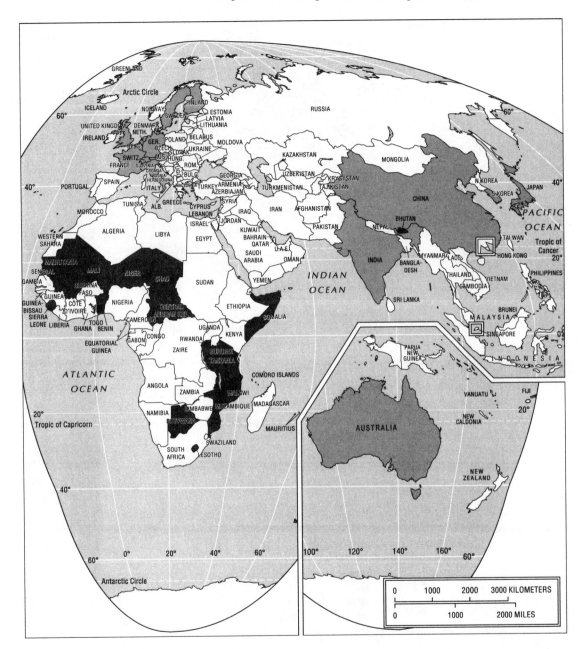

FIGURE 2.2   *(Continued)*

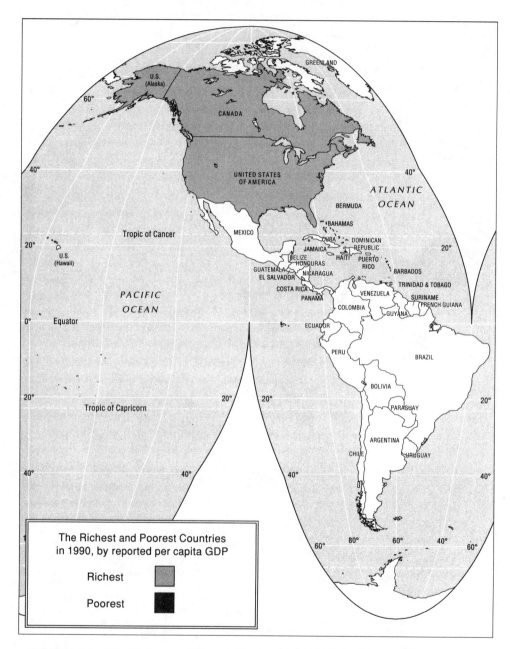

FIGURE 2.3   The Richest and Poorest Countries in 1990, by Reported Per Capita GDP

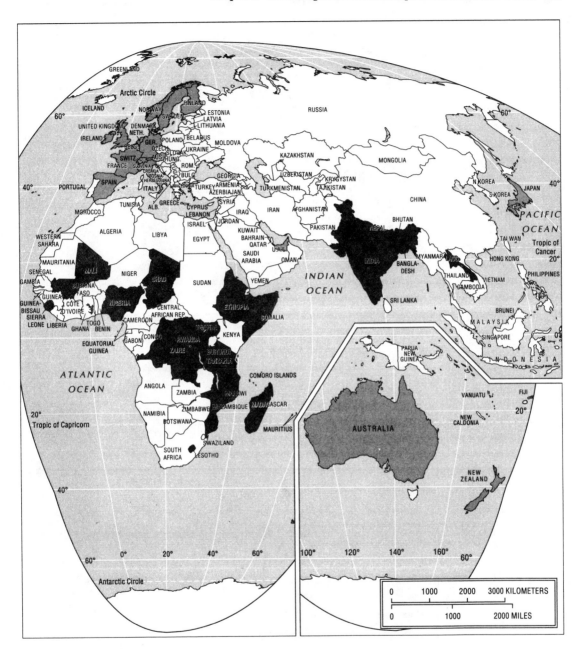

FIGURE 2.3 *(Continued)*

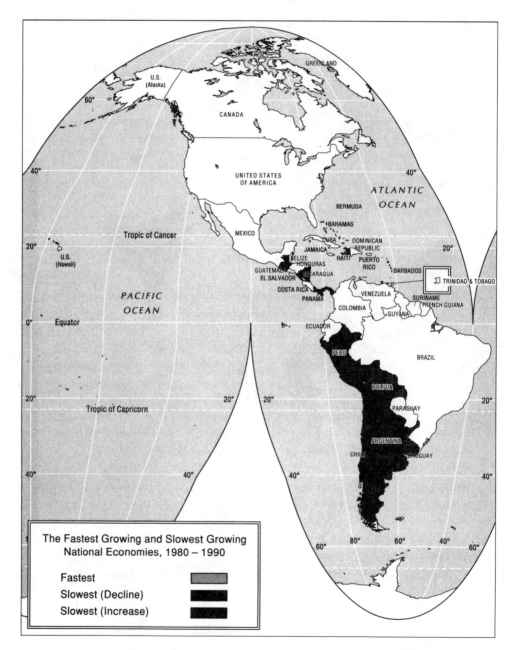

FIGURE 2.4   The Fastest Growing and Slowest Growing National Economies, 1980–1990

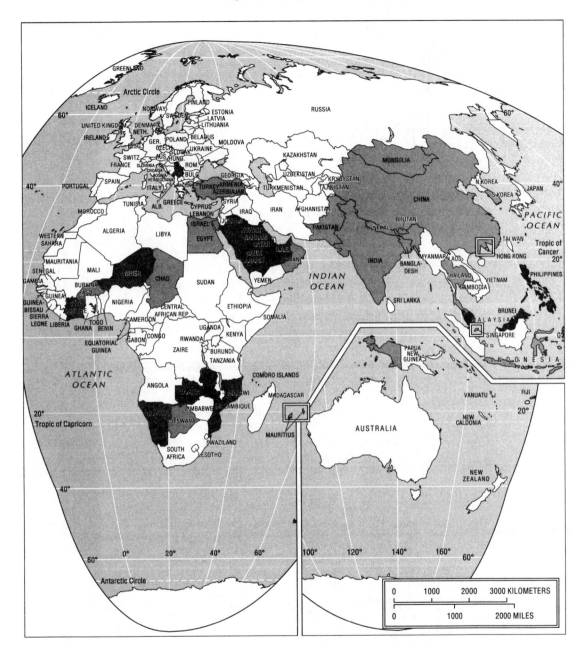

FIGURE 2.4   *(Continued)*

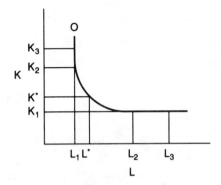

FIGURE 2.5   A Simple Production Function

The coefficients α and β define the partial elasticities, or responses, of output to the factors of production. If $\alpha + \beta = 1$, then there are constant returns to the the factors of production. If $\alpha + \beta < 1$ then there are decreasing returns. If $\alpha + \beta > 1$, then there are increasing returns to factors. The Cobb–Douglas production function is a neoclassical production function because technology, T, is disembodied from K and L and the function's multiplicative form makes it homogeneous.

Empirical estimation of the unknown values in the Cobb–Douglas function, T, α, and β, can be conducted by ordinary least squares regression in the form

$$lnQ = \hat{t} + \hat{a}lnK + \hat{b}lnL \qquad (2.2)$$

where lnQ, lnC, and lnL are the natural log transforms of the known variables. The parameter $\hat{t}$ is the estimated Y-axis intercept of the regression line defined by Equa-

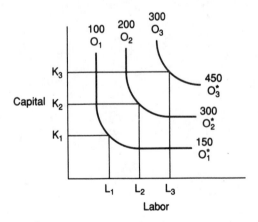

FIGURE 2.6   Constant Returns to Scale under Different Levels of Technology

tion 2.1, and is interpreted as the technological efficiency value, T, of the Cobb–Douglas function. The parameters $\hat{a}$ and $\hat{b}$ are the respective estimates of α and β in the Cobb–Douglas function. Equation 2.1 can be estimated over time, or cross-sectionally in geographical analyses of production.

2.8 PRODUCTIVITY DIFFERENCES BETWEEN RICH AND POOR COUNTRIES

As described in Chapter 3, many theories of economic growth concern the dynamic relationship between capital and labor as factors of production. For practical purposes, neither factor can act alone in production, even in a subsistence economy. Productivity can be defined, however, as the rate of output for a given level of input of a single factor. Production efficiency can be defined the same way. A more productive, or efficient, economy can produce more goods and services than a less productive economy can produce even when both pay the same factor costs and use the same factor combination. Rich economies are more productive than poor economies, by definition, when the measure of national wealth is per capita national income. Regardless of per capita factor combinations or even factor costs, a productivity difference is immediately revealed when one country has a higher per capita GDP than another country.

A simple method of defining productivity, P, is to measure marginal changes in output, Q, relative to marginal increments in factor inputs, F, in the following form:

$$P = \frac{\Delta Q}{\Delta F} \qquad (2.3)$$

If $P > 1$ then there are increasing returns in production, and if $P < 1$ then there are decreasing returns in production. Obviously, productivity increases with the value of P. Empirically, a measure of P can be determined by the equation

$$lnQ = a + P(lnF) \qquad (2.4)$$

where lnQ is the natural logarithm of the known measure of output, a is a derived constant, lnF is the natural logarithm of the known measure of input, and P is the unknown productivity coefficient. This type of equation frequently is solved using ordinary least squares regression.

Two crude measures of productivity in the World Bank (1992) income groups of countries were calculated using Equation 2.4. The first is a measure of changes in aggregate output, measured as GDP, as a response to changes in population. The second is a measure of changes in GDP relative to changes in energy consumption measured in equivalent kilograms of oil. Both measures were obtained using data for 1990. Before discussing the results, it is important to consider two points. First, the productivity measures are not derived from the analysis of true production functions. They are simple measures of geographical, or cross-sectional, changes in output relative to geographical variation in population and in energy consumption. Second, the productivity measures are averages used for descriptive purposes only. Their values should be interpreted as indicating productivity tendencies rather than defining fixed relationships.

A tendency toward decreasing "returns" when comparing productivity to population and energy consumption is exhibited by the productivity coefficients calculated for all countries reporting data in 1990 (Table 2.5). Overall, output increased at a rate of about 96% of the increase in population, and it increased at only about 83% of the rate of increase in energy consumption. In the low income countries, output increased by a virtual one-to-one relationship with population, but at a rate of only about 68% of the increase in energy consumption. Both the middle income groups had lower rates of productivity with respect to population increases than did the low income group, and the lower middle income group also had less productivity with respect to energy consumption. The high income group of countries, unlike the other three groups, had productivity coefficients greater than one with respect to both increases in population and increases in energy consumption. Output increased more than 6% faster than population and over 1.5% faster than energy consumption.

The differences in productivity coefficients are small across the income groups and have been calculated for only one year. Nevertheless, the productivity tendencies they describe, of increasing returns in the rich countries and decreasing returns in the others, neatly summarize the crux of the development problem. It is simple enough to state that the reason rich countries are richer than poor countries is because rich countries are more efficient producers, but why does the difference in productivity exist? An immediate response might focus on the availability of capital. Marx, Harrod and Domar, and the neoclassicists indicate that physical capital is the critical

TABLE 2.5 Aggregate Productivity Coefficients by World Bank Income Group, 1990

Income Group	Productivity Coefficients: to Population	to Energy
All	0.963	0.827
Low	1.009	0.683
Low Middle	0.983	0.648
High Middle	0.909	0.866
High	1.065	1.016

Source: World Bank, 1992. *World Development Report 1992* (New York: Oxford University Press).

factor of production (see Chapter 3). In addition, the factor of labor is always available and the size of the labor force, like population, does not seem to be correlated with per capita GDP. However, physical capital accumulation rarely has been found empirically to contribute significantly to variations in economic growth in either rich or poor countries (Thirlwall, 1977).

One possible explanation for the productivity differences between rich and poor countries is that rich countries are more able to achieve economies of scale in production. Economies of scale are defined simply as a decrease in the average cost of production with an increase in the volume of production. Ideally, average or unit costs decrease with increasing volumes of production for a number of reasons. One reason is that the fixed costs of production can be spread over more units as volume increases. For example, property taxes are a fixed annual charge to a business that diminish in per-unit cost as production increases. Another source of economies of scale is learning-by-doing, or experience. Learning-by-doing makes labor more productive, so labor costs per unit decrease as more units are produced. The effect of learning-by-doing is compounded by the ability of producers to specialize in their production as demand increases. In *The Wealth of Nations,* Adam Smith wrote, "The division of labor is limited by the extent of the market." He meant that occupational specialty is a positive function of demand. Stigler (1951) extended Smith's principle of specialization to firms, and showed how a greater "extent of the market" causes them to achieve lower costs through specialization. Given that, in the long run, production volume must equate approximately to demand, the greater the demand for a product the more likely its production will enjoy economies of scale. Rich countries not only have the highest per capita GDPs, they usually also have very large aggregate GDPs as well. Both per capita GDP and aggregate GDP are good approximate measures of demand and, therefore, good measures of potentially widespread economies of scale that induce high rates of measured productivity. Dennison (1967) found economies of scale to be one of a series of factors that accounted for productivity variations among the richer countries.

Another possible explanation of the different rates of productivity between rich and poor countries is in technological variation. Disembodied technology frequently has been offered as the explanation for the very large share of the economic growth of countries that cannot be accounted for by capital and labor in neoclassical models (Thirlwall, 1977). This point is discussed in Chapter 3. However, as noted by Kaldor (1961), it is very difficult to fully separate capital from technology in any practical way. For example, physical capital such as machinery is replaced not just because it is worn out but because it becomes technologically obsolete. A more broad concept than technology is that of innovation as described by Schumpeter (1951). His definition of innovation encompasses technological improvement in the physical sense and also improved ways of doing things in general. Schumpeter's innovation is very similar to the factor of "knowledge" found by Dennison (1967) to be important in explaining variations in economic growth rates among rich countries. Romer (1986) has considered knowledge as a separate factor of production that generates increasing returns.

Variations in human capital endowments, derived from sources such as educa-

TABLE 2.6 Geographical Variation in Selected Human Capital Variables by World Bank Income Group, 1989

Income Group	Mean Values		
	Secondary School Enrollment	Tertiary School Enrollment	Daily Calorie Consumption
All	50%	15%	2692
Low	21%	3%	2204
Low Middle	48%	15%	2611
High Middle	65%	18%	3102
High	91%	34%	3335

Source: World Bank, 1992. *World Development Report 1992* (New York: Oxford University Press).

tion (Ritzen, 1977) and nutrition (Rodgers, 1975), also may be an explanation for the productivity differences between rich and poor countries. Human capital is like a set of individually self-possessed tools. Just as labor productivity is augmented by physical capital, it also can be augmented by the human capital assets of good health and education. Places subjected to endemic disease or ignorance are not likely to have very productive labor forces. Human capital does tend to vary systematically with national income levels. Three human capital variables—percentage of secondary school enrollment (secondary school enrollment/population aged 12–17), percentage of tertiary school enrollment (tertiary school enrollment/population aged 20–24), and average daily calorie consumption—increase consistently from low to high income country groups (Table 2.6). On average, secondary school enrollment rates in the high income countries were 4.5 times greater than in the low income countries in 1989. Tertiary school enrollment rates were 10 times greater in the richest countries than in the poorest. Quantity of food does not directly equate with quality of nutrition, but the fact that average daily calorie consumption in the low income countries was only about 65% of calorie consumption in the high income countries does suggest that nutritional quality varies significantly between the two extreme income groups.

2.9 DIFFERENCES IN SECTORAL SHARES OF GDP BETWEEN RICH AND POOR COUNTRIES

In addition to productivity tendencies, the economic structure of countries tends to vary systematically by national income. Economies frequently are divided into broad sectoral aggregations, as described in Section 2.5. Sectoral shifts of labor force concentrations, from primary sector to secondary sector, and then from secondary sector to tertiary sector, have long been observed and associated with the process of economic development. Although sectoral shifts of the labor force have been discussed by a number of development analysts (e.g., Kuznets, 1965), their association with economic growth is frequently referred to as the *Clark–Fisher hypothesis* (Clark, 1951; Fisher, 1939). The Clark–Fisher hypothesis, like Rostow's stages of economic development, is part of a more general theory of modernization as a process of economic development. As poorer countries begin to achieve economic growth, it can be expected under the Clark–Fisher hypothesis that their labor forces will experience shifts through the sectors of the economy just as such shifts took place in most of the world's rich countries.

Why do sectoral shifts of the labor force occur during economic growth? One reason is based on Engel's law, named for Ernst Engel, which states that as income increases, decreasing portions of it are required to purchase necessities such as food. In different terms, the income elasticity of food and other necessities is less than one. The implication of Engel's law for sectoral shifts of the labor force is clear. As incomes increase during economic growth, increasing proportions of discretionary purchases are for non-necessities originating in the secondary and tertiary sectors. Employment in the primary sector remains stable, or decreases in relative proportion, as a type of demand ceiling for primary sector products is reached. Employment increases, both absolutely and in relative proportion, in the secondary and tertiary sectors as demand increases for their products.

Engel's law provides a basis for the shift of employment away from the primary sector, but not for the shift from the secondary to the tertiary sector. This shift has been explained by differences in productivity rates between the secondary and tertiary sectors. Technology is considered to be more labor saving in the secondary sector than it is in the tertiary sector. As technological advances take place, proportionately less labor is required in the secondary sector and, therefore, proportionately more labor is required in the service sector even if the relative level of demand for goods and services remains unchanged.

A related explanation for the shift from the secondary sector to the service sector has been provided by Kellerman (1985), who argued that service sector growth is induced by growth in the secondary sector. Increased secondary sector production, mostly in manufacturing, requires increases in the services of the tertiary sector, such as transportation and power utilities, that complement production of goods. In addition, other services, such as retail and wholesale trade, finance, and insurance, are directly or indirectly required for distribution of the increased volume of manufactured goods. Although growth in the secondary sector induces growth in the tertiary sector, the share of the the labor force increases disproportionately in the tertiary sector because of its inherently low labor productivity.

Variations across World Bank income groups in shares of GDP in agriculture, the major part of the primary sector; manufacturing, the major part of the secondary sector (sometimes construction is included); and all services are shown for 1990 in Table 2.7. Even though the values given are shares in GDP, and not labor force

TABLE 2.7   Variation in Sectoral Shares of GDP by World Bank Income Group, 1990*

Income Group	Mean Values		
	Agriculture	Manufacturing	Services
All	21%	16%	48%
Low	37%	13%	40%
Low Middle	17%	16%	49%
High Middle	10%	18%	47%
High	3%	21%	61%

Source: World Bank, 1992. *World Development Report 1992* (New York: Oxford University Press).

proportions, the allocations do seem to correspond generally to the Clark–Fisher hypothesis. The low income group has, on average, the largest share of GDP in agriculture, and the high income group has its largest share of GDP in services. Agriculture's share of GDP uniformly decreases as income increases, and the service sector's share of GDP uniformly increases with income. Worldwide, manufacturing has the smallest share of GDP among the three sectors, but it has an intermediate share in the two higher income groups as would be expected under the Clark–Fisher hypothesis.

Geographical, or cross-sectional, evidence is not fully appropriate for testing models of historical process, but the average relative GDP shares of manufacturing and services of the low income group countries are problematic for the Clark–Fisher hypothesis. Simply, the share of GDP in manufacturing should not be less than the shares of both agriculture and services. Manufacturing should have an intermediate share, as it does in the other income groups of countries. In a sense, the low income countries' share of GDP in services is too large given their concurrent large average share of GDP in agriculture. This nonconformance to the Clark–Fisher hypothesis has been addressed by Pandit and Casetti (1989). They have shown that despite the broad accuracy of the Clark–Fisher hypothesis, the process it describes is not invariant over time. They found that the sectoral labor force shifts now taking place in the poorer countries are different in form and degree than those that took place in rich countries in the past. By simulation, they predicted that manufacturing will have a smaller share of labor than both agriculture and services in poor countries experiencing economic growth. They attributed this relationship to particularly low levels of labor productivity in the service sector of poor countries, but high levels of manufacturing labor productivity. Due to their relatively high manufacturing labor productivity, achieved by easy adoption of widely available production technology, poorer countries have not and will not experience large labor shares in manufacturing. In effect, the sectoral shifts of developing countries are more of a leapfrog process from the primary to the tertiary sector.

Both services and agriculture do tend to be less productive than manufacturing. Using the same method as in Equation 2.4, productivity coefficients for 1990 were calculated for each of the three sectors on a worldwide basis and within each of the four World Bank income groups (Table 2.8). Whether measured at the global scale or within the income groups, manufacturing was found consistently to be the most productive of the three sectors. In addition, manufacturing was the only one of the three sectors that exhibited a trend toward increasing returns to population across the low income group of countries. In general, the least productive sector was services, which had a tendency toward decreasing returns in all but the high income group. The relatively high productivity of the service sector in the rich countries and its tendency toward low productivity in the other income groups is a further illustration of Pandit's and Casetti's point that there are real service sector differences between rich and poor countries. In addition, the relative uniformity of manufacturing productivity with respect to population may be attributed to relatively easy access to standard manufacturing technology. This proposition does not appear to be supported, however, by the disparate productivities of manufacturing with respect to energy. In any case, the difference in service sector productivity coefficients, for both population and energy, between rich and poor countries suggest that the service sector's technology is not widespread.

Technological difference, however, is not necessarily the reason that service sector productivity is higher in rich countries than in poor ones. An alternative explanation for the differences in service sector productivity is that the potential for economies of scale in services is greater in rich countries than in poor countries. An important difference between services and manufactured goods is that most services

TABLE 2.8 Sectoral Productivity Coefficients by World Bank Income Group, 1990*

	Population Productivity Coefficients		
Income Group	Agriculture	Manufacturing	Services
All	1.012	1.004	0.893
Low	0.976	1.169	0.988
Low Middle	1.125	1.086	0.916
High Middle	1.073	1.119	0.997
High	1.087	1.251	1.129
	Energy Productivity Coefficients		
Income Group	Agriculture	Manufacturing	Services
All	0.563	0.974	0.831
Low	0.613	0.812	0.678
Low Middle	0.651	0.903	0.605
High Middle	0.970	1.114	0.944
High	1.230	1.333	1.203

Source: World Bank, 1992. *World Development Report 1992* (New York: Oxford University Press).

cannot be stored. The inability to store services means that they must be purchased more frequently than storable manufactured goods. The service sector should achieve economies of scale more easily in rich countries than in poor ones because higher incomes should increase the frequency of service purchases. Increased purchase frequency should increase the efficiencies incurred in learning-by-doing and in specialization. In addition, rich countries have very high proportions of their populations living in cities (see Section 2.10). Geographical concentrations of population should lower unit costs in the tertiary sector by further increasing the already large potential for high frequencies of service purchases in the rich countries (Coffey and Polese, 1989; O'Huallachain, 1989).

2.10 DEMOGRAPHIC DIFFERENCES BETWEEN RICH AND POOR COUNTRIES

Demographic characteristics also tend to vary systematically with national income. Two characteristics, the difference between birth rates and death rates, and urbanization, frequently are considered to be correlates of the process of economic growth. The *demographic transition* is a model drawn from modernization theory that describes the relationship between these demographic characteristics and economic development (Alonso, 1980; Stolnitz, 1970; Rostow, 1978). This transition is a shift from concurrent high birth and death rates to concurrent low birth and death rates (Figure 2.7). The birth rate minus the death rate is called the demographic gap. Natural population increase, or population growth excluding migration, is a function of the size and sign of the demographic gap. If the demographic gap is positive, so is

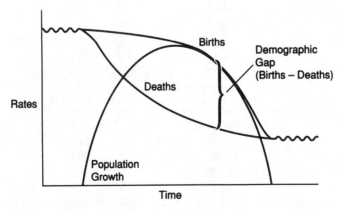

FIGURE 2.7   The Demographic Transition

the rate of natural population increase. If the demographic gap is negative, then population will decrease if net migration is not positive.

The first stage of the demographic transition is one of high birth rates being offset by high death rates and, therefore, no natural increase in population. The first stage is associated with an economy that consists mainly of subsistence agriculture. Low levels of technology make the economy very labor intensive. Large families are viewed as an asset because they provide large amounts of labor, so birth rates are high. Death rates are high because of low levels of health-care technology. Disease cannot be prevented or cured by widespread distribution of medicines. Obviously, given the emphasis on agriculture in the economy, the population is spread over rural areas and there is not much basis for significant urbanization.

The second stage of the demographic transition is marked by gradually decreasing birth rates and rapidly decreasing death rates. The demographic gap increases during the second stage so that the natural population growth rate increases as well. The general level of technology increases in the second stage, and technological adoptions in health-care practices rapidly reduce the death rate. Birth rates, however, remain high because of a strong tradition of large family size, held over from the first stage (its "roots" are in subsistence agriculture). The second stage is associated with the beginning of a shift from the primary sector of the economy to the secondary sector, as in the Clark–Fisher hypothesis. Agricultural productivity increases, creating surpluses that translate into demand for manufactured goods. The shift away from the primary sector leads to the beginning of urbanization as centers of industrial production and distribution develop.

The third stage of the demographic transition is one of decreasing rates of natural population growth brought about by a decreasing demographic gap. The demographic gap closes because birth rates decrease at a time when death rates have stabilized at a low level. The decline in birth rates is attributed to the increasing level of urbanization and significant removal of much of the population from the tradition of large families in a rural-agricultural economy. Death rates no longer decrease because the full range of health-care technology is being applied. In Clark–Fisher terms, the shift from the primary to the secondary sector nears completion during the third stage, and the shift from the secondary to the tertiary sector is underway. The third stage of the demographic transition provides a fundamental departure from the Malthusian model of population growth. Essentially, Malthus's view of population growth is one of the second stage of the demographic transition existing in perpetuity.

The demographic gap is closed, ending natural population increase, in the last stage of the demographic transition. The birth rate has receded to a level that is approximately equal to that of the already low death rate. The population is fully urbanized, and the economy has completed the sectoral shifts of the Clark–Fisher hypothesis. The last stage of the demographic transition equates well to Rostow's ultimate development stage of "high mass consumption."

As in the cases of other models drawn from modernization theory, such as Rostow's stages of development (see Chapter 3) and the Clark–Fisher hypothesis, much of the criticism of the model of the demographic transition concerns its posited geographical and temporal invariance of process. For example, Boserup (1981) has

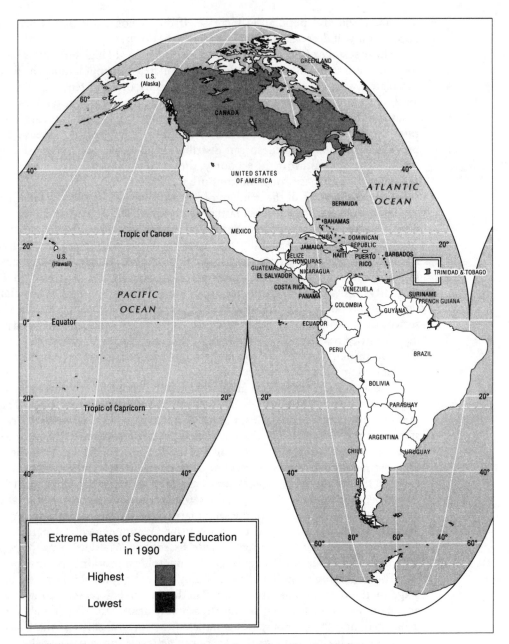

FIGURE 2.8   Extreme Rates of Secondary Education in 1990

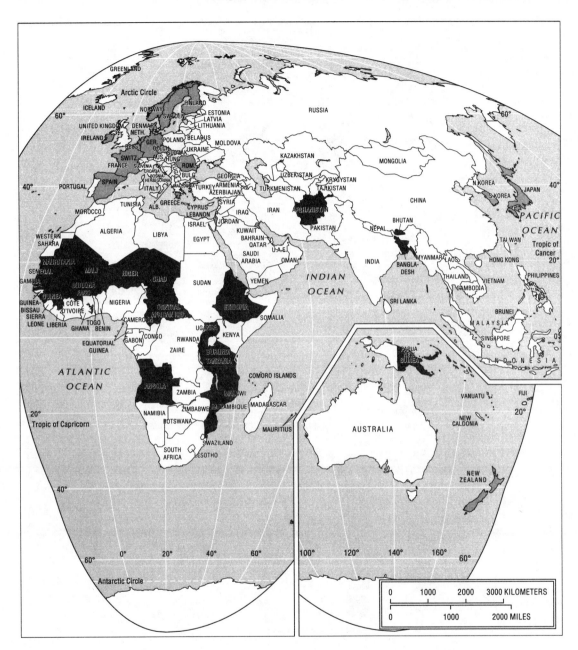

FIGURE 2.8   *(Continued)*

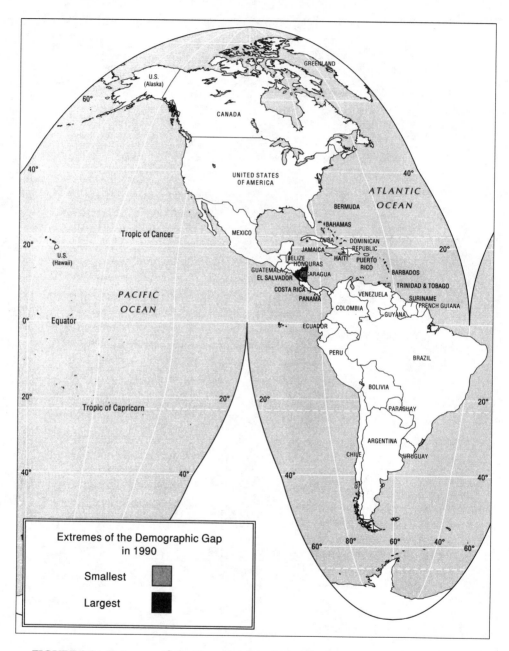

FIGURE 2.9 Extremes of the Demographic Gap in 1990

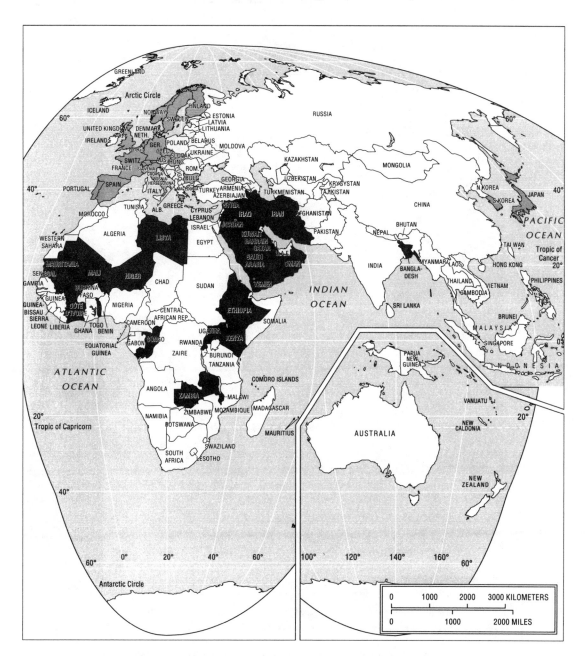

FIGURE 2.9 *(Continued)*

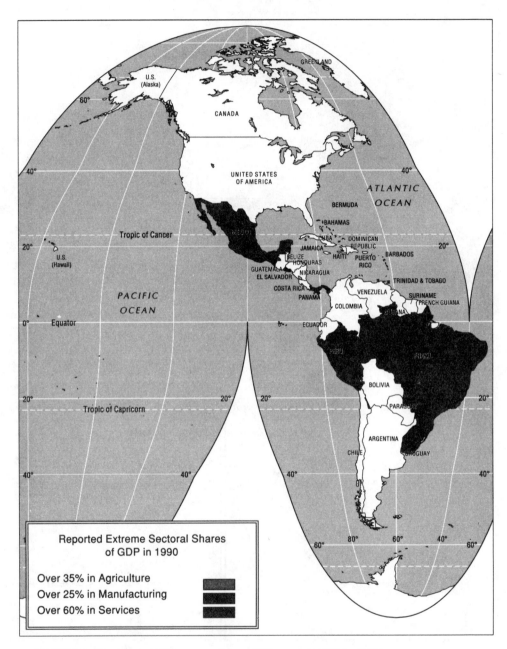

FIGURE 2.10   Reported Extreme Sectoral Shares of GDP in 1990

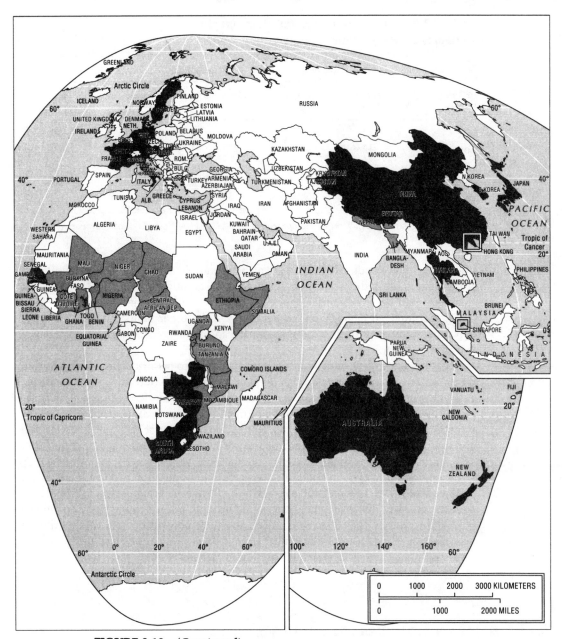

FIGURE 2.10   *(Continued)*

TABLE 2.9 Variation in Selected Demographic Variables by World Bank Income Group, 1990*

Income Group	Mean Values				
	Birth Rate	Death Rate	Demographic Gap	Urban Population	Rate of Urbanization
All	31	11	20	49%	4%
Low	42	15	27	27%	6%
Low Middle	32	9	23	48%	4%
High Middle	28	9	19	64%	3%
High	14	9	5	80%	1%

Source: World Bank, 1992. *World Development Report 1992* (New York: Oxford University Press).

noted that many countries with equivalent economic structures and technological levels have quite different demographic gaps. In addition, Grigg (1980) has found that birth and death rates now change at a more rapid rate than they did in earlier cases of completed demographic transition. On the other hand, Vining (1986) has concluded that urbanization is just as much a correlate of economic growth today as it was in the past.

Static geographical data do not provide insight into historical processes, but they do show the current demographic differences between rich and poor countries. Average crude birth rates (births per 1000 population) in 1990 decreased dramatically from the low Income group of countries to the high income group (Table 2.9). Average crude death rates (deaths per 1000 population) were the same in the middle and high income groups, but about two-thirds higher in the low income group. The systematic variation in birth rates with income leads to the same systematic variation in the demographic gap. In addition, average urban population proportions increase systematically with income, and average annual rates of urbanization (1980–1990) decrease consistently as income increases. In general, poorer countries have younger populations due to their high birth rates, and their populations are rural, although urbanization is increasing. Rich countries have older populations because their birth rates are low, and their populations are highly urbanized.

2.11 HUMAN CAPITAL, SECTORAL, AND DEMOGRAPHIC DIFFERENCES: GLOBAL PATTERNS

The regional patterns of countries with extreme values of secondary school enrollments, shown in Figure 2.8, is an approximate replication of the map of countries with extreme values of per capita GDP (Figure2.3). Countries with the highest levels of secondary school enrollment are clustered in Europe and also include the richer countries of the Pacific Rim. Countries reporting extremely low levels of secondary school enrollment largely are in Black Africa and South Asia. The pattern is approximately the same for extreme values of the demographic gap (Figure 2.9). The low end consists of an almost solid concentration of European countries. The richer countries of the Pacific Rim also have extremely low demographic gaps. Very high demographic gaps are found in several countries in Black Africa, and in the Islamic countries of the Middle East and Libya. Nicaragua, in Central America, is an exception to the concentrations.

The regional patterns of extreme sectoral shares of GDP are less clear than the patterns of secondary school enrollment and the demographic gap (Figure 2.10). Extreme shares of GDP in agriculture are found only in the poorer countries, mainly in Black Africa. However, extreme shares of GDP in both manufacturing and services are not so closely aligned with the geography of per capita national income. Extreme sectoral shares of GDP in manufacturing are found in very rich countries, such as Japan and the Federal Republic of Germany, and in the poorer countries of Zambia and the People's Republic of China. Extreme service sector shares of GDP are found in richer countries, but also in some of the poorer countries in Central America, Jordan, and Senegal in Africa.

The purpose of the three preceding sections was to draw out some of the systematic variations in selected economic and demographic characteristics that exist over levels of national income. Naturally, individual countries exhibit some degree of difference, but typically conform to the general patterns.

REFERENCES

Alonso, W. 1980. "Five Bell Shapes in Development." *Papers of the Regional Science Association* 45: 5–16.

Amin, S. 1974. *Accumulation on a World Scale: A Critique of the Theory of Underdevelopment* (New York: Monthly Review Press).

Amin, S. 1977. *Imperialism and Unequal Development* (New York: Monthly Review Press).

Bedjaoui, M. 1979. *Towards a New International Economic Order* (New York: Holmes & Meier).

Berentsen, W., J. Bowman, and G. Dinges. 1987. "Social and Economic Well-being in the United States." *Proceedings* of the New England-St. Lawrence Valley Geographical Society, Vol. XVI.

Berry, B. 1961. "Basic Patterns of Economic Development." In *Atlas of Economic Development,* edited by N. Ginsburg (Chicago: University of Chicago Press).

Boserup, E. 1981. *Population and Technological Change: A Study of Long-term Trends* (Chicago: University of Chicago Press).

Brandt, W. 1980. *North-South: Report of the Independent Commission on International Development* (London: Pan).

Chilcote, R. 1984. *Theories of Development and Underdevelopment* (Boulder: Westview Press).

Clark, C. 1951. *The Conditions of Economic Progress* (London: Macmillan).

Coffey, W., and M. Polese. 1989. "Producer Services and Regional Development: A Policy-Oriented Perspective." *Papers of the Regional Science Association* 67: 13–27.

Dennison, E. 1967. *Why Growth Rates Differ: Postwar Experiences in Nine Western Countries* (Washington: Brookings Institute).

Douglas, P. 1976. "The Cobb–Douglas Production Function Once Again: Its History, its Testing, and Some New Empirical Values." *Journal of Political Economy* 84: 903–915.

Eisner, R. 1988. "Extended Accounts for National Income and Product." *Journal of Economic Literature* 26: 1611–1684.

El Serafy, S., and E. Lutz. 1989. "Environmental and Natural Resource Accounting." In *Environmental Management and Economic Development,* edited by G. Schramm and J. Warford (Baltimore: Johns Hopkins University Press).

Fisher, A. 1939. "Production: Primary, Secondary, and Tertiary." *Economic Record* 15: 24–38.

Frank, A. 1979. *Dependent Accumulation and Underdevelopment* (New York: Monthly Review Press).

Ginsburg, N., J. Osborn, and G. Blank. 1986. *Geographic Perspectives on the Wealth of Nations.* Department of Geography, Research Paper No. 220 (Chicago: University of Chicago).

Grigg, D. 1980. *Population Growth and Agrarian Change: An Historical Perspective* (Cambridge: Cambridge University Press).

Grotewold, A. 1979. *The Regional Theory of World Trade* (Grove City, PA: Ptolemy).

Holloway, S., and K. Pandit. 1992. "The Disparity between the Level of Economic Development and Human Welfare." *The Professional Geographer* 44: 57–71.

International Comparison Program. 1986. *World Comparisons of Purchasing Power and Product for 1980* (New York: United Nations).

International Financial Statistics Yearbook. 1988. (Washington: International Monetary Fund).

Kaldor, N. 1961. "Capital Accumulation and Economic Growth." In *The Theory of Capital,* edited by F. Lutz and D. Hague (London: Macmillan).

Kellerman, A. 1985. "The Evolution of Service Economies." *The Professional Geographer* 37: 133–143.

Kendrick, J. 1972. *Economic Accounts and their Uses* (New York: McGraw-Hill).

Kuznets, S. 1951. *Economic Change* (New York: Norton).

Kuznets, S. 1965. *Economic Growth and Structure* (New York: Norton).

Lenin, V. 1948. *Imperialism: The Highest Stage of Capitalism* (London: Lawrence and Wishart). First published in 1917.

Lloyd, P., and P. Dicken. 1972. *Location in Space: A Theoretical Approach to Economic Geography* (New York: Harper & Row).

Marx, K. 1954. *Capital I* (London: Lawrence and Wishart). First published in 1867.

Miller, R., and P. Blair. 1985. *Input-Output Analysis: Foundations and Extensions* (Englewood Cliffs: Prentice-Hall).

Morris, M. 1979. *Measuring the Condition of the World's Poor: The Physical Quality of Life Index* (London: Frank Cass).

von Neumann, J. 1945. "A Model of General Equilibrium." *Review of Economic Studies* 13: 1–17.

Nordhaus, W., and J. Tobin. 1972. *Economic Growth* (New York: National Bureau of Economic Research).

O'Huallachian, B. 1989. "Agglomeration of Services in American Metropolitan Areas." *Growth and Change* 20/3: 34–49.

Pandit, K., and E. Casetti. 1989. "The Shifting Patterns of Sectoral Labor Allocation During Development: Developed Versus Developing Countries." *Annals of the Association of American Geographers* 79: 329–344.

Perrings, C. 1987. *Economy and Environment* (Cambridge: Cambridge University Press).

Reitsma, H., and J. Kleinpenning. 1985. *The Third World in Perspective* (Totawa, New Jersey: Rowman & Allanheld).

Ritzen, J. 1977. *Education, Economic Growth, and Income Distribution* (Amsterdam: North-Holland).

Rodgers, G. 1975. "Nutritionally Based Wage Determinations in the Low Income Labor Markets." *Oxford Economic Papers* 27: 61–81.

Romer, P. 1986. "Increasing Returns and Long Run Growth." *Journal of Political Economy* 94: 1002–1037.

Rostow, W. 1978. *The World Economy: History and Prospect* (Austin: University of Texas Press).

Schumpeter, J. 1951. *The Theory of Economic Development* (Cambridge: Harvard University Press).

Smith, D. 1987. *Geography, Inequality, and Society* (Cambridge: Cambridge University Press).

Stigler, G. 1951. "The Division of Labor is Limited by the Extent of the Market." *Journal of Political Economy* 59: 185–193.

Stolnitz, G. 1970. "The Demographic Transition: From High to Low Birth Rates and Death Rates." In *Population Geography: A Reader,* edited by G. Demko, H. Rose, and G. Schnell (New York: McGraw-Hill).

Tata, R., and R. Schultz. 1988. "World Variation in Human Welfare." *Annals of the Association of American Geographers* 78: 580–593.

Terlouw, C. 1989. "World-System Theory and Regional Geography: A Preliminary Exploration of the Context of Regional Geography." *Tijdschrift voor economische en sociale geografie* 80: 206–221.

Thirlwall, A. 1977. *Growth and Development,* 2d ed. (New York: John Wiley & Sons).

United Nations. 1986. *National Accounts Statistics: Analysis of Aggregates, 1983/1984* (New York: United Nations).

United Nations Development Program. 1990. *Human Development Report, 1990* (New York: United Nations).

Vining, D. 1986. "Population Redistribution towards Core Areas of Less Developed Countries, 1950–1980." *International Regional Science Review* 10: 1–45.

Wallerstein, I. 1979. *The Capitalist World-Economy* (Cambridge: Cambridge University Press).

World Bank. 1992. *World Development Report 1992* (New York: Oxford University Press).

Yapa, L., and W. Zelinsky. 1989. "How Not to Study the Geography of Human Welfare" *Annals of the Association of American Geographers* 79: 609–611.

CHAPTER 3

. . .

Models of Economic Growth and Development

. . .

3.1   INTRODUCTION

The state of a country's economic development is a complex thing to measure because there is no consensus as to its theoretical or practical definition. Almost by default, a country's per capita national product has become the standard by which its state of economic development is measured. Countries with large values of per capita GDP are considered, with few exceptions, to have achieved an advanced state of economic development. As briefly described in Chapter 2, not all countries have reached even a rough equality in per capita national product. The globe is highly differentiated along the lines of national income. Without such differentiation, a geography of national income would not exist. The geography does exist, but how did it come about? This is the question addressed in Chapters 3 and 4.

This chapter presents selected ideas concerning economic development that are quite varied. They share, however, an inward-looking perspective on the process of development that emphasizes domestic conditions as critical to a country's economic progress. The chapter begins with a presentation of two "single-factor fallacies" that at one time dominated thinking in the discipline of geography (and elsewhere) on a country's prospects for economic growth. That is followed by an outline of a more contemporary view of the processes of development and growth as one of "modernization." The chapter then focuses on problems associated with economic growth and concludes with some observations on the role of sectoral, social, and regional integration in solving those problems.

3.2 ENVIRONMENTAL DETERMINISM

The search by geographers for explanations of different development levels among countries has led to two broad generalizations concerning the foundations of Western-style economic growth: *environmental determinism* and *cultural determinism.* Both types of determinism are referred to as single-factor fallacies, mainly because in their extreme versions both focus myopically on one relevant factor of development, and neither works as a frame of general explanation of the economic development process.

Environmental determinism, in its strong version, usually is linked to the publications of Huntington (1915, 1945). Huntington's studies actually went beyond the role of the physical environment in effecting economic development and more broadly concerned the rise and fall of civilizations. His work was popular and influential both inside and outside the discipline of geography, but geographers liked it especially because it linked the physical environment and human action into one neat system. Extensions of Huntington's work to differential rates of economic growth provided an intuitively plausible explanation for the wealth of the United States and other midlatitude countries in Western Europe and the relative poverty of countries at extreme latitudes. Not unlike the three bears' porridge, low latitudes are too hot, high latitudes are too cold, but the middle latitudes are "just right."

The strong version of environmental determinism has been abandoned within the discipline of geography, but it does continue to have proponents among other groups of development analysts. One example of continued use of the strong version of environmental determinism is in the recent work of Kamarck (1976). Kamarck claimed that problems of poor soils, bad climate, insufficient mineral resources, and endemic diseases in the tropics virtually preclude low-latitude regions from economic growth. The strong version of environmental determinism fails because of the preponderance of exceptions to its rule. Seemingly inherent environmental constraints to economic growth really are functions of technological context. Many of the environmental barriers to economic development cited by Kamarck, for example, exist in Southern California.

A weak version of environmental determinism concerns the end of economic growth as much as its beginning. The weak version is an extension of Malthus's principle of population growth in relation to the problem of diminishing returns in agricultural production. In 1798, Malthus published his *Essay on the Principle of Population,* which contained the argument that human population tends to grow at a geometric rate and will do so unless limited by a scarcity of food. A scarcity of food, in turn, was guaranteed for large populations by the "law of diminishing returns" (recall from Chapter 2). Under a given level of technology, an increase in variable productive inputs relative to a fixed input will cause total output to increase. However, at some point of production, the increment of output will begin to diminish even as the increment of variable inputs is maintained. The fixed input is the limiting factor of production. In the case of agriculture, the limiting fixed input is land. In the Malthusian view, population growth inevitably leads to exhaustive use of all possible agricultural land. The addition of labor, the variable input, cannot overcome the fixity of land, so agricultural output is fundamentally limited. Because population tends to increase even in the face of limited food supplies, Malthus envisioned a continually miserable human condition.

The Malthusian perspective has been extended to encompass the perceived impasse between population growth and the use of natural resources and environmental pollution. A numerical simulation model representing this impasse at the global scale was built by Meadows et al. (1972). The model predicts that over time population outruns the environment's ability to carry it. Eventually, human population experiences a precipitous decline as the world is depleted of natural resources by production processes that concomitantly pollute the environment. The Earth becomes the ultimate fixed input to production, and its resources are not only being used up in a quantitative sense by population expansion but also in a qualitative sense by the pollution that is a by-product of increasing consumption. The environment ultimately controls the level of economic development in this weak version of environmental determinism just as much as in the strong version. So-called overpopulation is a problem in poor countries that limits their prospects of economic growth. Rich countries will be unable to maintain their levels of wealth because the ongoing process of wealth creation destroys the physical environment.

Newspaper and television accounts seem to bear continual evidence for the weak version of environmental determinism. Food shortages and other misallocations of resources are attributed to population pressures in poor countries. Environmental degradation is a real and pressing problem in most parts of the world, rich and poor alike. In addition, many environmental problems truly are international because atmospheric and oceanic currents are indifferent to political boundaries. Is the weak version of environmental determinism an accurate context for analyzing economic growth and decline?

The weak version of environmental determinism is fundamentally linked to the law of diminishing returns. However, the law of diminishing returns applies only under a condition of static technology. Technological improvements in production processes and product quality over time have led to more efficient use of resources and to substitutions of resources consumed. Boserup (1965) found that technological change actually is induced in many cases by increasing population. Based upon her research in poor regions, she suggested two types of technological change brought about increasing population density. One type is limited to improvements in agricultural production efficiency alone; the other leads to greater economy-wide efficiency.

According to the National Research Council's Working Group on Population Growth and Economic Development (1986), technological and institutional changes can be expected to limit population-resource problems. The Working Group examined a number of issues, including the relationships between population growth and use of exhaustible resources such as mineral ores and renewable resources such as forests, and the effect of population growth on pollution and other environmental degradation. The Group's somewhat guarded conclusions were that technological improvements in agriculture were, as suggested by Boserup, spurred by population growth, and that population growth tends to lead to organization of markets and formation of government policies that reduce both the inefficient use of resources and environmental abuses.

In the introduction to the Working Group's report, the authors remark that ". . . there is no statistical association between national rates of population growth and growth rates of income per capita" (p. 4). The lack of correlation between population variables and measures of national income has been noted frequently (e.g., Kelley, 1988; Simon, 1989). Using data for 1990 published by the World Bank (1992) for 109 countries, the Pearson correlation coefficients between population and per capita GDP (−.041), population density and per capita GDP (.114), and 1980–1990 annual population growth rate and 1980–1990 annual GDP growth (−.016) also show the lack of any real, measurable, simple association between population and national income. At this time, empirical evidence for the weak version of environmental determinism is more incidental than general.

3.3   CULTURAL DETERMINISM

The word "culture" has many definitions, but the one cited by Berry (1989, p. 5) is particularly appealing: "Culture is the collective programming of the mind that differentiates the motivations and behavior of members of one society from those of other societies." Cultural differentiation among societies can be seen in systems of production and distribution, government, life attitudes, and religious beliefs. At one time cultural determinism was viewed as an alternative to strong environmental determinism to explain European political and economic dominance of the globe during the age of imperialism. The dominant European powers found it fairly easy to subjugate most of Asia, Africa, and the New World because of their "superior" culture. European technology developed, according to the tenets of cultural determinism, because of a traditional Judeo-Christian attitude of antagonism toward the natural environment which could be traced to God's charge to Adam and Eve to multiply and subdue the Earth. Subduing the Earth was more easily accomplished by machine than by hand. Explanations for different levels of wealth within Christian regions were based on adherence to sect. The relative wealth of northern Europe was attributed to its majority of Protestants, whose work ethic contributed to a more rapid pace of industrialization. The relative poverty of southern Europe was attributed to its majority of Roman Catholics, who were inclined toward an agricultural economy.

Oishi (1985) called on the different emphases of two non-Western religious traditions to explain the economic differences between Thailand and Japan. Oishi argued that Confucianism is to East Asian economic development what Protestantism is to European economic development. Thrift and saving are important virtues in both Confucianism and Protestantism. These virtues lead to capital formation, which is a critical base for economic growth. Japan's economic development can be traced, according to Oishi, to its popular adoption of Confucianism. Thailand's dominant religion is Buddhism. To strict adherents of Buddhism, the world is a transitory state on the approach to Nirvana. Capital accumulation and investment are, at best, pointless in such a system. The impress of Buddhist philosophy on Thailand explains much of that country's poverty. Culture, according to Oishi, has determined the disparity in economic development between Japan and Thailand.

In 1990, Japan had a per capita GNP of U.S. $25,430, about 18 times larger than the per capita GNP of Thailand. However, the average annual rate of increase in GDP from 1980 through 1990 was 7.6% in Thailand and 4.1% in Japan. In addition, the annual average rate of increase in gross domestic investment from 1980 through 1990 was 8.7% in Thailand and 5.7% in Japan (World Bank, 1992). The disparity in rates of investment growth between the two countries especially suggests that any religious basis for the economic differences of Japan and Thailand seems to be disappearing, if it ever existed.

Peet (1989) has claimed that world capitalism is a global culture that is destroying regional cultures. On the other hand, Berry (1989) has suggested that economic location theory is inadequate because it does not incorporate cultural differences among many national economies. Cultural forces are strong but also appear to be flexible. Currently, economic and political systems, both of which are fundamental cultural characteristics, are undergoing real modification in many parts of the world. Berry linked market economies, or capitalism, and balanced-power political systems, or democracy, within the category of individualistic cultures. Capitalism and democracy, however, do not seem to be culturally specific in the way Berry describes. Instead, they can be viewed as providing a type of societal infrastructure that is necessary for economic growth on contemporary terms (Friedman and Friedman, 1980).

Johnston (1989) has suggested that democracy is not possible in the world's poorer countries because they are poor. Lewis (1992) has noted, however, that the growth of democracy and industrialization were mutually reinforcing in Turkey, and that its democratic system is more than partly responsible for Turkey's wealth relative to the other countries of the region. In fact, some suggest that poor countries may be poor because they are not democracies. Hayek (1944) has argued that political and economic centralization lead to national poverty. Useful economic knowledge is knowledge of specific opportunities, and such knowledge is too diffuse to be accommodated by central bodies. Innovation in economic processes is foregone under centralized control, and the economy cannot grow. Hirschman (1958) and Milanovic (1989), following Hayek, have insisted that the key to economic growth is individual entrepreneurship, which is stifled by government intervention in the economy. The focus on the role of the individual in economic growth was expressed earlier by Adam Smith in *The Wealth of Nations*, published in 1776. Smith claimed that the pursuit of individual self-interest led to economic growth.

According to the United Nations Development Program (1990), development is a process of increasing the choices people can make. Lack of political choice seems to limit economic choice, and lack of economic choice seems to limit political choice in a symbiotic relationship. Capitalist economies with right-wing dictatorships in South

America and elsewhere are experiencing a move toward democratically formed governments (Munck, 1989). In Eastern Europe, economic stagnation has led to the abandonment of centrally planned economies and governments controlled by Communist parties in favor of market economies and democratic political processes. Are capitalism and democracy fundamentally intertwined in the process of economic development? The answer appears to be yes, and the desire for economic growth effects cultural change rather than culture effecting economic growth.

3.4 THE EVOLUTIONARY APPROACH TO ECONOMIC DEVELOPMENT

Analysis of economic change often involves terms such as "growth" and "development," as in the present discussion. Use of these terms has invited analogies between biological processes and the processes that both drive and result from economic change (Nisbet, 1986). Several models of the process of economic development essentially are models of the evolution of society from some sort of primitive and simple initial state toward a more sophisticated and complex final state.

An early and influential model of this type was described by Marx and Engels in *The Communist Manifesto,* published in 1848. A type of primitive communism is the first form of economy, with tribal groups sustained by hunting and subsistence agriculture. The second form of economy is feudalism, with a defined class system in which the nobility dominates the rest of society. Feudalism gives way to capitalism. Workers, or proletariat, and a middle class, or petit bourgeoisie, become dominated by a class of capitalists, which controls society by its control of capital, the new means of production. Capitalism is transitory, too, according to this model of societal and economic evolution, because it entails self-destructive contradictions (see Section 3.6). Capitalism gives way to socialism, in which the political state acts for the people in controlling the means of production. Finally, socialism gives way to communism as the state withers and dies.

Rostow (1960) has provided an alternative to the Marxist stages of development in what has come to be called *modernization* theory. The Rostow model contains five stages that a country goes through in the process of economic development. The first stage is that of "traditional society," which is characterized by very limited technology, a great majority of the labor force and output found in agriculture, and low levels of capital formation. Political power is dispersed, and held by rural landlords who control the economy by their control of the agricultural sector.

The second stage of the model is one in which the "preconditions for take-off" are established. The preconditions are initiated by improvements in agricultural technology that lead to continual surpluses of agricultural output in certain regions. Increasing output induces capital formation by establishment of infrastructure, such as canals and roadways, that can be used to distribute surplus production beyond local areas. Interregional ties are formed by this developing transport infrastructure, leading not only to improved agricultural trade but also to trade in localized raw materials for nascent manufacturing. The establishment of fairly broad interregional flows defines an effective national market which, in turn, leads to establishment of a national government that provides an institutional infrastructure, primarily in its legal system, that allows continued economic growth. Facilitated by the national government, foreign export of domestically produced surpluses begins to take place during the preconditions for take-off. The external relationships of trade reinforce the strength of the national government and lead to a growing attitude of nationalism in the population. According to Rostow, the preconditions for take-off were first established in three countries: Great Britain, France, and the Netherlands.

Great Britain was the first country to "take off," or enter the third stage of modern economic development. Great Britain and France had equivalent stocks of raw materials, and Great Britain and the Netherlands had equivalent naval power. The development advantage among the three countries, however, fell to Great Britain because its raw material supplies were greater than those held by the Dutch, and its navy was superior to France's. The take-off is a stage of rapid industrial growth in a "propulsive" industry, cotton textiles in the British case. The propulsive industry generates growth in other types of manufacturing and the economy undergoes a general sectoral shift from agriculture to a manufacturing base. Countries escape the so-called Malthusian trap during the take-off through the development of industrial technology that overcomes the tendency toward diminishing returns in production.

In the fourth stage of the model—the "drive to maturity"—technological improvements extend to a wide range of industries. The initial propulsive industry is replaced by a series of others. The economy is broadened, however, as the once-critical role of any single industry is diminished by economic diversification. The last stage of economic development is one of "high mass consumption." In this ultimate stage, manufacturing is oriented toward the production of consumer goods and declines in relative importance as the service sector grows. Obviously, this final stage is marked by high average personal incomes.

Rostow's model represents an attempt to determine pertinent consistencies in the development process across countries of the world. Critical propulsive industries vary from country to country and over time, but according to Rostow the general process of development is one of stage-to-stage transition. With some exceptions, countries can expect to replicate the earlier European experience of economic growth and eventually reach the stage of high mass consumption. A list of stage transition dates for selected countries is given in Table 3.1. The richer countries on the list are in the stage of high mass consumption, while the poorer ones are in that stage's precursors. Rostow has been criticized heavily for declaring his model to be a universal growth experience, rather than just lessons from British history (e.g., Taylor, 1989). The focus of the criticism is that a country's context within the international economy is largely ignored in favor of an isolationist framework for economic development. Even allowing the accuracy of the years given in Table 3.1, can we really expect Thailand to follow the same development trail as that of Great Britain, given the

TABLE 3.1 Initial Years of Transition across Rostow's Stages of Economic Growth: Selected Countries

Country	Take-Off	Drive to Maturity	High Mass Consumption
Great Britain	1783	1830	1920
United States	1815	1870	1910
France	1830	1870	1920
Germany	1840	1870	1925
Sweden	1868	1890	1925
Japan	1885	1905	1955
Russia/USSR	1890	1905	1956
Italy	1895	1920	1950
Canada	1896	1915	1919
Australia	1901	1920	1925
Argentina	1933	1950	nr
Turkey	1933	1961	nr
Brazil	1933	1950	nr
Mexico	1940	1960	nr
Iran	1955	1965	nr
India	1952	1963	nr
China	1952	1968	nr
Taiwan	1953	1960	nr
Thailand	1960	nr	nr
Republic of Korea	1961	1968	nr

Note: "nr" indicates stage not reached as of 1978.
Source: Rostow, W. 1978. *The World Economy: History and Prospect* (Austin: University of Texas Press).

former's take-off in 1960 and the latter's take-off in 1783? Thailand faces an entirely different array of external relationships than Great Britain faced in the past, and external relationships are critical to economic growth and change.

Evolutionary models also have been developed for intranational regional development. Borchert (1967), for example, has described four epochs of American metropolitan location and growth in terms of broad technological change in transportation. The "sail wagon" epoch lasted from 1790 to 1830. Transportation was confined mainly to water routes during the period and America's major cities were either ocean ports or located on navigable inland waterways. The "iron horse" epoch, from 1830 to 1870, was marked by the development of the American railway system. Urban growth began to take place at interior sites served by the expanding railway network. The interior cities, however, served as feeders to the older ports, so port cities continued to grow but at slower rates than during the previous epoch. The "steel rail" epoch, lasting from 1870 to 1920, was the period in which the American rail system reached its greatest extent and had its maximum impact on the development of the American urban system. Cities grew in America's interior as railways expanded beyond their role of complements to waterways and became the dominant transportation mode. River ports, in particular, became much less important transport centers during the period, and high rates of urban growth occured in the Midwest and West. The "auto-air-amenity" epoch began in 1920 and, like Rostow's stage of high mass consumption, is the final period in an evolutionary process. The number of cities stabilized at the end of the steel rail epoch, and metropolitan growth rates generally have stabilized during the current epoch.

3.5 PROBLEMS OF ECONOMIC GROWTH AND DEVELOPMENT

Modernization theory probably tells us more about the history of economic growth and development among countries than about any current process. One historical feature of economic growth not addressed in modernization theory, however, is that it is not often an easy process, nor one that is smoothly linear in its advance. Short-term business cycles of growth and stagnation or recession occur in even the wealthiest countries. Growth and stagnation, or even decline, are considered to have a regular periodicity that is not too different from a circadian rhythm or generational reproduction. Recently, some emphasis has been placed on the analysis of long-term cycles of economic upswing and downswing called Kondratieff waves. These long economic waves are named for the Russian economist who either discovered or invented them, depending upon one's point of view. The waves supposedly can be found at both the global and national scales of analysis. They last about 50 years and are divided in half, with an initial period of strong growth, or upswing, followed by stagnation or downswing.

Maier (1987) defined four global Kondratieff waves with reference to periods of technological innovation. The first Kondratieff wave lasted from 1790 to 1849. Basic innovations during the period affected machine tools and steam engines. The second Kondratieff began in 1849 and ended in 1894. The dominant innovations during the second wave were in railroads and iron and steel production. The third Kondratieff, from 1894 to 1938, was a period of technological innovations in electrical engineering, chemicals, communications, and automotive transportation. According to Maier, the fourth Kondratieff began in 1938 and is just coming to an end. This Kondratieff has been driven by innovations in plastics, communications, and electronics.

Based upon examination of national production and income variables, Kleinknecht (1987) has found strong evidence of long-wave economic behavior in Germany, France, and the United States. He found weak evidence for national Kondratieffs in Belgium, Italy, and Sweden, and no evidence for long waves in the United Kingdom. However, validation of the long-wave hypothesis is hampered in two ways. First, empirical evidence of the existence of long waves has been developed on a data base that is quite thin. Reasonably accurate measures of national income and industrial production simply are not available for measuring the earlier waves, especially at the global scale. National production data covering the early periods is available for some countries, but the comparability of early data series to more current ones is questionable. Second, the theoretical basis for the existence of Kondratieff waves is weak, and nonexistent for their regular periodicity.

Monetary and financial contexts have been examined as theoretical bases for Kondratieff waves, but their existence is most frequently attributed, as by Maier (1987), to waves of technological innovation. The upswing of the Kondratieff is a period of increasing application of innovations that increases rates of growth. The downswing comes when the growth potential of technological innovation is used up due to its widespread application. Renewed growth requires new technology. Technological innovation can form the basis of the Kondratieff only if it is cyclical also. If innovation is a smooth, continuous process over time, it cannot be the basis of economic upswings and downswings.

Schumpeter (1951) argued for a lumpy rather than continuous progression of innovations, and his work can provide the beginning of a theoretical foundation for Kondratieff waves. Schumpeter drew a distinction between *invention,* the bringing about of new products and processes, and *innovation,* the adoption of inventions in the economy. Innovation comes about because of perceived profit opportunities, so not all inventions become innovations. Schumpeter divided innovations into two groups. Major innovations can generate substantial new profits in a particular industry. In addition, major innovations spawn minor innovations in related industries. For example, development of the automobile as a major innovation led to minor innovations in the related industries of steel and rubber production, and in highway and petroleum engineering, among others. Major innovations are infrequent, but when they occur they bring about bunches of minor innovations. Rapid growth takes place in spurts as bunches of innovations come along, so economic growth is cyclical as long as innovation is possible. Schumpeter's theory of innovations, therefore, can be taken as a theoretical basis for the existence of economic upswings and downswings related to technological advance, but it offers no explanation for the periodicity of the Kondratieffs.

3.6   MARX AND THE CRISES OF CAPITALIST GROWTH

In the early years of developing capitalist economies, Marx found reason to believe that such systems were not just cyclical, but doomed by internal inconsistencies. His analysis was, in fact, a reflection of the times in which he worked and the widespread abuses of laborers that took place during the beginnings of the industrial revolution. His thinking on the capitalist, or modern, economy became very influential by the early 1900s. Despite the failure of the centrally planned economies that it inspired, it remains an interesting analysis.

Marx (1954/56) relied on the labor theory of value in his economic analysis. All output ultimately results from labor alone, either in its present active state or in the form of "dead labor" embodied in machines and other capital. A machine, as a form of capital, can produce nothing by itself, and nature's free gift of ore in the ground is worthless until it is mined by labor. Capitalists economies are, by definition, controlled by the owners of capital, and not labor. The only way that capitalists can earn profits is to expropriate some of a product's value that should be attributed to labor. The expropriated share of a product's value is referred to as its surplus value. Under capitalism, production takes place not because a product is useful, as in a subsistence economy, but only because it has exchange value.

Initially, exchange value of a product tends to increase as the cost of its production decreases due to increases in productivity. Productivity is increased by capital deepening, or increasing the amount of capital per worker. Marx defined two types of capital. Constant capital, such as machinery, does not change in value over the production process. Variable capital consists of wages payed to employ labor. Surplus value, as value over and above the payment to labor, increases largely due to increases in constant capital. The production function described by Marx takes the form of the identity

$$Q = K_c + K_v + S \tag{3.1}$$

where Q is the value of output, K_c is the value of constant capital, K_v is the value of variable capital, and S is surplus value. This production function, as developed by Marx, leads to three types of crises that eventually bring about the self-destruction of capitalism: (1) a falling rate of profit, (2) a realization crisis, and (3) a disproportionality crisis.

The rate of profit, P_r, in Marx's theory is defined as

$$P_r = \frac{S}{K_c + K_v} \tag{3.2}$$

or the ratio of surplus value to the summed value of both types of capital. The rate of profit must fall because surplus value is always reinvested by capitalists in the interest of raising levels of constant capital. This continuous investment of surplus value, or profit, in new constant capital is a fundamental behavioral assumption in Marxist analysis. The ongoing investment in constant capital causes it to increase in relation to variable capital. The ratio K_c/K_v, called the organic composition of capital, always is increasing due to reinvestment of profits and technological improvements. As K_c increases in Equation 3.2, P_r must decrease. In order to raise the rate of profit, capitalists increase productivity by increasing the organic composition of capital, but obviously their effort is futile because increasing constant capital causes continued decline in the rate of profit. Eventually, the process causes bankruptcy.

The realization crisis also is based in the inevitable increase in the organic composition of capital. Employment of more constant capital leads to the technological unemployment of labor. The exchange value of a worker's only commodity, labor, decreases as a reserve army of unemployed grows. Capitalists cannot realize surplus value from consumer goods, however, because the consumer market is increasingly one of unemployed workers. The capital goods sector also is affected by the realization crisis because demand for capital goods in the bankrupt consumer goods sector no longer exists. This relationship is called the disproportionality crisis because it describes how two interrelated sectors cannot grow at different rates.

Marx's economic growth theory, which is part of a much larger sociological and philosophical work, has been criticized on a number of grounds. One criticism focuses on his use of the labor theory of value, which he did not originate but adopted from Smith and Ricardo. Most non-Marxist economists think that capital, as well as labor, is a true productive factor. Just as idle machines cannot produce a good without a labor input, labor cannot produce much without tools and other types of capital. A more important criticism of Marx's theory is that the inevitable fall in the rate of profit is not so much a true theoretical result as an extension of his assumption that the organic composition of capital is constantly increasing. Capitalists, like labor, do consume goods, so not all their profits are reinvested. In addition, labor must be employed in the production of new constant capital which is brought about by reinvested profits, so there is a possibility that the organic composition remains stable, and therefore the rate of profit. According to Samuelson (1970), real rates of profit actually have been stable over the long run in the industrial countries.

3.7 THE HARROD-DOMAR THEORY OF GROWTH

Many of the gross injustices observed by Marx were at least diminished, if not eliminated, by intervention of governments and the development of organized labor. The Great Depression of the1930s, however, was a strong reminder of the "fits and starts" characteristic of economic growth in even the most developed economies. One economic model, describing the economy as a series of adjustments that tended to encourage upswings or downswings, was developed by Harrod (1948), and by Domar (1957). Their analyses were independent, but their work has been linked due to its similarity in scope and purpose. Both versions are Keynesian in their use of broad aggregates, such as national savings and investment, to describe paths of economic growth. In a sense, Domar's work can be considered an extension of Harrod's, so only the basic format of Harrod's theory is described here.

Harrod defined a two-commodity economy of capital goods and consumer goods. There are only two activities as well, consumption and investment. The relative prices of the two commodities are known and constant. Their constant price ratio renders investment a reaction to changing demand alone, because price changes can have no bearing on profitability. Consumers, or households, save a known portion of their incomes, and savings are equal to investment. The fixed saving proportion, s, can be defined as

$$s = \frac{S_t}{Q_t} \qquad (3.3)$$

where S_t is current saving and Q_t is current output (note the instantaneous relationship). There is a given incremental capital-to-output ratio in production that defines the amount of additional productive capacity needed to produce an additional amount of output given current technology. The incremental capital-to-output ratio, a, is defined as

$$a = \frac{I_t}{Q_t - Q_{t-1}} \qquad (3.4)$$

where I_t is investment, which is equal to the increase in capital stock; Q_t is current output; and Q_{t-1} was the output in the preceding period. The given incremental capital-to-output ratio means that there is a given capital-to-labor ratio as well. Increased production is due to capital widening, or the spread of capital across the labor force, rather than by capital deepening as in Marx's theory.

In Harrod's theory, household consumption and investment are fixed in given proportions, but producers determine their levels of investment based on expectations of future demand. Production capacities are chosen with reference to least-cost production points for filling expected demand. Essentially, producers must determine an optimal incremental capital-to-output ratio so that output will neither exceed nor fall short of demand.

Harrod defined three types of growth rates in the economy: natural, actual, and warranted. The natural rate of growth, G_N, is defined as

$$G_N = \frac{L_t - L_{t-1}}{L_{t-1}} \qquad (3.5)$$

where L_t is the current size of the labor force, L_{t-1} was the size of the labor force in the preceding period, and λL is a labor augmentation term defining the degree of capital widening. Technological progress affects labor only and not the incremental capital-to-output ratio (technological progress of this sort is referred to as "Harrod neutral"). As long as λ is positive, labor is increasing its productivity.

The focus of Harrod's theory, however, is on the relationship between the actual and warranted rates of growth. The actual rate of growth, G_A, is defined as

$$G_A = \frac{Q_t - Q_{t-1}}{Q_{t-1}} \qquad (3.6)$$

where Q again refers to output. Note that $G_A = s/a$ because the actual rate of growth in output must be equal to the saving proportion, s, which determines the total increase in capital stock, divided by a, the incremental capital-to-output ratio. The warranted rate of growth, G_W, was defined by Harrod as

$$G_W = \frac{s}{a^*} \tag{3.7}$$

where a^* is the incremental capital-to-output ratio desired by producers to achieve the level of output they expect will just satisfy demand.

Instability in the economy is expected in Harrod's theory because the equilibrium case, in which the warranted rate of growth and the actual rate of growth are equal, need not occur. It is just as likely that the warranted rate will be either greater or less than the actual rate of growth. If the warranted rate is greater than the actual rate, producers will think that they have overestimated demand and decrease their investment and thereby decrease output. Recall that saving is defined as a constant proportion of output (Equation 3.3) and actual growth decreases as savings, or household investment, decreases ($G_A = s/a$). Therefore, a decrease in a^* effectively reduces demand in the next round of production. Once the warranted rate of growth exceeds the actual rate, the inequality becomes self-sustaining because producers always invest at a rate that meets the preceding period's demand and not the demand of the current period. A reversal of the relationship arises if the warranted rate is less than the actual rate, with ongoing instability in the economy due to underproduction. Harrod's theory is one of economic instability with ill-defined lower and upper limits to the disequilibrium paths in an economy.

Criticism of Harrod's theory is generally targeted at his behavioral assumption that producers invest only to meet expected demand in the next time period. This assumption eliminates any long-term investment plans, or anticipation of long-term demand trends, by producers. A related criticism is that producers are not required to respond to unanticipated demand levels only by varying their output. Price variations, of course, are another option that would be particularly useful in the short run.

3.8 THE NEOCLASSICAL THEORY OF GROWTH

Marx and Harrod both thought that capitalistic growth is an unstable process. Labor and/or capital would tend to be unemployed, or their shares in production in disequilibrium. Neoclassical theory, however, indicates that growth is an equilibrium process in which labor and capital both can be fully employed. Neoclassical growth theory essentially came about as a response to Harrod's theory. Important early contributions to neoclassical growth theory were made by Solow (1956), Swan (1956), and Uzawa (1961). The work of Solow usually is considered the pivotal contribution, and the basic format of his model is described here.

Solow assumed that output, Q, is a homogeneous commodity that can be either invested or consumed. The relative prices of investment, or capital, goods and consumption goods are not fixed as in the case of Harrod. Changing relative prices are, in fact, the focus of neoclassical theory. The production function in Solow's theory takes the form

$$Q = (K, L) \tag{3.8}$$

where K is capital and L is labor. This is an aggregate production function for the entire economy and is called "linear homogeneous" because it has the property

$$\lambda Q = (\lambda K, \lambda L) \tag{3.9}$$

where λ is a common multiple. For example, if $\lambda = 1.2$, a 20% increase in capital and 20% increase in labor results in a 20% increase in output, and not a 40% increase as easily might be assumed.

Capital and labor are imperfect but close substitutes in the neoclassical production function. They are imperfect because production cannot take place if only one or the other is employed. Away from the extremes, there is a wide range of possible factor combinations. The factors have a tendency to be used in fairly equal batches because they exhibit diminishing returns. That is, increments to one factor of production, while the other factor is held constant, result in decreasing increments of output. However, the increments in output always will be positive. In the case of variable capital and constant labor in production, the relationship takes the form

$$0 < \frac{\Delta Q}{\Delta K, L} < 1 \tag{3.10}$$

where the symbol Δ denotes any positive increment, or *marginal* change.

The choice of factor intensity, or which factor to employ in a relatively greater amount, depends upon the relative marginal productivities of the factors. The production function used by Solow is separable, so that the effect of the factors on production can be determined individually (as implied in Equation 3.10). The intensity rules are,

$$\text{if } \frac{\Delta Q}{\Delta K} > \frac{\Delta Q}{\Delta L}, \text{ then } \frac{\Delta K}{\Delta L} > 1 \tag{3.11a}$$

$$\text{if } \frac{\Delta Q}{\Delta K} = \frac{\Delta Q}{\Delta L}, \text{ then } \frac{\Delta K}{\Delta L} = 1 \tag{3.11b}$$

$$\text{if } \frac{\Delta Q}{\Delta K} < \frac{\Delta Q}{\Delta L}, \text{ then } \frac{\Delta K}{\Delta L} < 1 \tag{3.11c}$$

where ΔQ, ΔK, and ΔL are marginal values. If any factor's marginal productivity is greater than the other's, its use is intensified. Due to diminishing returns, however, the intensification eventually will lead to a relative decline in the factor's marginal productivity, and the production function will change fluidly so that more of the other factor is used. The factor switching in the production function inevitably leads to an equilibrium of capital and labor in production, and a tendency toward their full employment.

Solow's theory relies on capital deepening to induce gains in labor productivity, and it contains the assumption that technological progress is the main source of growth of output. Technological progress is neutral and disembodied, which means that it does not augment only labor or capital individually, but both in the same way and at the same time. This technology assumption suggests that the production function actually takes the form

$$Q = (K, L) + TP \tag{3.12}$$

where TP is technological progress.

Much of the criticism of Solow's and other's versions of neoclassical growth theory focuses on its aggregate production function. Influential critics, such as Robinson (1965) and Kaldor (1961), have argued that the microeconomic concept of the production function cannot be realistically aggregated to an entire national economy. (Samuelson [1962] has shown a link between the microeconomic and macroeconomic production functions, but it is not general.) In addition, the flexibility of the neoclassical production function is argued to be unrealistic. Machinery as capital, for example, cannot be reduced in size as the employment of labor increases. Further, the disembodiment of technology from capital is considered to be unrealistic because technological progress is intertwined with capital improvements. Recent work by Romer (1986) has extended the neoclassical model so that technology is considered a separate factor of production. Romer considers technology, or knowledge, as the cause of increasing returns to factors, or economies of scale. Such increasing returns, as illustrated in Chapter 2 by the high productivity tendencies of the rich countries, cannot be accommodated easily by conventional neoclassical models in which factor prices are determined in the kind of competitive markets associated with constant returns to scale. Increasing returns are commonly associated with monopolistic markets rather than competitive ones. Unfortunately, the "best" aggregate production function remains to be decided, and both the two-factor version and its extensions provide good empirical fits with reality.

3.9 THE DUAL ECONOMY

We can think of the transition from Marx's capitalist economy to the neoclassical economy as a historical process in which social institutions and perhaps technological progress combine with the market to smooth economic growth. It may be that this is the point at which economic growth and economic development become different things, with a developed economy defined as one that grows smoothly. Some insight concerning this type of distinction between growth and development can be drawn from the analysis of the *dual economy* made by Arthur Lewis (1954, 1972). According to Lewis's model, the existence of a dual economy provides the potential basis for economic growth in its contemporary sense. Although there are many definitions (see Peattie, 1980), Lewis's dual economy consists of a capitalist sector and a noncapitalist sector. The distinguishing characteristics of such economies are twofold. First, the capitalist sector is that in which labor is hired for a wage, and the product is sold for a profit; in the noncapitalist sector, profit does not enter the picture and the output of labor directly enters into consumption. Frequently, the capitalist sector is defined as manufacturing and the noncapitalist as agricultural, but that was not Lewis's intention. The method of production, and not the type of output, is a distinguishing characteristic. The second characteristic that distinguishes the two sectors is their prevailing wage rates, which are different but based together on significant labor surpluses in the noncapitalist sector.

The pivotal assumption in Lewis's model is that, in anything less than a long run, the marginal productivity of a worker in the noncapitalist sector is zero. In other words, reducing the number of workers on the farm does not cause a decrease in agricultural output, or reducing the number of workers in homespun textile production does not decrease the output of cloth. The large labor surplus in the noncapitalist sector can be drawn in to the capitalist sector as long as capitalist sector wages exceed noncapitalist sector wages by even a minimal amount. As long as the marginal productivity of a worker in the noncapitalist sector remains zero, the labor supply for the capitalist sector is virtually unlimited at a fixed low wage. The most interesting result in the Lewis model derives from this labor market condition; that increasing employment in the capitalist sector causes profits to increase as a proportion of national income at the same time per capita wages are increasing.

Lewis assumed that wages are spent on consumption and that profits are saved in the sense that they are reinvested. As additional labor is employed in the capitalist sector, any wage beyond the subsistence level is spent on consumption of capitalist sector goods and services. In turn, reinvested profits are deployed to capital broadening in order to maintain productivity levels in the expanding labor force, brought about by the increase in demand for the capitalist sector's goods and services. The share of profits in national income increases because output increases at a faster rate than wages, which do not increase at all on a per capita basis. Despite the fixity of wage rates, however, per capita incomes increase because workers who moved from the noncapitalist to the capitalist sector earn a minor wage premium, and at the same time workers in the noncapitalist sector earn a greater share of its total output, which does not decline despite the sectoral migration of labor.

Obviously, the ongoing supply of labor to the capitalist sector, which drives Lewis's model, is not unlimited. The condition can last for a long time, however, if population is undergoing rapid increase by natural means or by immigration, or if the labor force is expanding rapidly due to increased participation by women. Eventually, however, the fixed wage level in the capitalist sector will be driven up by the loss of the labor surplus in the noncapitalist sector. This is a critical turning point in the national economy for two reasons: (1) the wage rates of the capitalist and noncapitalist sectors should begin to equalize because workers in both sectors now have positive marginal productivities, and (2) shortages of labor in both sectors induce technological advances that are embodied in capital deepening. Thus productivity increases are accomplished by the substitution of capital for labor, and the share of wages in the national income can increase in proportion to profits.

The Lewis model begins with the classical economics of Marx, but ends with a much happier neoclassical result. Initial growth in the dual economy is largely in the form of increased profits made available from underpayment of wages. Instead of the inevitable crises of Marx, however, the dual economy of Lewis eventually runs smoothly as a single economy under neoclassical rules. The differences between the capitalist and noncapitalist sectors are eliminated by their shared labor shortage. Lewis's main point is that eventual widespread economic growth and development can be fueled by initial large supplies of cheap labor that result from the initial condition of economic duality. The Lewis model has been assessed in a variety of contexts, including the economic resurgence of Western Europe following World War II (Kindleberger, 1967) and the growth patterns of individual regions in the United States (Suarez-Villa, 1983).

3.10 ECONOMIC DEVELOPMENT AS INTEGRATION

The dual economy has been used as the conceptual basis for the existence of primate city-size distributions. A *primate city* is a national, or regional, city that is very much larger than the other places in a national urban system. Typically, it is the national political capital and the center of an economy's interactions with the international economy. Primacy in urban systems is found in countries at all levels of development but is particularly evident in poorer countries (Reitsma and Kleinpennig, 1985). Primacy seems a logical spatial expression of the dual economy in a poor country. The capitalist sector is small, but it agglomerates in one place in order to benefit from linkages and density of infrastructure. The noncapitalist sector is largely rural and spatially dispersed. The flow of low-cost labor is represented in large waves of rural to urban migration that are a common experience among a large number of countries during periods of rapid growth. Empirical evidence of the relationship between primacy and the dual economy, or any other economic conditions, is lacking, however. Richardson and Schwartz (1988), for example, were unable to find any measurable link between a series of economic variables and primacy in either a full set of countries or in a smaller set of poor countries.

The generalized association of primacy with low national income can be traced to the initial geographical concentration of physical capital that is common in most poorer economies due to scarcity of capital resources (Richardson, 1980). In earlier stages of economic growth, limited capital resources are more efficiently used in spatial concentrations, or agglomerations. *Agglomeration economies* can be achieved as average costs decrease because of the low transport and communications costs associated with the agglomeration. Agglomeration economies are an important basis for the tendency of national economies to have cores and peripheries. As the economy becomes richer, however, capital resources grow and can become more spatially widespread.

The initial concentration of physical capital and its subsequent dispersal with economic growth is one of a series of similar processes cited by Alonso (1980) as following a bell-shaped curve in their temporal association with economic development. The others included regional inequality, or disparity in per capita income across the parts of a country, and social inequality, made manifest in disparities in per capita income across subgroups of a country's population. To a great extent, the problem of regional inequality arises from the characteristic pattern of geographical concentration of capital resources. As capital resources become dispersed, peripheral regions experience an increase in their incomes as more labor can be employed, or employed more efficiently.

The development of interregional links in the form of transport and communications infrastructure is a vital part of the dispersal of physical capital. Banks (1974) found that the development of a country's interregional communications links was a common feature of industrialization in a large number of countries. The development of the Interstate Highway System was a critical element in the growth of that southern part of the United States called the Sunbelt (Cuadrado Roura and Suarez-Villa, 1992). It is not surprising that Borchert's (1967) growth eras are presented in the context of advances in transportation technology.

Physical linkages in the form of transportation and communications infrastructure effectively integrate a country's regions so that factors of production can be efficently distributed in a geographical sense. Their efficient distribution, according to the spatial neoclassical model, can lead to full employment and, by implication, income equality across a country's regions (see Chapter 4). Income inequality among social groups cannot be diminished by physical capital, but linkages among groups are as important in this effort as linkages between places are in the effort to reduce regional inequality. It is likely that the passage of civil rights legislation in the United States in the 1960s was just as important to sunbelt economic growth as the Interstate Highway System. The end of legal racial discrimination, which particularly affected the South at the time, enabled economic as well as racial integration. As in the case of regional integration, racial integration allows efficient employment of the factors of production, and raises incomes. Segregation, of the form still practiced throughout the United States, is not only morally reprehensible but economically inefficient. The same can be said of gender biases in labor markets, or any other socioeconomic condition that segments rather than integrates a country's population. Such biases effectively retard development by artificially maintaining conditions of "unlimited supplies of labor" when the economy should have otherwise passed that stage. As Alonso stated (1980, p. 13), ". . . economic development is a form of integration of the socioeconomy, over time, distance, and institutional barriers."

REFERENCES

Alonso, W. 1980. "Five Bell Shapes in Development." *Papers of the Regional Science Association* 45: 5–16.

Banks, A. 1974. "Industrialization and Development: A Longitudinal Analysis." *Economic Development and Cultural Change* 22: 320–337.

Berry, B. 1989. "Comparative Geography of the Global Economy: Cultures, Corporations, and the Nation-State." *Economic Geography* 65: 1–18.

Borchert, J. 1967. "American Metropolitan Evolution." *The Geographical Review* 57: 301–332.

Boserup, E. 1965. *The Conditions of Agricultural Growth: The Economics of Agrarian Change under Population Pressure* (Chicago: Aldine).

Cuadrado Roura, J., and L. Suarez-Villa. 1992. "Regional Economic Integration and the Evolution of Disparities." Paper presented at the 4th World Congress of the Regional Science Association International held in Palma de Mallorca, Spain.

Domar, E. 1957. *Essays in the Theory of Economic Growth* (Oxford: Oxford University Press).

Friedman, M., and R. Friedman. 1980. *Free to Choose* (London: Penguin).

Harrod, R. 1948. *Toward a Dynamic Economics* (London: Macmillan).

Hayek, F. 1944. *The Road to Serfdom* (Chicago: University of Chicago Press).

Hirschman, A. 1958. *The Strategy of Economic Development* (New Haven: Yale University Press).

Huntington, E. 1915. *Civilization and Climate* (New Haven: Yale University Press).

———— 1945. *Mainsprings of Civilization* (New York: John Wiley & Sons).

Johnston, R. 1989. "The Individual and the World Economy." In *A World in Crisis? Geographical Perspectives,* 2d ed., R. Johnston and P. Taylor, eds. (Cambridge: Basil Blackwell).

Kaldor, N. 1961. "Capital Accumulation and Economic Growth." In *The Theory of Capital,* F. Lutz and D. Hague, eds. (London: Macmillan).

Kamarck, A. 1976. *The Tropics and Economic Development: A Provocative Inquiry into the Poverty of Nations* (Baltimore: Johns Hopkins Press).

Kelley, A. 1988. "Economic Consequences of Population Change in the Third World." *Journal of Economic Literature* 26: 1685–1728.

Kindleberger, C. 1967. *Europe's Postwar Growth: The Role of Labor Supply* (Cambridge: Harvard University Press).

Kleinknecht, A. 1987. "Rates of Innovation and Profits in the Long Wave." In *The Long Wave Debate,* T. Vasko, ed. (New York: Springer-Verlag).

Lewis, A. 1954. "Economic Development with Unlimited Supplies of Labor." *Manchester School of Economic and Social Studies* 22: 139–191.

———— 1972. "Reflections on Unlimited Labor." In *International Economics and Development,* L. Di Marco, ed. (New York: Academic Press).

Lewis, B. 1992. "Rethinking the Middle East." *Foreign Affairs* 71/4: 99–119.

Maier, H. 1987. "Basic Innovations and the Next Long Wave of Productivity Growth: Socioeconomic Implications and Consequences." In *The Long Wave Debate.*

Marx, K. 1954/56. *Capital I, II, III* (London: Lawrence and Wishart). Capital I first published in 1867, Capital II first published in 1885, and Capital III first published in 1894.

Meadows, D.H., D.L. Meadows, J. Randers, and W. Behrens. 1972. *The Limits to Growth* (London: Pan).

Milanovic, B. 1989. *Liberalization and Entrepreneurship: Dynamics of Reform in Socialism and Capitalism* (Armonk, New York: M.E. Sharpe).

Munck, R. 1989. *Latin America: The Transition to Democracy* (London: Zed).

Nisbet, R. 1986. *The Making of Modern Society* (New York: New York University Press).

Oishi, Y. 1985. "Culture and Region: Prolegomena." *Papers of the Regional Science Association* 56: 1–3.

Peattie, L. 1980. "Anthropological Perspectives on the Concepts of Dualism, the Informal Sector, and Marginality in Developing Urban Economics." *International Regional Science Review* 5: 1–31.

Peet, R. 1989. "World Capitalism and the Destruction of Regional Cultures." In *A World in Crisis? Geographical Perspectives*, 2d. ed.

Reitsma, H., and J. Kleinpenning. 1985. *The Third World in Perspective* (Totawa, NJ: Rowman & Allanheld).

Richardson, H. 1980. "Polarization Reversal in Developing Countries." *Papers of the Regional Science Association* 45: 67–86.

Richardson, H., and G. Schwartz. 1988. "Economic Development, Population and Primacy." *Regional Studies* 22: 467–475.

Robinson, J. 1965. *Collected Economic Essays,* vol. 3 (Oxford: Oxford University Press).

Romer, P. 1986. "Increasing Returns and Long Run Growth." *Journal of Political Economy* 94: 1002–1037.

Rostow, W. 1960. *The Stages of Economic Growth: A Non-communist Manifesto* (New York: Cambridge University Press).

_____ 1978. *The World Economy: History and Prospect* (Austin: University of Texas Press).

Samuelson, P. 1962. "Parable and Realism in Capital Theory." *Review of Economic Studies* 30: 193–206.

_____ 1970. *Economics,* 8th ed. (New York: McGraw-Hill).

Schumpeter, J. 1951. *The Theory of Economic Development* (Cambridge: Harvard University Press).

Simon, L. 1989. "On Aggregate Empirical Studies Relating Population Variables to Economic Development." *Population and Development Review* 15: 323–332.

Solow, R. 1956. "A Contribution to the Theory of Economic Growth." *Quarterly Journal of Economics* 70: 65–94.

Suarez-Villa, L. 1983. "A Note on Dualism, Capital-Labor Ratios, and the Regions of the U.S." *Journal of Regional Science* 23: 547–552.

Swan, T. 1956. "Economic Growth and Capital Accumulation." *Economic Record* 32: 334–361.

Taylor, P. 1989. "The Error of Developmentalism in Human Geography." In *Horizons in Human Geography,* D. Gregory and R. Walford, eds. (Totawa, New Jersey: Barnes & Noble).

United Nations Development Program. 1990. *Human Development Report 1990* (New York: United Nations).

Uzawa, H. 1961. "Neutral Inventions and the Stability of Growth Equilibrium." *Review of Economic Studies* 28: 117–124.

Working Group on Population Growth and Economic Development. 1986. *Population Growth and Economic Development: Policy Questions* (Washington: National Academy Press).

World Bank. 1992. *World Development Report 1992* (New York: Oxford University Press).

CHAPTER 4

. . .

Spatial Interaction and
Economic Development

. . .

4.1 INTRODUCTION

The last chapter addressed economic growth and development from an inward-looking perspective and ended by considering the degree of a country's socio-economic integration as the measure of development. Essentially, the process of economic development can be viewed as the processes of advancing integration as an economy grows. There can be rich yet undeveloped countries, but developed countries are never poor. This chapter refocuses the analysis of economic growth and development to an outward-looking perspective, and emphasizes the role of spatial interaction between places, or flows, rather than internal characteristics.

How does the general nature of external relationships between countries affect their economic growth? These external relationships can be viewed as forms of spatial interaction in the international economy. The nature of spatial interaction in a system is as much a function of the system's place characteristics as it is of the flows themselves. In fact, the flows result in reaction to the place characteristics, and to the degree of spatial integration within the system. The chapter progresses from describing general models of spatial interaction to the particulars of measuring a country's interaction with the rest of the world by its balance of payments.

4.2 SPATIAL DIFFUSION

The differences between rich and poor countries, whether taken in conceptual form or on a case-by-case basis, are broad. Though it would be interesting to study the

79

initial causes of these differences, a more interesting direction to take is to analyze the near and distant prospects of equalization of international levels of wealth. External ties between countries, for better or worse, are very important in economic development. These ties can be considered as types of spatial interaction in the international economy. One type of spatial interaction is diffusion, the process of spread or movement over time and space. The inherently spatial characteristics of diffusion have been a major research concern in geography for decades, and most of the work done by geographers on this topic has its roots in the seminal contributions of Hagerstrand (1952, 1967). Geographical studies have considered the diffusion of a wide variety of items, including diseases, organizations, architectural styles, and technological innovations (Morrill et al., 1988). Whatever is being examined, the geographical domain of diffusion analysis is constant in its inclusion of at least one place or region that serves as the source of the diffusion process and a set of places or regions that act as receptors or destinations of whatever is being diffused. The spatial characteristics of diffusion frequently are classified into two types. One is *contagious diffusion* (Morrill, 1968), in which the process of geographical spread is limited by the distance between source and receptors. The other type is *hierarchical diffusion* (Hudson, 1969), which treats the economic and/or political linkages between source and receptors as complements and even alternatives to distance as the limiting factor(s) to spatial diffusion. Frequently, the distinction between contagious and hierarchical diffusion blurs because both processes can occur simultaneously.

The temporal and spatial characteristics of diffusion may be isolated for purposes of analytical focus. The temporal characteristic of diffusion is commonly viewed as a logistic process with the general form

$$P = \frac{L}{1 + ae^{-bt}} \tag{4.1}$$

where P is the proportion of individuals accepting the diffused item at time t, L is the ceiling limit of the accepting proportion, a is the initial proportion of acceptance (P at $t = 0$), and e is the base of the natural logarithms. A typical logistic curve is shown in Figure 4.1a. Logistic processes define a process of growth that begins slowly, accelerates, and then is slow again. Most empirical studies of temporal diffusion find this type of growth trajectory in the temporal adoption rates of the item being diffused. Casetti (1969) has provided an analytical rationale for temporal diffusion following a logistic trend.

The dominant spatial characteristic of diffusion is *distance decay,* which is identified in the function

$$I_{ij} = (D_{ij}^{-k}) \tag{4.2}$$

where I is the level of spatial interaction between the ith and jth places, D is their intervening distance, and k is a parameter. A typical distance decay function is graphed in Figure 4.1b. Basically, spatial interaction is a negative function of distance so that neighboring places are expected to have more interaction than distant places.

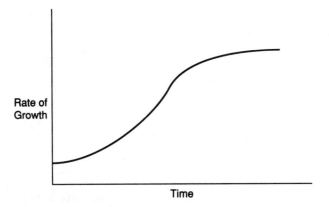

FIGURE 4.1*a*　A Logistic Growth Curve

Hierarchical diffusion was modelled by Hudson (1969) using a type of distance decay function amended to incorporate the relatively higher probability of interaction between larger places than between smaller places (see the discussion of gravity models in Section 4.3). In the hierarchical model, the largest center in a region is taken as the source of, for example, a technological innovation that is diffusing. The innovation initially and simultaneously spreads to the area immediately surrounding the largest center <u>and</u> to the next largest centers in the region, which may be some distance away. In this approach, population size and distance are equally important in determining the spatial diffusion of an innovation.

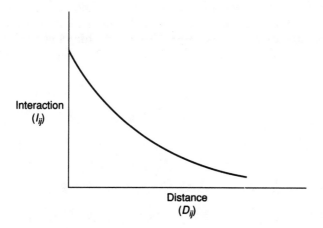

FIGURE 4.1*b*　A Distance Decay Function

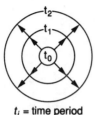

t_i = time period

FIGURE 4.2*a*   Diffusion in the Plane

The temporal and spatial characteristics of diffusion have been synthesized as a four-stage process (Brown, 1968). The first, or primary, stage consists of the establishment of diffusion sources during an initial time period. During the second time period, the diffusion stage entails a fairly rapid increase of the proportion of acceptors in close proximity to the sources (Figure 4.2). A condensing stage occupies the third time period, in which the rate of acceptance of the innovation is greater at locations more distant from the sources than at those nearby. This relationship occurs because, by the third period, distant centers are accepting the innovation at a rate that conforms to the rapid-growth segment of the logistic acceptance curve, while locations near the center now are beyond the rapid-growth segment of the curve and in its later slow-growth segment. The final time period consists of a saturation stage, by which all places within the geographical realm of the diffusion process are approaching their ceiling acceptance proportion as defined in the logistic model. Hanham and Brown (1976) have found empirical evidence supporting the temporal-spatial-stage process of diffusion.

In the 1950s and 1960s, economic development frequently was viewed as the outcome of a diffusion process (Reitsma and Klienpennig, 1985). Modernization theory (as described in Chapter 3) is essentially a theory of development that focuses on the acceptance of Western ways and rich-country technologies in poor countries. The rapid growth of Japan's economy following the Meiji restoration and again after World War II is often used as an example of successful adoption and adaptation of innovative technology diffused from distant sources (Blumenthal, 1976). Ongoing

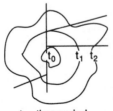

t_i = time period

FIGURE 4.2*b*   Diffusion over Spatial Structure

diffusion of cutting-edge technology from rich to poor countries should lead to an approximate equalization in levels of wealth around the world (Chisholm, 1982).

A less optimistic view of the efficacy of diffused technology in overcoming unequal levels of economic development was put forth by Friedmann (1972). He argued for the potential of diffused innovations to overcome the common predicament of different rates of growth in an economy characterized by core-periphery relationships. Friedmann regarded the core as being the geographical center of decisions controlling the international economy as well as innovative technology that generates wealth. Over time, a continous stream of technological innovation diffuses from the core in such a way that it eventually may lead to the development of corelike characteristics in once-peripheral regions. Friedmann's argues for a dynamic core-periphery demarcation of the international economy. *Upward transitional* regions, in Friedmann's dynamic model, are peripheral regions that have been able to break their traditional dependence on the core and are, in fact, becoming part of the core. Conversely, Friedmann defines *downward transitional* regions as those declining from core to periphery status.

Another influential proponent of diffusion as a critical process in economic development was Francois Perroux. Perroux (1950) described economic growth as being driven by the establishment of propulsive industries, or *growth poles,* that have positive effects on linked industries through a type of hierarchical diffusion of their growth. An increase in demand for the products or services of a propulsive industry generates an increase in secondary demand for the products of industries with which it is integrated. In a geographical context, the establishment of a growth pole in a peripheral region should trigger the region's take-off by serving as a leading industry for those already established in the region, and by inducing the establishment of new enterprises (Hirschman 1958). Perroux (1973) suggested a type of second-best result of economic development that could occur by the diffusion of growth through channels established by multinational corporations (MNCs). An MNC, based in a core country, could induce growth in a peripheral country's economy by establishing a subsidiary. Just as nonpropulsive industries benefit from their integration with growth poles, peripheral-country economies can benefit from their integration with core-country economies through MNCs. Perroux suggested that this integration should bring about increased investment, production, and incomes in peripheral countries, as well as improve their trade balances.

As described below, MNCs are not always effective channels for diffusion from rich to poor countries, but Perroux's suggestion for their use raises an important consideration for any diffusion process. Diffusion can be constrained in two ways. One constraint is spatial structure, or the connectivity among places. Spatial structure can be defined conventionally, at the international scale, by the immediate proximity of countries. Countries having mutual borders are connected in a primary way, and their close geographical proximity enhances the potential for spatial diffusion (Figure 4.2a). The effective spatial structure of an MNC, however, does not necessarily replicate the spatial structure of the world map. Instead, the spatial structure of an MNC is some subset of international nodes linked by the functional interrelationships among units of the corporation (Hanink, 1989). The intracorporate "proximity" of the MNCs' locations may, as suggested by Perroux, overcome the negative effect of geographical separation on the diffusion of economic growth. Another constraint to diffusion is the level of receptivity at places of potential acceptance. Whether or not a technological innovation, for example, is diffused successfully depends not only on the proximity between source and receptor, but also on the ability and willingness of the receptor to accept the innovation.

The geographical extent of the diffusion of leading technologies through MNCs actually seems quite limited at the international scale. Hagedoorn (1989), for example, has found that the diffusion of electronic process-control technology is bounded within a limited number of rich countries. The conduit for the diffusion of this technology is, in fact, the MNC. Its geographical spread, however, is not from core to periphery, but consists of flows and counterflows among the United States, Japan, Switzerland, and Germany. The diffusion is internal to the MNC and is accomplished by the acquisition of a related smaller company in one of these countries by an MNC headquartered in another. According to Dunning (1988), such multidirectional diffusion of technology within the set of rich countries is typical in those industries dominated by a limited number of MNCs. He found that there are agglomeration economies in technological development, so that geographical clusters of MNCs within the same industry yield an environment conducive to innovation. The number of technology sources, therefore, is limited, and so are their locations. In addition, Dunning found that many MNCs establish subsidiaries at technology sources, which represents a reversal of typical diffusion patterns. In this case, mobile acceptors move to the source of the innovation, rather than the innovation diffusing from the source.

Whether MNCs are drawn to innovation sources or technological innovation diffuses within and among MNCs, the bulk of leading-technology transfers are limited in their geography. In general, acceptance rates in technological diffusion appear to be positively associated with wealth levels (Pederson, 1970). Dunning (1988) and Chaudhuri (1989) have found, for example, that high quality of infrastructure and existing domestic technological capacity provide a country with a type of seedbed that facilitates acceptance of technological innovations from foreign sources. High infrastructural quality and technological capacity are characteristics of richer countries rather than poorer ones. Fransman (1986) has found that domestic improvements to leading foreign technologies has been a successful basis for economic growth in only a limited number of countries. Obviously, such a development strategy is not available to those countries lacking sufficient domestic technological capability. The end result is that only basic and even obsolete technology diffuses more rapidly to poor countries, rather than the leading technology that can more readily induce real economic growth (Malecki, 1983). There is a trickle-down of aging technology from rich countries to poor. Twenty-year-old machine tools are exported from the United States to Brazilian factories, and Indian plants use wire-producing machinery cast off as obsolete by its former American operators.

Even when diffusion of leading technology from rich to poor countries does take place within an MNC, it does not always have a positive effect on economic development. Dunning (1988) has found that the diffusion of technology within an MNC actually can weaken local sources of technological development in the poorer countries where subsidiaries are established, largely by overwhelming nascent domestic competition. This, of course, is the opposite of the growth-inducing effect of intra-MNC technological diffusion envisaged by Perroux. As noted by Gaile (1980), the general role of diffusion in economic development frequently is overemphasized because the critical roles of spatial structure and limits of receptivity often are ignored (Figure 4.2b).

4.3 THE GRAVITY MODEL OF SPATIAL INTERACTION

Spatial diffusion models suggest that spatial interaction is a negative function of the distance between places but a positive function of the size of places. Gravity models of spatial interaction directly encompass both the sizes and intervening distances of places in their specifications. In its basic form, the gravity model of spatial interaction is

$$I_{ij} = CM_i^k M_j^l D_{ij}^{-x} \qquad (4.3)$$

where I_{ij} is the volume of interaction between places i and j, C is a constant used for calibration, M_i and M_j are the "masses" of the places, with k and l as their respective weights, and D_{ij}^{-x} is the distance decay function. The model can be made linear by transforming all the variables to their common logarithm, and the unknown values of C, k, l, and x can be estimated from an empirical set of flows by ordinary least squares in the form (excluding subscripts)

$$\hat{I} = \hat{C} + \hat{k}M + \hat{j}M + \hat{x}D \qquad (4.4)$$

where the hat denotes an estimated value.

The basic gravity model describes two fundamental characteristics of spatial interaction: (1) holding distance constant, spatial interaction is an increasing function of the product of the masses of two places; and (2) holding masses constant, spatial interaction is a decreasing function of the distance between two places. Isard (1954) first suggested application of the gravity model to the analysis of flows in the international economy, and perhaps its most exhaustive use in that context was made by Linnemann (1966) in an analysis of world trade. Despite the conceptual simplicity of the gravity model, its analytical use has been subject to criticism on two grounds. One problem is selection of the appropriate measure of mass. Many gravity models applied in a subnational context rely on population as the appropriate measure of mass, but in an international context population measures of the mass variable generally are not useful. The mass measures in the basic gravity model are implicit measures of supply and demand. Within a single rich country, regional populations may be reasonable surrogates for supply and demand because incomes are fairly homogeneous. In international analysis, however, population and income are not consistent in their relationship. Frequently, a national income measure such as GNP or GDP is used as the measure of mass in gravity models applied at the international scale (e.g. Linnemann, 1966).

Another problem concerns the appropriate measure of distance. When treating countries as nodes rather than areas, intervening-distance calculations become difficult. For example, what is the distance between Canada and the United States? At one level, there is no distance at all because their boundary is a line with a nonmeasurable width. At another level, the distance may be quite variable because goods flowing between New York and Toronto or between Toronto and Los Angeles cross different distances. Linnemann (1966) used distances between economic centers of countries in his analysis, combining land distances to and from primary ports and nautical distances between ports where appropriate. Unfortunately, such calculations ignore the increasing importance of air freight in international trade. Actually, the definition of distance is not critical as long as a reasonable measure is used in a consistent fashion. However, the empirical results of these analyses must be interpreted as specific to the definition of distance employed. Importantly, despite the wide variety of mass and distance measures employed, gravity models of spatial interaction usually prove quite successful in replicating patterns of spatial interaction.

Problems in measuring mass and distance are important, but perhaps the more critical problem facing the basic gravity model is its lack of straightforward theoretical derivation. Isard and Dean (1987, p. 1063) state that the basic gravity model ". . . lays bare two key system-variables in operation: (1) mass, and (2) resistance to (energy requirement of) movement." This may be so; however, the analogy between physics and economic interactions is theoretically unsatisfactory. In general, three theoretical issues have been raised concerning the basic gravity model. One issue is that it has no basis in individualistic behavior. The argument is that spatial interaction patterns are the culmination of many individual choices. Without direct incorporation of behavioral characteristics, therefore, gravity models may be accurate in a descriptive sense but lack any explanatory power. In response to this criticism, spatial interaction models have been developed that directly incorporate behavioral theory, with the entropy model being one of the most widely used (Wilson, 1970).

The entropy model of spatial interaction has a basis in spatial behavior, but the gravity model also has been recast from the standpoint of Lancaster's (1966) theory of aspatial consumer behavior (Niedercorn and Bechdolt, 1969, 1972). (Lancaster's work in utility theory has been widely applied in the analysis of international trade. See Chapter 9.) The context of utility theory, and the addition of price variables in the gravity specification, provide the gravity model with a firm foundation in economic theory, and address the second theoretical issue.

Bergstrand (1985) has derived an extended gravity model from microeconomic theory and subjected it to empirical testing. The outcome is quite interesting in that Bergstrand lists results from a basic gravity model and the extended gravity model estimated from a single set of data. The basic gravity model took the form

$$E_{ij} = C + b_1 I_i + b_2 I_j + b_3 D_{ij} + b_4 A_{ij} + b_5 EEC_{ij} + b_6 EFTA_{ij} \qquad (4.5)$$

where E_{ij} is the value of exports from country i to country j, C is a constant, I_i and I_j are respective GDPs, D_{ij} is intervening distance, A_{ij} is an adjacency dummy variable (if the two countries i and j are adjacent, then $A = 1$; otherwise $A = 0$), EEC_{ij} is a European Economic Community dummy variable, and $EFTA_{ij}$ is a European Free Trade Association dummy variable. The values of b_1 through b_6 were estimated by ordinary least squares regression over 210 bilateral trade flows. In this model national incomes are used as the mass variables, and the distance employed is that between the countries' economic centers. The adjacency measure was used to capture the relatively increased trade possibilities between countries with mutual borders and in this context is complementary to the distance variable. The two variables EEC and $EFTA$ were used in order to capture the trade preference effects of mutual membership in either group. (Regional trade blocs are discussed in detail in Chapter 10.) Estimates of b_1 through b_6, from 1976, are fairly typical of those found in this type of analysis, and indeed in most applications of the basic gravity model (Table 4.1). Estimates for the national income variables were positive, as were Estimates for the adjacency and trade preference variables. Typically, the estimate for the distance variable was negative. Altogether, the basic model represented in Equation 4.5 accounts for about 80% of the variation in bilateral exports.

Bergrstrand's extended gravity model took the form

$$E_{ij} = BASIC + b_7 P_i + b_8 P_j + b_9 INF_i + b_{10} INF_j + b_{11} EXC_{ij} \quad (4.6)$$

where $BASIC$ consists of the model represented in Equation 4.5, P_i is the average

TABLE 4.1   Selected Estimated Coefficients from Bergstrand's Gravity Model Analyses of International Trade

	Basic Model	Extended Model
I_i	0.84*	0.84*
I_j	0.69*	0.56*
D_{ij}	−0.72*	−0.77*
A_{ij}	0.74*	0.76*
EEC_{ij}	0.30	0.18
$EFTA_{ij}$	0.69*	0.73*
P_i	ne	−0.96
P_j	ne	1.85*
INF_i	ne	−0.05
INF_j	ne	−1.12*
EXC_{ij}	ne	0.73
R^2	0.79	0.81

Note: "ne" indicates not estimated. * indicates that the estimate is significantly different than zero at $\alpha = .01$.

Source: Bergstrand, J. 1985. "The Gravity Equation in International Trade: Some Microeconomic Foundations and Empirical Evidence." *Review of Economics and Statistics* 67: 474–481.

price of exports, P_j is the average price of imports, INF_i and INF_j are the inflation rates of the bilateral pair of countries, and EXC_{ij} is their currency exchange rate tendency, with a value greater than one indicating that the importing country's currency appreciated over the exporting country's currency during the year. All the variables added to the basic model are either price or price related. In conjunction with the original GDP, distance, and trade preference variables, Equation 4.6 represents a complete system of production, price, and transfer costs. However, despite its representation as an economic system, the extended model does not effectively improve on the accountability for export values provided in the basic model (Table 4.1). The values of the estimates of b_1 through b_6 remain virtually unchanged between the basic and extended, or economic, model. While the additional variables of P_j and INF_j contribute to trade, the other additional variables do not in a significant way. Like the basic model, the extended model also accounts for about 80% of the variation in bilateral exports.

As for the third theoretical issue, in addition to its lack of behavioral and economic content, the basic gravity model has been criticized for its lack of explicit spatial content. As it stands, the model defined in Equation 4.3 does not contain any allowance for the effect of spatial structure on interaction over a set of geographically dispersed nodes. This issue was first addressed by Curry (1972), who argued that an implicit recognition of spatial structure exists in most applications of the basic gravity model if nodal populations are spatially autocorrelated, or geographically clustered. Curry's paper was the first in a series that investigated the relationship between spatial structure and the parameters of the gravity model (Fotheringham, 1981). The primary spatial problem of the basic gravity model is that it does not accommodate potentially competing flows between nodes. For example, an intervening node k directly between nodes i and j has no impact on the flow I_{ij} because this flow is simply a function of M_i, M_j, and D_{ij}.

Fotheringham (1983) has extended the basic gravity model in the following way:

$$I_{ij} = CM_j^k A_{ij}^l D_{ij}^{-x} \qquad (4.7)$$

where M_j and D_{ij}^{-x} are interpreted as in the basic gravity model. The extension made by Fotheringham is the addition of the variable A_{ij}, which represents market, or population, potential and encompasses spatial structure of a geographical system. In Fotheringham's specification, the potential measure is taken as

$$A_{ij} = \sum_{j=1}^{n-2} \frac{M_j}{D_{ij}} \qquad (4.8a)$$

where M_j is the mass at j and D_{ij} is interving distance. The term A_{ij} is evaluated for all $n - 2$ nodes ($n \ne i$, $n \ne j$) that may compete for flow I_{ij}.

The concept of geographic potential was originated by Warntz (1964, 1965) and fully developed by Sheppard (1979). It is a weighted measure of centrality within a set of spatial nodes. Holding distance between places constant, a node's geographic potential is a simple function of its size. Conversely, if all nodal sizes are held constant, then geographic potential is an inverse function of a node's aggregate distance to all other nodes in the system. Importantly, if the potential of all nodes within a geographic set is known, then the relevant spatial structure of the set of nodes is known as well. Because the potential measure A_{ij} incorporates both nodal size and internodal distances in a single term, it is as much an operator as it is a variable in spatial interaction models (see the appendix).

4.4 THE ECONOMIC BASE MULTIPLIER

Spatial diffusion, gravity, and geographic potential models tell us something about the volume and direction of spatial flows, but they don't directly reveal the impact of such flows. Two interregional multipliers have been developed that serve to quantify the nodal impact of spatial flows: (1) the economic base multiplier, and (2) the central place multiplier. The two multipliers can be described independently, but, as will be shown, they describe virtually the same thing. While both multipliers are conventionally considered to operate in the context of interregional, intranational exchange, there is no reason why they cannot provide insight concerning international exchange as well.

The *economic base multiplier* is an interregional employment multiplier drawn from the Keynesian income multiplier. The economy of a place, in economic base terms, can be divided into two broad sectors. The first sector consists of exports, which are comprised of any goods or services produced in a place but consumed anywhere outside that place. (Sometimes the economic base multiplier is called the export base multiplier.) The other sector, the service sector, although it encompasses both goods and services produced and consumed within a place's boundaries. It is called the service sector because its goods and services "serve" the residents of the place and its firms directly. The theory of the economic base is that the export sector is a place's source of economic growth (North, 1955). As the export sector grows, it generates increased demand for the goods and services it purchases locally, and its growing (by assumption) labor force generates increased demand for goods and services consumed by local households.

In an outline form, the economic base multiplier can be derived in the following way. First, allocate a place's total employment between the export and service sectors, so that

$$E = X + S \tag{4.9}$$

where E is total employment and X and S are export and service shares, respectively. Service employment can be taken as some share, k, of total employment, so that

$$S = kE \tag{4.10}$$

By substitution in Equation 4.9,

$$E = X + kE, \qquad 0 < k < 1 \tag{4.11}$$

which in multiplier notation is

$$E = \left(\frac{1}{(1-k)}\right) X \tag{4.12}$$

defining total employment as a multiple of export employment. The value of k defines the total employment generated by an increment to export employment. For example, assume that export employment increases by 500 jobs. If $k = 0.1$, then $E = 556$; if $k = 0.5$, then $E = 1000$; if $k = 0.9$, then $E = 5000$.

Tiebout (1956), among others, has discussed the conceptual problems of the economic base model. One problem is that the definition of an export is scale dependent. Small regions have higher probabilities of trade with the outside world than larger regions have, and at the global scale exporting is impossible. This scale relationship is evident in international trade, in what Magee (1980, p. 10) refers to as "the law of the declining share of trade with respect to country size." Another problem in the export base model is the explicit assumption that service employment is a function of export employment in a unidirectional way. Pred (1966) has demonstrated that the relationship between the export sector and the service sector is more likely to be circular. For example, regional infrastructure is viewed as a component of the service sector that provides a foundation for increasing a region's exports. In turn, export growth, or its potential, induces continued development of the region's infrastructure.

4.5 THE CENTRAL PLACE MULTIPLIER

Central place theory is perhaps the most important theoretical contribution toward our understanding of geographical economies. It was initially developed by Christaller (1933) in explanation of the size and areal spacing of cities as points of distribution, and it was soon extended by Lösch (1940) to include cities as points of production. The fundamental characteristics of a central place system are determined by its hierarchical production and trade principles. In its most basic form, central place theory concerns a homogeneous region in which household size and income are constant. Therefore, the salient regional market characteristics are defined by population alone. In the basic case, the variety of goods produced at a place is a function of that place's population. Any individual good is produced as a response to achievement of some local, systematically consistent, minimal level of demand that defines the good's *market threshold population*. The *order of a good* is defined by its requisite threshold population, with the production of lower order goods supported by smaller populations and the production of higher order goods requiring larger populations. In sum, threshold populations define the minimum operating scale for the goods produced. Threshold populations are considered nested, and so is production of goods by their order. For example, consider three goods with different thresholds. Good 1 has a threshold population of 1000, good 2 has a threshold of 2000, and good 3 has a threshold of 4000. A place with a population of 4000 would contain production of goods 1, 2, and 3 because it has the requisite thresholds for all three goods. A place with a population of 3500 would contain production only of goods 1 and 2, because its population is insufficient to support local production of the highest order good 3.

The trade principle of central place theory is that each good has a *range* over which it can be traded. The range of a good is a function of its order, so that longer trading ranges exist for higher order goods than for lower order goods. Any consumer surplus would be maximized by purchasing a good from the closest place in which it is produced. The highest order place in a system of central places need not import anything because it contains local production of all goods, in conformance with the principle of nested production thresholds. A place with a small population, however, must import all goods for which it does not contain sufficient threshold populations for local production. It will import these goods from the nearest place in which they are produced. Trade in a basic central place system is purely hierarchical. Higher order goods are exported from larger places to smaller places, and only to those smaller places within the range of the good in question.

Exports in a central place system have been treated in the same way as exports in the economic base model; that is, as the basis of total employment or population growth (Dacey, 1966; Beckman and McPherson, 1970). Using the Beckman and McPherson central place multiplier, the population of the smallest sized center, C_1, in a central place system is defined as

$$C_1 = k(C_1 + R) \tag{4.13}$$

where k is the proportion of the population of C_1 required to supply the market and R is the rural population that imports the low order good(s) produced at the smallest central place. In multiplier notation, this relationship is

$$C_1 = \left(\frac{1}{1-k}\right) kR \tag{4.14}$$

The equivalence of the central place multiplier has been addressed by Parr, Denike, and Mulligan (1975) and by Nourse (1978). Following Nourse's approach, let L be the labor force participation rate, or the proportion of the population employed. Then

$$E_n = L_{Cn} \tag{4.15}$$

where E is total employment in an nth order place. Rearranging,

$$\frac{E_n}{L_n} = C_n \tag{4.16}$$

By substituting Equation 4.12 for E,

$$C_n = \frac{\left(\dfrac{1}{1-k}\right)X}{L} \tag{4.17}$$

or

$$C_n = \left(\frac{1}{1-k}\right)\left(\frac{X}{L}\right) \tag{4.18}$$

where the term X/L is the population needed to provide the exports of C_n, and is equal to kR in Equation 4.14.

4.6 THE INTERREGIONAL MULTIPLIER AND UNEQUAL EXCHANGE

In their basic form, central place systems represent an economically unsustainable flow of exchange (Henderson, 1972). Smaller places are continually purchasing goods and services from larger places, but the largest place exports everything and imports nothing. Small places in such a system eventually must run large deficits in their balance of payments and the largest place must enjoy an increasing surplus in its balance of payments. The balance of payments problem in a central place system can be reduced in a conceptual way by the incorporation of transfer payments or variable prices in the basic model, but those extensions may cloud the real issue of unbalanced exchange in any spatial economic system. This imbalance in exchange is revealed in a simple examination of the central place multiplier defined in Equation 4.15. Mulligan (1979) has shown analytically that the base multiplier increases with city size in the type of hierarchy represented in central place systems. In addition, Horn and Prescott (1978) and Thompson (1982) have provided empirical evidence of the multiplier's relationship to city size. Thompson's analysis indicated that the reason base multipliers increase with city size is that larger centers have sectoral compositions different from smaller centers. This is a major point of central place theory.

In and of themselves, divergent multipliers do not mean that smaller places grow at a slower rate than larger places. Growth is not completely a function of external exchange. Even a fully isolated place can experience economic growth because additional stocks of natural resources are discovered, or technological advances induce higher production efficiency. At the extreme, our world is a closed system that does experience economic growth. However, in any realistic context, external exchange between economies is an important factor in their economic growth, but spatial exchange is inherently unbalanced. The imbalance in spatial exchange is encompassed in the geographic, or market potential, model (re: Equation 4.8a), which has the basic form

$$A_i = \sum_{j=1}^{n} \frac{M_i}{D_{ij}} \qquad (4.8b)$$

If M is defined in terms of national income, as it is in most gravity analyses of international trade, then Equation 4.8b becomes a geographic *income potential* model. Holding distance constant, as M increases, so does A, and a large value of M can counteract the potential diminishing effects of large values of D, distance. In turn, as A increases, flows to the place can be expected to increase, and M is continually augmented. Fotheringham and Webber (1980) have incorporated this relationship in a gravity model of spatial interaction that has simultaneous equations encompassing flow and growth as positive functions of each other. In summary, rich countries have an inherent edge over poor countries in spatial exchange, simply because they are rich (see the appendix).

4.7   THE SPATIAL DUAL ECONOMY

The initial growth in Lewis's dual economy takes place in the capitalist sector, but its root cause is in the cheap labor drawn from the noncapitalist sector. The capitalist sector could not grow without utilizing the noncapitalist sector's labor resources. The analogy between the dual economy, as described by Lewis, and a geographical economy split into core and periphery is not hard to draw. Amin (1977) has argued that the international division of labor is constructed in such a way that labor on the periphery is underpaid in the same way that redundant noncapitalist labor is underpaid in the capitalist sector of the dual economy. Underpayment of peripheral labor is the cause of growth in the core in the same way that underpaid noncapitalist labor is the cause of growth in the capitalist sector.

The issue becomes one of outcomes, however. Does the core always grow at a more rapid rate than the periphery, or, as in the case of the Lewis model, is eventual convergence between the two regional types likely to take place? Myrdal (1957) has suggested that convergence of wealth across rich and poor regions or countries is an unlikely prospect. He defined a process of *circular cumulative causation*, which consists of a long-term trend of increasing inequality among regional levels of wealth; or, at best, persistent differences. Myrdal's system is a constant dual economy in a geographical context (Thirlwall, 1977), but with rich regions growing richer at the expense of poor regions.

A good way to illustrate Myrdal's model is by contrast to a neoclassical description of income convergence across regions of disparate wealth. Recall from Chapter 3 that a basic proposition of the neoclassical growth model is that the factors of production flow to their greatest marginal productivities. The extension to an interregional growth process is made simply by taking the flows as literal across space. Begin with a two-region (X and Y) geographical economy in which per capita incomes and fixed populations are equal. Each region has equal amounts of mobile factors of production, capital, and labor, employed in the production of a single product. For additional simplicity, let the two regions have the same level of entrepreneurial and technological expertise. Each region is in supply-and-demand equilibrium in its factor and product markets, with supply just matching demand. The coexistence of individual regional market equilibria further indicates an interregional equilibrium, with equal prices for factors and products across both regions. Ignoring a reason, let the general level of demand increase in region X relative to region Y, including increases in demand for the factors of production, and the product. Prices in region X rise relative to prices in region Y, so that interregional disequilibria occur in the product and factor markets.

From a neoclassical standpoint, any interregional disequilibrium is a temporary condition when both factors and products are (perfectly) mobile. On the one hand, increased prices for a product in region X induce imports of the product produced in region Y. Prices for the product in region X decrease, due to the additional supply, and prices for the product in region Y increase due to the decrease in the product's regional availability. On the other hand, the increases in prices paid to the factors in region X induce factors from region Y to migrate. The relative price reactions to these flows are the same as in the product market, with decreasing prices in region X and increasing prices in region Y. Flows of both the product and the factors stop when regional prices converge and interregional equilibrium is restored. Region X is now larger than region Y, with greater population and more productive capacity after factor migrations. However, per capita incomes are equal across regions, and although price levels are higher, the increase in wages just offsets the increase in product prices so that real incomes are unchanged from the original equilibrium conditions. An important point is that interregional equilibrium would be restored even if only the product or a single factor was mobile. Even if only one of the factors, or the product, was imperfectly mobile—due to transportation costs, for example—interregional equilibrium would be restored. Prices would not be equalized between the regions, with their difference being the cost of transport. However, the incidence of the transport cost would be split between the regions in equilibrium, with imports and exports fixed in relative proportions, but at lower levels than in the case of perfect factor and/or product mobility.

Myrdal argued that convergence toward price equalization or even price equilibrium between regional markets was unlikely. Any initial trigger to rapid growth in one region, or the core, leads to a self-perpetuating cycle of continued growth relative to other regions in the periphery. Whether the differences in wealth between a core region and a peripheral region simply remain constant or actually become greater is a function of the relative balance between what are termed *spread* and *backwash* effects. Spread effects are related to positive flows from the core to the periphery. For example, the increased wealth in the core may raise its demand for products produced in the periphery, so that core growth actually induces peripheral growth. Backwash effects are related to flows from the periphery to the core. Greater opportunities in the core can induce capital flows from the periphery, undermining much of its base for regional income growth. In addition, labor migration from the periphery to the core may drain the periphery of its best and brightest in a "brain drain" that diminishes the human capital stock of the periphery. Unless the net effects are positive in spread, the gap between the core and periphery will be maintained and probably increase. Romer (1986) has suggested that mobile knowledge factors, embodied in capital as technology or in people as human capital, will migrate from poor to rich countries in a circular process. These knowledge factors provide increasing returns, but only where they are in large supply, so they are more productive and earn more in rich countries than in poor ones.

As long as backwash effects are net positive, the process of circular cumulative causation results in consistent interregional disequilibrium. With respect to region X and region Y, the initial increase in demand in region X is self-perpetuating in its effect because the change in prices could change the nature of production in region X as well. For example, the initial increase in demand in region X could lead to the achievment of more efficient regional production due to economies of scale. Rather than the product being imported from region Y, the product would be exported to region Y because of its lower production cost in region X. Output in region Y would fall and so would its regional income due to unemployment. Increased production efficiency in region X would raise its per capita income level, but at the same time limit any immigration of labor and capital because factor demand would increase at a slower rate than product demand. The core region, X, would undergo an upward spiral in economic growth at the partial expense of a downward spiral in the peripheral region, Y. Rather than eventual convergence in prices and an ultimate return to equalization across the markets in both regions, growth would become *polarized*, with region X being rich and region Y being poor.

The spread-backwash process is really a spatial one (Gaile, 1979), and it is multiregional. In spatial terms, the initial trigger to rapid growth in core regions alters the geographic potentials of the whole system. While aspatial market economics eventually must yield interregional equalization, the impress of any real spatial structure over a regional system can easily counter the tendency toward equalization, or even unbalanced equilibrium (see the appendix). In the simplest case, differing intervening distances between regions results in differing incidences of any spread-backwash process. In an international context, however, spatial structure is not a simple function of intervening physical distances, but also economic distances and

TABLE 4.2   Mean Annual Growth Rates of GDP and of Population by World Bank Income Group, 1980–1990

Income Group	GDP Growth	Population Growth
All	2.7%	2.0%
Low	3.1%	2.7%
Low Middle	2.6%	2.1%
High Middle	2.2%	1.8%
High	2.7%	0.7%

Source of data: World Bank. 1992. *World Development Report 1992* (New York: Oxford University Press).

cultural distances which, can and do change. In addition, the nodal characteristics that comprise a large share of a country's geographical potential are fashioned as much by a country's policies toward international exchange as by the exchange itself.

Pure economic theory of the neoclassical sort yields balanced growth among the world's countries. Pure spatial theory, on the other hand, yields unbalanced growth. It is likely that good theory rests somewhere in between, because economic growth rates are not fully consistent along lines of per capita national income. Between 1980 and 1990, for example, average real growth rates were higher in the World Bank's low income countries than in any other income group (Table 4.2). However, the high income countries averaged the second fastest rate. In addition, when population growth is considered, the decade of the 1980s saw per capita growth in national income occur at the fastest rate in the high income countries and at the lowest rate in the low income and high middle income countries.

4.8   MEASURING GEOGRAPHICAL INTEGRATION AND LINKAGE

Economic development results from a mix of internal and external conditions that interact with one another (Lewis, 1977). Trade has been called the engine of growth, but a national economy cannot grow unless domestic institutions facilitate growth and allow more international integration of their economies. Such integration both broadens the domestic resource supply and provides access to wider markets. The degree of any country's integration into the international economy varies from circumstance to circumstance. Some markets are more open than others. Trade in goods, for example, tends to be more open than trade in services. In addition, factors may have different degrees of mobility, so geographical integration is more easily achieved in some factor markets than in others.

There are different approaches to measuring economic integration. One used frequently in regional analysis divides an economy into two components: the region's link to the national economy, and the region's particular component. The decomposition can be represented in the following function (Hanink, 1988):

$$E_R = (N, R_i) \qquad (4.19)$$

where E_R is the economy of a region, N is the national economy component, and R_i is the ith region's particular component. This approach is a scale-wise partitioning of economic space, with each scale contributing or transmitting economic impulses to the immediate lower scale (Jones, 1984). In turn, national economies can be derived as the function

$$E_N = (G, N_i) \qquad (4.20)$$

where E_N is the economy of a nation-state, G is the international economy component, and N_i is the ith country's's particular component. Equations 4.19 and 4.20 represent a top-down or distributive system of multiregional spatial economies, with higher-scale economic conditions distributed at next lower scales. As linear regression models, they have been used to assess linkage and integration among regions (Thirlwall, 1966; Jeffrey, 1974; Hanink, 1988). (Conceptually, such models are similar to the single-index portfolio model described in Chapter 6.) At the regional scale, the smaller the unique regional effect, the more integrated the region within the national economy; the larger the unique effect, the less integrated the region's economy. The same concepts can be extended to the international economy, so that a national economy is composed partially of global economic effects and partially of unique national effects. The linear regression specification of the relationships is

$$E_n = a + \beta I + e \qquad (4.21)$$

where E_n is some characteristic of the nth country's economy and I is a relevant international index of the characteristic.

Two numerical results of these types of regressions are of interest. One is the sign and value of the calculated β coefficient. The β coefficient can be taken as a measure of the type of linkage between the national and the international economy, and it can be interpreted in much the same way as a stock market beta (see Chapter 6). If the β is approximately one, then the national and international economies are tracking in much the same way. If the β is significantly less (more) than one, then the national economy is tracking in a significantly dampened (amplified) way compared to the international economy.

The other interesting numerical result is the coefficient of determination, R^2, which describes the degree of integration between the national and international economies. The value of R^2 ranges from 0, indicating that none of the variance in a dependent variable is determined as a function of the independent variable's variance, to 1.00, indicating that all of the variance in a dependent variable is determined as a function of the independent variable's variance. As the relative size of the residual value of the regression equation decreases, the value of R^2 increases. Relatively large values of R^2—for instance, $R^2 > 0.500$—suggest that a national economy is fairly well integrated into the international economy, while smaller values suggest a poorly integrated national economy.

For purposes of illustration, linear regressions linking national to international indices of industrial production and employment were estimated. The data are published by the International Monetary Fund (1989) as indices, and so do not have to be manipulated in any way for the calculated beta coefficients to have the numerical properties described above. It should be noted that most models of the type specified in Equation 4.21 are estimated as time-series. Time-series regressions calculated by ordinary least squares frequently suffer from serially autocorrelated residuals, or errors. In order to avoid that problem here, a method of generalized least squares, which controls for serial autocorrelation, was used to estimate the industrial output and employment models.

The results from regression equations linking national economic characteristics of industrial production and employment to international indices are listed in Table 4.3. The degree of integration, as measured by R^2, is much greater in the case of industrial production than it is for employment, where it is virtually nonexistent. Only 4 countries—Austria, Luxembourg, Denmark, and Switzerland—had R^2 values greater than 0.5 in the case of employment, while all 19 countries had R^2 values greater than 0.5 in the case of industrial production. This result is not unexpected, because labor markets are usually much less integrated than goods markets. Especially among the set of rich countries examined here, trade in goods is significantly less regulated than migration of labor, and trade and migration are important mechanisms for integrating the goods (industrial production) and labor (employment) markets, respectively.

There does not seem to be any immediate pattern to the measured levels of international integration in either case. An economy's size, for example, which can be problematic in this regard (Johnston, 1979), does not seem to play any role in conditioning the values of R^2 or beta. Note that some of the betas in the Employment column of Table 8.13 are negative, indicating a countercyclical relationship between those countries and the international labor market. However, the R^2 values in all of the cases are very low, suggesting the countercyclical track of employment in those countries is nothing more than a random association, at least as measured here.

Using an alternative perspective of international economic links, Bennet and Kelleher (1988) used linear regression to identify degree of integration among the world's leading stock markets (Chapter 6). Their approach was in the context of the single-index portfolio model, but linked one market to another rather than linking one market to some international index. The assumption is that X's stock market is a function of Y's stock market. This assumption, of course, can be generalized to the full economy, so that one country's economic characteristics can be taken as a function of another country's characteristics. In the stock market analysis, different

TABLE 4.3   Economic Integration (R^2) and Linkage (beta) among Selected Countries: Industrial Production and Employment, 1978–1987

Country	Industrial Production beta/R^2	Employment beta/R^2
Sweden	1.127/0.956	1.368/0.451
United States	1.293/0.952	1.937/0.390
Belgium	0.514/0.921	no data
Austria	0.955/0.919	0.495/0.582
France	0.324/0.901	−0.061/0.001
Ireland	2.410/0.885	0.424/0.013
Canada	1.160/0.877	1.213/0.089
Spain	0.599/0.875	0.210/0.004
Japan	1.511/0.870	0.450/0.107
Luxembourg	1.699/0.857	0.833/0.516
Denmark	1.635/0.856	2.269/0.526
Netherlands	0.662/0.845	0.910/0.084
Norway	2.101/0.830	1.116/0.226
Switzerland	0.706/0.790	2.403/0.646
West Germany	0.555/0.742	1.094/0.201
Finland	1.476/0.689	−0.122/0.002
United Kingdom	0.658/0.569	0.669/0.113
Australia	0.624/0.564	0.425/0.036
Italy	0.548/0.548	−0.485/0.037

functional relationships were tested with respect to market openings. For example, following the clock, the Tokyo market can have a later or earlier opening than the New York and London markets. It simply depends on one's starting point.

As a geographical model, one reasonable assumption is that a smaller economy has characteristics that are functions of a a larger and neighboring economy's characteristics. As examples, such relationships were estimated taking Canadian industrial production and employment as a function of those variables in the United States, and Austrian industrial production and employment as functions of those characteristics in West Germany. As before, industrial production seems more integrated than employment. In the case of industrial production, the Canada-United States beta is 0.923, with $R^2 = 0.900$. In the case of employment, the beta is negative, at −0.499, but the R^2 of only 0.162 suggests that the labor markets are not integrated. The Austria-Germany linkages are weaker than those of Canada and the United States, perhaps because Austria is not a co-member of Germany in the EC. The beta in the case of industrial production is 1.211, with $R^2 = 0.707$. In the case of employment, the beta is 0.124, and the $R^2 = 0.271$.

4.9 NATIONAL BALANCE OF PAYMENTS ACCOUNTS

Links between a country's economy and the rest of the world are measured in a fairly standard accounting system that is often linked with the country's product account. While a national product account focuses primarily on a country's domestic economy, the international components of a country's economy are measured by its *balance of payments*. A country's balance of payments is divided into three separate accounts: the current account, the capital account, and the international reserves account (*Balance of Payments Manual*, 1977). Together, these three accounts provide a record of the international transactions of a country over a certain period of time. Like the national product account, the balance of payments accounts are used to guide policy formulation both by national governments and many international institutions.

Balance of payment accounting usually follows the double-entry method used by many financial institutions. Each international transaction is viewed either as a credit or a debit. Further, the sum total of the sheet (current account + capital account + reserves) should equal zero, just like the sum of a bank's assets and liabilities. The current account consists of all nonfinancial transactions between foreign and domestic individual and corporate residents. Financial items are considered in the capital account (*Balance of Payments Manual*, 1977). Transactions that require payments by foreigners are considered to be assets to the domestic economy, and transactions that require payments to foreigners are considered to be debits to the domestic economy. In the capital account, the country that receives a financial flow carries it as an asset, while the country in which the financial flow originates records it as a debit. While it does seem incongruous, exports of current account items are considered to be assets and exports of capital account items are considered as debits. Ideally, this distinction leads to a balancing of these accounts. If both accounts were accurately measured in their entirety, and reserves could be held constant, their sum would be zero. Any country holding a current account surplus (deficit) would also hold a capital account deficit (surplus) of the same absolute value; hence the term "balance of payments."

In order to simplify presentation, a generalized balance of payments sheet showing all items net is given in Table 4.4. Items A–G comprise the current account. Item A, Net Merchandise Trade, is the value of exports minus the value of imports. Merchandise is defined as any moveable good, and so includes agricultural products and raw materials as well as manufactured products. Items B–D concern different types of services. Item B, Net Nonfactor Services, includes things such as communications, construction, and film rentals, as well as financial services such as insurance and brokerage. Item C, Net Transportation, includes shipping of both goods and passengers, and insurance on goods entered into trade. Item D, Net Travel, covers both goods and services purchased in a country by nonresidents. Travellers are defined as those people staying within a foreign country for less than one year.

Items E–G might be considered financial items in a different context, but are

TABLE 4.4   A Generalized Balance of Payments Account

I. Current Account
   A. Net Merchandise Trade
   B. Net Nonfactor Service Trade
   C. Net Transportation
   D. Net Travel
   E. Net Investment Income
   F. Net Other Income
   G. Net Unrequited Transfers

II. Capital Account
   H. Net Direct Investment
   I. Net Portfolio Investment
   J. Net Other Capital
   K. Net Short-Term Capital

III. Net Reserves

IV. Net Errors and Omissions

Note: I + II + III + IV = 0.
Source: Balance of Payments Manual, 4th ed. 1977
(Washington: International Monetary Fund).

carried in the current account in a balance of payments statement. Item E, Net Investment Income, includes earnings from stock dividends and interest. Capital gains and losses are not included here but are considered to be, respectively, additions and subtractions from capital and therefore are entered in the capital account. Reinvested earnings, including stock dividends and bonus shares, are entered in both the current account and the capital account. For example, if a resident of country A receives a two-for-one split on shares of stock in a corporation of country B, country A records a credit in its current account and a debit in its capital account, while country B records a debit in its current account and a credit in its capital account. This treatment results because the resident of country A is receiving a payment (assuming less than full dilution), but the "destination" of the payment is country B. Item F, Net Other Income, includes both labor income and payments of royalties and license fees. All of these are considered types of payments to factor services. Labor income may accrue to seasonal migrant workers who reside in other countries or to border residents who commute internationally on a day-to-day basis. Item G, Net Unrequited Transfers, includes one-sided transfers from private sources; for example, remittances made by migrant workers to their families in their home countries. This item also includes inter-official transfers between governments, such as military and economic aid, and transfers such as taxes and fees that take place between governments and individuals.

   The capital account is a record of transactions that entail changes of legal ownership of an economy's foreign financial assets and liabilities (*Balance of Payments Manual,* 1977). These transactions include the creation of claims, or investment, by foreigners, and the liquidation of claims. Item H, Net Direct Investment, is the value of domestic direct investment by foreigners minus the value of foreign direct investment by domestic residents. Direct investment is defined as one in which the investor holds a lasting interest. This lasting interest is usually maintained by the investor holding a substantial equity interest. Wholly owned incorporated subsidiaries and wholly owned unincorporated branches are always viewed as direct investment because of the 100% equity position involved. The low-end equity requirement for designation of an investment as direct varies from country to country, but most definitions are within the range of 10 to 25%. Item I, Net Portfolio Investment, contains those equity investments lower than direct investment proportions, and long-term bonds, debentures, and other similar instruments. Both direct and portfolio investments are considered long-term if their maturity debts are greater than one year, or, as in the case of equities, if they have no term at all. Item J, Net Other Capital, contains some long-term loans such as certificates of deposit which are not covered under either Items H or I. Item K, Net Short-Term Capital, includes demand deposits, currency holdings by nongovernmental entities, and bonds and other debt instruments that mature in less than one year.

The last major category of the balance of payments is Net Reserves (III). International reserves are forms of exchange that can be used by governments to settle international claims. International reserves include monetary gold and foreign exchange assets. They also consist of special drawing rights (SDRs) and other International Monetary Fund (IMF) credits. SDRs are a type of currency, or "facility" in IMF parlance, that was developed to increase the supply of international reserves. Essentially, SDRs are a type of weighted currency unit that is heavily tied to the value of the U.S. dollar. (Selected operations of the IMF, including the use of SDRs, are described in Chapter 7.)

The final line in the balance of payments is IV, Net Errors and Omissions. This value, frequently referred to as the "statistical discrepancy," is the ultimate balancing item in the balance of payments. If the sum of the current account, capital account, and net reserves is negative (positive), the statistical discrepancy will be positive (negative). Conceptually, the sums of the two accounts and net reserves should be zero, but in practice this balance is unlikely to be achieved due to errors in valuation and omissions of transactions from the record. Sometimes the statistical discrepancy is rather large, but the IMF notes a rule of thumb that as long as the discrepancy is less than 5% of the total of merchandise exports and imports, a balance of payments statement is reasonably accurate (*Balance of Payments Manual*, 1977, p. 62).

Short versions of the current and capital accounts of the United States, Japan, the United Kingdom, and Nigeria are given in Table 4.5. The entries are for 1979 and 1985, representing weak and strong U.S. dollar years, respectively. The IMF publishes both annual and quarterly balances of payments for all its member countries in its *Balance of Payments Yearbook*. Values in this publication are given in SDRs, which facilitates comparison among countries.

In 1979 America's current account was roughly in balance because its merchandise trade deficit was more than offset by its surplus in service trade. Its capital account was in deficit, with all three long-term items showing more American invest-

TABLE 4.5 Generalized Current and Capital Accounts for Selected Countries: 1979 and 1985*

	United States		United Kingdom	
	1979	1985	1979	1985
Merchandise Trade	−21.29	−119.71	−5.58	−2.55
Other Goods and Service Trade	25.28	20.29	8.25	11.58
Transfers	−4.72	−15.00	−3.74	−4.37
CURRENT ACCOUNT	−0.73	−114.42	−1.07	4.66
Direct Investment	−10.35	2.19	−4.69	−5.60
Portfolio Investment	−1.68	62.42	0.17	−16.74
Other Long-Term Investment	−6.26	7.63	−0.91	0.34
Short-Term Investment	7.18	29.61	−8.70	6.84
CAPITAL ACCOUNT	−11.11	101.85	−14.13	−15.17
National Currency/SDR	1.2920	1.0153	0.6101	0.7912

	Japan		Nigeria	
	1979	1985	1979	1985
Merchandise Trade	1.37	54.72	3.81	4.19
Other Goods and Service Trade	−7.24	−5.09	−2.22	−2.72
Transfers	−0.87	−1.63	−0.30	−0.25
CURRENT ACCOUNT	−6.74	48.00	1.29	1.22
Direct Investment	−2.06	−5.72	0.24	0.34
Portfolio Investment	−0.97	−40.81	———	———
Other Long-Term Investment	−6.75	−15.45	0.79	−1.95
Short-Term Investment	4.44	9.68	−0.07	−0.77
CAPITAL ACCOUNT	−5.34	−52.30	1.22	−2.38
National Currency/SDR	283.13	242.19	0.7787	0.9068

* All items are net in billions of Special Drawing Rights (SDR). The symbol "_____" indicates none.
Source: Balance of Payments Statistics Yearbook, Part 1. 1987 (Washington: International Monetary Fund).

ment abroad than foreign investment in the United States. By 1985, the American current account had gone into deep deficit. Service trade was still in surplus, but the American merchandise trade deficit was the largest recorded up to that time. As should be expected with such a deep current account deficit, the U.S. capital account ran a large surplus in 1985. All investment items were positive, with portfolio investment contributing the single largest share to the surplus.

Japan's current account in 1979 was in deficit, despite a small surplus in merchandise trade. Its capital account was in deficit in 1979, with short-term investment as the only surplus item. By 1985 the Japanese current account was in large surplus

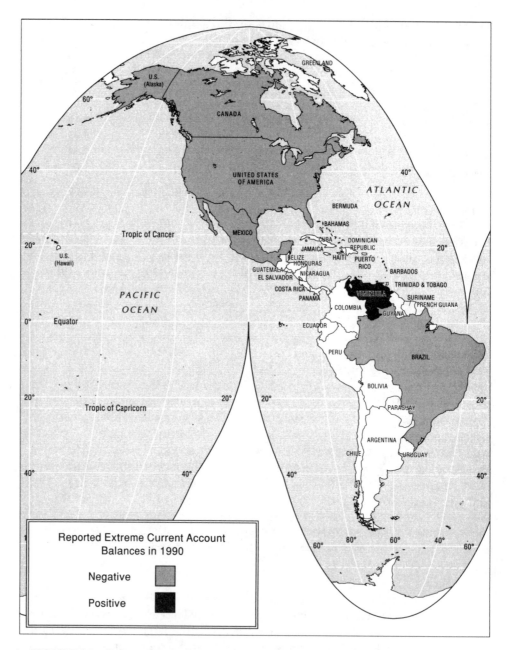

FIGURE 4.3   Reported Extreme Current Account Balances in 1990

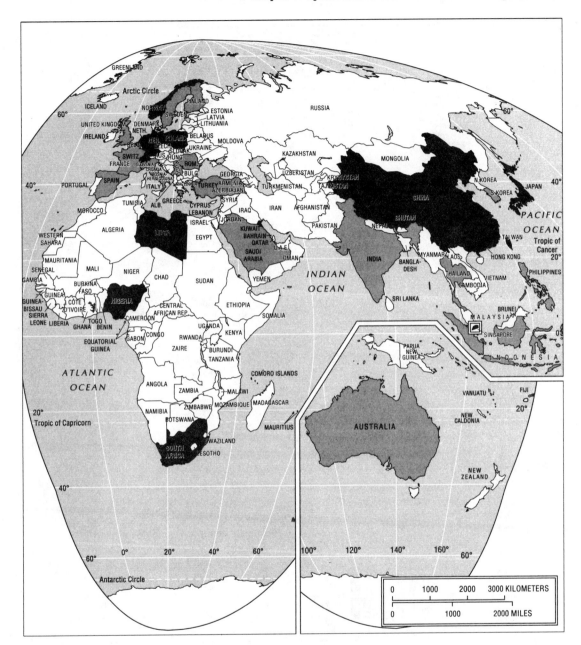

FIGURE 4.3 (Continued)

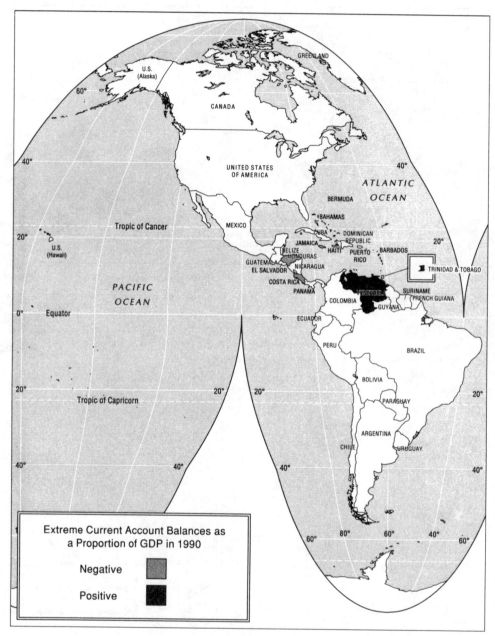

FIGURE 4.4   Extreme Current Account Balances as a Proportion of GDP in 1990

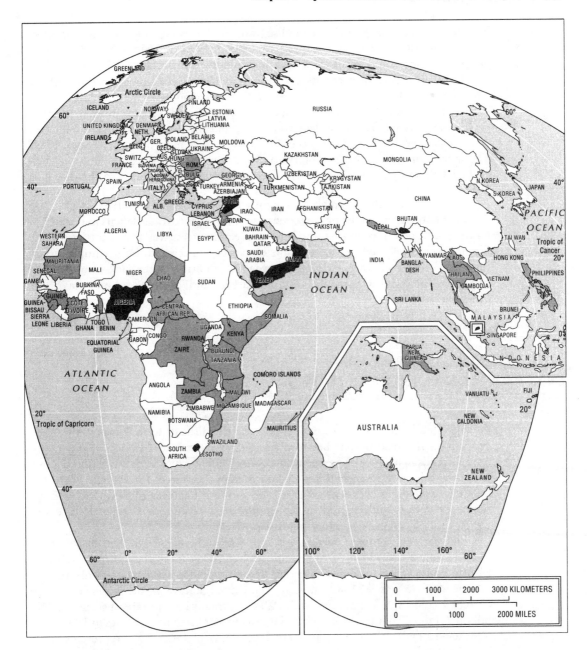

FIGURE 4.4   *(Continued)*

because of its net receipts in merchandise trade. Both service trade and transfers were in deficit in 1985, as they were in 1979. By 1985, Japan's capital account was in deep deficit, due mostly to sizeable Japanese portfolio investment abroad.

The British current accounts for 1979 and 1985 were similar to those of the United States. Both countries had deficits in merchandise trade and surpluses in service trade. In the British case, however, the service trade surplus more than made up for the merchandise trade deficit in 1985, and the British current account was in surplus. The British capital accounts were in deficit in both 1979 and 1985. The short-term item was the primary contributor to the British capital account deficit in 1979, and portfolio investment was the primary contributor to the deficit in 1985.

The three cases discussed above are for wealthy industrial countries. Nigeria, on the other hand, is one of the poorer countries. It ran service trade deficits in both 1979 and 1985. As described in Chapter 2, service sectors in less wealthy countries usually are not well developed, so such countries can be expected to be net importers of services. Another characteristic of less wealthy countries is the lack of a sophisticated, well-developed portfolio capital market, and Nigeria did not have any observed portfolio capital flows in either 1979 or 1985.

4.10 THE GEOGRAPHY OF INTERNATIONAL INCOME FLOWS

As suggested by the examples in Section 4.9, it is difficult to make generalizations concerning the relationship between national income and balance of payments. Again, trends in balance of payments accounts yield much more information about a country's role in the international economy than the results for a single year. The difficulty in making pertinent generalizations about balances of payments and national incomes is underscored by an examination of current account balances in 1990.

Like national incomes, current accounts tend to be skewed in their distribution. In 1990 only 33 of 117 reporting countries had surpluses in their current accounts (World Bank, 1992). The mean current account balance was about −$938 million and the median was −$158.5 million. The United States had the largest deficit on current account at −$92 billion, while (West) Germany had the largest surplus at $47 billion. Of those countries with the 20 largest current account surpluses in 1990, only Venezuela is in the Western Hemisphere (Figure 4.3), and Africa was represented only by Libya and Nigeria. All three countries are oil exporters and have been limiting imports. The two regional concentrations of countries with current account surpluses in 1990 were in Europe and East Asia. The greatest regional concentrations of countries in deficit were in the Western Hemisphere and Western Europe. Additional countries with such deficits were in the Pacific basin.

The regional picture does change, however, when current account balances in absolute terms are taken as proportions of GDP. The absolute value of the current account balance as a proportion of GDP is an indicator of the relative impact of international economic links on a national economy. The mean proportion in 1990 was (negative) greater than 0.02 and the median was (negative) 0.028, indicating that a "typical" country had a current account deficit equal to 2–3% of its GDP. The value for Kuwait was 0.36, the extreme case for a country running a current account surplus in 1990. The largest regional concentration of extreme cases with current account deficits was in Africa (Figure 4.4); there is another concentration in Europe.

What a particular balance of payments result means, however, is not as straightforward as a national income account result. A country's current account, for example, can be negative, zero, or positive. Any of these three results is not directly indicative of a country's economic health. Countries with low GDP can have a positive current account and countries with a high GDP can have a negative current account. Most governments prefer their country's current account to be positive in any given year, but this preference seems driven mostly by nationalism rather than by economic rationality, given the degree of internationalization in almost all national economies. However, underline{trends} in a country's balance of payments are useful when analyzing a country's position in the international economy, and collectively the individual trends virtually define the gross flow characteristics of the international economy. On average, the gross flow characteristics exhibit the relationships of the core-periphery models and the tendency toward polarization described by Myrdal. Only the high income countries, on average, have positive current accounts (Table 4.6). Each of the countries in the other income groups has a deficit, on average. As a proportion of GDP, the current account deficits follow a sort of perverse gradation, with the low income countries having the largest average deficits.

TABLE 4.6 Median Current Account Balances and Current Account Balances as a Proportion of GDP by World Bank Income Group, 1990

Income Group	$U.S. millions Balance	As % of GDP
All	−159	−3%
Low	−153	−5%
Low Middle	−200	−3%
High Middle	−139	(−)0
High	830	1%

Source of data: World Bank. 1992. *World Development Report 1992* (New York: Oxford University Press).

REFERENCES

Amin, S. 1977. *Imperialism and Unequal Development* (New York: Monthly Review Press).

Balance of Payments Manual, 4th ed. 1977 (Washington: International Monetary Fund).

Balance of Payments Statistics Yearbook. 1987. Vol. 38, part 1 (Washington: International Monetary Fund).

Beckman, M., and J. McPherson. 1970. "City Size Distribution in a Central Place Hierarchy: An Alternative Approach." *Journal of Regional Science* 10: 25–33.

Bergstrand, J. 1985. "The Gravity Equation in International Trade: Some Microeconomic Foundations and Empirical Evidence." *Review of Economics and Statistics* 67: 474–481.

Blumenthal, T. 1976. "Japan's Technological Strategy." *Journal of Development Economics* 3: 245–255.

Brown, L. 1968. *Diffusion Processes and Location* (Philadelphia: Regional Science Research Institute).

Casetti, E. 1969. "Why Do Diffusion Processes Conform to Logistic Trends?" *Geographical Analysis* 1: 101–105.

Chaudhuri, P. 1989. *The Economic Theory of Growth* (Ames: Iowa State University Press).

Chisholm, M. 1982. *Modern World Development: A Geographical Perspective* (Totawa, New Jersey: Barnes & Noble).

Christaller, W. 1933. *Die zentralen Orte in Suddeutschland* (Jena: Gustav Fischer). English translation by C. Baskin. 1966. *Central Places in Southern Germany* (Englewood Cliffs, New Jersey: Prentice-Hall).

Curry, L. 1972. "A Spatial Analysis of Gravity Flows." *Regional Studies* 6: 131–147.

Dacey, M. 1966. "Population of Places in a Central Place Hierarchy." *Journal of Regional Science* 6: 27–33.

Dunning, J. 1988. *Multinationals, Technology, and Competitiveness* (London: Unwin Hyman).

Fotheringham, A. 1981. "Spatial Structure and Distance Decay Parameters." *Annals of the Association of American Geographers* 71: 425–436.

———. 1983. "A New Set of Spatial Interaction Models: The Theory of Competing Destinations." *Environment and Planning A* 15: 15–36.

Fotheringham, A., and M. Webber. 1980. "Spatial Structure and the Parameters of Spatial Interaction Models." *Geographical Analysis* 12: 33–46.

Fransman, M. 1986. *Technology and Economic Development* (Boulder: Westview Press).

Friedmann, J. 1972. *Urbanization, Planning, and National Development* (Beverly Hills: Sage).

Gaile, G. 1979. "Spatial Models of Spread-Backwash Processes." *Geographical Analysis* 11: 273–288.

———. 1980. "The Spread-Backwash Concept." *Regional Studies* 14: 15–25.

Hagedoorn, J. 1989. *The Dynamic Analysis of Innovation and Diffusion: A Study in Process Control* (London: Pinter).

Hagerstrand, T. 1952. *The Propagation of Innovation Waves.* Lund Studies in Geography, series B, no. 4.

———. 1967. *Innovation Diffusion as a Spatial Process* (Chicago: University of Chicago Press).

Hanham, R., and L. Brown. 1976. "Diffusion Waves within the Context of Regional Economic Development." *Journal of Regional Science* 16: 65–71.

Hanink, D. 1988. "Nonintegration of Regional Labor Markets: The Case of Large U.S. Cities from February 1980 through December 1983." *Environment and Planning A* 21: 705–713.

———. 1989. "Introduction: Trade Theories, Scale, and Structure." *Economic Geography* 65: 267–270.

Henderson, J. 1972. "Hierarchy Models of City Size: An Economic Evaluation." *Journal of Regional Science* 12: 435–441.

Hirschman, A. 1958. *The Strategy of Economic Development* (New Haven: Yale University Press).

Horn, R., and J. Prescott. 1978. "Central Place Models and the Economic Base: Some Empirical Results." *Journal of Regional Science* 18: 229–241.

Hudson, J. 1969. "Diffusion in a Central Place System." *Geographical Analysis* 1: 45–58.

International Monetary Fund. 1989. *Balance of Payments Statistics Yearbook*, vol. 40, part 1 (Washington: International Monetary Fund).

Isard, W. 1954. "Location Theory and Trade Theory: A Short Run Analysis." *Quarterly Journal of Economics* 68: 305–320.

Isard, W., and W. Dean. 1987. "The Projection of World (Multiregional) Trade Matrices." *Environment and Planning A* 19: 1059–1066.

Jeffrey, D. 1974. "Regional Fluctuations in Unemployment within the U.S. Urban Economic System." *Economic Geography* 50: 111–123.

Johnston, R. 1979. "On Urban and Regional Systems in Lagged Correlation Analyses." *Environment and Planning A* 11: 705–713.

Jones, D. 1984. "Geographical Transmission of Economic Events." *Economic Geography* 60: 132–149.

Lancaster, K. 1966. "A New Approach to Consumer Theory." *Journal of Political Economy* 74: 132–157.

Lewis, A. 1977. *The Evolution of the International Economic Order* (Princeton: Princeton University Press).

Linnemann, H. 1966. *An Econometric Study of International Trade Flows* (Amsterdam: North-Holland).

Lösch, A. 1940. 2nd ed. *Die raumliche Ordnung der Wirtschaft*, 2d ed. (Jena: Gustav Fischer). English translation by W. Woglom. 1954. *The Economics of Location* (New Haven: Yale University Press).

Magee, S. *International Trade* (Reading: Addison-Wesley).

Malecki, E. 1983. "Technology and Regional Development: A Survey." *International Regional Science Review* 8: 89–126.

Morrill, R. 1968. "Waves of Spatial Diffusion." *Journal of Regional Science* 8: 1–19.

Morrill, R., G. Gaile, and G. Thrall. 1988. *Spatial Diffusion* (Beverly Hills: Sage).

Mulligan, G. 1979. "Additional Properties of a Hierarchical City Size Model." *Journal of Regional Science* 19: 57–66.

Myrdal, G. 1957. *Economic Theory and Under-developed Regions* (London: Duckworth).

Niedercorn, J., and B. Bechdolt. 1969. "An Economic Derivation of the 'Gravity Law' of Spatial Interaction." *Journal of Regional Science* 10: 273–281.

————. 1972. "An Economic Derivation of the 'Gravity Law' of Spatial Interaction: A Further Reply and Reformulation." *Journal of Regional Science* 12: 127–136.

North, D. 1955. "Location Theory and Regional Economic Growth." *Journal of Political Economy* 63: 243–258.

Nourse, H. 1978. "Equivalence of Central Place and Economic Base Theories of Urban Growth." *Journal of Urban Economics* 5: 543–549.

Parr, J., K. Denike, and G. Mulligan. 1975. "City Size Models and the Economic Base: A Recent Controversy." *Journal of Regional Science* 15: 1–8.

Pedersen, P. 1970. "Innovation Diffusion within and between National Urban Systems." *Geographical Analysis* 2: 203–254.

Perroux, F. 1950. "Economic Space: Theory and Application." *Quarterly Journal of Economics* 64: 89–104.

————. 1973. "Multinational Investments and the Analysis of Development and Integration Poles." *Economies et Societes* 24: 831–868.

Pred, A. 1966. *The Spatial Dynamics of U.S. Urban-industrial Growth, 1800–1914* (Cambridge: MIT Press).

Reitsma, H., and J. Kleinpenning. 1985. *The Third World in Perspective* (Totawa, New Jersey: Rowman & Allanheld).

Romer, P. 1986. "Increasing Returns and Long-Run Growth." *Journal of Political Economy* 94: 1002–1037.

Sheppard, E. 1979. "Geographic Potentials." *Annals of the Association of American Geographers* 69: 438–447.

Thirlwall, A. 1966. "Regional Unemployment as a Cyclical Phenomenon." *Scottish Journal of Political Economy* 13: 205–219.

————. 1977. *Growth and Development*, 2d ed. (New York: John Wiley & Sons).

Thompson, J. 1982. "An Empirical Note on the Compatability of Central Place Models and Economic Base Theory." *Journal of Regional Science* 22: 97–103.

Tiebout, C. 1956. "Exports and Regional Economic Growth." *Journal of Political Economy* 64: 160–169.

Warntz, W. 1964. "A New Map of the Surface of Population Potentials for the United States 1960." *Geographical Review* 54: 170–184.

————. 1965. *Macrogeography and Income Fronts* (Philadelphia: Regional Science Research Institute).

Wilson, A. 1970. *Entropy in Urban and Regional Modelling* (London: Pion).

World Bank. 1992. *World Development Report 1992* (New York: Oxford University Press).

INTERNATIONAL FINANCE

*P*ART II CONTAINS DISCUSSIONS OF THE geography of financial capital in the international economy. The flow of capital has two forms: investment and lending. In turn, there are two basic types of investment: portfolio and direct. International direct investment is different from portfolio investment and lending, although all three ultimately are methods of financing activities in foreign countries. Direct investment is unlike portfolio investment because it entails control of the activities financed; it is unlike lending because it entails ownership.

The first chapter of this section, "Currency Exchange Rates," is a precursor to the chapters on lending and investment and also to the material in Section III on international trade. Exchange rate variations can have widespread impacts on the international economy. Chapter 5 begins by addressing currency exchange rates and their variability. Exchange rate variability is the single most important characteristic that distinguishes domestic from international investment. Exchange rates are considered with respect to their market determination and also to the exchange rate management practices of both governments and investors.

Chapter 6, "International Portfolio Investment," begins with a discussion of the relative immobility of capital in the international economy. Focusing on equity markets, the chapter then proceeds to describe contemporary financial portfolio models which, in the case of the capital asset pricing model (CAPM), emphasize the role of risk in the investment decision and, in the case of the arbitrage model, the potential for multiple sources of return. The chapter includes consideration of selected factors of risk and return in the international economy, maintaining the context of the financial portfolio models. After an examination of the degree of integration of the world's stock markets, the chapter ends with a brief description of selected stock markets and measures of their relationships between 1978 and 1987.

Chapter 7, "International Lending and Debt," is more concerned than Chapter 6 with economic development problems. It begins by casting lending as a spatial flow under neoclassical terms, but then discusses the segmented characteristics of international debt markets that undermine equilibrating processes. The first type of segmentation considered is that between Core and Periphery. The more sophisticated debt instruments available in the Core are discussed, as is the more active role of commercial banks. Commercial bank lending in the Periphery is covered, but the chapter quickly turns to the activities of the leading multilateral lending agencies: the IMF and the World Bank. The chapter ends with a discussion of recent efforts to reduce foreign debt as an impediment to economic development in the Periphery.

The material in Chapter 8, "The Location of Foreign Direct Investment and the Multinational Corporation," begins with an examination of the variety of theories of the location of capital assets and linked theories of the formation of the MNC. The chapter then turns to a brief description of current broad geographical and sectoral patterns of foreign direct investment (FDI). As should be expected, the major national sources of FDI are the countries of the Core; virtually by definition the capital surplus, capital exporting countries. Major national destinations of FDI, however, are found in both Core and Periphery. The chapter ends by returning to the geography of economic growth and development, examining FDI effectiveness in strengthening or diminishing the differences between Core and Periphery.

CHAPTER 5

· · ·

Currency Exchange Rates

· · ·

5.1 INTRODUCTION

Surprisingly, given their importance, currency exchange rates are not directly considered in international trade theory. Instead, as discussed in Chapter 9, international prices are set in barter terms so that country X trades so many units of a commodity for so many units of another commodity produced in country Y. The absence of currency in such theoretical transactions allows us to study the process of trade more closely. Unfortunately, theory and reality are separated in a number of ways, and currency issues are vital in the series of spatial interactions that comprise the geography of the international economy. Differences in currency may, in fact, be the single most important factor in distinguishing international from domestic economic flows.

For example, international investors face one problem not typically faced, at least directly, by domestic investors: exchange rate volatility. Although perfect stability was far from achieved, the exchange rates of many currencies were basically fixed in U.S. dollar terms under the Bretton Woods agreement from the end of World War II until 1971. Since that time, exchange rates among the world's currencies have been determined both by markets and management by countries. First we will consider market determination of exchange rates, then government management of exchange rates and some international cooperative agreements.

5.2 EXCHANGE RATE DETERMINATION

When national currencies are coins made of precious metals, particularly gold coins, currency exchange rates can be defined in barter terms. For example, given equal purities, if the gold dollar of country X weighs 20 grams and the gold dollar of country Y weighs 40 grams, then Y's dollar is worth twice X's dollar. The same type of barter rates can be determined if paper currency backed by a fixed amount of gold is used. This was the Bretton Woods system; the U.S. dollar was fixed in its exchange value for gold, which in turn meant that any currency fixed in its exchange rate to the U.S. dollar was also effectively fixed in its exchange value for gold. The Bretton Woods system ended when the United States no longer guaranteed the value of its dollar in terms of gold, thus undermining the entire system.

How do markets determine exchange rates? There are three basic and interrelated theories of exchange rate determination. One holds that exchange rates are ultimately determined by *purchasing power parity* (Baillie and McMahon, 1989). In a static context, PPP is a simple barter rate of exchange based on the relative prices of goods between two countries. For example, if a loaf of bread costs one of country X's dollars in country X and two of country Y's dollars in Country Y, then the exchange rate between the two countries should be the simple ratio of the prices; that is, X/Y or 1/2. The PPP-based exchange rate is simple to determine for two countries and one product, but beyond the most basic level it becomes quite difficult. When more than one good is considered in more than two countries, the relative prices of the goods must be calculated across a number of countries. Countries with relatively high prices, other things being equal, would have cheap currencies in international markets, and countries with relatively low prices would have relatively expensive currencies. Exchange rates would then effectively bring about the "law of one price" in an international economy segmented by multiple currencies. In fact, relative prices are not the same across all countries. Recall, for example, that the relative prices of services tend to be lower in poor countries than in rich ones. Only goods entered into international trade on a competitive basis or goods that are everywhere the same should be considered in calculating PPP values.

Another basic theory of exchange rate determination by markets is monetarist (Humphrey and Kelleher, 1982; Boughton, 1988). The monetarist theory focuses, in the static case, on a simple money supply equation. For example, if countries X and Y are fully identical except that country X has 5,000 units of currency in circulation and country Y has 10,000 units of currency in circulation, then the simple ratio X/Y or 1/2 again defines the exchange rate. Niehans (1980) has described the similarity of the monetarist and PPP theories of exchange rate determination. For example, in the case just described, the purchasing power of country X's currency is twice that of country Y's, given the condition that the two countries are identical beyond their money stocks. Both monetarist and PPP theories also describe exchange rate fluctuations as the result of changing relative prices of goods. Under PPP, changes in the relative prices of goods are the source of exchange rate fluctuations. As the goods in country X decrease in price relative to the goods in country Y, country X's currency appreciates in value against country Y's currency. The monetarist view is that the change in relative prices is induced by changing the relative supplies of money between the two countries, so that the relative decrease in prices in country X is the result of the relative increase of country Y's money supply. In a dynamic context, the monetarist view is that the expectation of the future exchange rate is a determinant of the current exchange rate (Somanath, 1984). This assumes a very efficient currency market, with virtually perfect knowledge of future differences in purchasing power between two countries.

Both PPP and monetarist theories assume exchange rates are tied to goods prices. An alternative theory is that exchange rates are a function of relative prices of financial capital across countries, or asset market price parity (Gross, 1987). If the real rate of interest on deposits in country X is 10% and the real rate on deposits in country Y is 5%, and if capital is mobile between the two countries, then country X's currency will appreciate relative to Country Y's. As in the case of PPP, the exchange rate tends to equalize payments between the two countries. Note that differences in the rate of interest could easily be a function of different additions to money supplies between two countries.

Essentially, PPP, monetarist, and asset market theories are very interrelated, and it has been suggested that PPP determines exchange rates in the long term and asset markets determine them in the short term. Dornbusch (1976) has provided a model of exchange rate volatility based on the relatively slow speed of price adjustments in goods markets (PPP) and the fast speed of price adjustments in asset markets across countries. His model suggests that exchange rates are "too" volatile; that they tend to overshoot or undershoot some equilibrium level. Krugman (1989) has also argued that exchange rates are too volatile and that currency exchange markets fail to recognize both short-term trends and long-term equilibria.

An important period of exchange rate volatility took place from 1978 to 1987 (see Epilogue). The volatility was not uniformly spread but was experienced differently, on average, by countries of different World Bank income groups (Table 5.1). By the end of the period, the high income countries generally were experiencing strengthening exchange rates, but the exchange rates in the poorer income groups, particularly in the low and low middle incomes, continued to weaken. At the global scale, the exchange rate volatility of the period was related to the rise and fall of the price of oil during the period as much as any other single factor. The high income countries, as a group, were hard-hit by the higher oil prices of the first part of the period, and their currencies, on average, declined in value. However, the rich economies were also able to recover rapidly as oil prices declined later in the period, and the exchange value of their currencies increased as their economies grew. On the other hand, the economies of the poorer countries were devastated by the high oil prices, and their economies were virtually bankrupted. The poorer economies were unable to recover from the second oil shock in the same way that the rich countries did, so their

TABLE 5.1   Median Exchange Rates Indexes by
World Bank Income Group, 1978–1987*

Year	All	Low Income	Low Middle Income	High Middle Income	High Income
1978	.941	.939	.932	.960	1.000
1979	.928	.946	.972	.960	1.000
1980	.961	.958	.948	.947	1.000
1981	.928	.935	.854	.953	.962
1982	.851	.863	.770	.944	.938
1983	.738	.721	.656	.944	.856
1984	.660	.621	.606	.825	.772
1985	.686	.675	.490	.715	.838
1986	.618	.565	.400	.691	.802
1987	.571	.489	.392	.634	.973

* 1977 = 1.000.

Source of original data: International Monetary Fund. 1989. *Balance of Payments Statistics Yearbook,* vol. 40, part 1 (Washington: International Monetary Fund).

currencies continued to decline in value even after the price of oil greatly declined. Examining a different, and longer, period, Wood (1991) found that oil prices were the primary determinant of exchange rate trends among the developing countries.

With respect to the theories of exchange rate determination, the exchange rate declines in the poorer countries from 1978 through 1987 were a good example of integrated PPP and monetarist models of exchange rate determination. As the price of oil increased, it induced inflation on a global scale. The rate of inflation, however, tended to be higher in the poor countries than the rich ones because poor countries had less capacity in their economies to absorb price increases. To some degree, the price increases were offset by the too-rapid expansion of money supplies, which inevitably led to increasing rates of inflation, or decreasing purchasing power. The generally greater price increases in poorer countries relative to the price increases in richer countries caused depreciation of the poor countries' currencies. (In addition to printing money, many poor countries financed their oil and other purchases by borrowing. See Chapter 7.)

Differential asset returns and interest rates across international markets did not play much, if any, role in determining the declining currency values of the poor countries during this period. Essentially, the poorer countries did not have asset markets, of either equities or bonds, that could be equated during the period to the asset markets of the richer countries. In addition, capital controls frequently were used to limit and direct the (legal) flow of finance between countries. Given the circumstances, tradeable goods prices are the only basis for defining market-based exchange rates between two poor countries, or between a rich country (one with an asset market) and a poor country. Currency valuations taken from asset market prices are limited largely to the set of rich countries. It seems that exchange rate models are not only limited temporally, but also geographically. Over the long term, and between poor countries or countries with greatly disparate wealth levels, exchange rates are most likely determined by PPP with respect to goods. Over the short term and among rich countries, it may be that exchange rates are most likely determined by PPP with respect to financial assets.

The changes in exchange rates from 1978 to 1987 are very long-term ones in the context of foreign exchange markets, so despite any fundamental differences between rich and poor countries it could be expected that PPP would play the key role in currency valuations. Over a few days, or the true short term, changes in PPP could not be expected to play any real role in exchange rate markets. An extreme example of short-term volatility in exchange rates took place in the U.S. dollar market between August 16 and August 21,1991. August 16 was the last day of currency trading in New York before the Stalinist coup d'etat in the Soviet Union; by August 21 it was clear that the coup had failed and the liberal Gorbachev was returned to power.

Rates of exchange between selected currencies and the American dollar for the period are listed in Table 5.2. At first glance, the changes in the rates of exchange seem small, but note that they are for trades of at least U.S. $1 million so a 1% change translates into a $10,000 difference. Two different exchange rate paths are taken by the four different national currencies listed in the table. The expected path is that followed by the British pound, Japanese yen, and Korean won. Each rapidly declined in value against the American dollar between August 16 and August 19 and then gained in exchange value from August 19 to August 21. Each of the three currencies was, in fact, stronger against the American dollar on August 21 than on August 16.

TABLE 5.2   Selected Exchange Rates for Trades of U.S. Dollars: August 16, and 19–21, 1991*

	U.S. Dollar in Foreign Currency			
Country	Friday, August 16	Monday, August 19	Tuesday, August 20	Wednesday, August 21
Canada	1.1448	1.1432	1.1410	1.1445
United Kingdom	.6025	.6148	.6124	.5929
Japan	137.4000	138.1000	137.5000	136.4300
Republic of Korea	733.8000	734.1000	732.3000	730.1000
European Currency Unit (ECU)	.8482	.8543	.8852	.8760
Federal Reserve Board Index	94.44	96.33	96.05	93.24

* Trades were for U.S. $1 million minimum in New York City as of 3:00 P.M. Eastern Daylight Time on the designated dates.
Source: Hartford Courant, August 20, 1991, p. B4, and August 22, 1991, p. D5.

The Canadian dollar followed the opposite path, strengthening against the American dollar from August 16 to August 20, and then declining in exchange value from August 20 to August 21.

A reasonable explanation for the exchange rate volatility over this short period can be found in the asset market model of exchange rate determination. The perceived failure of liberalization in the Soviet Union and the return of inward-looking totalitarianism had a stronger negative affect on European and East Asian asset markets than on the asset markets in the United States. Both the South Korean and German markets could be viewed by an alarmist as being under an actual physical threat. A more reasonable perception was that a renewal of strong East-West tension would seriously undermine prospects for German growth by making the reunification process less tractable because the Soviet Union still had Red Army divisions stationed in the former German Democratic Republic (East Germany). Further, there was uncertainty over the constancy of Soviet oil exports to Western Europe. The most realistic view was that a large part of the potential expansion of markets in the Soviet Union, by all corporations, had been eliminated by the coup d'etat. American companies would also be affected, but to a smaller degree than Western European or East Asian companies simply because of the large size of the American domestic market. American assets were expected to have greater future returns than the assets held in most other countries, so the value of the American dollar increased relative to most other currencies. When the coup d'etat failed, the threat of declining asset returns in East Asia and Western Europe disappeared, and those currencies not only gained back lost exchange value but actually increased against the American dollar. The failure of the coup appeared to insure more rapid opening and liberalization of the Soviet economy, and now the corporations that would have been most hurt by the coup were most helped by its failure, greatly appreciating their asset values relative to asset values in the United States.

The general increase and then decrease in the value of the American dollar during the short period of unrest is evident in two broad exchange indicators (Table 5.2). The Federal Reserve Board's index of the dollar's weighted multilateral exchange value increased by almost two points between Friday and Monday, and dropped by over three points from Monday to Wednesday. The exchange value of the American dollar against the European Currency Unit (ECU; see Section 5.4) continued to increase strongly from Monday to Tuesday, but by Wednesday began to decline. The additional day of dollar increase against the ECU, and the dollar's slow decline, resulted from the more immediate and severe implications of problems in the Soviet Union for Europe than for the rest of the world.

The Canadian dollar, unlike most other currencies, gained in value against the American dollar at the beginning of the coup and then lost value as the more liberal government was restored. The basis for this exchange rate track was likely more political than economic, because the American and Canadian economies are so close. This specific market probably considered that the United States could be more significantly affected in political and military contexts than Canada. The uncertainty led to a type of premium on Canadian currency relative to the American dollar. When the uncertainty ended, the premium was removed.

The case of Canadian and American dollar exchange rates during the period was unusual because any type of uncertainty in international affairs, whether economic or political, usually causes the American dollar to increase in value against other currencies. At the same time that the American dollar was generally increasing in value, the price of gold was increasing as well. Both gold and the American dollar are viewed as safe havens of liquidity because both have purchasing power virtually throughout the world. Despite the abandonment of any type of gold standard by the United States, the American dollar effectively remains almost "as good as gold" in international markets.

The American dollar currently holds special status among the world's currencies. In addition to its status as a safe haven, its role in the international economy is maintained by the convention of denominating commodity prices in American dollars. Oil, for example, and even gold itself, are priced in American dollars regardless of country of production or consumption. When the price of oil is raised, consumers must effectively buy more American dollars to meet the increase, thereby raising the exchange value of dollar (other things remaining equal). In financial markets, international bond issues from both private and public sector sources are more frequently denominated in American dollars than any other currency, and both governments and individuals still have more than half of their foreign currency holdings in American dollars (*Economist,* 1991).

This is not to say, however, that the American dollar is beyond significant fluctuation in value. A long-term fluctuation is represented in the period 1978–1987. A severe slide in the value of the dollar occurred in the late summer of 1992 in response to a mix of factors. High interest rates in Western Europe and low ones in the United States, the American recession, and fear of inflationary expansion of spending by an expected Democratic administration all combined to severely depress the value of the dollar relative to the yen and the deutsche mark. In addition, the Bush administration did not intervene because it saw the weak dollar as a method of stimulating exports and replacing imports with cheaper domestic production, therefore providing an opportunity for economic growth.

Despite its volatility, the dollar still plays a special role in the international economy because of the size of the American market. Commodities and bond issues are priced in American dollars because their single most likely point of sale, for some time, has been the United States. Private wealth is held in American dollars because the United States has the single largest unsegmented financial market in the world. Even when rates of return are relatively low in the United States, the wide variety and large number of investment opportunities in the U.S. market allow investors to avoid the transaction costs of moving between smaller markets using different currencies. One of the aims of the European Monetary Union (see Section 5.4) is to provide a base for unification of European financial markets that can eliminate these transaction costs. Krugman (1990) has developed a model of international currency exchange in which avoidance of transaction costs leads to the development of a dominant international currency. Such a result is expected, however, because reduction of transaction costs is the basic reason that money rather than barter is used as a means of exchange.

5.3 EXCHANGE RATE MANAGEMENT: GOVERNMENT POLICY

Since the end of the Bretton Woods sytem of fixed exchange rates, currencies, in effect, have become commodities with their own prices. Unlike the case of most commodities, however, price swings on a currency can be quite rapid and dramatic and almost always of interest to national governments. In a market system, prices and their changes are supposed to convey information. For example, if the price of a loaf of rye bread is twice that of a loaf of wheat bread, then the market values rye twice as much as wheat. Further, if wheat bread's price begins to increase relative to that of rye, it is because wheat bread is getting in relatively short supply. The prices of currencies, under a floating system, should convey the same sort of useful information. An increase in one currency's value relative to another's should result, for example, because of changes in relative supplies of the currencies that effect changes in their relative purchasing power.

The kind of exchange rate volatility described above is more a function of speculation concerning future events than a reaction to any fundamental change in relative prices (Frenkel, 1987). If this is so, then elimination of speculative concern should go a long way toward elimination of short-term exchange rate volatility. Obviously, if the future value of a currency is guaranteed—by fixing its value with respect to gold, for example—then true speculation is unfounded. One reason that governments intervene in currency markets is at least to dampen the volatility of their currency's value.

Actually, governments take as much of an interest in the value of their currency as in its short-term volatility. In theory, the relative value of a country's currency is taken as a function of the country's domestic prices compared to others. In reality, exchange rates also have an impact on domestic prices. The value of a country's currency can affect both production and consumption decisions of "domestic" interests (Williamson and Miller, 1987). When the exchange value of a country's currency is high, that country's producers may limit production of goods for foreign markets where the price of the goods is high, and the country's consumers may prefer the goods of foreign producers with their low prices (Dornbusch, 1987). In open economies, currency exchange values can be as much of a determinant as they are a result of international trade patterns.

The impact of variable rather than fixed exchange rates on trade has been addressed in two areas. One concerns the effect on trade of the increased risk and uncertainty that should be engendered in the international economy by flexible exchange rates. Trade requiring foreign currency that itself changes in price can cause uncertainty over the true price of the goods being exchanged. Producers would prefer the safety of trading within their own countries to the potential of significant currency losses in international markets. It appears, however, that the uncertainty of foreign trade is outweighed by its rewards (Balassa, 1980; Ghosal and Snyder, 1986). World trade generally has been growing faster than world production and income since the end of the fixed exchange system of the Bretton Woods agreement.

In addition to concerns over the effect of flexible exchange rates on trade volume, there are concerns for their impact on trade patterns. As import prices decrease (increase) and the prices of exports increase (decrease) because of the appreciation (depreciation) of a country's currency, both the structural and geographical pattern of the country's trade obviously would change. However, the link between changes in currency values and changes in import and export prices is not all that clear. Recall Bergstrand's (1985) application of an extended gravity model to international trade (see Table 4.1). He found that exchange rate changes had no significant impact on the patterns of trade that he examined. Other related studies have suggested that exchange rate changes are not as strongly linked to trade pattern dynamics as might be expected (e.g., Bailey et al., 1986).

There are several reasons why changes in exchange rates are not immediately and directly translated into changes in trade patterns. The importance of product differentiation in international trade, for example, means that product qualities other than price play important roles in buying decisions (Dornbusch, 1987; Laffer, 1986). In addition, Krugman (1989, p. 40) has raised the point that producers "price to the market"; that is, producers lower or raise their prices to offset changes in exchange rates in order to stabilize market shares. Losses during one period can be made up by exchange-rate-based gains in another. Volkswagen learned this lesson the hard way during the early 1970s when the deutsche mark increased rapidly in value against the American dollar. As the price of Volkswagen's cars increased rapidly in the American market, it lost significant market share to its Japanese competitors, which held the line on prices even as the yen appreciated (Srinivasulu, 1981).

Eventually, however, exchange rates do affect the pattern of trade. Di Liberto (1988) has found that the lag between exchange rate changes and trade changes runs about three years for American trade in general. Childs and Hammig (1987) found a lag of between two and three years in American trade of agricultural commodities. Warner and Kreinen (1983) found that as the duration of an exchange rate movement extended, its impact was more immediately felt. For example, American trade was more immediately affected by the dollar's appreciation during the early 1980s because the appreciation was long-term, rather than episodic. The effect that exchange rates have on trade patterns, if long-lived, can be extended to patterns of domestic production. Trade losses may result in losses of domestic production and employment. These losses, in addition to declining merchandise trade balances, are a reason that governments may choose to intervene in currency markets.

The exchange rate management practices that governments employ in the attempt to stem losses in trade and related production are essentially reactive. In other instances, governments employ exchange rate management in a proactive manner that attempts to use the international economy as a basis for domestic growth. Some governments, especially of countries that are very successful in export markets, have been accused of keeping their currencies artificially low in order to undercut competitors in international markets (*World Financial Markets,* 1989). Other governments have kept their currencies at artificially high rates in order to reduce domestic inflation. When currencies have high values they buy more on international markets, and domestic producers must keep prices low in order maintain market share. Several countries, including Chile, Israel, and Argentina, have used exchange rate management in attempts to reduce domestic inflation rates (Dornbusch, 1986). Several countries use multi-tiered exchange rates for different types of transactions. For example, the Soviet Union in 1991 quoted a tourist exchange rate, a commercial exchange rate, and an official exchange rate. Each was different from the other and was used, in addition to a black market rate, only within the Soviet Union.

To say that a government can force its currency's value to some artificially low or high rate means that there is a definable equilibrium exchange rate. For example, a bilateral exchange rate defined by purchasing power parity (PPP) would theoretically be an equilibrium rate. Holders of one of the pair of currencies could not gain by holding the other with respect to the consumption of goods. An equilibrium exchange rate based on PPP, however, is only one of several types of exchange rate equilibria defined by Williamson (1983). Williamson refers to the exchange rate equilibrium based on purchasing power parity as the *fundamental equilibrium exchange rate*. This rate is the most commonly used baseline for determination of a currency's tendency to be over- or undervalued.

Another exchange rate equilibrium defined by Williamson is the *market equilibrium exchange rate,* which is the rate that clears the market in the absence of government intervention. This is the rate usually in force when governments are most active in exchange rate markets. The stability of this equilibrium requires a very high degree of capital mobility in the short term. However, actual financial flows in the international economy vary in their temporal flexibility. Trade, for example, seems to react fairly slowly to exchange rate movements. Again, if actual exchange rates are responsive to both short-term (financial asset prices) and long-term (goods prices) conditions, then the conditions must be coincident for stability to be achieved. If short-term conditions appear to run counter to long-term conditions, then a stable equilibrium is unlikely; thus any given rate of exchange could depend, for example, more on the timing of transactions rather than fundamental economic relationships. In this case, the currency becomes as much of a commodity as the means of acquiring a commodity.

Finally, Williamson defines the *current equilibrium exchange rate* as the rate that would obtain under complete knowledge of the relevant economic fundamentals of purchasing power parity and asset prices, and the relevant macroeconomic policy variables. This is the rate that would be expected to yield equal returns on comparable investments between two countries and to deliver the same amount of goods. As indicated in the definition of this rate, macroeconomic policy can be an important determinant of exchange rates and is commonly used by governments to guide exchange rate values.

Fiscal policy and monetary policy are the two basic macroeconomic tools available to governments of countries with market-oriented economies. Fiscal policy concerns taxation and spending, and monetary policy ultimately concerns interest rates. Common purposes of macroeconomic policy include rapid growth, low inflation, and high levels of employment; ideally, fiscal and monetary policies are formulated to achieve all three. There are two related problems, however, in achieving the three basic goals of macroeconomic policy.

One problem is that the goals, to a degree, are mutually exclusive. For example, rapid growth frequently leads to high inflation, and high employment can also have inflationary effects. Low inflation frequently is achieved only when rates of employment are depressed. Typically, a balance among the three goals is sought, but it becomes easy for policy to become cyclical as counterweights to any particular direction are sought. For example, low interest rates follow high interest rates in a monetary policy cycle that attempts to fine-tune economic growth. The second problem in achieving domestic policy goals is that most countries are integrated enough within the international economy that domestic policy can no longer be considered separately from international policy. This means that "cause and effect" of domestic and international policies becomes clouded as the two become more and more intertwined. For example, exchange rate policy and policy towards a country's current account balance can be considered elements of a domestic growth policy as much as they can be considered responses to a country's current level of growth (Crockett and Goldstein, 1987; Williamson and Miller, 1987).

Take two hypothetical and simplified cases. In the first case, assume that a country decreases its money supply in an attempt to raise interest rates so that the rate of growth, and thereby the rate of inflation, may be depressed. Other things being equal, the increase in interest rates may attract foreign investment so that the rate of growth is maintained, as is the rate of inflation. In the second case, consider a country that deliberately undervalues its own currency in order to increase growth rates by export expansion. If the policy was successful, imports would become less competitive in the country's markets as their prices increase, and price inflation could easily result due to a lack of foreign competition.

Perhaps the strongest example of the declining distinction between domestic and international economic policy is the case of the fiscal and trade deficits of the United States during the Reagan administration (1981–1989). Bird (1991) divides the period into two phases, one of expansionary fiscal policy and U.S. dollar appreciation (1981–1984), and one of dollar depreciation (1985–1989). The expansionary fiscal policy of the first Reagan administration was accomplished by a significant reduction in taxes and a significant increase in spending by the federal government. At the same time, monetary policy was restrictive, so that real rates of interest in the United States reached very high levels. Compared to most of the rest of the world, the United States experienced strong growth under high interest rates, and the dollar appreciated in value considerably as foreign interests became attracted to the American economy.

The dollar's increase in value during the first phase led to its decline during the second, as described by Bird. First of all, the high value of the dollar led to an increasing merchandise trade deficit, and eventually a deficit on the entire current account. As dollars earned in merchandise trade with the United States accumulated offshore, their exchange value began to stabilize as matching inflows were generated on America's capital account and liberal foreign investment compensated for American tight money policy. In retrospect, the seeming success of Reagan's "domestic" policy was due largely to the ability of the American economy to draw on the international economy for financial capital.

The dollar actually began to depreciate as monetary policy was relaxed, and American interest rates became less favorable compared to those of other industrial countries. Obviously, American policy during the period cannot be taken in isolation. Rates of interest as determinants of exchange rates are meaningful only when taken in their international market context. Aliber (1990) has argued that the American trade deficit of the 1980s was as much a result of German and Japanese policies of low interest rates as the American policy of high interest rates. In fact, one of the reasons that the dollar began its decline in value during the second half of the 1980s was the development of a coordinated interest rate policy among the world's richest countries. In September of 1985, the Group of Five, or G-5, consisting of the United States, Japan, United Kingdom, France, and West Germany, announced a policy of interest rate coordination. The G-5's immediate intention was to attempt to halt the rapid growth of the United States' merchandise trade deficit by realigning exchange rates within the group (Kenen, 1988). The announcement of coordinated intervention in the foreign exchange market may have been as important in reducing the value of the dollar as was the actual implementation of the policy. As noted by Mayer (1982), just a government's expression of concern with the exchange market can have a strong effect on exchange rates.

5.4   COOPERATIVE AGREEMENTS

The difficulty of unilateral management of exchange rates has led to a variety of cooperative agreements among countries. The Bretton Woods system of fixed exchange rates was, of course, a cooperative arrangement among the countries that were members of the International Monetary Fund. The Bretton Woods system was also similar to other systems of exchange rate cooperation in that, while it was cooperative, it was based on the maintainance of several currency values relative, or "pegged," to a single strong currency. The strength of that currency was defined by two characteristics: a relatively high value with respect to international purchasing power, and the stability of that value. Alternatively, macroeconomic policy coordination, of the sort used to decrease the value of the American dollar in the second half of the 1980s, can be used instead of a strong currency peg as the basis for a system of fixed exchange rates.

Many former French colonies of West Africa gained political independence in the 1950s and 1960s but maintained currency links to the French franc. The French franc (FF) zone includes Burkina Faso, Burundi, Cameroon, the Central African Republic, Comoros, the Congo Peoples Republic, Gabon, Cote d'Ivoire, Niger, and Senegal, all of which are classified among the world's poor countries. The currencies of these countries are pegged to the French franc in a sort of regional version of the Bretton

Woods system. (The British at one time anchored a sterling area in East Africa also comprised of former colonies, such as Kenya.) Unfortunately, it may be that the FF peg held by these countries is at least partly to blame for their poverty. Essentially, their currency prices are those of France and not determined by market evaluation of their individual economies in the context of the international economy. Frequently the strong currency peg has led to FF zone overvaluation that limits the ability of these countries to export their products.

The FF zone is a remnant of one-time conventional thinking on the problems posed by flexible exchange rates for the economies of developing countries. For example, Lal (1980) notes the view that floating exchange rates contributed to uncertainty that diminished trade in general. Further, poorer countries do not have the requisite institutional support in the form of financial markets that allow flexible exchange rate regimes to operate efficiently. Another view was that exchange rate movements led to wasteful resource allocations, based only on current prices, in poor countries. Given these ideas, it was argued that a poor country could benefit from stability and efficiency of both trade and production if it could peg its currency to a strong one.

Lal argues that the objections to floating exchange rates for poor-country currencies were ill-conceived, and recent evidence suggests that freeing exchange rates, in concert with other policies of financial and trade liberalization, provides benefits to poorer countries. For example, the World Bank (1991) indicates that a competitive exchange rate is a critical ingredient in the expansion of a country's export sector, and that countries with overvalued currencies have experienced both declining exports and capital flight (see Chapter 7). Related analysis by Nunnenkamp and Schweickert (1990) suggests that currency devaluation by developing countries does lead to economic contraction initially, but soon leads to expansion of the economy, particularly in the pivotal agricultural sector.

The FF zone of currency pegs will probably not last much longer. At the same time that system begins to fold, a larger and more visible system of fixed exchange rates has been developing in the European Community. The move toward a single *European Monetary System (EMS)* began in 1979 (Fraser, 1987). Initially, eight of the nine nations that were members of the EC at the time joined the EMS. The United Kingdom held out, for reasons to be described, until 1991. The unit of account in the EMS is the *European Currency Unit (ECU)*. The ECU actually is a basket of EMS member currencies; thus far it has not reached the status of legal tender in any but the most limited central banking transactions. Some bonds are ECU-denominated but in fact represent the weighted collections of the individual currencies that comprise the ECU. The initial composition, or weighting, of the ECU ranged from about 33% deutsche mark to just over 1% Irish punt, and was largely determined by the relative sizes of national income among the member countries. Importantly, while the British would not accept the EMS's *exchange rate mechanism (ERM)*, the pound sterling was made a constituent part (about 13%) of the ECU at its inception.

The focus of the EMS is *convergence,* which has many meanings in this context but began with reference to stable currency exchange rates among EMS members (Ungerer, 1989). The ERM has a two-tiered band of exchange rate flexibility with respect to the ECU. There is a relatively loose band, designed as a transition band for the EC's weaker economies, that allows a fluctuation of 6% in a currency's value against the ECU. The stricter standard band is only 2.25% and is currently used by all EMS members. Although it does not serve this role in an official sense, the deutsche mark is the so-called anchor currency of the EMS and serves a role similar to the U.S. dollar under the Bretton Woods system. For practical purposes, the exchange bands of the EMS are defined as much with respect to the deutsche mark as with respect to the ECU. In order for its currency to remain within the band, a country's government must employ monetary and/or fiscal policy to control inflation in the same way as the German government. Failure to do so would tend to force the currency to diverge beyond the band and void the whole purpose of the EMS, which is exchange rate stability within the single market.

The convergence of relative exchange rates essentially requires the convergence of macroeconomic policies among EMS members that is possible only among countries with at least roughly equivalent economies (Branson, 1990). Convergence of exchange rates is unlikely unless inflation rates, interest rates, and government budget deficits as proportions of GDP also converge. All three of these are related measures, to a large degree fashioned by government policy. For now, Portugal and Greece remain outside the EMS because their economies currently cannot be expected to follow the same policies as the stronger European economies. It may be, in fact, that these relatively weak economies would suffer under the EMS, because exchange rate changes would no longer compensate for their differences from the stronger economies in factor prices and productivities (de Cecco and Giovannini, 1989).

The British, under the government of Margaret Thatcher, felt that the ERM went too far in taking away their sovereign power with respect to fiscal and monetary matters and handing that sovereignty to the EC in general and the Germans in particular. Governments typically use fiscal policy for what appears to be purely domestic purposes, and the loss of such policy tools seems a loss of governmental power. Under the government of John Major, the British appear willing to make concessions that will further their integration within Europe. Ultimately, however, free movement of goods and services requires a single currency. If the European market is to become a truly single market, as is the United States, then it will need a single currency and a single central bank (*World Financial Markets,*1990). Central banks, such as the U.S. Federal Reserve, control a country's money supply and credit conditions. Whether the British will ever abandon these functions of the Bank of England to a central European authority, or whether any other country is willing to give up these functions, remains to be seen.

In mid-1992, the basis for the EMS began to collapse because of problems with the coordination of macroeconomic policy convergence. The United Kingdom, in deep economic recession, found the pound slipping below its assigned parity within the ERM. In order to raise the pound's value, the British government was forced to raise interest rates which, of course, helped deepen the recession. At the time, German rates were very high because the German central bank feared that the expenses associated with the reunification of West and East Germany would be inflationary. It was the mark, of course, that was actually putting pressure on the pound because of the mark's leading role in the EMS. The British wanted the Germans to lower their rates, and the Germans wanted the British to raise theirs. Finally, in September, the United Kingdom and Italy, which was being affected in the same way, effectively withdrew from the ERM temporarily. The entire system will have to be redesigned if a true European currency is ever to be developed.

5.5 EXCHANGE RATE MANAGEMENT: BUSINESS AND INVESTOR PRACTICES

The preceding discussion has concerned government policies toward exchange rate management, but exchange rates are also "managed" by people, companies, and governments as they use foreign currencies in a wide variety of transactions. While most of this section concerns private exchange rate management practices, some recent trends in the use of foreign currencies by governments provide an interesting overview of the general importance of geographical diversification in the international economy.

With the demise of the Bretton Woods system, use of the U.S. dollar as an official reserve currency has declined. A country's official reserves are used in its official foreign transactions. When the U.S. dollar was the international numeraire, many countries held almost their entire reserves in dollars. The dollar was a *vehicle currency,* bought and sold as an intermediary to buying and selling other currencies. Now that few currencies are pegged to the U.S. dollar, its role as a vehicle currency has declined. Further, the relatively long-term growth rates of Japan and Germany have led to an increase in the use of the deutsche mark and the yen as reserve currencies in favor of the dollar. At one time, the pound sterling was an important reserve currency, but its use in this regard has declined greatly since the 1960s (Bank for International Settlements, 1988).

One of the chief purposes of reserve currency diversification is to achieve risk-return benefits of the kind described in the next chapter (Horii, 1986). As fewer and fewer currencies are pegged to the dollar, governments can reduce the risk of dollar depreciation in their reserves by holding a larger variety of currencies. As long as individual currencies are not perfectly and positively correlated with each other, the aggregate value of the reserves should be relatively stable. (The ECU, even within the limits of the ERM, is relatively stable simply due to its weighted composition of still-individual currencies.) Further, if a country tries to manage an otherwise floating currency exchange rate, it needs to hold sufficient amounts of the relevant foreign currencies in order to buy and sell its own currency in international markets.

While governments are faced with problems of reserve currency management brought on by fluctuations in exchange markets, the principal players in foreign exchange markets are corporations and individuals. Tourism plays an important role in foreign exchange transactions, but the business roles of trade and finance are generally much greater and are focused upon here. The management of exchange rates by multinational corporations is very complex (Belkaoui, 1991); thus we can only generalize about three responses to exchange rate volatility, or risk. The three responses are *absorption, temporal hedging,* and *geographical hedging.* They are not mutually exclusive. In fact, it would not be unrealistic for a multinational corporation to be using all three at the same time.

The absorption of exchange rate volatility occurs if a corporation, for example, views such volatility as a short-term fluctuation around an otherwise long-term acceptable rate of exchange. Krugman (1989) has argued for this view as a reason that very volatile swings in exchange rates have dampened effects in international trade markets. He noted that the rise and fall of the value of the American dollar during the 1980s should have had an even more marked effect on trade and production than what actually occurred. Again, it seems that real prices in international markets are stabilized by the producer practice of pricing to the market, with the purpose of maintaining a share of the market that was very costly to establish. Obviously, absorption of unfavorable exchange rates must be a temporary response because anticipation of long-term losses would have to lead to abandonment of the market unless the producer wishes to become bankrupt.

The absorption of exchange rate changes by modifying prices is only one practice of managing exchange rate volatility, and one that is available only in the area of trade and not in investment. A more general view of exchange rate volatility is in the context of risk to be avoided rather than a cost to be incurred. Whilborg (1978) has defined exchange rate risk as the variance of an investment's real rate of return due to variance in an exchange rate that is not matched by corresponding variance in the purchasing power of the currency in question. This type of real economic risk is not limited to investment alone but can also be anticipated in international trade. In addition to such real economic risk, two types of financial risk, *translation (accounting) risk* and *transaction (economic) risk* have been described (Siegel, 1983; Choi, 1986).

Translation risk concerns the valuation of assets in a "home" currency and a foreign currency when their exchange rates are fluctuating. Apparent losses or gains in an asset's worth can take place due to currency swings that have no true impact on the asset's economic value. Translation risk is primarily an accounting and reporting problem (Oxelheim, 1985). It does not exist when accounts are maintained in a single, "local," currency (Demirag, 1988). Translation risk is not an actual financial problem unless the asset is sold at the wrong time, and the issue of timing is actually associated with transaction risk.

Transaction risk exists because the relative values of currencies change over time at different rates. Orders are placed during one period and at a certain price in a foreign currency, but by the period in which payment is due, the exchange rate may have moved (Hekman, 1985). If a foreign currency's price is falling, then the exchange rate becomes more favorable to buyers of the the foreign country's products and purchasers of the foreign country's real assets. On the other hand, purchases of shares in the country's corporations and lending to interests in the foreign country become less favorable.

Changes in exchange rates are like inflation, which affects lenders and investors in opposite ways. Similarly, just as a portfolio's risk can be reduced by holding both stocks and bonds (see Chapter 6), foreign exchange transaction risk can be reduced by conducting transactions of opposite direction across the foreign currency. With respect to trade, for example, buying and selling goods across a pair of currencies tends to cancel out any exchange losses in the short term. With respect to finance, a stock holding or loan can be offset by borrowing the foreign currency. These kinds of simultaneous exchange hedges are less common than either temporal or geographical hedges because they typically are available only to those engaged in wholesale activities or in the direct provision of financial services.

Perhaps the most commonly used hedge against foreign exchange risk is the temporal one of the *forward foreign exchange contract* (Jones and Jones,1987; Swanson and Caples, 1987). A *hedge* is an offsetting position, or counterweight, to any exposure to risk. Automobile collision insurance, for example, is a hedge against the risk of future car wreck by providing for a future payment if the wreck takes place. Forward exchange contracts are agreements between a bank and its customer on an exchange of currency at a given rate. By locking in an exchange rate, the owner (bank customer) of the foreign exchange contract can eliminate transaction risk. For example, if a Canadian wishes to purchase a German machine by a payment due in 90 days, the Canadian takes the risk of the Canadian dollar depreciating against the deutsche mark, therefore raising the machine's cost. The forward contract simply fixes the price for 90 days. If the Canadian dollar depreciates against the mark, the increase in the machine's price is offset by a gain in the currency market, and any appreciation of the Canadian dollar is offset by a decrease in the machine's price. Like insurance, forward contracts are not free, and the payment to the bank when the contract is purchased includes a transaction cost.

An outgrowth of the forward exchange contract is the *currency futures contract.* Forward contracts typically are used with respect to a specific purchase as described in the example above. Futures contracts are more general in that they are standardized and have their own market, including trade in a U.S. dollar index and ECUs. On the other hand, futures contracts are available only in a limited number of currencies widely used in international trade and finance. In addition to their uses as a hedge, currency futures contracts are traded in anticipation of profits. If a futures' price is below the *spot price,* or current exchange rate, on the day the contract expires, the holder of the contract makes a profit. While individual traders do make significant profits (and incur losses) in currency futures, the evidence for any systematic relationship between futures' prices and the actual spot exchange rate at a future time is weak (Jung and Weiland, 1990; Kindleberger, 1980; Kohers, 1987; Lewis, 1988).

The geographical hedge is simply geographical diversification of currency holdings in such a way that offsets occur across the currencies. Effectively, the ECU was a geographical currency hedge due to its diverse composition before the ERM was established. Now that most of the ECU's constituent currencies are within the ERM, they track together, and the relative stability of the ECU derives more from central bank discipline than diversified portfolio effects. On the other hand, the American dollar index that sells in the currency futures markets combines both temporal and geographical hedges against exchange rate risk. The temporal hedge has been discussed; the geographical hedge is similar to that provided by the ECU before the ERM. The typical index consists of a trade-weighted basket of currencies that are not pegged to the dollar. Some rise and some fall against the dollar, so, on average, the exchange value of the index is fairly stable. The availability of indexes lowers the transaction costs of currency diversification because only one instrument is purchased, not the complete set of currencies that it represents. Multiple currency bonds, carrying ECU denominations, for example, also reduce transaction costs.

The critical factor in a geographical diversification strategy is that the currencies held in a portfolio are not correlated in their exchange values (see Chapter 6). In a statistical sense, if two variables are perfectly and positively correlated ($r = 1.00$) they may as well be a single variable. (This is with respect to the Pearson product-moment correlation coefficient, r, which is a standardized measure of covariance. Minimizing covariance among asset returns is one of the objectives of the mean-variance portfolio model described in Chapter 6.) Two currencies with such a correlation might as well be the same currency and cannot provide any diversification

TABLE 5.3 Exchange Rate Indexes and Correlations: West German Mark, Japanese Yen, and American Dollar, 1978–1987

Exchange Rate Indexes

Year	Mark	Yen	Dollar
1978	1.071	1.150	0.923
1979	1.118	0.923	0.923
1980	1.024	1.127	1.000
1981	0.973	1.141	1.090
1982	0.973	1.123	1.090
1983	0.894	1.197	1.200
1984	0.827	1.182	1.224
1985	0.944	1.322	1.100
1986	1.075	1.500	1.000
1987	1.138	1.662	0.857

Pearson Correlation Coefficients

	Mark	Yen	Dollar
Mark	———	0.249	−0.975
Yen		———	−0.255
Dollar			———

Source of original data: International Monetary Fund. 1989. *Balance of Payments Statistics Yearbook,* vol. 40, part 1 (Washington: International Monetary Fund).

benefits with respect to risk reduction. As long as the correlation of the exchange values is less than 1.00, some of the exchange volatility can be diversified away. At an extreme, if two currencies are perfectly and negatively correlated ($r = -1.00$), then they are perfect offsets. As an example, three currency indexes are listed in Table 5.3 along with their correlations. Between 1978 and 1987, the mark, yen, and dollar moved on different tracks with respect to their exchange rates against the IMF's special drawing right, an artificial unit of account composed of a number of currencies (see Chapter 7). Each currency could have served as a hedge against any of the other two during the period because of the fairly low correlations among all three. However, deutsche marks and American dollars ($r = -0.975$) were almost perfect offsets during the period.

The best mix of foreign and domestic currencies in a portfolio can vary from one country's viewpoint to another's (Biger, 1979). In Table 5.3, for example, the yen-mark correlation is weak but positive while the dollar-mark and dollar-yen correlations are negative. As long as a currency portfolio is significantly anchored by a particular domestic currency, then this determines the composition of the other currencies in the portfolio. In the example represented in Table 5.3, it might have been expected that a German would have found dollars more effective than a Japanese would have in offsetting exchange risk. In general, however, a currency portfolio consisting of yen, marks, and dollars would have provided good stability of value during the period at very low transaction cost. Unfortunately, describing the past is much easier than predicting the future.

REFERENCES

Aliber, R. 1990. "The U.S. Trade Deficit and the U.S. Fiscal Deficit: Cause and Effect." In *International Finance and Financial Policy.* H. Stoll, ed. (New York: Quorum Books).

Bailey, M., G. Tavals, and M. Ulan. 1986. "Exchange-Rate Variability and Trade Performance: Evidence for the Big Seven Industrial Countries." *Weltwirtschaftliches Archiv* 122: 466–477.

Baillie, R., and P. McMahon. 1989. *The Foreign Exchange Market: Theory and Econometric Evidence* (Cambridge: Cambridge University Press).

Balassa, B. 1980. "Flexible Exchange Rates and International Trade." In *Flexible Exchange Rates and the Balance of Payments.* J. Chipman and C. Kindleberger, eds. (Amsterdam: North-Holland).

Bank for International Settlements. 1988. *Reserves and International Liquidity* (Basle: Bank for International Settlements).

Belkaoui, A. 1991. *Multinational Management Accounting* (New York: Quorum Books).

Bergstrand, J. 1985. "The Gravity Equation in International Trade: Some Microeconomic Foundations and Empirical Evidence." *Review of Economics and Statistics* 67: 474–481.

Biger, N. 1979. "Exchange Risk Implications of International Portfolio Diversification." *Journal of International Business Studies* 10/2: 64–74.

Bird, G. 1991. "Debt, Deficits, and Dollars: The World Economy in 3-D." *World Development* 19: 245–254.

Boughton, J. 1988. *The Monetary Approach to Exchange Rates: What Now Remains?* (Princeton: International Finance Section, Department of Economics, Princeton University).

Branson, W. 1990. "Financial Market Integration, Macroeconomic Policy, and the EMS." In *Unity with Diversity in the European Economy,* C. Bliss and J. Braga de Macedo, eds. (Cambridge: Cambridge University Press).

Childs, N., and M. Hammig. 1987. "An Examination of the Impact of Real Exchange Rates on U.S. Exports of Agricultural Commodities." *The International Trade Journal* 2: 37–54.

Choi, J. 1986. "A Model of Firm Valuation with Exchange Exposure." *Journal of International Business Studies* 17/2: 153–160.

Crockett, A., and M. Goldstein. 1987. *Strengthening the International Monetary System: Exchange Rates, Surveillance, and Objective Indicators* (Washington: International Monetary Fund).

de Cecco, M., and A. Giovannini. 1989. "Does Europe Need its Own Central Bank?" In *A European Central Bank? Perspectives on Monetary Unification after Ten Years of the EMS,* M. de Cecco and A. Giovannini, eds. (Cambridge: Cambridge University Press).

Demirag, I. 1988. "Assessing Foreign Subsidiary Performance: The Currency Choice of U.K. MNCs." *Journal of International Business Studies* 19/2: 257–275.

Di Liberto, M. 1988. "A Test for Structural Change in U.S. Real Trade and Trade Prices: Fixed Exchange Rate Period vs. Flexible Exchange Rate Period." *The International Trade Journal* 2: 337–376.

Dornbusch, R. 1976. "Expectations and Exchange Rate Dynamics." *Journal of Political Economy* 84: 1161–1176.

——— . 1986. *Inflation, Exchange Rates, and Stabilization* (Princeton: International Finance Section, Department of Economics, Princeton University).

——— . 1987. "Exchange Rates and Prices." *American Economic Review* 77: 93–106.

Economist. 1991. "A Fistful of ECUs." July 13, p. 83.

Fraser, R. 1987. *The World Financial System* (Burnt Mill, England: Longman).

Frenkel, J. 1987. "The International Monetary System: Should it be Reformed?" *American Economic Review* 77: 205–210.

Ghoshal, A., and J. Snyder. 1986. "Flexible Exchange Rates and International Trade: An Empirical Investigation of Bilateral Flows." *The International Trade Journal* 1: 27–46.

Gross, A. 1987. *The Role of the Current Account in Asset Market Models of Exchange Rate Determination* (Berlin: Walter de Gruyter).

Hekman, C. 1985. "A Financial Model of Foreign Exchange Exposure." *Journal of International Business Studies* 16/2: 83–99.

Horii, A. 1986. *The Evolution of Reserve Currency Diversification* (Basle: Bank for International Settlements).

Humphrey, T., and R. Kelleher. 1982. *The Monetary Approach to the Balance of Payments, Exchange Rates, and World Inflation* (New York: Praeger).

International Monetary Fund. 1989. *Balance of Payments Statistics Yearbook,* vol. 40, part 1 (Washington: International Monetary Fund).

Jones, E., and D. Jones. 1987. *Hedging Foreign Exchange: Converting Risk to Profit* (New York: John Wiley & Sons).

Jung, A., and V. Wieland. 1990. "Forward Rates and Spot Rates in the European Monetary System-Forward Market Efficiency." *Weltwirtschaftliches Archiv* 126: 615–629.

Kenen, P. 1988. *Managing Exchange Rates* (New York: Council on Foreign Relations Press).

Kindleberger, C., 1980. "Myths and Realities of the Forward Exchange Market." In *Flexible Exchange Rates and the Balance of Payments*, J. Chipman and C. Kindleberger, eds. (Amsterdam: North-Holland).

Kohers, T. 1987. "Testing the Rate Forecasting Consistency of Major Foreign Currency Futures." *The International Trade Journal* 1: 359–370.

Krugman, P. 1989. *Exchange-Rate Instability* (Cambridge: MIT Press).

_____ . 1990. *Rethinking International Trade* (Cambridge: MIT Press).

Laffer, A. 1986. "Minding our Ps and Qs: Exchange Rates and Foreign Trade." *The International Trade Journal* 1: 1–26.

Lal, D. 1980. *A Liberal International Economic Order: The International Monetary System and Economic Development* (Princeton: International Finance Section, Department of Economics, Princeton University).

Lewis, K. 1988. "Inflation Risk and Asset Market Disturbances: The Mean-Variance Model Revisited." *Journal of International Money and Finance* 7: 273–288.

Mayer, H. 1982. *The Theory and Practice of Floating Exchange Rates and the Role of Official Exchange Rate Intervention* (Basle: Bank for International Settlements).

Niehans, J. 1980. "Dynamic Purchasing Power as a Monetary Rule." In *Flexible Exchange Rates and the Balance of Payments*.

Nunnenkamp, P., and R. Schweickert. 1990. "Adjustment Policies and Economic Growth in Developing Countries-Is Devaluation Contractionary?" *Weltwirtschaftliches Archiv* 126: 474–493.

Oxelheim, L. 1985. *International Financial Market Fluctuations: Corporate Forecasting and Reporting Problems* (Chichester: John Wiley & Sons).

Siegel, M. 1983. *Foreign Exchange Risk and Direct Foreign Investment* (Ann Arbor: UMI Research Press).

Somanath, V. 1984. "Exchange Rate Expectations and the Current Exchange Rate: A Test of the Monetarist Approach." *Journal of International Business Studies* 15/1: 131–140.

Srinivasulu, S. 1981. "Strategic Response to Foreign Exchange Risks." *Columbia Journal of World Business* 16/1: 13–23.

Swanson, P., and S. Caples. 1987. "Hedging Foreign Exchange Risk Using Forward Foreign Exchange Markets: An Extension." *Journal of International Business Studies* 18/1: 75–93.

Ungerer, H. 1989. "The European Monetary System and the International Monetary System." *Journal of Common Market Studies* 27: 231–248.

Warner, D., and M. Kreinin. 1983. "Determinants of International Trade Flows." *Review of Economics and Statistics* 65: 96–104.

Wihlborg, C. 1978. *Currency Risks in International Financial Markets* (Princeton: International Finance Section, Department of Economics, Princeton University).

Williamson, J. 1983. *The Exchange Rate System* (Washington: Institute for International Economics).

Williamson, J., and M. Miller. 1987. *Targets and Indicators: A Blueprint for the International Coordination of Economic Policy* (Washington: Institute for International Economics).

Wood, A. 1991. "Global Trends in Real Exchange Rates 1960–84." *World Development* 19: 317–332.

World Bank. 1991. *World Development Report 1991* (New York: Oxford University Press).

World Financial Markets. 1989. "The Asian NICs: Wrestling with Success." April 17, pp. 7–9.

———. 1990. "The Decade of Europe?" February 14, pp. 1–11.

CHAPTER 6

. . .

International Portfolio Investment

. . .

6.1   INTRODUCTION

Recall from Chapter 4 that a country's international balance of payments consists of two accounts of flows: the current account, and the capital account. Part III of this book concerns the flows of merchandise trade and trade in services that are carried in the current account. With the exception of current payments of interest and dividends, which are considered payments to current factor services, financial flows are carried in the capital account. At least on a conceptual basis, the capital account offsets the current account, so when the current account is in deficit (surplus) the capital account is in surplus (deficit). If one thinks of national income as the sum of investment and consumption, then the relationship between the accounts is clear. A current account deficit indicates that a country is, in a sense, consuming at a rate that detracts from investment. The domestic shortfall in savings is made up from foreign sources. On the other hand, a current account surplus indicates that a country is consuming at a rate low enough to build up a surplus of savings, which can be exported. Two points here are important. The first is that this accounting concept suggests that international financial flows are generated, like all flows in a system of spatial interaction, by place characteristics. A country's consumption behavior affects the flow of finance. The second point is that if the world economy was perfectly integrated, no country could experience a balance of payments problem because every country's surplus in one account would ultimately offset another country's deficit in another account, even in the short run. The reality is that many countries have suffered balance of payments problems for long periods of time, which means that the international economy is less than perfectly integrated.

This chapter addresses the degree of integration in the international economy in the context of portfolio investment. As described in Chapter 4, portfolio investment includes both equity investments not engendering control of an enterprise, and long-term bonds and debentures. As will be shown, equity and debt are linked both analytically and practically, but the focus in this chapter is on the equity investments of a portfolio, while debt is focused upon in Chapter 7. The first major section of this chapter begins with an overview of the degree of mobility of capital in the international economy. As is demonstrated, capital is not as mobile as might be expected under conventional neoclassical theory. However, when risk as well as return on international investment is considered, the relative immobility of capital in the international economy is not so surprising. The primary source of risk in the international economy is currency exchange fluctuations, which were considered in Chapter 5. This chapter contains a discussion of other sources of risk and return, some of which are common to both domestic and international investment. The last part of the chapter describes the role of geographical diversification in limiting the riskiness of investment, and some current trends toward fuller integration of the world's national financial markets.

6.2   CAPITAL MOBILITY IN THE INTERNATIONAL ECONOMY

So far, the discussion of capital in this book has dealt with physical capital rather than financial capital, but there is no real theoretical distinction. Any excess of income over consumption, in the absence of wasteful behavior, can be defined as savings, which, in turn, can be considered as investment. Inventories aside, the difference between financial capital and physical capital is the time it takes to build a machine or erect a building. The lack of a true distinction between physical capital and financial capital makes capital in general quite mobile. Any distance decay in capital flows, especially given current financial service technology, is not due to transportation costs but to uncertainty about distant markets. Other barriers to trade in capital result from the same sort of management barriers that impede flows of goods.

A good starting point for a discussion of international portfolio investment is the basic neoclassical model, limited to a two-country case and employing discrete periods of production and investment. Let each of the two countries, X and Y, produce one good and have equal supplies of labor. Let the law of diminishing returns be fully enforced. Let pKx and pKy be the payments to capital in countries X and Y, respectively. In addition, let the capital payment function take the form

$$pK = \frac{1}{(K/L)} \qquad (6.1)$$

The capital payment function expresses the payment as a function of capital supply in the context of decreasing returns. Given a constant supply of labor, pK decreases as K increases because capital's marginal productivity is decreasing. In the neoclassical model, the payment to a factor is derived as the factor's marginal productivity.

The country with the lower value of K/L would have the higher payment to capital. Capital would flow from the country with the the the higher value of K/L, seeking the higher payment, until both countries have the same capital supply and the same payments to capital. In this context, the expected return on a unit of capital is simply a function of a common capital to labor ratio. The commonality of capital to labor ratios between the two countries is due to the instantaneous flow of capital that would eliminate any disparity. In short, capital should obey the "law of one price." In theory, capital is almost perfectly mobile between countries, but in reality it is not.

Evidence of international capital mobility should be observed in two forms. One form is a lack of correlation between national saving and national investment. If national saving and investment are not correlated, it means that the source of investment funds is outside the country of investment. On the other hand, if saving and investment are highly correlated it means that domestic investment is largely financed domestically rather than by foreign sources. Feldstein and Horioka (1980) were the first to investigate the correlation between national investment and saving. They examined both coincident and lagged relationships for individual years and over time. In all cases they found very high rates of correlation between national saving and investment, which meant that capital is largely immobile and its mobility was not increasing over time. The other form of evidence for international capital mobility is equal real rates of interest across countries (Chinn, 1989). The real rate of interest is nominal interest discounted for inflation. Nominal rates can be expected to vary but, under the law of one price, real rates should equalize. If real rates are not at the same level across countries, then the capital flows that would bring about their equalization must not be taking place.

As in the case of high correlations between national saving and investment, the evidence from an examination of real interest rates suggests that capital is not very mobile in the international economy. Both real rates of interest and saving-investment correlations for all countries and by World Bank Income Group during 1990 are given in Table 6.1. Both types of measures illustrate the low degree of capital mobility between countries. The saving-investment correlations are high in each case and suggest that capital mobility is no greater for rich countries than for poor ones. Real interest rates were quite variable during 1990, and the extreme cases can rightfully be considered aberrations. However, the variability in median interest rates from income group to income group is a reasonable measure of a true disparity in world interest rates that should not exist in a world with a high degree of capital mobility.

Critics of both measures of capital mobility have countered the evidence for capital immobility with empirical and theoretical arguments. The foremost empirical argument for capital mobility is the extremely high value of sales of foreign currency that take place every year. In recent years, sales volumes of foreign exchange around the world have come to nearly U.S. $1 trillion (thousand billion) a month. Compared

TABLE 6.1 Capital Mobility Indicators by World Bank Income Group, 1990

Income Group	Savings-Investment Correlation	Median Lending Interest Rate (%)
All	0.996	6.8
Low	0.996	6.4
Low Middle	0.962	7.3
High Middle	0.991	9.3
High	0.996	7.8

Source of original data: World Bank. 1992. *World Development Report 1992* (New York: Oxford University Press).

to the value of world trade in goods and services, capital trade is greater by about 5.5 times on an annual basis. Golub (1990), however, has noted that foreign exchange sales are not really measures of the amount of capital that crosses borders but are more a function of the frequency of transaction. They inflate the value of capital flows in the same way that counting each sale of stock during a year would be misleading as to the value of the stock. Golub showed that, in fact, gross capital flows are actually quite small proportions of gross domestic investment.

On the theoretical side, Wong (1990) has argued that high correlations between domestic saving and investment do not really tell us anything about capital mobility. The relationship between saving and investment is a measure of a country's ratio of traded goods to nontraded goods, and not of capital mobility. A country with a relatively closed economy, with a very high proportion of nontraded goods in consumption, generates by necessity most of its own financing for investment. Capital flows counteract trade flows in national accounting, so countries with relatively small trade flows will also have relatively small capital flows.

Perhaps the best evidence for capital mobility across countries is the existence of a difference between national saving and national investment. Obviously, if a country's economy is investing more than it saves, there must be some flow of external finance. On the other hand, if a country is saving more than it invests, then the surplus is being invested in other countries. While they may last for years, such imbalances are not perpetually sustainable on financial economic terms or on the terms of welfare economics. Without such capital mobility, both the rich and the poor would get continually poorer (Brennan and Solnik, 1989). In 1990, on net, over half the countries reporting to the World Bank had negative savings-investment gaps (Table 6.2). The capital inflow this represents, however, was typical only of the world's poorer countries. The capital inflows to the poorer countries originated, as should be expected, in the world's richer countries. The high income countries had positive gaps, on average, of over one billion dollars. The source of the disparity in gaps rests more on the side of the savings proportion than the investment proportion. In the

TABLE 6.2 Median Values of Saving-Investment Gap and Savings and Investment Proportions of GDP by World Bank Income Group, 1990*

| Income Group | Gap* | As a Proportion of GDP: | |
		Savings	Investment
All	−154.0	0.20	0.21
Low	−247.5	0.08	0.17
Low Middle	−188.1	0.19	0.21
High Middle	287.7	0.24	0.21
High	1,038.0	0.24	0.21

* In millions of $U.S.
Source of original data: World Bank. 1992. *World Development Report 1992* (New York: Oxford University Press).

spirit of Engel's law, savings proportions in poor countries should be expected to be low because immediate consumption of food and shelter requires most of the poor's income. The single largest gap in savings proportions is between the low income group and the low middle income group. Investment proportions are much more uniform, with the median rate differing only at the low income group. The differences in savings and investment proportions suggest that capital is quite mobile in the international economy, but the fairly small values of the median gaps suggest that international supply and demand for capital is quite thin compared to domestic markets. It seems that the potential mobility of one unit of capital is very high, but in aggregate terms capital mobility is actually fairly low.

6.3 FINANCIAL PORTFOLIO THEORY

The low level of capital mobility in the international economy can be attributed to several impeding factors. For example, government restrictions on cross-border capital flows are significant barriers (Bayoumi, 1990). In addition, time and transaction costs are impeding capital flows. Real transactions take time, effectively limiting capital mobility because any lag between recognition of a capital deficit in one country and an inflow of capital from other countries means that payments to capital would be unequal. In fact, any such lag would insure that payments to capital follow a short-term adjustment track, both within and across countries, that approximates but never equals the long-term trend of equal payments to capital between the countries. In addition, transactions are costly, so payments to capital must be dis-counted every time it moves from one market to another. In order to achieve the long-term average international payment to capital on a short-term basis, an investor must own capital in both countries, so that lower payments to capital in one country are offset by the higher payments in the other, and so that transaction costs are not always accumulating. As long as capital is not perfectly mobile, short-term fluctua-tions in its payments can be eliminated by geographical diversification.

The fluctuation in payments to capital is called *asset risk*. Concern for such risk is the basis of an important extension to the neoclassical model of investment called *contemporary portfolio theory*. A portfolio is a collection of assets that may include stocks and bonds, and other less liquid items such as real estate and baseball cards. Different assets are held in a portfolio for the same reason that the investor described above should own capital in both countries, to decrease fluctuation in asset earnings. Perhaps the most basic kind of portfolio mix is stocks and bonds (or bond-equivalent stocks). Over time, stock returns and bond returns tend to track in opposite direc-tions. High (low) stock returns and low (high) bond returns are concurrent so that one counteracts the other.

An investor indifferent toward the potential for fluctuations in asset prices will simply hold either stocks or bonds, based on his or her perception of which will yield the highest return at the moment. In general, the investor's evaluation of asset risk determines the mix of assets in a portfolio. The more averse to risk the investor is, the more diversified the portfolio; the less averse to risk, the more specialized the portfo-lio. In addition, the payment to an asset and its riskiness are linked, because almost all investors have some aversion to risk. Risk premiums are paid to assets; thus the riskier the asset, the higher its average payment. The higher average payment counteracts the fluctuations so that an investor can trade risk for return. If all investors had the same preference toward risk-return balances, then all individual assets would be valued by their return alone. But because investor preferences vary and the determination of risk is not free of error, assets do vary in risk-return proportions and, therefore, in value. The variability of risk-return proportions and in investor risk-return preferences mean that most portfolios require some diversifi-cation.

Tobin (1952), in economics, and Markowitz (1959), in finance, developed early models of optimum, or efficient, portfolio diversification based upon the relationship between the payment, or return, to a portfolio, and the covariation of the returns to the portfolio's assets. The *mean-variance portfolio model* takes the form

$$E(\bar{R}_P) = \sum_{i=1}^{n} X_i E_i \tag{6.2}$$

where $E(\bar{R}_P)$ is the expected mean return to the portfolio, P; E_i is the expected return on the ith asset; and X is the percentage of the portfolio's n total investments in the asset. The risk of a portfolio is taken as

$$\sigma^2(R_P) = COV(E_i E_j) \tag{6.3}$$

where COV is the covariance of the returns among the portfolio's individual assets.

The risk of a portfolio is at a maximum when its assets' returns are perfectly and positively correlated, and at a minimum when the returns are perfectly but negatively correlated. An *efficient portfolio* is one that maximizes return for a given level of risk or minimizes risk for a given level of return, regardless of an investor's preferences for combinations of risk and return. An *optimum portfolio* is one that maximizes return for an investor-specified risk level. For example, if an investor is willing to take on 5 units of risk, and of two such risk-bearing portfolios one has an expected return of 8 and the other an expected return of 9, the latter is the optimum portfolio.

There are two problems with the mean-variance portfolio model. One is that it is mathematically difficult in practice because its form is quadratic. The other and more important problem is that it is information-intensive. In order for an optimum portfolio to be determined, an investor would have to know the expected returns and their variances for all possible assets. Even limiting the portfolio's domain to stocks, for example, requires an awful lot of information. The *capital asset pricing model* (*CAPM*—say "CAP M") was developed by Sharpe (1963), Lintner (1965), and Mossin (1966) as a simplified linear version of the mean-variance portfolio model that is less knowledge-intensive in practice.

The CAPM is

$$E(R_P) = R + \theta_P \sigma_P \tag{6.4}$$

where $E(R_P)$ is the expected return on efficient portfolios, R is risk-free return, θ_P is the risk premium for efficient portfolios, and σ_P is the standard deviation of efficient portfolio returns. Note that the risk premium is essentially a weight on the portfolio's risk. For example, if $\sigma_P = 0$, then $\theta_P = 0$, so that $E(R_P) = R$. The relationship between return and risk is linear in this form and is called the capital market line. A *market portfolio*, or one that contains all the market's assets in exact proportion to their percentage of the entire market, and all other efficient portfolios follow the capital market line. Therefore,

$$E(R_M) = R + \theta_M \sigma_M \tag{6.5}$$

where the subscript M refers to the market, and

$$\theta_M = \frac{[E(R_M) - R]}{\sigma_M} \tag{6.6}$$

indicating that the market risk premium is the difference between the returns of the market portfolio and risk-free return, scaled to market volatility.

Unlike the mean-variance model, the CAPM form easily accomodates the valuation of a single asset:

$$E(R_i) = R + \theta_M r_{iM} \sigma_i \sigma_M \tag{6.7}$$

where the subscript i indicates a single asset, and r is a correlation coefficient.

The expected return to any asset can be measured in the form

$$E(R_i) = a_i + b_i M + c_i \tag{6.8}$$

where a is a constant, b is the *portfolio beta*, M is the risk in the market portfolio, and c is the asset's individual risk. This linear expression indicates that each asset has two components of risk. The value of c defines the asset's *diversifiable risk*. The sum of the c values of all the assets in the market is assumed to be zero, so diversification of a portfolio in the correct proportions can eliminate individual risks. Because individual risks can be eliminated by diversification, investors can't expect to be paid a premium for bearing such risk. The risk premium paid to an asset is defined through the portfolio beta, which expresses the asset's *systematic risk*. The portfolio beta measures the covariation between the asset's payment fluctuation, or risk, and the risk on the market portfolio as measured by M, which is a broad market indicator such as one of the Wall Street stock indexes. If $b_i = 1$, then the stock is perfectly correlated with the entire market. In effect, it is a substitute for the full market portfolio. If $b_i > 1$, then a risk premium greater than one would be required, and if $b_i < 1$, then the investor would expect a lower return than on a proportional market portfolio. For example, letting all values of a and c be zero, if stock A has a beta of 0.5, stock B has a beta of 1, and stock C has a beta of 2, then the value of stock A would be one-half the value of stock B and the value of stock B would be one-half stock C's value. (Note that the single-index portfolio model measures a stock's integration with the rest of the stock market in the same way that a country's economic integration with the rest of the world was measured in Chapter 4.)

One problem with the CAPM is the definition of the market portfolio, or M in Equation 6.8, and its effect on the value of asset betas. For example, if two different stock indexes are used then it can be expected that two different betas would be calculated for a single stock. If all assets are included in the market portfolio, however, much of the convenience of the CAPM is lost and one might as well go back to the quadratic mean-variance model. Ross (1976) has developed an *arbitrage theory of capital asset pricing* that avoids the problem of defining a full market portfolio. In fact, the market portfolio is of no particular interest. In a simplified manner, the arbitrage model can be expressed

$$E_i = R + b_1 F_1 + b_2 F_2 + \cdots + b_n F_n \tag{6.9}$$

where E_i is the expected return on the ith asset, R is risk-free return, and $b_1, \ldots, b_n$ are links between the asset and $F_1, \ldots, F_n$, which are return factors. The b coefficients are similar to the portfolio beta because they quantify systematic relationships between the asset's return and and a general index. While one of the return factors, F, could be a market index, this is not usually the case. Typical measures of F are inflation, interest rates, and industrial production. Stulz (1984) has described an international version of the CAPM which also requires such a multiple-index form because of the variability of inflation and exchange rates across countries.

Arbitrage is the purchase of an item at a lower price for immediate resale at a higher price. It was developed in commodity markets when communications systems were crude. For example, if grain was $1 per bushel in village A and $1.20 per bushel in not-too-distant village B, someone with that scarce knowledge would purchase grain in village A for immediate resale in village B. Such opportunities are infrequent in most commodity markets today, and arbitrage has come to be associated with stock markets. In addition, the scarce knowledge required for successful arbitrage is frequently acquired illegally as inside information. The arbitrage model described above is used for what its name indicates, and in a legal fashion. When used correctly, which is not an easy thing to do, it gives very good price signals that allow its user to buy and sell stocks at favorable prices. For example, it can identify stocks that are very downward sensitive to inflation and, given inflationary tendencies and actual stock prices, indicate profitable buy and sell opportunities.

The mean-variance portfolio model, the CAPM, and the arbitrage model of asset pricing each tell us something a little different about investment in general and in an international context in particular. The CAPM is an extension of the mean-variance model. It maintains the concept of diversification as a method of risk reduction but also defines a type of uniform target for rate of return in its use of a market portfolio as a systematic measure. In turn, the arbitrage model is an extension of the CAPM because it maintains the link between individual asset prices and one or more systematic factors. In a way, it simply divides the source of systematic risk in the market portfolio into a series of components that are weighted to individual assets or groups of similar assets. The typical return factors of inflation, rates of industrial production, and interest rates are of as much interest to an international investor as to one holding assets in a single market. Geographical variability in these and other factors of an investment's return provide a type of international arbitrage potential in the compound context of sector and country or region of investment. This last point underlines some of the complexity of international investment. A generalized assessment of the major potential sources of risk and return in international investment and the potential benefits of the geographical diversification of financial portfolios are discussed in the remaining parts of this chapter.

6.4 SELECTED RISK AND RETURN FACTORS OF AN INTERNATIONAL PORTFOLIO

The Europeans are finding that exchange rate stability within the ERM is best achieved by international convergence of economic characteristics. Convergence means a large positive correlation among key economic characteristics such as inflation. The larger the correlation, the more similar the characteristics and the smaller the basis for divergence in currency values. Exchange rate trends are good summary indicators of economic similarity in general, but investments in specific sectors or industries may require analysis of other measures. Recall that while the CAPM can be taken as a single-index investment model, the arbitrage model is typically multivariate in conception and more specific with respect to critical factors determining an asset's return. In this section of the chapter, three potential return factors are first described with respect to their similarities across the World Bank Income Groups. These factors are consumer prices, real growth of national income, and interest rates, during the 1978 to 1987 period of exchange rate volatility. This description gives a mixed picture of the general degree of integration in the international economy.

Globally, inflation was a problem from 1978 to 1987 (Table 6.3). The major source of inflation was the increase in oil prices resulting from the Iranian revolution. The depth of incidence of inflation and its rate of increase varied by income group. Between 1980 and 1987, for example, prices increased by about 150% in the middle income groups of countries, about 100% in the low income group, and only about 55% in the high income countries. In general, these variations indicate a more severe

TABLE 6.3 Median Consumer Price Indexes and Their Correlation by World Bank Income Group, 1978–1987*

Year	All	Low Income	Low Middle Income	High Middle Income	High Income
1978	.786	.781	.765	.742	.832
1979	.879	.884	.852	.840	.903
1980	1.000	1.000	1.000	1.000	1.000
1981	1.127	1.128	1.129	1.200	1.117
1982	1.252	1.273	1.249	1.301	1.217
1983	1.373	1.394	1.405	1.468	1.315
1984	1.517	1.517	1.616	1.663	1.375
1985	1.648	1.646	1.926	1.790	1.430
1986	1.844	1.844	2.297	1.907	1.489
1987	1.914	1.991	2.643	2.416	1.554

Pearson Correlation Coefficients

Income Group	Low Income	Low Middle Income	High Middle Income	High Income
Low Income	——	.983	.988	.984
Low Middle Income		——	.982	.936
High Middle Income			——	.966
High Income				——

* 1980 = 1.00.

Source of original data: International Monetary Fund. 1989B. *Balance of Payments Statistics Yearbook,* vol. 40, part 1 (Washington: International Monetary Fund).

decrease in purchasing power during the period in the poor countries than in the rich countries.

In terms of the trend of inflation, however, there was virtually no difference among the income groups. The correlations of the price series' are all very high (Table 6.3), and this suggests that markets are well-integrated with respect to price variation. It may be that a general "law of one price" is in operation, but is more applicable to trend than actual level. With regard to investment, such high correlations indicate that inflation-sensitive investments cannot be arbitraged in a geographical way. The geographical demarcation used here, World Bank Income Groups, is much too coarse for any practical interpretation, but the same approach may be used in more specific contexts.

Differences in lending rates were briefly discussed (see Table 6.1); here, deposit rates are of interest (Table 6.4). In general, average rates of interest on deposits followed price trends by rising and then tailing off from 1978 through 1987. However, there are large differences in both rates and trends across the income groups. The low income group of countries, on average, had the lowest deposit

TABLE 6.4   Median Nominal Interest Rates and Their Correlation by World Bank Income Group, 1978–1987*

Year	All	Low Income	Low Middle Income	High Middle Income	High Income
1978	6.00	6.00	6.00	9.20	6.33
1979	6.01	6.00	6.90	10.40	8.00
1980	6.80	6.10	7.50	11.90	9.37
1981	8.65	6.25	9.67	9.40	10.38
1982	9.30	7.70	11.70	9.30	8.76
1983	9.00	7.50	12.80	9.00	8.09
1984	9.40	7.50	10.64	10.79	7.75
1985	8.87	7.71	9.77	10.26	7.51
1986	8.29	7.35	9.50	8.93	6.51
1987	8.00	7.79	9.37	8.94	6.21

Pearson Correlation Coefficients

Income Group	Low Income	Low Middle Income	High Middle Income	High Income
Low Income	——	.774	−.354	−.331
Low Middle Income		——	−.323	.200
High Middle Income			——	.400
High Income				——

* Deposit rates.

Source of original data: International Monetary Fund. 1989B. *Balance of Payments Statistics Yearbook,* vol. 40, part 1 (Washington: International Monetary Fund).

interest rates during the period, but the rates were more functions of government policy than inflation. The stability of average interest rates is also a function of their control by governments rather than by markets. The interest rates of the other three income groups fluctuated more in response to changes in price levels, but government controls on capital were still fairly widespread during the period in many countries regardless of their income group.

Correlations of the interest rate trends of the income groups suggest that capital markets remained strongly segmented during the period. Low and even negative values of interest rate correlations are only possible if capital cannot flow from one set of markets to another. In comparison to the high correlations of inflation rates, the low correlations in this case provide additional evidence that goods markets are more integrated than capital markets, at least on a global basis. The segmentation of capital markets, rather than integration, is the primary reason that capital is fairly immobile. Again, the two major sources of capital market segmentation at the international scale are government controls of capital flows and the fairly high transaction costs of investing in foreign markets, including the costs of obtaining the appropriate information. (The problems arising from government controls of financial activity are discussed in Chapter 7.)

On average, real growth in national incomes experienced a full cycle over the period (Table 6.5). The peak occurred in 1978 and 1979, the trough in 1982 and 1983, and recovery from 1984 through 1987. The cycle was more pronounced in the middle income groups than in the other two, and the high income group of countries had the smallest average range between highest and lowest rates of real growth. Correlations of real growth of national income among the income groups are intermediate to the high correlations of rates of inflation and the low and negative correlations of interest rates on deposits. The fact that the correlations are all positive indicates that, again at a very coarse scale, there are no real countercyclical economies. On the other hand, the relative weakness of the correlations does suggest that gains to investment, of the kind described in the arbitrage model, are potentially available in the international economy. In addition, the low correlations suggest that geographical diversification, in an international context, can reduce the risk associated with a financial portfolio.

Any investor wishing to geographically diversify a portfolio can use three different methods. One method is to accumulate equities (and bonds, realistically) of corporations located in different countries around the world. This approach, however, would generate transaction costs that would probably negate any benefits achieved from diversification. This is especially true of individual attempts to purchase stocks on markets in the poorer countries, which may otherwise present the greatest potential for diversification (Errunza, 1978). Two other methods rely on the use of intermediaries in international markets, either MNCs or international mutual funds.

It has been suggested that MNCs provide a geographically diversified portfolio in and of themselves, simply by their own corporate geographical diversification. The evidence varies concerning the effectiveness of holding stock in an MNC as a substitute for holding stocks of several geographically dispersed corporations. Aggarwal (1980) and Mathur and Hanagan (1980) provided evidence that MNC equities are a

TABLE 6.5 Median Real National Income Growth, 1978–1987, by World Bank Income Group*

Year	All	Low Income	Low Middle Income	High Middle Income	High Income
1978	4.6	4.8	6.4	5.0	3.0
1979	4.6	4.6	4.9	6.1	3.8
1980	3.4	3.0	5.0	2.1	2.8
1981	2.7	4.1	4.1	1.4	1.1
1982	1.2	1.8	0.9	0.9	0.9
1983	1.5	1.3	1.5	0.3	1.9
1984	2.7	3.2	2.7	1.9	3.3
1985	2.8	4.0	2.4	0.4	2.7
1986	2.7	3.8	2.4	5.0	2.4
1987	3.2	0.9	4.8	3.8	2.7

Pearson Correlation Coefficients

Income Group	Low Income	Low Middle Income	High Middle Income	High Income
Low Income	———	.440	.435	.375
Low Middle Income		———	.628	.526
High Middle Income			———	.594
High Income				———

* In %, by 1980 currency values.
Source of original data: International Monetary Fund. 1989B. *Balance of Payments Statistics Yearbook*, vol. 40, part 1 (Washington: International Monetary Fund).

good substitute for direct geographical diversification, while Jacquillat and Solnik (1978) provided contrary evidence. The diversification effect may be temporally inconsistent. In an early work, Brewer (1981) found no benefits to investors from the MNCs' geographical diversification, but more recently found evidence that holders of MNC common stock derive geographical diversification benefits (Brewer, 1989). An interesting line of related research concerns investor recognition of the diversification benefits associated with MNC stock. If MNC stock provides such benefits it should command a premium in its price that reduces its rate of return in a way that matches the reduction in risk. Imagine two corporations that are entirely similar except that one is geographically diversified. The stock price of the diversified corporation should be higher, reducing its rate of return, than the stock price of the nondiversified corporation simply because the diversified corporation's stock has a lower level of diversifiable risk. Again, results are mixed, with some evidence that stock prices are conditioned in this way (Aggarwal, 1979; Mikhail and Shawky, 1979; Agmon and Lessard, 1981), and some that they are not (Adler, 1981). The major problem of measurement is finding companies that are completely similar except with respect to their geography.

International mutual funds are widely available as sources of portfolio diversification benefits with low transaction costs. The general purpose of mutual funds is to provide portfolio diversification at low transaction cost. International mutual funds may be like domestic mutual funds except that they cover a single foreign market. However, most international mutual funds are diversified by both industrial and geographical composition. Obviously, this type of dual diversification would be very costly for an individual investor to manage well.

The characteristics of a typical international mutual fund are illustrated in the prospectus of the Kemper International Fund (1987), used here for example only. The Kemper International Fund was advertised as a method of using an intermediary to provide the expertise on international markets, especially concerning exchange risk, that is not typical of the individual investor. At the time, it owned equities and warrants (debt convertible to equity at a future date) in nine foreign markets, and the prospectus stated that at least 80% of the fund's investments were outside the United States under usual conditions. The largest number of foreign holdings, 40, was in the Japanese market, and the smallest number, 3, was held in Belgium and Canada. The Hong Kong market was the only market in the fund that could be considered as peripheral, but only in the sense that it is not among the three dominant markets and is not European. The fund's portfolio was sectorally diversified both within and across the national markets, and held approximately balanced proportions of heavy manufacturers, light manufacturers, and financial and other service sector corporations.

The prospectus contains the standard material required of any U.S.-based mutual fund, but, due to the fund's geography, it contained additional material. For example, the fund's use of financial futures in the interest of limiting its exposure to foreign exchange risk is described. Potential investors are advised that the fund may make investments in developing countries, and that such investments usually offer very high rates of return but also are very risky. Exchange risk and political risk are emphasized in a section of the prospectus entitled "Special Risk Considerations" (p. 4). There it indicates that foreign markets are often difficult to work in, as compared to the American market, because of their relative illiquidity and high transaction costs. In addition, the prospectus warns of the possibility, although low probability, that its assets in any single foreign market may be subject to changing regulations, confiscatory taxation, or even outright confiscation. Given the fund's geographical exposure noted above, there was no actual exposure to any of these problems.

The Kemper International Fund was allocated across only industrial world markets in 1987. While international funds are broader now in a geographical sense, most funds still prefer to keep most of their eggs in the fairly similar baskets of the Core's stock markets. One reason for this investment geography is that bigger markets are found in the Core economies and, on a proportional basis, peripheral countries have less than their share of the world's equity markets (Table 6.6). This is not surprising, of course, because rich countries are, almost by definition, those countries well-endowed with capital, including financial capital. In turn, poor countries suffer capital deficits of the most general sort, including financial capital deficits which are usually met by the loans, and not the investments, of foreigners (see

**TABLE 6.6   Shares of Global
Stock Market Capitalization in
1991 and GDP: Selected Countries***

Country	Percent of Market Capitalization	Percent Share of World GDP
United States	38.1	24.2
Japan	28.4	13.2
United Kingdom	11.0	4.4
Germany	3.8	6.7
France	3.3	5.3
Canada	2.8	2.6
Switzerland	1.7	1.0
Australia	1.6	1.3
Netherlands	1.6	1.3
Italy	1.3	4.9
Hong Kong	1.1	0.3
Singapore	0.7	0.2
Others	4.6	34.7

* GDP is for 1990, and World GDP includes only reporting
countries.
Source: Economist, September 28, 1991, p. 85, and World Bank,
1992. *World Development Report 1992* (New York: Oxford
University).

Chapter 7). The concentration of the world's equity markets is particularly telling in a
Core-Periphery context, with only three countries—the United States, Japan, and the
United Kingdom—having proportional market capitalizations each greater than
10%, and each much greater than their individual proportions of world income. In
Table 6.6, "Others" approximates the Periphery, with almost 35% of the world's
income, but less than 5% of its stock market capitalization.

6.5   THE INTEGRATION OF
INTERNATIONAL EQUITY MARKETS

The potential for portfolio risk reduction by international diversification has been
described by a number of analysts (e.g., Lessard, 1976; Rugman, 1977; Jorion,
1989). Typically, the presence of correlation coefficients of less than one across
national stock indexes are provided as simple evidence, as are the variable beta
coefficients estimated from some sort of international CAPM. Low correlation coef-

ficients can be taken as evidence of segmentation, or dis-integration, among markets and economies, and can encompass the intentions of the arbitrage model. However, the use of the single-index version of the CAPM requires that the markets and economies of interest be fairly integrated, otherwise the functional relationship between the single investment and the systematic (world) index may be spurious. The question, then, becomes whether national equity markets are internationally integrated or segmented.

The evidence for low capital mobility provided earlier in this chapter indicates that capital markets, including equity markets, are segmented. However, there is also evidence that equity markets are well integrated in that the stock markets of different countries tend to move together. It is unusual, albeit not unknown, for any single market to maintain a sustained increase (bull market) or sustained decrease (bear market) by itself. In general, there does seem to be an integrated set of national markets that move up and down together. An interesting example of the seeming integration of individual national stock markets is their behavior during the 1980s.

From 1981 through September 1987, world stock market capitalization, or the value of stock at market price, grew at a rate of 17% per year. Naturally, some stock markets grew at a faster rate and some at a slower rate, but most of the 1980s could be characterized as a global bull market (International Monetary Fund, 1989A). The bull market ended, however, with a crash in October of 1987 that affected each of the world's active stock markets. The steepest declines took place in the smaller Pacific Basin markets; Australian stock prices dropped by over 58% and those in Hong Kong dropped by more than 56%. In Japan, however, the biggest market in the region (see Section 6.6), the drop was much smaller at 12.6%.

Economists of the Federal Reserve Bank of New York examined the relationships among price changes in the Japanese stock market, the American market (−21.5% during the month), the British market (−26.1%), and, secondarily, the German market (−22.9%) before and during the crash in an effort to measure the functional relationships between these large equity markets in particular and international financial markets in general (Aderhold et al., 1989; Bennet and Kelleher, 1989). Their analyses suggest that major markets are integrated, but not in a mechanically functional way.

Statistical analyses of the stock market linkages included correlation analysis and beta analysis of the type suggested in the single-index portfolio model (Bennet and Kelleher, 1989). Three results of the correlation analysis are quite interesting. First, the correlations between each pair of stock market indexes examined was higher for the period 1980–1987 than for the period 1972–1979. This general increase can be taken as good evidence that the major stock markets are becoming more integrated with time. Second, the correlations increased, usually in a significant way, during times of extreme upward or downward volatility, especially 1980–1987. This indicates that the markets become more integrated during stressful periods, perhaps because international conditions become more important relative to domestic market conditions. The third result, however, is that even during the times of greatest volatility, the correlations between the markets are not very large. For example, the largest correlation under volatile circumstances is 0.56 between the West German and British stock indexes. During average markets, the correlation drops to 0.27. The highest correlation under average market conditions is 0.36 between the American and West German indexes. The generally low correlations among the major markets suggest that they are not well integrated.

Statistical evidence for the low level of integration between the markets also is provided by beta analysis. This type of analysis is similar to the single-index model of the CAPM (Equation 6.8), but in this case takes the form

$$V_i = a + bV_j + e \qquad (6.10)$$

where V_i is the change in the price index of the ith market, a is a constant, b is the beta (or linkage coefficient), V_j is the change in the price index of the jth, and e is an error term. This specification indicates that price changes in the ith market <u>depend</u> on price changes in the jth market. The values of the beta coefficients are interpreted in the same way as in the single-index and economic integration models. For example, if $b = 1$, then the markets are linked on a one-to-one basis, and if $b = 0$ the markets are not linked at all. The best linkage equations were those that used the British market as the index. In this case, the beta for the West German and American markets was 0.38 and 0.43 for Japan, during the period 1980–1987. However, an extension to the analysis suggests that domestic economic variables, including interest rates, inflation, output, and unemployment, were more powerful in explaining stock price changes than any linkages to foreign stock markets.

The actual trading linkages between the major markets were also investigated (Aderhold et al., 1989). Two types of trading linkages should lead toward integration of stock markets. One is cross-border equity purchases in which citizens and firms of one country buy equities of corporations sold on another country's stock exchange. The other is the trading of a single stock on many exchanges, so-called *24-hour trading*. Under 24-hour trading, for example, a single stock is sold on the New York, Tokyo, and London exchanges in a nonstop fashion due to their locations in greatly different time zones. Obviously, the greater the number of stocks sold on a 24-hour basis, the more integrated markets must become as the "law of one price" begins to prevail. During the 1980s both cross-border stock purchases and 24-hour trading increased dramatically. However, they both still remained in such small proportion on the major exchanges, with the exception of London (see Section 6.6), that they cannot be considered as integrating mechanisms during the coordinated stock market crashes of 1987.

It appears that the strongest link among the the world's stock markets during 1987 was psychological. Major sell-offs in individual markets did spur major sell-offs in the others, but not because of fundamental reasons such as general declines in corporate earnings, for example. It seems, in hindsight, that a type of hierarchical diffusion of uncertainty, originating in New York on October 14 and spreading to London on October 19 and Tokyo on October 20, generated a global herd mentality among investors around the world to get out of the (any) stock market. Again, price changes are more correlated during volatile markets, and it may be that such international diffusion can take place only during those periods of heightened uncertainty of domestic information in which investors are more receptive to international information.

Only major stock markets were considered in the analyses cited above, and each of the major markets is in one of the World Bank's high income countries. There are, however, many other stock markets around the world and some are found even in low income countries. While most of the stock markets in lower income countries are quite small compared to the major stock markets, a few are relatively large (World Bank, 1989). India's major stock market, in Bombay, has more listed companies than the Tokyo market, and the rate of sales on the Mexican market is greater than that in the United States. For the most part, however, developing-country stock markets are fairly isolated due to continuing capital flow restrictions and simple lack of information among rich-country investors. Improvements in communications technology and a growing trend toward deregulation of national financial markets suggest that, whatever its current status, the international market for equities is becoming more integrated. To date, however, much of the improvement in communications between stock exchanges and much of the impact, by value of transactions, of government deregulation have been limited to the largest exchanges and the world's biggest economies (Allen, 1989; Honeygold, 1989).

Perhaps just as important as technological advances and regulatory reform, convergence among macroeconomic policies will lead to more integration of international financial markets. As found by Bennet and Kelleher (1989), macroeconomic variables are strong predictors of stock market price changes. Convergence of macroeconomic policy among members of the EMS has been discussed, but convergence of Japanese, American, and EC policies is not out of the question. Some of these policies have been coordinated in the past in the interest of guiding financial and goods markets, and the recognition of the growing integration of financial markets may encourage further direct efforts, or markets may bring about the same result indirectly (Burdekin, 1989). If, in fact, macroeconomic policy convergence is the true key to financial market integration, then rich-country markets are more likely to benefit from continuing integration than poor-country markets, because the convergence of macroeconomic policy among countries with highly disparate national incomes is unlikely.

6.6   SELECTED STOCK MARKETS

The relative immobility of financial capital is surprising in that the two dominant models of stock valuation, the portfolio model and the arbitrage model, indicate the potential benefits of investing in international markets rather than a domestic market alone. In the context of the portfolio model, stock holdings could be diversified internationally as an effective method of portfolio risk reduction. In the context of the arbitrage model, portfolio gains should be more widely available in an international rather than domestic portfolio simply because economic conditions are much more diverse internationally than domestically.

Both financial models, however, as well as the general neoclassical model, hold transaction costs as an implicit brake on the capital flows they encourage. Importantly, it does not matter if the transaction costs are known and current or uncertain and anticipated. Transaction costs depress real rates of return on any single asset and can modify the critical relationships among assets that can determine the overall value of a portfolio, and therefore the portfolio's composition. The portfolio effects of transaction costs are typically more severe in the international market than in the domestic one. At a general level, for example, domestic markets are not encumbered by currency exchange costs and uncertainty of future rates of exchange. In a more specific context, knowledge of foreign stock markets is simply more expensive than knowledge of any domestic market.

Notably, international stock market transactions are generally confined within the small set of the world's rich countries. The rich countries provide the most opportunities for equity investment and are the greatest source, almost by definition, of financial capital. In turn, equity markets tend to be thin in the Periphery, although not in all cases, and government regulation of foreign investment in peripheral markets also tends to be strict.

As of 1991, there were stock markets operating in 57 countries around the world (Blackwell Finance, 1991). Many of these countries are sites of one market, but many others contain several. For example, the United States contains two large national stock exchanges, the dominant New York Stock Exchange and the American Stock Exchange, and also regional stock exchanges, such as in Cincinnati. In Germany, the regional stock exchanges have developed in such a way that no dominant one has emerged, although the Frankfurt exchange is the largest.

While most of the world's stock exchange transactions take place in the traditional venues of the Core, smaller and peripheral stock markets are emerging around the world. Three of the more important of these markets are in Hungary, Argentina, and the Republic of Korea. The Hungarian stock market was opened in June 1990 and now lists just over a dozen shares. Foreigners may own 100% of a company's stock, but any proportion of 50% or more requires the government's approval. The stock market is open for trading only one hour each business day (Blackwell Finance, 1991). The exchange, located in Budapest, may become important regionally in Eastern Europe as markets continue to replace centrally planned economic systems.

Until recently, hyperinflation has been an almost continent-wide problem in South America. It devastated the principal Argentine stock market in Buenos Aires and still limits its investment potential to most outsiders. However, the Argentine government is now actively pursuing foreign investment under the administration of Carlos Menem, and foreign investors are treated in the same manner as Argentine citizens. Further, restrictions on Argentinian holdings of foreign currency, bank accounts, and investments are virtually nonexistent, so Argentina is increasing its integration into the global economy. If current policies hold, it appears that Buenos Aires may become the financial center of South America.

The Korea Stock Exchange, in Seoul, is fairly large with over 600 listed companies and a capitalization at the end of 1989 of over U.S. $140 billion (Blackwell Finance, 1991). The exchange was operated by the government until 1988, when it became a membership organization. The privatization of the stock exchange marked the initiation of a process of internationalization scheduled to be completed in 1992. The Republic of Korea's relationship to the international economy is highly regulated by its government (Cowitt, 1991). Korean citizens are restricted in their ability to exchange the won for foreign currency, hold foreign bank deposits, and own foreign stocks. In turn, foreigners are restricted in their ability to broker transactions on the Korean stock exchange and to hold Korean equities in their portfolios.

At the end of 1989, the Tokyo Stock Exchange was the largest in the world when measured by capitalization, at over U.S. $4.3 trillion (1,000,000,000,000). It lists about 1600 companies. While the yen is still subject to some exchange controls, Japanese citizens are free to hold foreign currency and bank deposits, and to own stock in foreign corporations. About 120 foreign stocks are listed on the exchange, as is a U.S. Treasury bond future. Foreign access to the Japanese stock market was greatly improved in 1980 by the passage of a law that allows foreign investors to purchase up to 10% of a company's total shares by filing a prior notice with the Minister of Finance (Blackwell Finance, 1991). Purchases in greater proportions, however, may be prohibited. Purchases of Japanese bonds by foreigners are treated in the same way as their purchase of stocks.

When measured by number of listed companies, the New York Stock Exchange is the world's largest with over 2200. Its capitalization at the end of 1989 was just over $3 trillion. Of the three largest exchanges (Tokyo and London are the other two), New York has the smallest listing of foreign stocks; 87 at the end of 1989. There are few restrictions on foreign ownership of American equities and bonds, and American citizens are not restricted in any meaningful way from holding foreign currency or bank deposits, or owning stock in foreign corporations. The Toronto Stock Exchange is the largest equity market in Canada, and on a proportional basis is more international than the New York Stock Exchange. At the end of 1989, 72 of Toronto's 1632 listed companies were foreign, and the exchange's market capitalization was about U.S. $700 billion (Blackwell Finance, 1991). Canadian ownership of foreign currency and stocks is unrestricted, as is ownership of Canadian equities in portfolio proportions.

The most important stock exchange with respect to international capital flows is the International Stock Exchange of the United Kingdom and the Republic of Ireland, or more simply, *The London Exchange*. Over 550 of its nearly 2000 listings are foreign corporations, and foreign equities accounted for nearly one-half the London Exchange's U.S. $3.4 trillion in mid-1990 (Blackwell Finance, 1991). British citizens are not restricted from holding foreign currency or bank deposits, or from foreign stock ownership. Foreigners are not restricted in their abilities to own U.K. equities. Given its location, London has long had the potential to play a leading role in international stock trading. Because of its geographical position, London's open hours encompass all the trading hours in Europe and the morning hours of the chief exchanges in Canada and the United States. However, London's potential was not realized until October 1986, when the so-called *Big Bang* took place. The Big Bang refers to the liberalization of stock trading regulations and automation of the trading system on the London Exchange, which greatly reduced its transaction costs. The intention of the London market is to soon provide "paperless" trading, with the business of the exchange taking place completely by electronic transfer.

A major reason that the London Exchange became the most important in Europe is that the United Kingdom is only one of three Western European countries that do not require any significant government authorizations of stock, lending, or banking transactions (*World Financial Markets*, 1988). The other two countries are the Netherlands and West Germany, but the size of the domestic stock market in the Netherlands is small compared to the British market, and the German stock market is fragmented along regional lines. If British regulatory freedom is a major reason for continental dominance of the London Exchange, then the European Community's initiatives concerning financial market integration by community-wide regulatory uniformity may mean the end of London's leading role.

Such a decline seems unlikely, however, for two reasons, both involving links with the American market. One reason is that communication between the United Kingdom and United States is fairly easy. The common language of British and American stock traders cannot be considered a trivial feature of the fairly strong links between the stock markets of the two countries. The second reason is that British and American styles of stock trading are quite similar. Both stock markets are characterized by a large proportion of equity and bond financing of corporations brokered by specialized financial intermediaries (Masera, 1990). On the other hand, Germany, the United Kingdom's greatest potential rival in the financial arena, as well as France and Italy, have financial markets dominated by large banks, and strong links between banks and industrial corporations arising from bank ownership of sizeable numbers of their shares. Perhaps the bank-dominated system will gain supremacy. Deutsche Bank, among others, is very active in handling international stock sales in the *Euro equity market*, in which stocks are sold outside their corporation's home country (Honeygold, 1989). The advantage is small, however, because the market is relatively small and highly fragmented. Again, the similarity between the United Kingdom and United States should serve to bolster the British position in European finance because it bolsters Europe's linkage with another large market.

Data in the form of national indexes are available for the five larger markets for the period 1978 through 1987, but in their national context rather than for specific exchanges (International Monetary Fund, 1989B). They are used here to demonstrate some specific relationships among the markets and to illustrate the effects of changing exchange rates and differential rates of inflation on risk-return relationships in international equity markets.

Ignoring both rates of inflation and exchange rates, the Japanese stock market grew the most from 1978 through 1987, and the Canadian market grew the least (Table 6.7). With respect to trends, however, all five markets were approximately in step with one another. The smallest correlation between any two markets, $r = .725$, is between Canada's and South Korea's, the two smallest markets. Given the magnitude of this lowest correlation, hindsight tells us there was little benefit to be achieved by diversification over the period, and lucky the investor in the Japanese market.

The potential portfolio relationships change considerably when domestic rates of inflation are taken into account. Domestic inflation rates would be a primary consid-

TABLE 6.7   Selected Nominal Annual Stock Exchange Indexes and Their Correlations: 1978–1987*

Stock Exchange Indexes

Year	Canada	Japan	South Korea	United Kingdom	United States
1978	0.506	0.876	1.321	0.824	0.789
1979	0.733	0.949	1.109	0.936	0.854
1980	1.000	1.000	1.000	1.000	1.000
1981	0.974	1.163	1.161	1.128	1.072
1982	0.768	1.158	1.122	1.307	0.993
1983	1.114	1.365	1.119	1.649	1.342
1984	1.102	1.721	1.212	1.962	1.347
1985	1.305	2.102	1.278	2.422	1.545
1986	1.439	2.792	2.094	3.005	1.949
1987	1.680	4.129	3.840	3.968	2.460

Correlations

	Canada	Japan	South Korea	United Kingdom	United States
Canada	——	.902	.725	.928	.951
Japan		——	.929	.987	.984
South Korea			——	.864	.874
United Kingdom				——	.990
United States					——

* 1980 = 1.00.

Source of original data: International Monetary Fund. 1989B. *Balance of Payments Statistics Yearbook*, vol. 40, part 1 (Washington: International Monetary Fund).

eration for domestic investors and for foreign investors intending to keep their money in a foreign market, but not necessarily in equities. The superior performance of the Japanese market from 1978 through 1987 is not diminished by inflation because Japanese inflation was quite low during the period. The performance of the Korean stock market was most seriously affected by high rates of inflation during the period, and a trough between 1978 and 1987 is fairly apparent (Table 6.8). British, Canadian, and American performances are subdued as well, and, in turn, the correlations among the indexes are different here than in the nominal case. In general, the correlations between each index are subdued when inflation is taken into account. In one case, the difference is very small, as the correlation between the Japanese and American markets declines by .010 when inflation is taken into account. On the other hand, the correlations between the Korean and all other markets are markedly depressed, especially in the case of Canada. These low correlations suggest that, again in hindsight, real diversification benefits were available within the set of countries during the period simply by investing in the Korean market. The problem, however, was that the Korean market was highly restricted to foreign investors during the

TABLE 6.8   Selected Annual Stock Exchange Indexes Derived Using Real Domestic Prices and Their Correlations: 1978–1987*

Stock Exchange Indexes

Year	Canada	Japan	South Korea	United Kingdom	United States
1978	0.608	0.978	2.010	1.103	0.996
1979	0.808	1.022	1.427	1.103	0.969
1980	1.000	1.000	1.000	1.000	1.000
1981	0.866	1.108	0.957	1.008	0.971
1982	0.616	1.074	0.862	1.075	0.847
1983	0.845	1.242	0.831	1.297	1.110
1984	0.801	1.532	0.880	1.469	1.068
1985	0.912	1.834	0.906	1.710	1.183
1986	0.966	2.421	1.444	2.052	1.464
1987	1.081	3.577	2.572	2.601	1.784

Correlations

	Canada	Japan	South Korea	United Kingdom	United States
Canada	———	.665	.226	.630	.721
Japan		———	.629	.987	.974
South Korea			———	.593	.670
United Kingdom				———	.969
United States					———

* 1980 = 1.00.

Source of original data: International Monetary Fund. 1989B. *Balance of Payments Statistics Yearbook*, vol. 40, part 1 (Washington: International Monetary Fund).

period, and foreign stock markets were restricted to Koreans by their own government. In fact, the low correlations between the Korean and other stock markets is due in no small part to the lack of integration between the Korean equity markets and others.

Differential inflation rates among countries are discounted in foreign exchange markets, of course, because they affect both asset prices and purchasing power. When exchange rate change and its stock price effect are taken into account, the high degree of integration among the four less-restricted markets during the period is evident (Table 6.9). Except when the Korean market is considered, the lowest correlation among the indexes incorporating currency exchange rate changes is between Canada and Japan, and the coefficient of .717 is a high one. In general, these coefficients indicate that capital flowed quite freely among the unrestricted markets, again excluding South Korea. These are the correlations that would have been of interest to a truly global investor who compares returns internationally.

In hindsight, the fairly high correlations indicate that geographical portfolio diversification would not have been particularly beneficial during the period, and that

TABLE 6.9 Selected Annual Stock Exchange Indexes Derived Using Exchange Rate Changes and Their Correlations: 1978–1987*

Stock Exchange Indexes

Year	Canada	Japan	South Korea	United Kingdom	United States
1978	0.539	0.980	1.724	0.707	0.821
1979	0.737	0.989	1.403	0.860	0.860
1980	1.000	1.000	1.000	1.000	1.000
1981	1.049	1.320	1.143	1.085	1.184
1982	0.858	1.243	1.100	1.159	1.170
1983	1.286	1.587	1.067	1.309	1.634
1984	1.263	2.088	1.160	1.432	1.711
1985	1.432	2.563	1.144	1.731	1.980
1986	1.343	4.173	1.600	2.102	2.163
1987	1.490	6.522	2.855	2.814	2.477

Correlations

	Canada	Japan	South Korea	United Kingdom	United States
Canada	——	.717	.234	.833	.922
Japan		——	.818	.977	.895
South Korea			——	.688	.513
United Kingdom				——	.957
United States					——

* 1980 = 1.00. See text for additional information.

Source of original data: International Monetary Fund. 1989B. *Balance of Payments Statistics Yearbook,* vol. 40, part 1 (Washington: International Monetary Fund).

leaving one's money in the Japanese market alone would have been the best investment strategy. To some degree, however, the very success of the Japanese stock market caused Japanese foreign portfolio investment to increase during the 1980s. An excess of price to earnings ratios on the Tokyo market is partly responsible for the rapid rise of the Japanese stock index. Essentially, the large savings pool accumulated by the Japanese caused "excessive" stock pricing that became unsustainable and very risky. (The excessive pricing extended to real estate in Japan. Both markets crashed in 1991.) More realistic and more sustainable price to earnings ratios were available overseas, and Japanese foreign portfolio investment increased from about U.S. $30 billion to $290 billion during the 1980s (*World Financial Markets,* 1989). In the first part of that decade, the United States was the major recipient of Japanese portfolio investment, but by its end just over 50% of such investment was in European markets. (However, much of Japan's "European" portfolio investment is actually in Japanese stock warrants, sold in Europe and denominated in U.S. dollars!)

REFERENCES

Aderhold, R., C. Cumming, and A. Harwood. 1989. "International Linkages Among Equities Markets and the October 1987 Market Break." *Quarterly Review* (Federal Reserve Bank of New York), 13/2: 34–46.

Adler, M. 1981. "Investor Recognition of Corporation International Diversification: Comment." *Journal of Finance* 36: 187–190.

Aggarwal, R. 1979. "Multinationality and Stock Market Valuation: An Empirical Study of U.S. Markets and Companies." *Management International Review* 19/2: 5–21.

_____. 1980. "Investment Performance of U.S.-Based Multinational Companies: Comments and a Perspective on International Diversification of Real Assets." *Journal of International Business Studies* 11/1: 98–106.

Agmon, T., and D. Lessard. 1981. "Investor Recognition of Corporation International Diversification: Reply." *Journal of Finance* 36: 190–191.

Allen, R. 1989. "Globalisation of the U.S. Financial Markets: The New Structure for Monetary Policy." In *International Economics and Financial Markets*, R. O'Brien and T. Datta, eds. (Oxford: Oxford University Press).

Bayoumi, T. 1990. "Saving Investment Correlations: Immobile Capital, Government Policy, or Endogenous Behavior?" *IMF Staff Papers* 37: 360–387.

Bennet, P., and J. Kelleher. 1989. "The International Transmission of Stock Price Disruption in October 1987." *Quarterly Review* (Federal Reserve Bank of New York), 13/2: 17–33.

Blackwell Finance. 1991. *The 1991 Handbook of World Stock and Commodity Exchanges* (Oxford: Basil Blackwell).

Brennan, M., and B. Solnik. 1989. "International Risk Sharing and Capital Mobility." *Journal of International Money and Finance* 8: 359–373.

Brewer, H. 1981. "Investor Benefits from Corporate International Diversification." *Journal of Financial and Quantitative Analysis* 16: 113–126.

_____. 1989. "Components of Investment Risk and Return: The Effects on Common Shareholders from Firm-Level International Involvement." *Management International Review* 29/1: 17–28.

Burdekin, R. 1989. "International Transmission of U.S. Macroeconomic Policy and the Inflation Record of Western Europe." *Journal of International Money and Finance* 8: 401–423.

Chinn, M. 1989. "A Tale of Two Markets: Capital Market Integration and the Determination of Exchange Rates." In *International Economics and Financial Markets*.

Cowitt, P. 1991. *World Currency Yearbook, 1988–89* (Brooklyn: International Currency Analysis, Inc.).

Errunza, V. 1978. "Gains from Portfolio Diversification into Less Developed Countries' Securities: A Reply." *Journal of International Business Studies* 9/1: 117–123.

Feldstein, M., and C. Horioka. 1980. "Domestic Saving and International Capital Flows." *Economic Journal* 90: 314–329.

Golub, S. 1990. "International Capital Mobility: Net Versus Gross Stocks and Flows." *Journal of International Money and Finance* 9: 424–439.

Honeygold, D. 1989. *International Financial Markets* (New York: Nichols Publishing).

International Monetary Fund. 1989A. *International Capital Markets: Developments and Prospects* (Washington: International Monetary Fund).

————. 1989B. *Balance of Payments Statistics Yearbook,* vol. 40, part 1 (Washington: International Monetary Fund).

Jacquillat, B., and B. Solnik. 1978. "Multinationals are Poor Tools for Diversification." *Journal of Portfolio Management* 4/2: 8–12.

Jorion, P. 1989. "Asset Allocation with Hedged and Unhedged Foreign Stocks and Bonds." *Journal of Portfolio Management* 15/4: 49–54.

Kemper Group. 1987. *Kemper International Fund Prospectus.*

Lessard, D. 1976. "World, Country, and Industry Relationships in Equity Returns: Implications for Risk Reduction through International Diversification." *Financial Analysts Journal* 32/1: 32–38.

Lintner, J. 1965. "The Valuation of Risk Assets and the Selection of Risky Investments in Stock Portfolios and Capital Budgets." *Review of Economics and Statistics* 47: 13–37.

Markowitz, H. 1959. *Portfolio Selection: Efficient Diversification of Assets* (New York: John Wiley & Sons).

Masera, R. 1990. "Issues in Financial Regulation: Efficiency, Stability, Information." In *Financial Institutions in Europe under New Competitive Conditions.* D. Fair and C. de Boissieu, eds. (Dordrecht: Kluwer Academic Publishers).

Mathur, I., and K. Hanagan. 1980. "Risk Management by MNCs: The Investors' Perspective." *Management International Review* 21/2: 22–35.

Mikhail, A., and H. Shawky. 1979. "Investment Performance of U.S.-Based Multinational Corporations." *Journal of International Business Studies* 10/1: 53–66.

Mossin, J. 1966. "Equilibrium in a Capital Asset Model." *Econometrica* 34: 768–783.

Ross, S. 1976. "The Arbitrage Theory of Capital Asset Pricing." *Journal of Economic Theory* 13: 341–360.

Rugman, D. 1977. "International Diversification by Financial and Direct Investment." *Journal of Economics and Business* 30: 31–37.

Sharpe, W. 1963. "A Simplified Model for Portfolio Analysis." *Management Science* 9: 277–293.

Stulz, R. 1984. "Pricing Capital Assets in an International Setting: An Introduction." *Journal of International Business Studies* 15/3: 55–73.

Tobin, J. 1952. "Liquidity Preference as Behavior towards Risk." *Review of Economic Studies* 26: 65–86.

Wong, D. 1990. "What do Saving-Investment Relationships Tell Us about Capital Mobility?" *Journal of International Money and Finance* 9: 60–74.

World Bank. 1989. *World Development Report 1989* (New York: Oxford University Press).

————. 1992. *World Development Report 1992* (New York: Oxford University Press).

World Financial Markets. 1988. "Financial Markets in Europe: Toward 1992." February 14, pp. 1–11.

World Financial Markets. 1989. "Japan: The World's Leading Foreign Investor." April 17, pp. 1–12.

CHAPTER 7

. . .

International Lending
and International Debt

. . .

7.1 INTRODUCTION

While international flows of equity capital increased rapidly during the 1970s and 1980s, the primary method of finance in the international economy remained debt. In fact, future historians of the international economy may think of the 1980s as the "decade of debt" because of the problems of massive international debt faced by so many borrowing countries and lending institutions during the period. International debt, however, is certainly not a product of the 1970s and 1980s; debt is the oldest mode of international finance. In addition, international debt should not be associated only with the poorer countries of the world, nor should international borrowing be automatically considered a sign of weakness in a country's economy. International debt has many forms and each must be considered in a variety of contexts. The purpose of this chapter is to provide an overview of the different forms of international debt in their geographical contexts.

The chapter begins with a discussion of debt within the framework of the neoclassical model of geographical flows. It proceeds by drawing distinctions between the international debt of core and peripheral economies. Differences in the international debt structures of the set of individual countries focused upon in the text also are considered. The chapter then turns to the instruments and institutions of international debt financing. Private sources of debt finance are considered as well as the development and current operations of the two major quasi-governmental international financial institutions, the International Monetary Fund and the World Bank.

Finally, the chapter considers lending and debt with special regard to the financial links between Core and Periphery and problems of economic development.

7.2   DEBT AS A FINANCIAL FLOW

Just as oil price increases dominated the news of the international economy in the 1970s, the international economy of the 1980s was most often discussed with reference to debt. Usually, the decade's *debt crisis* is traced to the Mexican government's declaration of a moratorium on its payments of interest on international loans. The moratorium was announced in August of 1982 but, like most pivotal events in the international economy, the crisis took some time to come to a head. Mexico's moratorium was short-lived (see Section 7.8), but the general problem of disruption and shortfalls in repayments of international debt remains to be faced by creditors, and burdensome debt payments drag down the economies of a number of debtor countries.

The international debt crisis is a complex issue in many respects, not least of which in its origin. As noted by Bird (1991), any country's international debt problem has sources in internal fiscal and monetary management and in the international economy. As indicated in Chapter 5, drawing distinctions between internal and external conditions of government finance is difficult because they are effectively integrated. According to Dornbusch (1989), four factors led to the debt crisis of the 1980s. First, the global recession of the late 1970s and early 1980s brought about stagnation in export markets for manufactured goods and decreases in raw material and commodity prices. Second, the increase in oil prices, particularly with the second shock, generated significant international payments problems for oil importers while not being particularly helpful to oil exporters. The third factor was outright economic mismanagement by debtor countries, including currency overvaluation. The fourth factor was outright mismanagement by lenders, particularly commercial banks that relied on insufficient risk analysis in their lending practices. To these factors, Solomon (1990) adds high interest rates on international loans, and *capital flight*, or very high levels of legal and illegal export of capital by the citizens of a country.

Capital flight contributes to the demand for debt in fairly unusual circumstances. Typically, it is associated with the hyperinflation that results from economic mismanagement of governments (see Section 7.8). Its contribution to the demand for international debt, or foreign financing of economic growth, derives from its reduction of domestic savings available for domestic investment. Simply, a country will be a net importer of financial capital, either in the form of loans or investments, in the international economy, if its domestic savings are less than its domestic requirements for investment (see Chapter 6). In turn, any country that has more savings than investment requires will export financial capital. Again, while portfolio investment (Chapter 6) and direct investment (Chapter 8) are increasing in their importance, international lending remains the predominant form of international financial flow.

Its importance will continue until governments sell shares; most international debt is either incurred by governments or carries government guarantees.

Recall from Chapter 6 that a capital payment function might take the form

$$pK = \frac{1}{(K/L)} \tag{6.1}$$

expressing the payment as a function of capital supply in the context of decreasing returns. Given a constant supply of labor, pK decreases as K increases because capital's marginal productivity is decreasing. In the neoclassical model, the payment to a factor is derived as the factor's marginal productivity. In the case of a loan, the payment is collected as interest. Any interest payment can be divided into three parts. All three parts are effectively integrated, but each can be taken as having a separate influence on an interest rate's determination. One part of the interest payment is compensation for the time value of the money lent. The time value of money is an assessment of the opportunity cost of forgoing its immediate use in favor of its use in the future, when the loan is repaid. Another part is the payment required to offset the risk of the loan's interest payments, or even principal, not being (re)paid by the debtor. Finally, there is that part of the interest rate determined on the demand side as payment for the marginal productivity of the financial capital of the loan.

The interest rate effect of a loan's duration is fairly consistent. Typically, the longer the term of the loan, the higher the rate of interest. Lenders expect a premium in association with the long term largely due to the increase of uncertainty over the value of money in the future. Most often, lenders expect inflation to continually erode money's value over time, making long-term rates higher than short-term rates. Occasionally, government bond prices may result in long-term interest rates falling below short-term rates. This fairly unusual circumstance is due to a sudden tightening of a money supply, which raises current rates. A sudden contraction of the money supply makes money scarcer, increasing its marginal productivity and raising its payment, or interest rate. This effect of monetary contraction cannot be found immediately in long-term rates because many long-term bonds were bought before the contraction. In addition, the long-term market may literally discount the money supply contraction if it is perceived as a temporary policy. Interest rate spreads between long- and short-term loans are based on inflationary expectations, which, like many exchange rate expectations, are in turn based on perceptions of government monetary and fiscal policy.

If there were no distinctions of rich and poor among the world's countries, that part of the interest rate representing a payment to the marginal productivity of financial capital would be geographically constant. Homogeneity of incomes is equivalent to homogeneity of capital, so capital productivity would be geographically homogeneous as well. That portion of interest rates comprised of the factor payment would follow the law of one price in such a world. Differences in income, however, which result from differences in capital endowment, would lead to differences in capital's marginal productivity under neoclassical rules. Countries well-endowed with capital would export its services to poor countries where marginal productivities and payments would be greater. Under basic neoclassical rules, capital flows, including loans, are expected to be from rich to poor countries (see Chapter 6).

The flow from rich to poor does not always take place as expected. Harrod (1973) has noted that technological differences between rich and poor have a role to play in the flow of capital that may be as important as differences in capital endowments. The marginal productivity of a unit of capital is not simply a function of the capital-labor ratio, as expressed in Equation 6.1. As observed in Chapter 3, the level of technology may be as critical as factor quantities in producing a particular level of output. Higher technological endowments in some rich countries may lead to equal or greater payments to capital than can be earned in poor countries due to their capital shortages. In a neoclassical context, however, payments to capital would tend toward geographical equalization as technology diffuses from sources of technological innovations to places of technological deficiency. Equalization of capital service payments across countries due to technology's diffusion would be unlikely because the diffusion would have to be instantaneous. It is more likely that payments to capital services would equalize because capital's marginal productivity had equalized across countries. In a neoclassical world, the flow of capital between places would lead to equalization of marginal productivities and, therefore, payments to capital. The original cause(s) of disequilibrium do not affect the realization of equilibrium.

Despite the neoclassical argument's logic, interest rates on international loans are not equalized across countries. Actually, it is hard to expect international equalization when interest rates on mortgage loans seem to differ significantly between lenders located across the street from each other. Perhaps the major reason that mortgage rates in such close proximity differ is that the lenders have different attitudes toward risk. The type of risk considered in the case of lending is different than the portfolio risk discussed in Chapter 6. While portfolio risk is of interest to lenders as well as investors, the risk associated with an individual loan is usually taken as the risk that the borrower will be unable to pay the loan's interest and/or repay the loan's principal (see the appendix).

Mortgage lenders assess the risk of their loans by appraising the property intended for purchase, and by examining the income and credit history of the borrower. The property is appraised so that the lender may determine if its value can support the loan as collateral. If a house, for example, is worth less than the loan, then the borrower has no compelling reason to pay off the loan's full value. If a house, for example, is worth more than the value of the loan, then the borrower has a vested interest in keeping the house by paying off the loan. During times of declining or even stable housing prices, lenders should require higher down payments so that the value of the loan remains relatively small in proportion to the house's market value. The borrower's income is examined by the lender in order to determine the borrower's ability to pay off the loan. There are rules of thumb concerning ability to pay; one is that a mortgage loan should not exceed 2.5 times the borrower's annual gross income. Finally, the borrower's credit history is examined by the lender to determine if the borrower intends to pay off the obligation. A poor credit record that includes a foreclosure on an earlier mortgage loan would not be helpful to the borrower's cause.

The mortgage analogy may be overdrawn, but it is not inappropriate. Many international loans are made for specific projects and are based on a feasibility analysis. Loans to governments for infrastructural improvements, for example, frequently have been treated this way by the World Bank. Governments also sell bonds for this purpose in private markets. The feasibility of such a project is based on its value, so it is appraised in much the same way as a house for lending purposes. However, the bulk of international lending is as much for operational purposes as it is for investment. The single largest borrower in international markets is the government of the United States, which borrows to meet fiscal operating deficits. In international markets, most scrutiny is focused upon a borrower's ability to pay a loan's interest, and, occasionally, the borrower's ability to repay the principal.

Domar (1950) included repayment of principal in his measure of the rate of lending required to contribute to a borrowing country's growth:

$$L\frac{O}{I} = \frac{p + i}{p + g} \tag{7.1}$$

where L (O/I) is the ratio of debt charges, or outflow, to annual lending, or inflow; p is the rate of amortization of principal; i is the rate of interest; and g is the borrowing country's rate of economic growth. In order for lending to contribute to the borrower's economy, it must increase at a rate greater than the rate of interest. If the rate of lending and the rate of interest are equal, debt charges equal new lending so the loans are simply returned as $I - O = 0$. More problematic is the case where the rate of interest is greater than the borrowing country's rate of growth, which leads to a net outflow of financial capital from a borrower to a lender because $I - O < 0$. In the cases where $I - O = 0$ and $I - O < 0$, the rate of lending must be greater than the rate of interest or lending won't contribute to a country's growth. This suggests the realistic proposition that, in international lending, payments problems require additional lending and not a lending reduction.

A country's exports usually are its primary source of the foreign exchange earnings generally required for loan repayments. Therefore, the rate of growth in exports is considered the relevant economic growth rate with respect to repayment of loans. Simonson (1985) has provided a debt dynamics equation that directly incorporates a debt/export ratio as the variable of interest:

$$\Delta Z = (I - X)Z + G \tag{7.2}$$

where ΔZ is the change in the net debt to export ratio, with net debt defined as total foreign debt minus international reserves; I is the average rate of interest on current loans; X is the growth rate of exports; and G is the ratio of the resource gap to exports. The *resource gap* is defined as the current account deficit (less interest payments) minus direct investment, plus capital exports. Simonson indicated that the heavy lending by commercial banks to poorer countries during the 1960s and 1970s occurred under conditions where $I - X < 0$. He cites (p. 53) a typical interest rate, from 1974 to 1980, of 10.7%, while exports grew at 21.1% annually. Prospects for repayment of loans were very good under such conditions, so lenders readily refinanced loans, effectively setting G to 0. Basically, total debt was declining or remaining stable even as loan levels increased. The debt crisis developed when $I - X$ became positive in the early 1980s. Interest rates on loans to poorer countries rose to over 16% while increases in exports dropped to a rate of 1% annually. Ultimately, the world's debt crisis is a result of global recession and the decline in international trade that took place after the second oil shock.

Globally, and for individual countries, international debt levels seem to be tied to the business cycle. Cohen (1989), for example, has described the cyclical nature of the industrial countries' balance of payments since World War II. Further, the debt crisis of the 1980s and 1990s is not the world's first. There was a wave of loan defaults during the Great Depression of the 1930s in Latin America and in many of the now wealthier European countries (Dornbusch, 1989). Lewis (1977) wrote of the seemingly crushing debt burdens faced by India and China about one hundred years ago. The same level of debt was faced at the time by Australia, Canada, and Japan, all rich countries today. It seems that countries can grow and export themselves out of debt problems, although not all of them do (Meier, 1989). Debt is not inherently the problem; slow or no growth is the problem from a financial perspective.

The relationship between growth and debt is the basis for a *stages of debt model* that conforms to the more general constructs of modernization theory (recall from Chapter 3). The simplest version of the model contains four stages (Hitiris, 1988, p. 249). Stage 1 is that of "immature debtor"; the country is young and relatively poor and has net payments balances in merchandise trade and in finance that are negative. The merchandise trade balance is negative because the country's young economy is not diversified enough to provide sufficient domestic production to meet domestic demand (Kindleberger, 1937). Its financial account is negative because it requires considerable foreign capital to build the infrastructure necessary for economic growth. Eventually, a country's domestic growth allows it to enter stage 2, "mature debtor," during which its merchandise trade account moves to the positive but its financial account remains negative. Both private and public investment are still heavily dependent upon foreign sources of finance in this stage.

By stage 3, the country has become an "immature creditor" with surpluses in both merchandise trade and financial accounts. Due to growth, the country's economy is diversified enough so that its import bill is reduced at the same time that its exports are growing. In addition, its domestic industry is producing sufficient financial capital surpluses that the country can now contribute to financing growth in other countries. The financial account remains positive when the country enters stage 4, that of "mature creditor," but its merchandise trade account is again negative. The signs on the accounts are related because the country's economy is heavily specialized in services, including the financial capital it exports, and so must import a large volume of manufactured goods. As indicated by the "creditor" label of stage 4, the value of the country's financial exports more than compensates for the costs of its merchandise imports.

The stages of debt model is actually a statement of stylized facts that captures the neoclassical expectations of financial flows in the international economy. Capital exporters have surpluses of capital that are beneficially employed in poor, capital-deficient countries. Furthermore, the model illustrates the expected effect of growth diminishing a country's debt burden. While the general relationships described in the model may be accurate, there does not appear to be any actual systematic evidence that the stages are in fact temporal sequences (Halevi, 1971; Hitiris, 1988).

The flow of finance in general, including the flow of loans in particular, is typical of most spatial flows. With respect to determination of interest rates, for example, the nodal characteristics of importance include domestic marginal rates of return to financial capital, domestic growth rates, and government policy. In addition, the flow of finance is conditioned by another flow, that of merchandise trade. So far, systems of spatial interaction have been framed as nodes effecting flows and flows affecting nodes. In the case of international lending, the spatial interaction must be extended to account for the additional interdependency of different types of flows.

7.3   DEBT DISTINCTIONS: CORE AND PERIPHERY

The map of aggregate international debt in 1990 suggests that it was a particular problem of the Western Hemisphere (Figure 7.1). In fact, four of the six leading international debtors were countries of the hemisphere, in the following order:

1. United States, with external debt of nearly U.S. $350 billion ($349,690,000,000);
2. West Germany, with external debt of nearly $150 billion;
3. Brazil, with external debt over $82 billion;
4. Mexico, with external debt over $76 billion;
5. Canada, with external debt of nearly $69 billion;
6. India, with external debt over $61 billion.

Of the remaining reporting countries, only Italy, with an external debt of about $53.3 billion, also had international debt obligations over $50 billion (International Monetary Fund, 1991; World Bank, 1992).

The ordering of countries changes when external debt is taken per capita. On a per capita basis, the external debt of the United States in 1990 was about $1860, much less than Canada's, at $5084 the world's highest. Canada's per capita debt was followed by Norway's at $5042, Finland with $4329, Gabon with $3315, and

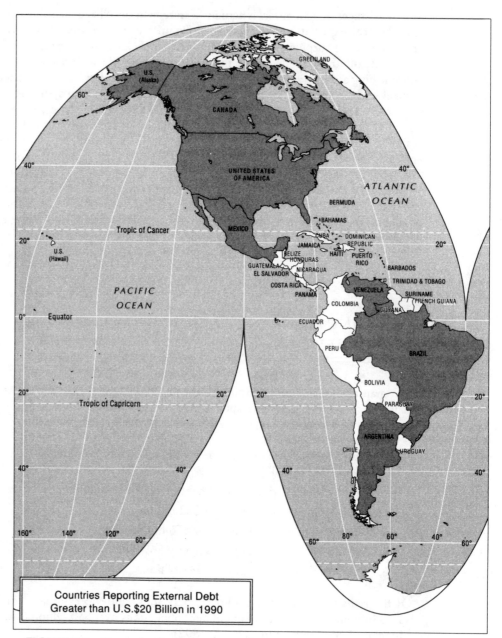

FIGURE 7.1 **Countries Reporting External Debt Greater than U.S. $20 Billion in 1990**

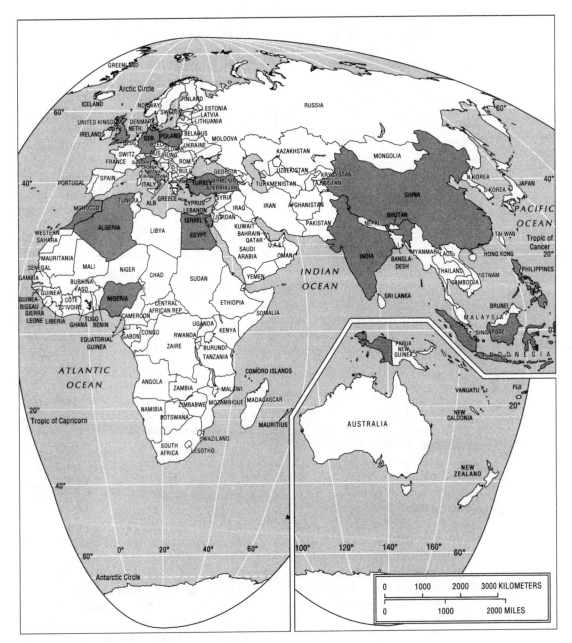

FIGURE 7.1   *(Continued)*

Panama at $2781. Other countries in 1990 with per capita foreign debt of over $2000 were Nicaragua at $2692, Jordan at $2400, Congo at $2225, Israel at $2168, and Hungary with per capita external debt of $2011. Importantly, a distinct pattern of Core and Periphery does not really emerge in the geography of debt in 1990, whether it is taken as an aggregate or per capita. Both rich and poor countries alike can depend on external debt financing.

A Core-Periphery pattern does appear, however, when debt is assessed in the context of ability to pay. The largest share of highly indebted countries—those with external debt more than their GDPs—was in Africa. None of the Core economies had such extreme debt burdens. In 1990, 15 reporting countries, 11 of them in Africa, had external debt greater than their GDPs. By contrast, the United States' external debt was only 6.5% of its GDP in 1990, and Canada's was about 12% of its GDP. Three countries had external debts more than twice as large as their GDPs—Mozambique (307%), Tanzania (257%), and Somalia (216%).

An alternative measure of debt burden is the ratio of debt to exports. At the extreme, the geographical pattern of this measure also conforms to Core and Periphery (Figure 7.2). Two regional concentrations are apparent: a major one in Africa and a minor one in South Asia. Altogether, 21 countries reported volumes of external debt greater than 500% of their merchandise exports in 1990 (International Monetary Fund, 1991; World Bank, 1992). Sudan, Nicaragua, Tanzania, and Uganda each had external debts greater than 1500% of the value of their merchandise exports. By contrast, the United States' external debt was equal to 94% of its merchandise exports and Canada's external debt was equal to 55% of its merchandise exports in 1990.

As indicated in Figure 7.2, debt burden varied in a geographically systematic way in 1990. In addition, there were important patterns among income levels as well. On average, the greatest aggregate and per capita external debt was held by the World Bank's high middle income group in 1990 (Table 7.1). To a large degree, the relationship is driven by the high debts of the Latin American countries. When considered in proportion to GNP, however, the average debt burden of the high middle income countries is not so pronounced, and is less than the average debt burden in the low middle income and low income groups. The same basic relationship exists when debt burden is framed with respect to merchandise exports. In this case, the average debt burden of a high middle income country is about one-third the debt burden of the average country in the low middle income group, and one-fifth the debt burden in the low income group. The difference between debt burdens with respect to GNP and exports is an important one. If foreign earnings rather than growth of output is the critical factor in external debt repayment, then the high middle income countries are in a much better debt position than the world's poorest countries (World Bank, 1990). The differences in the debt problems of the low and middle income groups are considered in more detail in Section 7.8.

An important difference between rich country and poor country debt is made clear in Table 7.1. While aggregate debt levels are high in the rich countries on average, debt burdens are very low by international standards. The average debt in the World Bank's high income countries represents only 5% of GNP and 32% of annual exports, so the rich countries do not have any fundamental problems in repaying loans. The relative creditworthiness of the rich countries also is represented in their ratio of external private to external public debt. In 1990, private interests in the low income countries were able to borrow, on average, U.S. $2 for every $1000 debt incurred by the public sector. The average was $9 of private debt to every $1000 of public debt in the low middle income group, and $6 in the high middle income group. In the high income countries, the external debt incurred by the private sector averaged $850 per $1000 dollars of external borrowing by the public sector (International Monetary Fund, 1991; World Bank, 1992).

A brief examination of the international debt positions in 1990 of a selected set of countries illustrates some of the variations within the broader patterns. The items on debt and equity in Table 7.2 are from the capital account (recall from Chapter 4), so negative values represent outflows while positive values represent inflows. One important feature of the table is that it illustrates some of the portfolio effects in international finance. With the exception of France and the Republic of Korea, there is a lack of consistency among the signs of the three financial flows. For example, the United States, found itself a net destination for government debt finance in 1990, but effectively exported financial capital to both private borrowers and stock markets in foreign countries. Japan in 1990 was in a position of lending money to foreign governments and buying foreign stocks, but its private sector borrowed from foreign interests. In the 1980s, the Japanese current account was so large that it financed the public debt of most of the rest of the world, including the United States (Yoshitomi, 1985). The disparity among most of the individual countries' net positions suggests some of the geographical diversification that can be expected among even such aggregate financial flows (Chapter 6).

International lending and debt tend to draw out the degree of integration in the international economy (Rotberg, 1989). The high interest rates on international loans, for example, that led to the debt crisis in Latin America originated in the fiscal deficits of the United States (Feldstein, 1985). In turn, the debt problems of Latin America limited its demand for American products and contributed to the American merchandise trade deficit (Sachs, 1989). At the same time that international debt illustrates the degree of integration in the international economy, significant differences exist between the external debts of the rich and poor countries. While rich-country debt is generally large, it is relatively affordable compared to the debt of poor countries. In addition, rich-country external debt is much more likely to be incurred by private interests than it is in poor countries. Even the external public debt of the rich countries is different than that of the poor countries. Rich governments are much more likely than poor governments to be able to borrow for general operating deficits, because poor governments are more likely to have to borrow to finance specific projects. In addition to these distinctions between the debt of rich and poor countries, there are distinctions between Core and Periphery in methods of financing debt and in lending institutions. These distinctions are taken up in the following sections.

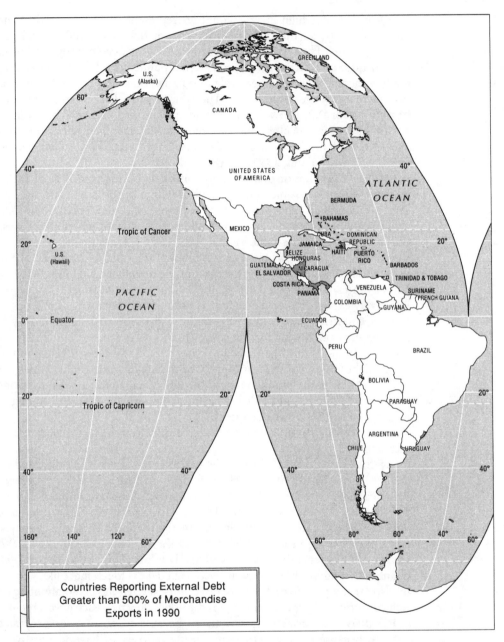

FIGURE 7.2   Countries Reporting External Debt Greater than 500% of Merchandise Exports in 1990

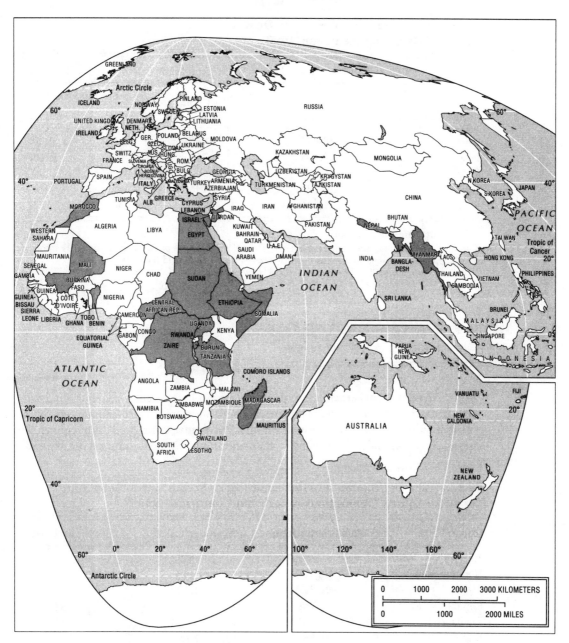

FIGURE 7.2 *(Continued)*

**TABLE 7.1   Measures of External Debt
by World Bank Income Group, 1990***

| Income Group | External Debt | | | |
| | Total (millions, U.S.$) | Per Capita (U.S.$) | As a Proportion of: | |
			GNP	Exports
All	4,447	480	48%	288%
Low	2,303	265	70%	504%
Low Middle	6,486	903	49%	298%
High Middle	20,298	1,196	29%	94%
High	11,541	446	5%	32%

* Values listed are group medians.
Source of original data: International Monetary Fund. 1991. *Balance of Payments Statistics Yearbook,*
vol. 42, part 1 (Washington: International Monetary Fund); and World Bank. 1992. *World
Development Report 1992* (New York: Oxford University Press).

7.4   DEBT FINANCING IN THE CORE
1: MONEY MARKETS AND BONDS

While Chapter 6 concerned international portfolio investment in general, it particularly focused on international equity markets. As indicated in that chapter, one of the easiest methods of portfolio diversification is for an investor to hold both equities, or shares of stock, and debt, usually in the form of government and corporate bonds.

**TABLE 7.2   Net External Public Sector Debt, Private Sector Debt, and
Corporate Equity Transactions of Selected Countries, 1990***

Country	Public Sector Debt	Private Sector Debt	Corporate Equity
Australia	−643	178	2,795
West Germany	10,960	−11,900	730
Japan	−16,370	21,400	−19,520
Republic of Korea	299	132	380
Thailand	−445	−33	447
France	10,336	11,659	807
United Kingdom	−8,047	−10,544	3,495
United States	27,350	−10,820	−21,470

* Values are in millions of $U.S.
Source: International Monetary Fund. 1991. *Balance of Payments Statistics Yearbook,* vol. 42, part 1
(Washington: International Monetary Fund).

Recall that the yields on debt and on equity tend to be countercyclical, thus reducing portfolio risk. As in the case of equities, distinctive national markets are still important, but international debt markets are increasingly easy for both borrowers and lenders to use (Meerschwam, 1989). Also like the international equity markets, however, the largest share of private debt transactions, whether borrowing, lending, or both, remains within the Core economies (*World Financial Markets*, 1989B).

Any investor holding foreign debt faces all the risks of a foreign portfolio that affect investment in foreign equities. In turn, the holder of foreign debt can obtain the same benefits that affect the owner of foreign stock. To some degree, the decision to lend is similar to the decision to invest. A question in common to lending and investing is whether to enter the international markets or simply stay at home. Of course, the geography of lending is not exclusive. As in the case of equity investments, international diversification of lending may be beneficial with respect to portfolio risk reduction.

There are important differences between lending and investing. Loans are made, in most instances, over fixed terms of various lengths. The duration of the loan, as defined by a bond's date of maturity, for example, should have a bearing on the lending decision in a geographical sense as well as with respect to lender liquidity requirements and interest rates. A lender may feel more confident lending to borrowers in a particular country for five years than for thirty years. The duration of a commitment is not an actual issue in most equity investment, an exception being stock warrants or otherwise convertible debt. In addition to duration, a lender can choose between private, typically corporate, borrowers and government borrowers or borrowers offering government guarantees that the interest and principal of the loan will be paid. Equity investors are, of course, limited to investing in corporations. Typically, government bonds offer their holders lower yields than private ones offer because governments are taken to be more reliable borrowers. The gap between higher corporate bond yields and lower government bond yields is called the *yield differential*.

Barret and Kolb (1986) have found that the yield differential tends to increase systematically with interest rates in all the major, Core-economy bond markets of the world. Although Barret and Kolb found a geographically consistent relationship between the yield differential and interest rates, relationships between the yield differential and other macroeconomic characteristics were not as uniform across the markets examined. Apparently the yield differential, holding interest rates constant, varies from country to country in a way that may provide opportunities of geographical diversification for portfolio risk reduction.

Reducing exchange rate risk, however, is the primary role of geographical diversification in international lending, just as it is for international investment in equities. Exchange rate risk can be reduced by a geographical diversification strategy, but in many cases it is reduced or eliminated by the borrower in international markets. By eliminating exchange rate risk, the borrower can expect to pay a lower rate of interest. Much exchange rate risk is shifted from American lenders to foreign borrowers in international markets because so much borrowing is denominated in American dollars in the form of *Yankee bonds*. In addition, many borrowers issue dual currency and multiple currency bonds that automatically carry any benefits of geographical diversification of exchange rate risk. In 1990, the International Capital Market, a consortium of bond dealers headquartered in Switzerland, listed 20 different single-currency denominations in its traded bonds (Blackwell Finance, 1991). It also listed dual currency and multicurrency denominated bonds, including those valued in European Currency Units (see Chapter 5) and in special drawing rights (see Section 7.7).

Debt financing takes place in *money markets* as well as *bond markets.* Money markets are used to borrow money for short periods to cover operating expenses and maintain the borrower's liquidity. Bond markets are used to borrow money for longer periods and the borrowed funds frequently are dedicated to a specific purpose. Bond markets, as opposed to money markets, are true capital markets because they usually finance investment and not operating expenses (Honeygold, 1989). Banks operate both as borrowers and lenders in the international economy and in both money markets and bond markets (see Section 7.5).

The international dimension of financial markets can be realized in two ways. One is the ability of a citizen of country X to lend or borrow or invest money in the domestic market of country Y. For example, the purchase of a U.S. Treasury note by a Japanese corporation is a part of international finance. This aspect of international finance is important, but the market can be quite segmented along national boundaries. Different countries have their own specific regulations concerning their domestic debt markets just as they do with respect to domestic equity markets. Foreign borrowers and lenders must contend with each country's applicable regulations in this part of the international financial market.

An alternative realization of the international financial market is found in the *Euromarkets,* which is a collective set of debt markets not regulated by any individual country. The development of the Euromarkets is linked to the demand for American dollars in Western Europe that led to the creation of *Eurodollars.* Initially, Eurodollars were deposits of American dollars by the Soviet Union and other Eastern European countries in Western European banks (Hogendorn and Brown, 1979). The governments of these countries used their U.S. dollar accounts to finance transactions in international trade, but were afraid that their holdings would be confiscated by the American government if held as deposits in American banks. Initially held in France, Eurodollar accounts soon spread to England, and deposits grew from a number of sources. In addition to the original depositors, American corporations started Eurodollar accounts for use in their transactions in Europe, and because interest rates on American dollars deposited in European banks were greater than the regulated interest rates paid by American banks. In the 1970s, the supply of Eurodollars expanded considerably in the form of deposits of American dollars by oil-exporting countries.

Eurodollars have changed dramatically since their inception in two ways. First, Eurodollars are no longer confined to actual American dollars. Any deposit of a foreign currency in a bank that pays interest in that foreign currency is called a Eurodollar. Japanese yen, in particular, but also deutsche marks and Swiss francs are among the more frequently found "Eurodollars," which are now more often called, in aggregate, *Eurocurrency* (not to be confused with European Currency Units). As the dollar part of Eurodollar is declining in use, the geographical part is also becoming a misnomer. This is because of a second, locational, change in the Eurodollar. These deposits are now frequently held outside of Europe, in the Bahamas or Singapore, for example. The bulk of Eurodollar deposits remains in Europe, however, forming the basis of the Euromarkets.

The Euromarkets provide both short-term money market instruments, such as Eurocommercial paper (Heller, 1988), and long-term debt instruments called Euro-bonds (Fisher, 1988). The popularity of the Euromarkets is strongly related to the gap between its interest rates and interest rates on domestic debt (International Monetary Fund, 1990). Borrowers frequently prefer Euromarkets because, while interest rates typically are higher than on domestic loans, the lack of regulation allows more lending to less creditworthy customers. The Euromarkets are attractive to lenders because they use more discreet bearer instruments rather than the publicly registered ones required of most issues of domestic debt.

7.5   DEBT FINANCING IN THE CORE 2: PRIVATE BANKS

Although direct lending does take place, most bonds and other paper are handled by brokers in order to reduce the transaction costs of borrowing and lending. Financial intermediaries bring together large numbers of borrowers and lenders which, combined with their specialized knowledge and expertise, provide economies of scale in financial transactions. With respect to frequency of transaction and average size, banks are the most important financial intermediaries in the international economy. Banking may be divided into two basic forms: *investment banking* and *commercial banking*. Investment banking is more like brokering than true banking. Investment banks underwrite bond and equity issues and act as intermediaries in arranging other forms of long-term financing. They earn money from charging fees for their services rather than from the difference between their interest rates on loans and deposits. Commercial, or retail, banks are true banks that do make loans and accept deposits, which comprise their loanable funds. In addition, retail banks tend to lend money for relatively short periods and in relatively small amounts as compared to the typical investment bank transaction. Some banks act only as investment banks or commercial banks and some act as both, usually depending upon government regulations. Some general characteristics of international banking within the Core are described in this section, and those affecting the Periphery are described in Section 7.6.

The international bank was pioneered by the French and British through their colonial empires (Lewis, 1977). The basic role of international banking early on was financing international trade, and that purpose remains important today (Korth, 1985). Banks issue *letters of credit* and *banker's acceptances*, which are guarantees of bank payment of obligations incurred in international trade. Importers pay a fee for these instruments, which assure the exporter that the bank is liable for a certain payment for goods received by the importer. International banks also provide short-term financing that is competitive with commercial paper, and long-term financing competitive with the bond market. In addition to services directly connected with lending, international banks provide related financial services such as foreign exchange trading.

International banks are a form of multinational corporation (see Chapter 8). Their operations can take on a variety of forms (Choi, 1985). The simplest type of international presence is provided by *correspondent banks,* which act on each other's behalf in foreign countries (and in different states in the highly segmented American banking market). When a bank uses a foreign correspondent, it does not directly offer banking services in the country in question, usually because of government restrictions or insufficient demand. *Representative offices* are also used in circumstances in which government restrictions do not allow the direct provision of banking services by foreign banks. Unlike a correspondent bank, a representative office allows direct contact between a bank and the foreign market, which facilitates transactions affecting third countries.

Direct provision of bank services is made through agencies, branches, and subsidiaries of foreign banks (Korth, 1985). *Agencies* may make loans but not accept deposits. Agency banking is encouraged in those countries that are trying to facilitate foreign financing of domestic debt. Foreign *branches* can take deposits as well as make loans. Branches are legal extensions of a parent bank, while *subsidiaries* are legally distinct from their parents and may be different types of banks. For example, a commercial bank in one country may have a wholly owned subsidiary in another country that practices only investment banking.

The extent of bank activity is usually strongly regulated by government. In the United States, the Glass-Steagal Act of 1934, a federal law, prohibits retail banks from operating as investment banks. Operating outside the country, however, foreign subsidiaries of American commercial banks can carry on investment banking as long as they comply with the foreign government's regulations. It seems that the two major forces in international banking are to serve markets and avoid regulations (Damanpour, 1990). In tandem, these forces drive the geography of international banking.

Private international banking markets are almost completely within the Core, and that's where the great majority of international banking is located (Table 7.3). On average, the banks in a low income country have foreign liabilities, or deposits, that total about U.S. $1.4 billion, and total foreign assets, or loans, of about $1.3 billion. While both average foreign assets and foreign liabilities increase from low to low middle to high middle income countries, the difference between bank foreign assets and liabilities in the average high middle income country and the average high income country is well over U.S. $140 billion on each side of the ledger. The intra-Core concentration is also indicated by the headquarters of the world's largest banks. At the end of 1990, 10 of the world's 15 largest banks were Japanese, three were French, and one each was headquartered in Germany and the United Kingdom (*Economist,* 1991A).

TABLE 7.3   Foreign Assets and Foreign Liabilities of Banks by World Bank Income Group, 1990*

Income Group	Assets	Liabilities
All	101.4	110.9
Low	1.4	1.3
Low Middle	1.9	4.1
High Middle	6.1	6.9
High	247.6	268.6

* Values listed are group means in billions of $U.S.
Source: International Monetary Fund, 1992.
International Financial Statistics Yearbook, 1992
(Washington: International Monetary Fund).

There are some deviations, however, from the Core concentration of international banking. In 1990, the banks of 13 countries had foreign assets (loans) of more than 100 billion American dollars, and banks of 15 countries had foreign liabilities (deposits) greater than that amount (Table 7.4). Both lists are dominated by Core countries, with the United Kingdom, Japan, and the United States ranked

TABLE 7.4   Leading National Money Centers by Bank Foreign Assets and Bank Foreign Liabilities, 1990*

Assets		Liabilities	
United Kingdom	1069.9	United Kingdom	1205.8
Japan	950.6	Japan	958.5
United States	652.2	United States	733.3
Hong Kong	463.8	France	519.7
France	458.7	Hong Kong	402.7
Switzerland	444.1	Cayman Islands	401.0
West Germany	394.8	Singapore	354.9
Cayman Islands	389.4	Switzerland	353.0
Luxembourg	355.1	Luxembourg	296.0
Singapore	346.7	Belgium	239.8
Belgium	192.0	West Germany	226.4
Netherlands	185.3	Italy	196.9
Bahamas	174.7	Bahamas	182.0
		Netherlands	153.4
		Sweden	104.6

* Assets or liabilities of more than $100 billion expressed in billions of $U.S.
Source: International Monetary Fund. 1992. *International Financial Statistics Yearbook* (Washington: International Monetary Fund).

first to third, respectively, in both categories. Hong Kong, Singapore, the Cayman Islands, and the Bahamas are centers outside the set of Core countries. Hong Kong and Singapore are important financial centers, in addition to Japan, in East Asia. Both places have strong economies that generate significant domestic supply and demand for loanable funds, and they are also centers of "Asian currency" markets that function much like Eurocurrency markets. Unlike Hong Kong and Singapore, the Cayman Islands and the Bahamas do not have strong domestic financial markets. They do, however, provide significant tax benefits in international finance, and significant secrecy that enhances their use as so-called *off-shore banks.*

Frequently, offshore banks provide services that are illegal in many other jurisdictions. While most are legitimate, some offshore banks have developed a reputation for laundering dirty money earned from illicit drug and weapons sales. Sometimes offshore locations are integrated within a bank's other units in order to hide transactions. An extreme example of some of the geographical complexity of international banking used for nefarious purposes is found in the case of Bank of Credit & Commerce International (BCCI). It's been said that BCCI brought new meaning to the phrase "full service bank." BCCI was associated with arms sales, narcotic trafficking, and the finances of terrorist groups and the CIA, in addition to more typical investment and commercial banking activities. The primary financing of BCCI's investment banking came from small but oil-rich Abu Dhabi. The government of that country had become the principal stockholder by the time of BCCI's liquidation in 1992 (*Economist,* 1992). BCCI's second largest shareholder was an investment company headquartered in the Cayman Islands, and the bank's headquarters were in Luxembourg. Directly, BCCI had about 30 offices of some sort spread over 30 countries. In addition, it had a subsidiary, also headquartered in Luxembourg, which had almost 50 branches in about 10 countries and its own subsidiaries in Canada and Gibraltar. BCCI also owned a subsidiary headquartered in the Cayman Islands, which in turn had over 60 offices in about 30 countries. In addition to these official holdings, BCCI appears to have had several secretly held operations in other countries, including the United States.

Tax codes and secrecy laws are part of a system of domestic bank regulation that varies from country to country. A more important form of commercial bank regulation that also varies internationally concerns *capital adequacy requirements.* Capital adequacy is defined as the ratio of a bank's net worth to its total liabilities. Another form of regulation concerns *reserve requirements,* usually defined with respect to capital reserve requirements, or the proportion of deposits that cannot be used in a bank's loans. An alternative requirement is made with respect to all capital, not just deposits. For example, if a bank borrows money itself, a certain proportion of the borrowed money cannot be used for the bank's loans. Capital adequacy standards and reserve requirements are imposed by governments to ensure confidence in the banking system and adequate capital bases so that all usual transactions are covered. Other things being equal, the higher the capital adequacy requirement the less profitable the bank, because money not on loan is not earning interest. Eurocurrency markets are profitable for lenders because their foreign currency loans, such as

Euronotes (International Monetary Fund, 1986), are not subject to capital reserve requirements.

A guarantee of capital adequacy is required to maintain a national banking system as an integral part of a country's financial infrastructure. Surprisingly, some countries do not have capital adequacy standards or do not enforce the ones they have (Maxwell and Gitman, 1990). Capital adequacy standards are usually enforced by central banks. While there is no true central bank for the international economy, the *Bank for International Settlements (BIS)* serves as a coordinating agency for transactions between many of the world's central banks and for selected international financial transactions. Under BIS auspices, international supervision of banking practices among the so-called Group of Ten (G-10) began in 1974 (Fraser, 1987), in the wake of the first oil shock. G-10 includes Belgium, Canada, France, Germany, Italy, Japan, the Netherlands, Sweden, the United Kingdom, and the United States. In 1988, the BIS established a risk-weighted capital adequacy standard of 8% for G-10 domiciled international banks, to be phased in over a four-year period (International Monetary Fund, 1989). This capital adequacy standard was designed to promote confidence in the international banking system and ensure international bank liquidity in the same way that such standards are designed to work in domestic bank markets.

The establishment of capital adequacy standards in international banking facilitates the integration of international capital markets by creating confidence across national market lines. Uniformity of banking requirements across national borders facilitates the primary activity of international banks, which is trade in financial services. As previously indicated, an early and still important purpose of international banking is trade finance. The locational pattern of international banking is almost a replication of international trade patterns (Damanpour, 1991). Jain (1986) has shown that the lending patterns of international banks are explained by trade and direct-investment flows. The international loans of American commercial banks follow the geographical pattern of American trade and investment, while Japanese commercial loans have about the same international geography as Japanese trade and investment. The link between trade and the location of international banking has also been found at the regional level within the United States (Goldberg et al., 1989).

The link between trade and international banking is being accommodated relatively slowly in geographically discriminatory trade agreements (International Monetary Fund, 1990). In the Canada-U.S. agreement, American banks are given preference over third-country banks in the Canadian market, but some limitations on non-Canadian ownership of large Canadian banks still apply (Harrington, 1989). Intra-Community banking has lagged behind merchandise trade in the European Community. Until the EC '92 directives were established, banks were subject to typical national requirements with respect to items such as operating licenses and capital adequacy requirements. A single operating license is established in the EC '92 legislation, and the uniform capital adequacy requirement is established at 8%, the BIS level for international banks (Eurofli, 1989). Steinherr (1990) has argued, however, that a single European banking market cannot be achieved until certain technical problems, such as diversity in national accounting standards for banks, are solved.

7.6 DEBT FINANCING IN THE PERIPHERY 1: PRIVATE BANKS

While the discussion of private bank lending has emphasized intra-Core finance, private banks are also active in the Periphery. Private bank financing in the Periphery is different than in the Core in three important ways. As already described, private bank lending to the Periphery is significantly less than in the Core. Also, private bank lending in the Periphery is primarily to governments, with proportionately much smaller volumes of lending to corporate or other private borrowers than is common in the Core. The third difference between bank lending in the Core and the Periphery is that loans to the Periphery are taken to be inherently more risky than loans to the Core. The extra risk accounts for smaller volumes of loans to the Periphery and their somewhat safer placement with governments rather than private borrowers.

The inherently greater risk of loans to the periphery is largely a function of export prices (see Section 7.2). Private lending to the Periphery expanded rapidly during the late 1960s, when export markets were growing rapidly (Committee for Economic Development, 1987). Improved trade markets caused a general increase in credit-worthiness among many Periphery countries and provided additional reasons for increased lending (O'Brien, 1990). The increased volume of trade required increased volumes of the export and import financing traditionally provided by banks. In addition, export earnings in the Periphery were frequently deposited in international banks which were then able to recycle those funds as loans. The volume of loanable funds, and therefore loans to the Periphery, skyrocketed in the 1970s when many members of OPEC deposited their oil earnings in international banks.

The international recession that began as a result of the second oil shock led to the stagnation of export earnings in general, and oil revenues actually declined. The result was the debt crisis of 1982, which had a dramatic effect on international banks. The locus of the debt crisis of the 1980s was Latin America (see Sections 7.7 and 7.8). A number of international banks were highly exposed in their loans to the region (Khoury, 1985). Manufacturers' Hanover had combined loans to Argentina, Brazil, Mexico, and Venezuela (the latter two oil exporters) equivalent to more than 200% of its capital. Bank America, Chemical Bank, and Citibank had loans to the region representing more than 150% of capital, and Bankers' Trust, Chase Manhattan, Morgan Guaranty, and First Chicago had exposures of over 120% of capital.

Not surprisingly, the delay of payments on loans of those magnitudes created a true debt crisis for the lenders (see Section 7.8). All of the banks listed faced some threat to their solvency, and many were effectively bailed out of bankruptcy by the International Monetary Fund (Solomon, 1990), which continued to finance peripheral debt (see Section 7.7). The stock prices of international banks tumbled as their profitability decreased (Sachs, 1989). Many regional banks, and even smaller ones normally operating in very local markets, also had been active in lending to peripheral borrowers (Heldring, 1989). For example, Colonial Bank of Waterbury, Connecticut, was forced into insolvency by its losses in foreign markets in the early 1980s.

While the debt crisis did have a significant impact on the international banking system, its strongest effects had dissipated by the late 1980s as bank exposure in peripheral markets declined. Of all the banks previously listed, only Manufacturers' Hanover (no longer in existence after its acquisition by Chemical Bank) had loans to Argentina, Brazil, Mexico, and Venezuela still equivalent to over 100% of its capital by the end of 1987 (Huhne, 1989). Bankers' Trust, Citicorp, First Chicago, and Morgan Guaranty all had loans to the four countries totalling less than 60% of capital. In general, a result of the debt crisis was a reduction of bank lending to borrowers in the Periphery (Rotberg, 1989). The crisis dissipated by the end of 1991, as debt was reduced and foreign investment increased (see Chapter 8).

Banks have reallocated their geographical portfolio of loans away from the Periphery for two reasons. First, the ability of borrowers in the Periphery to make good their loans has been drawn into question not so much by the debt crisis itself, but by the stagnation in the international economy that brought on the crisis. Second, bank regulators have been strengthening the loan loss provisions and capital adequacy requirements of banks on a risk-weighted basis. For example, the 8% capital adequacy standard established by the BIS is an average value. Loans to peripheral customers require a higher proportion, while loans in the Core have smaller capital base requirements. Ironically, at the same time loans have become more difficult to come by in the Periphery, the focus on risk reduction has had the effect of lowering interest rates. The average spread between the effective international prime rate, the *London Inter-Bank Offer Rate (LIBOR),* and the higher rates charged to borrowers in the Periphery began to decline after 1983. Unfortunately, the decrease in the average rate is due largely to the geographical reduction in loan portfolios that has virtually eliminated all but the best credit risks in the Periphery (International Monetary Fund, 1990).

The determination of a country's credit risk is conducted in many different formats. Khoury (1985) has listed the four basic models for assessing *country risk* and *sovereign risk*. One model is completely qualitative so that a country's risk rating is based completely on an evaluator's judgement. Another model, called "structured qualitative," is a qualitative model that also incorporates data. A third type adds a scoring procedure to the structured qualitative model. The fourth type of model is completely quantitative and usually takes on an econometric form. Country risk assessments are made for extending loans on an individual country basis and can have a bearing on both the value of the loan and the interest rate. In addition, individual country risk assessments can be used in fashioning a bank's international loan portfolio (Cataquet, 1989). High-risk, high-interest countries are offset by low-risk countries, depending upon the bank's risk preference and the prevailing attitude of bank regulators.

The quantitative models are frequently designed to calculate the probability of a country defaulting on its debt. These econometric models usually are specified as logit regression equations. Dymski and Pastor (1991) used a logit regression model to calculate the probability of payment problems across a set of Latin American countries. They found that past debt rescheduling and current high debt loads increase the probability of current debt repayment problems. More rapid growth rates decrease the probability of debt problems. They also found that the probability of debt problems decreases with the openness of a country's economy, measured as trade turnover divided by GNP, and that the probability of debt problems decreases with a government's ability to suppress wages in favor of making debt payments.

The more qualitative country risk models usually take a wide variety of factors into consideration (Johnson et al., 1990). In addition to economic risk, *political risk* is also evaluated (Davis, 1981). Government stability, processes of political succession, and the friendliness of relations between the borrowing country and the bank's headquarters' country all have a bearing on risk of a loan. The internal politics of borrowing may be just as important as external politics if vested interests in a country can gain from its default on foreign obligations (Conybeare, 1990). Many of the qualitative risk assessment models are quite exhaustive in the factors they consider, but Cosset and Roy (1991) have found that three factors—GNP per capita, the national savings rate, and current debt—are excellent predictors of qualitative assessments.

7.7 DEBT FINANCING IN THE PERIPHERY 2: THE IMF AND DEVELOPMENT BANKS

Despite the level of sophistication in country risk assessment models, they cannot predict the future with certainty. In the late 1970s, by any method of assessment, Mexico was considered a risk-free borrower in international financial markets (Katz, 1989). It had strong export earnings from oil and a very stable political and economic system. By 1982, however, Mexico was unable to keep to its debt repayment schedule, illustrating the ability of good credit risks to go bad fairly quickly in the international economy. It also illustrated the level of uncertainty in the international economy that tends to pervade relationships between Core and Periphery. Actually, uncertainty is more problematic than risk in the lending patterns between rich and poor. Because it can't be quantified like risk, uncertainty can't be offset accurately by a particular interest rate.

The problem of uncertainty, as much as anything else, has led to the large role played by the *International Monetary Fund (IMF),* the *World Bank,* and other quasi-governmental, multilateral lending institutions in financing peripheral economies (Crockett and Goldstein, 1987). Altogether, there are about 20 regional development banks around the world. Recently, the European Bank for Reconstruction and Development was established for the benefit of Eastern European countries as they move toward market economies. Another regional development bank operates only within the Nordic countries. Most regional development banks, however, provide debt finance in the Periphery. Examples include the Asian Development Bank and African Development Bank. These banks are consortiums of peripheral country borrowers and Core country lenders. For example, the African Development Bank has about 50 African states and about 25 non-African states, primarily from Western Europe, as members (Mingst, 1990).

Although the number of regional development banks is large, the IMF and the International Bank for Reconstruction and Development, or World Bank, stand out as the most important multilateral lenders in the international economy. The IMF and the World Bank are both United Nations organizations established at the Bretton Woods conference in 1944. Their ties to the United Nations, however, are less than integral. The UN is headquartered in New York, while both the IMF and World Bank are headquartered in Washington, D.C. The IMF and World Bank are frequently linked in discussions of the international economy and, in fact, are frequently linked in their efforts. They are, however, distinct institutions and have distinctly different original charters (Fraser, 1987).

The IMF is not a bank but a monetary organization that was designed to provide an international institutional framework for the expansion of international trade and finance. It was intended to provide a mechanism for international monetary cooperation; recall that the Bretton Woods exchange rate system was established under IMF auspices. The IMF had 29 member countries at the end of 1945. By the beginning of 1992 it had about 170 members, including the independent republics that emerged from the USSR's demise. The IMF is operated by a Board of Governors elected by the members. The voting power of the individual members is based on their *IMF quotas,* which are measured in *special drawing rights (SDRs)*.

SDRs were established by the IMF as an international reserve asset in 1969. The IMF's intention was for SDRs to replace gold and the American dollar in international exchange (Chrystal, 1978). They were intended to preserve liquidity in reserve balances that had both gold and U.S. dollar shortages (International Monetary Fund, 1987). Originally, the SDR was valued in reference to the American dollar and, therefore, gold. With the end of the fixed exchange rates of Bretton Woods, however, the SDR was revalued in 1974 as a basket of the American, British, French, Japanese, and West German currencies. In 1991, SDRs were composed as 40% U.S. dollars, 21% German marks, 17% Japanese yen, and 11% each of French francs and British pounds (International Monetary Fund, 1992). SDRs can be used only for official transfers between governments and are not actual currency. Because of their composition of multiple strong currencies, however, some Eurobond issues carry SDR denominations that provide built-in benefits of geographical exchange rate diversification. SDRs are also used as a unit of account by a number of regional development banks, including both the African Development Bank and Asian Development Bank.

The IMF quota system ensures that the world's largest economies control IMF operations. Quotas are equal to a country's subscription, or capital contribution, to the IMF. A country's quota is taken as a function of its GDP, average monthly international reserves, average payments on current account, average receipts on current account, and the variability of current receipts measured as a moving average. Obviously, the use of national income as a basis for the quotas favors the world's largest economies, especially the United States, which has about 20% of all IMF quotas. The United States also provides about 20% of the IMF's capital. Each member of the IMF has 250 votes as a baseline allocation and is allocated one additional vote for each 100,000 SDRs in its quota. For example, in 1990 Peru had a quota of 330,900,000 SDRs and the United States had a quota of 17,918,300,000. Peru had 3559 votes (250 + 3309) while the United States had 179,433 (250 + 179,183) in the IMF. (The late American billionaire H.L. Hunt, known for political conservatism, once suggested that Americans should have one vote for every dollar they paid in taxes. Was he inspired by the IMF?)

Quotas also determine the amount of assistance from the IMF that is available to a member. IMF lending programs, covering eight different areas, were established to meet a problem in a country's balance of payments or its international reserves position. All of the programs, or *IMF facilities,* were intended for short-term finance, but some have been extended for fairly long periods under special conditions. Members are allowed to draw on five different IMF facilities generally concerned with steep declines in reserve accounts or balance of payments that are caused by general conditions. Special facilities are available to offset declines specifically related to oil prices, to finance purchases of primary commodities, and to finance structural adjustment (see Section 7.8 for more detail on IMF policies).

The Periphery has not been the only user of the IMF's several facilities. As recently as 1979, the British had drawn on the greatest number of SDRs, over 800 million, of any country borrowing from the IMF (International Monetary Fund, 1991). The Philippines was second, at just over 500 million SDRs. Several industrial countries relied on IMF facilities to manage balance of payments problems into the early 1980s (Table 7.5). The use of IMF facilities in the mid- and late 1970s and early 1980s by industrial economies was due mainly to the oil shocks. By the mid-1980s, however, the flow of finance from the IMF to its members was almost entirely toward the Periphery. In 1985, four countries had IMF drawings of more than two billion SDRs: India, with about 4.5 billion; Brazil, at over 4.2 billion; Mexico, at about 2.7 billion; and Argentina, at just over 2.1 billion SDRs. By 1990, the number had been reduced to three: Mexico, at over 4.6 billion; Argentina, nearly 2.2 billion; and Venezuela, with just over 2.1 billion SDRs.

The change in IMF lending and borrowing patterns is illustrated in Table 7.5. In 1980, countries from the high income group were borrowing the greatest amounts, on average. They did not, however, approach the borrowing ceiling expressed in their quotas. In fact, the average country that borrowed from the IMF in 1980 was well under its limits, regardless of income group. In 1985, the average country was still under its limit of IMF borrowing, but not if it was among the low or low middle income countries. Quotas were frequently exceeded, under special facilities, in 1985 so that the average IMF lending in both low and high middle income groups was over 100% of quota. By 1990, with lower oil prices and concerted efforts toward debt reduction, IMF lending was again below quota, on average.

TABLE 7.5   Average Use of International Monetary Fund Credit in Special Drawing Rights (SDR) and Percent of Quota by World Bank Income Group, 1980, 1985, and 1990*

| | External Debt | | | | | |
| | Millions of SDRs | | | Percent of Quota | | |
Income Group (1992)	1980	1985	1990	1980	1985	1990
All	39	79	26	42	56	36
Low	43	91	69	94	163	95
Low Middle	25	150	49	44	126	59
High Middle	0	122	36	0	47	22
High	84	0	0	11	0	0

* Values listed are group medians.
Source: International Monetary Fund. 1992. *International Financial Statistics Yearbook* (Washington: International Monetary Fund).

Unlike the IMF, which is primarily concerned with balance of payments problems, the World Bank is a development bank designed to finance the development and post–World War II reconstruction of its members. While the IMF makes loans to cover shortfalls in operating funds, the World Bank has been more concerned with capital projects. Because of the nature of the projects, loans are usually long-term. The World Bank generally makes loans to governments or to related public borrowers. It does lend to private sector borrowers, including small and medium-sized enterprises since 1973 (Webster, 1991). The member countries of the World Bank are the same as those of the IMF. Voting procedures and the allocation of votes are similar to those used by the IMF, as well. By tradition, although not by rule, the president of the World Bank is an American and its managing director is a West European.

Until recently, World Bank lending has been very much oriented toward financing capital projects, its original purpose. Transportation projects such as port and railway development, water supply and sewerage systems, manufacturing-plant construction, and capital projects in agriculture dominated the World Bank's lending. Proposals for these types of projects are submitted by potential borrowers and evaluated by the World Bank's staff using cost-benefit analysis (Little and Mirrlees, 1991). Potential loans are judged on the creditworthiness of the borrowing country as well. Poorer countries are able to borrow from a World Bank affiliate, the *International Development Association (IDA)*, which was established as a supplementary source of credit, under World Bank management, for the world's poorest countries (Committee for Economic Development, 1987). Recently, the World Bank has become much less project-oriented and has been lending for human capital development in the areas of education and health as much as for physical capital development.

Over time, it seems that the lending practices and policies of the World Bank and the IMF have been converging. Both institutions joined together in development banking during the 1980s because the severity of the debt crisis required such a concerted focus (Miller, 1989). In its discussion of the "two sisters," the *Economist* (1991B) stated that the IMF's role in Eastern Europe will be more that of a development bank than a provider of short-term balance of payments supports. The IMF and World Bank started to coordinate their lending to African countries in the mid-1980s. In some cases, such as Nigeria, the IMF and World Bank have been coordinating their efforts with commercial banks as well (International Monetary Fund, 1986). The purpose of their policy coordination is to bring about so-called structural economic adjustments that are intended to provide a basis for real economic growth.

7.8 THE CHALLENGE OF DEBT REDUCTION FOR ECONOMIC DEVELOPMENT

One of the more interesting points raised in Chapter 6 is that financial capital is relatively immobile in the international economy. Despite the growing importance of international investment and the continued importance of international lending, aggregate measures of saving and investment indicate that most countries are practically self-sufficient in their supply of capital for domestic investment. The average case, however, is accompanied by extremes in both the short and long runs, otherwise an international debt crisis could never arise. In one respect, international debt problems are a function of the mobility of capital between the capital-exporting countries and poorer capital-importing countries.

Countries must import financial capital when their demand for investment is greater than their supply of domestic savings. Capital imports may be in the form of portfolio investment (Chapter 6), direct investment (Chapter 8), or borrowing. Among poorer countries—those with the greatest savings-investment gaps—foreign borrowing is the primary method of importing financial capital. If foreign debt is to decrease in these countries, one of two things must happen. Either domestic savings must increase at a faster rate than domestic investment, or exports must increase at a faster rate than imports. From the viewpoint of *dual gap analysis,* the difference between domestic savings and investment and between imports and exports is equivalent (Thirlwall, 1977). Let I be national income, C be consumption of domestic production, M be imports, and S be national saving. By national accounting,

$$I = C + M + S \tag{7.3}$$

which equates income to total consumption plus saving. Let Q be domestic output, X be exports, and N be investment. Again, by national accounting,

$$Q = C + X + N \tag{7.4}$$

which equates output to production of consumption and capital goods. Recall that output, Q, and income, I, are equivalent in the national accounts. Then, by manipulation,

$$S - N \equiv M - X \qquad (7.5)$$

indicating the equivalence of the savings-investment gap and the import-export gap. Closing either gap, of course, closes the gap between resources used and resources supplied in an economy. Increasing either gap, on the other hand, requires an increase in foreign indebtedness.

The recent debt crisis is the result of certain countries being unable to close either side of the dual gaps. Explanations vary, but because one of the gaps, investment-saving, is measured in the domestic economy, and the other, imports-exports, is measured in the external economy, both domestic and external causes have been suggested (Corbridge, 1989). The relationship between debt problems and rates of exporting has already been described (see Section 7.2), and related issues of trade and debt have been raised. Peet (1987), for example, argued that much peripheral debt resulted from ill-advised attempts to create export-driven economies as a development strategy. The related industrialization strategies required poorer countries to import expensive capital equipment, but the exports that were produced were not competitive in world markets, due largely to the trade management practices of the Core economies (see Chapter 10). Macroeconomic policies that discourage domestic investment and general governmental interference in the domestic economy have been considered primary causes of severe debt problems (Committee for Economic Development, 1987; World Bank, 1989). Although external causes of debt are emphasized in some cases and domestic causes are emphasized in others, in reality they work with each other in a typical system of spatial interaction.

Perhaps the most contentious type of flow in the international economy, *capital flight,* is frequently linked to problems of international debt. There is no generally accepted definition of capital flight, but in general it is considered to be an outflow of financial capital from a country that is greatly disproportionate to any purpose of geographical diversification of financial portfolios (Williamson and Lessard, 1987). Capital flight can be a severe drain on the stock of domestic savings available to finance capital investment, and it has been considered a significant contributor to the borrowing requirements of countries it affects. Kindleberger (1987) has described the history of capital flight, noting its past occurrences in France, Italy, Germany, and more recently in Latin America. While different specific conditions appeared to precipitate capital flight at different times and from different places, Kindleberger found that a common condition of lack of confidence in government existed in all cases.

About 30 countries have been identified as suffering from capital flight during the 1980s, with Argentina, Mexico, and Venezuela being the most affected (Williamson and Lessard, 1987). Not coincidentally, these three countries have had significant problems of international debt. As in any type of spatial interaction, the flows entailed in capital flight are driven by the nodal characteristics of source and destination. In addition, the flow itself has an effect on the nodal characteristics. Cuddington (1987) found that high real interest rates in the Core, especially in the United States, attracted fleeing capital from Venezuela, Mexico, and Argentina. High American interest rates were particularly attractive because the return on capital placed in the United States was felt to be virtually risk-free. As capital fled those countries, their borrowing had to increase, which in turn led to more capital flight. One explanation for increased borrowing leading to increased capital flight is that holders of financial capital are afraid that higher debt burdens will result in higher tax rates and higher rates of inflation developing as methods of debt reduction.

High taxes and high rates of inflation are two reasons typically mentioned as causes of capital flight (Walter, 1987). In addition to these macroeconomic reasons, problems in domestic financial markets can also effect capital flight. Some governments use domestic financial markets as sources of significant revenue and tools of economic control in a policy that is called *financial repression* (McKinnon and Mathieson, 1981). In general, financially repressed systems have low interest rate ceilings on deposits and loans, and very high reserve requirements. These policies make the government a very important source of financial capital, which it can ration on a political basis. It is the low interest rates on deposits, however, that lead to capital flight in search of higher rates, further shrinking the domestic supply of loanable funds. In this respect, Leite and Sundararajan (1990) have suggested that interest rate management by governments is effective only when domestic rates are fixed reasonably close to international rates.

Dual-gap analysis indicates that foreign debt can be alleviated either by generating a surplus of savings or a foreign trade surplus. While analytically consistent, however, the identity of the two gaps is not always realistic. Zini (1989), for example, has described a fundamental problem of Brazilian foreign debt. During the 1980s, Brazilian debt increased at the same time its merchandise trade balance was running large surpluses. The inconsistency with dual-gap conditions is due to the separation of debt from trade: the debt is held by the government while the trade account is in private hands. This is not always the case, but the degree of sovereign debt in the international economy has led to a decreasing emphasis on a foreign trade remedy to debt problems in favor of other approaches.

The spatial system of the international debt crisis has two basic nodes: the lending Core and the borrowing Periphery. Each node, in turn, can be internally differentiated. Institutionally, Core lenders can be divided between private enterprises such as the commercial banks, and government and quasi-government multilateral institutions such as the IMF and World Bank. Borrowers in the Periphery can be differentiated with respect to income level and geography. These distinctions are expressed in the IMF's listing of 15 heavily indebted countries (International Monetary Fund, 1986). Ten are Latin American countries: Argentina, Bolivia, Brazil, Chile, Colombia, Ecuador, Mexico, Peru, Uruguay, and Venezuela. This geographical concentration is extreme, and the problem of foreign debt continues to be a leading issue in Latin American economic and political policy formulation (Aguilar and Zejan, 1989). Three other heavily indebted countries are in Africa:—Cote d'Ivoire, Morocco, and Nigeria—and the remaining countries are the Philippines and the former Yugoslavia.

The geography of the IMF's list is similar to the geography of severe debt portrayed in Figure 7.2. However, the IMF's list of African countries is limited because it is based on debt volumes more than debt proportions. Essentially, the list of 15 is a list of large heavily indebted countries; it doesn't contain the high number of African countries that are severely indebted in proportional terms but do not carry very large nominal debt burdens (Greene, 1989; Kwasa, 1989). The heavily indebted countries were singled out because their debt burdens posed significant problems to Core-based lenders rather than to growth in their domestic economies. Ultimately, the wealth distinction of peripheral borrowers is between those with middle income and those with low income classifications using the World Bank's system. Geographically, the primary concentrations of borrowers are in middle income countries in Latin America, and mainly low income countries in Africa.

Lewis (1977) has stated that international debt is a problem from the lender's point of view only when interest payments are not made. Repayment of a loan's principal is not important because the money was lent to earn interest and bankers are happy as long as the interest is paid. However, when interest payments are not made, the loan's principal is considered to be threatened as well. This is the making of a debt "crisis," and this is what happened in the early 1980s, especially in Latin American markets. In order for any debt crisis to be reduced to a debt problem, methods of repayment have to be devised and payment schedules have to remade so the safety of the loan's principal is assured and interest payments can resume. For example, the debt crisis that began with Mexico's declaration of a payments moratorium in August 1982 ended in that same month with renegotiation of the structure of Mexican debt and its repayment schedule. Additional rearrangements were made in 1984 and again in 1987, 1989, and 1990 (International Monetary Fund, 1990).

Debt reduction is a problem that is institutionally and geographically complex. Lenders and borrowers act as individuals and within groups. In addition, private, government, and multilateral agencies frequently use coordinated policies to try to alleviate international debt problems, and much of the effort toward debt reduction during the 1980s and the beginning of the 1990s has been of a coordinated nature. Certain innovative practices have been developed for purposes of voluntary debt reduction (Williamson, 1988). The reduction is considered to be voluntary when procedures are adopted at the lender's option, and not coordinated or coerced by a government or multilateral institution. So-called menu approaches to debt reduction were developed in the late 1980s; such approaches allow banks several methods of debt reduction, including simply exiting a market (Diwan and Kletzer, 1992). Conventional forms of debt reduction found in the menus include debt buy-backs, debt exchanges, and debt conversions to equity (International Monetary Fund, 1990).

The benefits of these three forms are as much a function of accounting standards as anything else. Debt buy-backs allow countries to buy their own debt at a discount, usually by issuing new debt. Debt exchanges also are forms of substituting new debt for old. Debt conversions to equity, on the other hand, can contain some real benefits to domestic economies. These programs allow foreign interests to exchange external debt for domestic equities, thereby providing potential for productive investment within the debtor economy. Particularly innovative measures that are variants of debt-to-equity conversions include debt for education exchanges (Czinkota with

Kohn, 1988) and *debt-for-nature swaps* (Moran, 1991). Debt-for-nature swaps allow banks to sell their peripheral country debt at a discount, either in the country itself or in other secondary debt markets. The debt is then cancelled in return for the borrowing country's dedication of land for some kind of environmental preservation. Under this method, for example, rain forest acreage has been set aside for preservation in exchange for the forgiveness of foreign debt.

Voluntary debt reduction is growing in frequency but has not had the large-scale effect of larger coordinated policies. One type of international coordination of debt reduction is represented in the *Paris Club* (Trichet, 1989). The Paris Club is actually an informal forum for establishing international cooperation among lenders and debtors; over time it has facilitated debt reschedulings of about 50 countries. An important feature of the Paris Club is that it recommends the use of different policies for different classes of debtors. Extension of repayment periods and concessional interest rates are stressed for the poorest African countries, while the menu approaches are considered more appropriate to reduce the debt of the higher-income Latin American countries.

The IMF, World Bank, and other multilateral lending institutions are asked to observe at the Paris Club. The largest-scale debt reduction initiatives, however, have required active and concerted efforts by these institutions with private lenders. The two most widely considered comprehensive plans for reducing problematic levels of foreign debt have been designed under the direction of their namesakes, James Baker and Nicholas Brady, each the American Secretary of the Treasury at the time of their plan's inception (Hobbs, 1990). The *Baker Plan*, presented in 1985, called for concerted lending by both commercial banks and the leading multilateral institutions of the IMF and World Bank. The Baker Plan was not well received by either debtors or lenders. Commercial banks, in particular, were not forthcoming with new and increased lending, especially in Latin America (recall from Section 7.6). The *Brady Plan*, presented in 1989, was a modification of the Baker Plan that emphasized debt reduction rather than refinancing. Although the emphasis was changed toward debt reduction, both the Baker and Brady plans focus on domestic growth and domestic capital formation, including the return of flight capital, as the long-term solution to the problem of recurring debt crises in the international economy (*World Financial Markets,* 1988). Both the Baker and Brady plans called for the IMF and World Bank to maintain policies that could facilitate the establishment of strong potential for domestic growth.

Until the mid-1980s, IMF policy generally was to reschedule debt payments over longer terms in order to relieve debt payment problems (Dillon and Oliveros, 1987). Some of the rescheduling was conducted through what is called an *extended fund facility*. In addition, the IMF provided a standby facility to provide short-term relief to countries experiencing a significant shortfall in their balances of payments; extended fund facilities are for longer-term relief. The extended fund facilities were usually offered under what is called *conditionality*. IMF conditionality required those countries that were extended the special facilities to implement policies that would, according to the IMF, improve the balance of payments in a fundamental way (Mosley, 1987). For example, IMF financing might be extended under the condition that a country allows its currency's exchange rate to float, thereby improving exports by currency depreciation. Another condition might be relaxation of policies of financial repression. Essentially, IMF conditionality was an attempt to ensure domestic solutions to the severe external debt problems.

In the mid-1980s, the IMF began to extend *structural adjustment facilities (SAFs),* which were parallel offerings to the World Bank's *structural adjustment loans (SALs)* (Bird, 1989). Both programs complied with the call in the Baker and Brady plans for large-scale reformation in the economies of the highly indebted countries. Essentially, both are loans that provide financing to carry out the conditions required under IMF conditionality. They provide financial resources to governments to supply export incentives and maintain revenues as tax systems are changed. Additional lending by the World Bank consists of *sectoral adjustment loans,* which finance deregulation of agriculture and manufacturing in countries, with the aim of making those sectors competitive domestically and internationally. They also are available to support changes in financial sectors and to provide support for freeing energy prices. An important focus of adjustment lending has been stabilization of prices in indebted countries where high rates of inflation have diminished rates of saving and investment (Dornbusch, 1991). Both IMF and World Bank structural lending and World Bank sectoral lending were used to help solve the Mexican debt problem in the late 1980s and in 1990 (Rodriguez, 1991).

The conditionality of the IMF facilities and the adjustment loans of the World Bank have not been welcomed by all borrowers (Periera, 1989). Many borrowers feel that the IMF and World Bank are imposing on their sovereignty with these new lending regimes. One concern is the fairly strict limits placed on uses of new loans, and the strict limits on government domestic policy. Another concern is that the liberal nature of the rich Core economies cannot be rapidly imposed on the poor Periphery economies where market failure seems to have lead to their poverty (Colclough and Manor, 1992). The World Bank (1991) has pointed to the generally higher profitability of freer markets than of those restricted by governments. Both private and public sector projects, including agricultural ones, have higher rates of return in those countries with less government intervention in markets than in those countries where government is very active in the economy.

Rates of return on various projects, however, are calculated over relatively long terms, while the immediate imposition of conditions can lead to severe short-term problems that the governments and citizens of borrowing countries may not wish to take on. Both conditionality and adjustment lending policies have been controversial in both clusters of indebted countries. African nations in particular have had strong disagreements with the IMF over imposed price changes and removal of subsidies (Mingst, 1990). Further, because most of the government-imposed price distortions affect agriculture, conditions are intertwined with the sectoral adjustment loans of the World Bank so that most new commitments directly result in higher food prices in the short run (Chege, 1992; Perrings, 1989).

Latin American problems with the multilateral agencies have most often concerned conditions imposed on macroeconomic policy that are designed to limit inflation rates (Rubli-Kaiser, 1989). The short-term result of these policies is usually higher unemployment (Feinberg, 1989). This has been the result in Peru, a country that has experienced foreign debt problems for some time (Scheetz, 1986). The strictness of IMF conditions on new lending led to the unilateral relief of the country's debt burden in 1985, as its president at the time, Alan Garcia, limited repayments on foreign loans to 10% of export earnings. The policy may have been justified because debt payments were a significant obstacle to Peru's domestic economic growth (Dornbusch, 1989), but it led to the crash of the Peruvian economy because new foreign capital was cut off. The government simply inflated the money supply to maintain employment and spending, with the ensuing hyperinflation of prices. Subsequently, a new president, Alberto Fujimori, adopted the strict fiscal regime prescribed by the multilateral agencies and Peru again became eligible for a wide range of foreign credits. The cost was high, however, as reduced government spending and employment threw the country into deep economic recession. The level of hardship became so severe that, by 1991, a cholera epidemic had developed in Lima. The outbreak of cholera resulted from an overload on the city's already overburdened sanitation facilities as migrants fled extreme rural poverty and the bloodshed of the rural insurgency of the radical Shining Path.

Despite the volume of lending between Core and Periphery, many of the world's poorest countries receive most of their external financing in the form of aid and grants (World Bank, 1990). A large number of international aid organizations sponsored by multilateral and national public and private agencies provide aid, but most is given by governments as bilateral donors. Ruttan (1989) has cited several motives for grants of foreign aid. One is the simple moral responsibility of rich countries to help poor ones. A related motive is compensation for injustices committed under the rule of colonial empires. All too frequently, aid is tied to specific projects in the form of forgiven loans. This type of aid is really a form of subsidy to the source country's domestic enterprises, because it is granted on the condition it is spent on particular goods produced in the granting country. At one time, a great deal of Japanese foreign aid was considered to be of this type (*World Financial Markets,* 1989A), but much of Japan's aid is now directed through international organizations with no strings attached. Whatever the motive, foreign aid usually falls well short of desired levels. In recent years, only Norway, Denmark, and the Netherlands have granted amounts that approach or exceed 1% of GNP, the target established by the Organization for Economic Cooperation and Development (OECD) (see Chapter 11). It is unlikely that foreign aid will ever be of a sufficient amount to provide significant assistance in the economic development of the Periphery.

REFERENCES

Aguilar, R., and M. Zejan. 1989. "Debt Repayment Capacity in Argentina and Uruguay." In *Economic Development and World Debt,* H. Singer and S. Sharma, eds. (New York: St. Martins Press).

Barret, W., and R. Kolb. 1986. "The Structure of International Bond Risk Differentials." *Journal of International Business Studies* 17: 107–118.

Bird, G. 1989. "World Debt, Financing, Structural Adjustment and the Official Sector." In *Economic Development and World Debt*.

_____. 1991. "Debt, Deficits, and Dollars: The World Economy in 3-D." *World Development* 19: 245–254.

Blackwell Finance. 1991. *The 1991 Handbook of World Stock and Commodity Exchanges* (Oxford: Basil Blackwell).

Cataquet, H. 1989. "Country Risk Management: How to Juggle with Your Arms in a Straitjacket?" In *Economic Development and World Debt*.

Chege, M. 1992. "Remembering Africa." *Foreign Affairs* 71: 146–163.

Choi, K. 1985. *Multinational Banks: Their Identities and their Determinants* (Ann Arbor: UMI Research Press).

Chrystal, K. 1978. *International Money and the Future of the SDR*. Essays in International Finance, no. 128 (Princeton: Princeton University, Department of Economics, International Finance Section).

Cohen, R. 1989. *World Trade and Payments Cycles: The Advance and Retreat of the Postwar Order* (New York: Praeger).

Colclough, C., and J. Manor, eds. 1992. *States and Markets: Neo-liberalism and the Development Policy Debate* (Oxford: Oxford University Press).

Committee for Economic Development. 1987. *Finance and Third World Economic Growth* (New York: Committee for Economic Development).

Conybeare, J. 1990. "On the Repudiation of Sovereign Debt: Sources of Stability and Risk." *Columbia Journal of World Business* 25/1: 46–52.

Corbridge, S. 1989. "Debt, the Nation-State and Theories of the World Economy." In *Horizons in Human Geography*, D. Gregory and R. Walford, eds. (Totawa, New Jersey: Barnes & Noble).

Cosset, J.-C., and J. Roy. 1991. "The Determinants of Country Risk Ratings." *Journal of International Business Studies* 22: 135–142.

Crockett, A., and M. Goldstein. 1987. *Strengthening the International Monetary System: Exchange Rates, Surveillance, and Objective Indicators* (Washington: International Monetary Fund).

Cuddington, J. 1987. "Macroeconomic Determinants of Capital Flight: An Econometric Investigation." In *Capital Flight and Third World Debt*, D. Lessard and J. Williamson, eds. (Washington: Institute for International Economics).

Czinkota, M., with M. Kohn. 1988. *Improving U.S. Competitiveness: Swapping Debt for Education* (Washington: U.S. Department of Commerce, International Trade Administration).

Damanpour, F. 1990. *The Evolution of Foreign Banking Institutions in the United States* (New York: Quorum Books).

_____. 1991. "Developments in the Market Structure and Activities of Foreign Banks in the United States." *Columbia Journal of World Business* 26 (Fall): 58–69.

Davis, R. 1981. "Alternative Techniques for Country Risk Evaluation." *Business Economics* 16/3: 34–41.

Dillon, K., and G. Oliveros. 1987. *Recent Experience with Multilateral Official Debt Rescheduling* (Washington: International Monetary Fund).

Diwan, I., and K. Kletzer. 1992. "Voluntary Choices in Concerted Deals: The Menu Approach to Debt Reduction in Developing Countries." *The World Bank Economic Review* 6: 91–108.

Domar, E. 1950. "Foreign Investment and the Cycle of Payments." *American Economic Review* 40: 805–826.

Dornbusch, R. 1989. *Background Paper, The Road to Recovery*. Report of the Twentieth Century Fund Task Force on International Debt (New York: Priority Press).

———. 1991. "Policies to Move from Stabilization to Growth." In *Proceedings of the World Bank Annual Conference on Development Economics 1990*, S. Fischer, D. de Tray, and S. Shah, eds. (Washington: World Bank).

Dymski, G., and M. Pastor, Jr. 1990. "Bank Lending, Misleading Signals, and the Latin American Debt Crisis." *The International Trade Journal* 6: 151–191.

Economist. 1991A. "The World's Biggest Banks." July 27, p. 90.

———. 1991B. " 'Sisters in the Wood': A survey of the IMF and World Bank." October 12, inset.

———. 1992. "Bank of Credit & Commerce International: Statement by Majority Share-holders." February 29, p. 81.

Eurofi. 1989. *1992-Planning for Financial Services and the Insurance Sector* (London: But-terworths).

Feinberg, R. 1989. "The International Institutions and Latin American Debt." In *Solving the Global Debt Crisis: Strategies and Controversies by Key Stakeholders*, C. Bogdanowicz-Bindert, ed. (New York: Harper & Row).

Feldstein, M. 1985. "The View from North America." In *Global Economic Imbalances*, C. Bergsten, ed. (Washington: Institute for International Economics).

Fisher, F. 1988. *Eurobonds* (London: Euromoney Publications).

Fraser, R. 1987. *The World Financial System* (Burnt Mill, England: Longman).

Goldberg, M., R. Helsley, and M. Levi. 1989. "The Location of International Financial Activity." *Regional Studies* 23: 1–7.

Greene, J. 1989. "The African Debt Problem." In *International Economics and Financial Markets*, R. O'Brien and T. Datta, eds. (Oxford: Oxford University Press).

Halevi, N. 1971. "An Empirical Test of the 'Balance of Payments Stages' Hypothesis." *Journal of International Economics* 1: 103–117.

Harrington, J. 1989. "Implications of the Canada-United States Free Trade Agreement for the Provision of Producer Services." *Economic Geography* 65: 314–328.

Harrod, R. 1973. *Economic Dynamics* (London: Macmillan).

Heldring, F. 1989. "The Debt Crisis: A Regional Bank's Point of View." In *Solving the Global Debt Crisis: Strategies and Controversies by Key Stakeholders*.

Heller, L., ed. 1988. *Eurocommercial Paper* (London: Euromoney Publications).

Hitiris, T. 1988. "U.S. Balance-of-Payments Stages 1790–1985: A Statistical Investigation." *The International Trade Journal* 2: 247–262.

Hobbs, M. 1990. "Debt Policies for an Evolving Crisis." In *The Global Debt Crisis: Forecast-ing for the Future*, S. MacDonald, M. Lindsay, and D. Crum, eds. (London: Pinter Publishers).

Hogendorn, J., and W. Brown. 1979. *The New International Economics* (Reading: Addison-Wesley).

Honeygold, D. 1989. *International Financial Markets* (New York: Nichols Publishing).

Huhne, C. 1989. "Some Lessons of the Debt Crisis: Never Again?" In *International Economics and Financial Markets*.

International Monetary Fund. 1986. *International Capital Markets: Developments and Prospects* (Washington: International Monetary Fund).

————. 1987. *The Role of the SDR in the International Monetary System*. Occasional Paper no. 51 (Washington: International Monetary Fund).

————. 1989. *International Capital Markets: Developments and Prospects* (Washington: International Monetary Fund).

————. 1990. *International Capital Markets: Developments and Prospects* (Washington: International Monetary Fund).

————. 1991. *Balance of Payments Statistics Yearbook,* vol. 42, part 1 (Washington: International Monetary Fund).

————. 1992. *International Financial Statistics Yearbook* (Washington: International Monetary Fund).

Jain, A. 1986. "International Lending Patterns of U.S. Commercial Banks." *Journal of International Business Studies* 17/3: 73–88.

Johnson, R., V. Srinivasan, and P. Bolster. 1990. "Sovereign Debt Ratings: A Judgmental Model Based on the Analytic Hierarchy Process." *Journal of International Business Studies* 21: 95–117.

Katz, M. 1989. "Mexico: Anatomy of a Debt Crisis." In *Economic Development and World Debt*.

Khoury, S. 1985. *Sovereign Debt: A Critical Look at the Causes and the Nature of the Problem*. Essays in International Business, no. 5 (Columbia: Center for International Business Studies, College of Business Administration, University of South Carolina).

Kindleberger, C. 1937, reprinted 1965. *International Short-term Capital Movements*. (New York: Augustus M. Kelley).

Kindleberger, C. 1987. "A Historical Perspective." In *Capital Flight and Third World Debt*.

Korth, C. 1985. *International Business: Environment and Management*. 2d ed. (Englewood Cliffs, New Jersey: Prentice-Hall).

Kwasa, S. 1989. "The Debt Problem of Eastern and Southern Africa." In *Economic Development and World Debt*.

Leite, S., and V. Sundararajan. 1990. "Issues in Interest Rate Management and Liberalization." *IMF Staff Papers* 37: 735–752.

Lewis, A. 1977. *The Evolution of the International Economic Order* (Princeton: Princeton University Press).

Little, I., and J. Mirrlees. 1991. "Project Appraisal and Planning Twenty Years On." In *Proceedings of the World Bank Annual Conference on Development Economics 1990*.

Maxwell, C., and L. Gitman. 1990. "Capital Adequacy and Asset Securitization: An Assessment of the World's Central Banks." *The International Trade Journal* 5: 183–215.

McKinnon, R., and D. Mathieson. 1981. *How to Manage a Repressed Economy*. Essays in International Finance, no. 145 (Princeton: Princeton University, Department of Economics, International Finance Section).

Meerschwam, D. 1989. "International Capital Imbalances: The Demise of Local Financial Boundaries." In *International Economics and Financial Markets*.

Meier, G. 1989. "Misconceptions about External Debt." In *Economic Development and World Debt.*

Miller, M. 1989. "The World Bank and the International Monetary Fund: Roles in and Beyond the Debt Crisis." In *Economic Development and World Debt.*

Mingst, K. 1990. *Politics and the African Development Bank* (Lexington: The University Press of Kentucky).

Moran, K. 1991. "Debt-for-Nature Swaps: U.S. Policy Issues and Options." *Renewable Resources Journal* 9: 19–24.

Mosley, P. 1987. *Conditionality as Bargaining Process: Structural Adjustment Lending, 1980–86.* Essays in International Finance, no. 168 (Princeton: Princeton University, Department of Economics, International Finance Section).

O'Brien, R. 1990. "Introduction—a Perspective on Debt." In *The Global Debt Crisis: Forecasting for the Future.*

Peet, R. 1987. "The New International Division of Labor and Debt Crisis in the Third World." *The Professional Geographer* 39: 172–178.

Pereira, L. 1989. "A Debtor's Approach to the Debt Crisis." In *Solving the Global Debt Crisis: Strategies and Controversies by Key Stakeholders.*

Perrings, C. 1989. "The Adjustment Programme and the Perverse Effects of Poverty in Sub-Saharan Africa." In *Economic Development and World Debt.*

Rodriguez, A. 1991. "Actors in the Latin American Debt Crisis II: International Financial Institutions." In *Latin American Debt in the 1990s: Lessons from the Past and Forecasts for the Future,* S. MacDonald, J. Hughes, and U. Bott, eds. (New York: Praeger).

Rotberg, E. 1989. "The Politics of the Debt Crisis." In *Solving the Global Debt Crisis: Strategies and Controversies by Key Stakeholders.*

Rubli-Kaiser, F. 1989. "The Economic Adjustment Process in Latin America: A Conceptual Evaluation." In *Economic Development and World Debt.*

Ruttan, V. 1989. "Why Foreign Economic Assistance?" *Economic Development and Cultural Change* 37: 411–422.

Sachs, J. 1989. *New Approaches to the Latin American Debt Crisis.* Essays in International Finance, no. 174 (Princeton: Princeton University, Department of Economics, International Finance Section).

Scheetz, T. 1986. *Peru and the International Monetary Fund* (Pittsburgh: University of Pittsburgh Press).

Simonson, M. 1985. "Indebted Developing-Country Prospects and Macroeconomic Policies in the OECD." In *Global Economic Imbalances,* C. Bergsten, ed. (Washington: Institute for International Economics).

Solomon, R. 1990. "An Overview of the International Debt Crisis." in *International Finance and Financial Policy,* H. Stoll, ed. (New York: Quorum Books).

Steinherr, A. 1990. "Financial Innovation, Internationalization, Deregulation and Market Integration in Europe: Why Does it Happen Now?" In *Financial Institutions in Europe under New Competitive Conditions,* D. Fair and C. de Boissieu, eds. (Dordrecht: Kluwer Academic Publishers).

Thirlwall, A. 1977. *Growth and Development.* 2d ed. (New York: John Wiley & Sons).

Trichet, J. 1989. "Official Debt Rescheduling: The Paris Club." In *Solving the Global Debt Crisis: Strategies and Controversies by Key Stakeholders.*

Walter, I. 1987. "The Mechanisms of Capital Flight." In *Capital Flight and Third World Debt*.

Webster, L. 1991. *World Bank Lending for Small and Medium Enterprises: Fifteen Years of Experience*. Discussion Paper No. 113 (Washington: World Bank).

Williamson, J. 1988. *Voluntary Approaches to Debt Relief*. Policy Analyses in International Economics, no. 25 (Washington: Institute for International Economics).

Williamson, J., and D. Lessard. 1987. *Capital Flight: The Problem and Policy Responses*. Policy Analyses in International Economics, no. 23 (Washington: Institute for International Economics).

World Bank. 1989. *World Development Report 1989*. (New York: Oxford University Press).

_____. 1990. *World Development Report 1990*. (New York: Oxford University Press).

_____. 1991. *World Development Report 1991*. (New York: Oxford University Press).

_____. 1992. *World Development Report 1992*. (New York: Oxford University Press).

World Financial Markets. 1988. "LDC Debt Reduction: A Critical Appraisal." December 30, pp. 1–12.

_____. 1989A. "Japan: The World's Leading Foreign Investor." November 10, pp. 1–12.

_____. 1989B. "Government Bonds and Global Diversification." November 22, pp. 1–5.

Yoshitomi, M. 1985. "Japan's View of Current External Imbalances." In *Global Economic Imbalances*.

Zini, A., Jr. 1989. "Brazil at the Crossroads: Foreign Debt and Fiscal Exhaustion." In *International Economics and Financial Markets*.

CHAPTER 8

· · ·

The Location of Foreign
Direct Investment and the
Multinational Corporation

· · ·

8.1 INTRODUCTION

Before the debt crisis of the 1980s, growth in exports was taken by lenders as a form of insurance that loans would be repaid. Much of the debt crisis, however, resulted from a global slowdown in international trade. The decline in trade led to more broadly based solutions to debt problems that require adjustments to the economies of heavily indebted countries. While increasing exports is still the primary focus of most growth policy in both rich and poor countries, other initiatives to establish conditions for domestic growth are being pursued. In the cases of the middle income Latin American economies, these conditions seem best established by reformation of macroeconomic policies to encourage domestic investment. For the poorer African countries, domestic growth may be encouraged more by establishing microeconomic policies that will enhance productivity, particularly in agriculture. Common across both sets of countries, however, is an increasing interest in replacing foreign loans with *foreign direct investment (FDI),* which is the topic of this chapter.

One way to analyze FDI's geographical patterns is to use least-cost location theory. This approach considers FDI primarily as a location-of-production issue. The optimal location of foreign production can be determined by weighing the relative locational costs of a product's inputs and the transportation and other costs of serving a market. Many of the costs of operating in distant countries have been decreasing for some time, allowing an increase in both trade and FDI in the international economy that conforms easily to conventional trade and location theory. Most often, least-cost location theory seems most effective in accounting for FDI flowing from Core to Periphery, but intra-Core flows that are market oriented can also conform to least-cost models.

While least-cost location theory is most applicable to perfectly competitive product markets, much of the international economy is characterized by less perfect competition. Both monopolistic and oligopolistic competitive forms have been cited as rationales for FDI. In these markets, FDI does not so much maximize profits, at least in any short-run sense, as it maintains market share. This type of FDI is more likely to be intra-Core than to flow from Core to Periphery because the world's major markets are, by definition, in the Core. The result of FDI due to oligopolistic reaction is cross-FDI, or FDI in both directions across a pair of countries. This type of cross-investment is also typical of investments that are managed as portfolios. An MNC's collection of productive assets can be managed in a way that reduces its risk by geographical diversification. Even though geographical diversification can be only a secondary aspect of FDI, it indicates that investment theory, as well as location theory, is useful in assessing FDI patterns.

The application of conventional location theory to FDI can be made in a fairly straightforward manner. *Normative location theory* provides rules for determining an optimal location of a firm; for example, with respect to minimizing costs of production. *Positive location theory* provides generalizing frameworks that account for the actual pattern of locations, which are typically suboptimal by normative rules. In either form, location theory is applicable at an international scale. In a normative context, it might be used to determine the best country in which to locate a particular type of production. In a positive context, it may be used to explain, or even predict, the geographical pattern of an individual industry or production in general. Unfortunately, while considerable location theory is applicable at the international scale with only minor modification, much of it must be more thoroughly recast for it to be useful in understanding foreign direct investment. For the most part, location theory comes out of the geographical extension of microeconomic production theory (Isard, 1956), but when considering FDI, we must draw on the geographical extensions of investment theory as well.

This chapter begins by taking up location theory in its two forms. The supply-oriented theory of cost minimization is presented first, and then the demand-oriented revenue maximization theory is discussed. The differentiated market model of revenue maximization theory is related to theories of FDI that are based on the existence of imperfect factor and financial markets, and the market imperfection models are used to provide the link between investment location, production location, and the theory of the firm. That part of the chapter turns more specifically to models of the formation of the MNC as opposed to models of foreign production, and two models that effectively synthesize otherwise distinctive approaches to the location of FDI are described. The discussion then turns from theory to the reality of the recent geography of FDI. Both source and destination countries are considered at the international scale, and current patterns of intranational FDI investment are discussed. The chapter concludes with some consideration of the the role played by FDI in economic development.

8.2   COMPARATIVE COSTS

If FDI was simply foreign "production," then we could expect a map of FDI to approximate closely a map of world output, or simply be a proportional version of a map of country GDP. The same thing could be said if FDI was simply one variety of foreign "investment." When capital controls exercised by governments are taken into account, the location of FDI should be a proportional version of the map of investment, which for practical purposes takes us back to the map of GDP. As shown in Figure 8.1A, the sources of FDI do approximate the map of world GDP, but the destinations shown in Figure 8.1B correspond less so. The difference in the maps brings out the complexity of FDI theory. With respect to the sources of FDI, it may be more useful to think of FDI in the context of investment theory. With respect to FDI destinations, however, it may be more useful to draw on location theory. Whether measured as a stock or as a flow, FDI and source income are more highly correlated than FDI and destination income. Also, while many countries have high correlations between their incoming and outgoing FDI, those correlations are far from perfect. Simply, while there are similarities between sources and destinations of FDI, there must also be some important differences. The role of those differences, as revealed in geographically variable costs of business operations, in affecting the location and volume of FDI are described in this section.

The theory of location is one of *profit maximization*. Producing units, which we will call firms, locate where their profits will be maximized as long as they are operating in a market economy. If firms produce products under conditions of perfect competition, then they are price-takers and can maximize their profits only by operating at the lowest possible cost (Webber, 1972). *Least-cost location theory* attempts to determine the place where operating costs are lowest, which will be the optimal location of the firm.

Alfred Weber (1909) provided the most influential work on least-cost location theory. While many of its particulars are obsolete, its general framework remains very effective for analysis of location problems. Weber's primary focus in cost minimization was reduction of transportation costs. His model considered a production function that can be taken as

$$Q = (M_1, M_2, L, C) \tag{8.1}$$

where Q is output, M_1 and M_2 are two different types of raw materials, L is labor, and C is some fixed demand. The last "factor," C, is not usually taken as a variable in production functions because it is not an input. In spatial production models, however, any factor that has a locational characteristic must be considered in the production function because it has a bearing on the volume of output. In the Weber model, the locations of demand sites, labor supply sites, and raw material sites are limited and punctiform in their geography (Figure 8.2). The firm may require some materials that are ubiquitous, but since these have spatially invariant costs they are

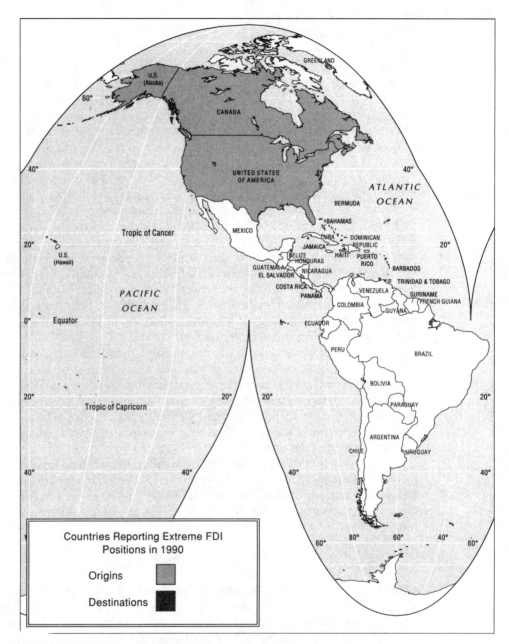

FIGURE 8.1   Countries Reporting Extreme FDI Positions in 1990

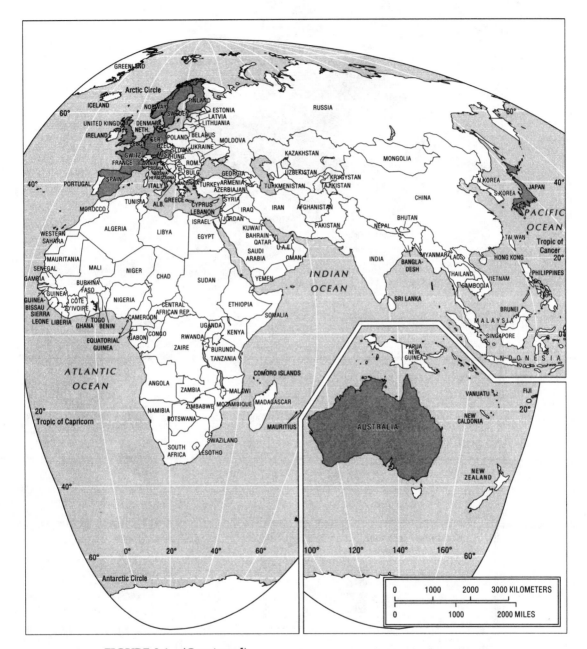

FIGURE 8.1 *(Continued)*

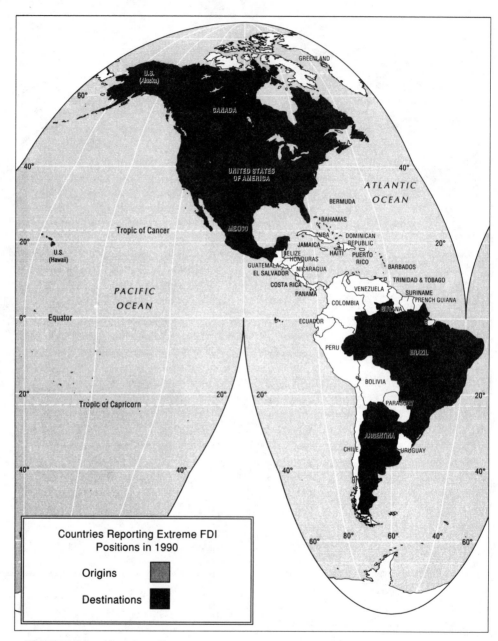

FIGURE 8.1 *(Continued)*

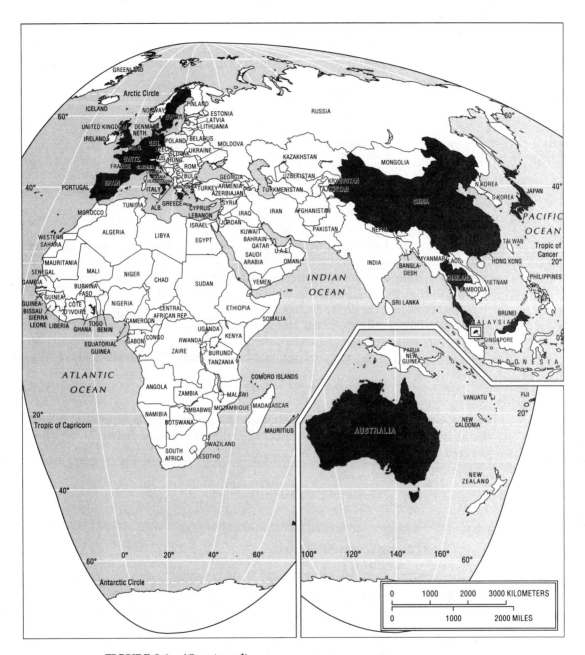

FIGURE 8.1   *(Continued)*

A Potential Distribution of the
Factors of Production in Weber's Model

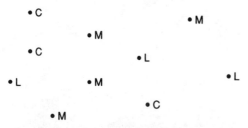

FIGURE 8.2A   A Potential Distribution of the Factors of Production in Weber's Model

not important to the location of production and can be ignored in the production function. The costs of interest in the Weber model are the cost of transporting the raw materials to their point of processing, the cost of transporting the finished product to its point of consumption, and the cost of labor. Weber considered these costs directly in terms of ton-miles of transport, but here they are taken as financial expenditures, such as dollars per mile in a linear cost function.

The optimal location of production is considered primarily with respect to transport costs, t, of raw materials and finished products. That location where

$$(tM_1 + tM_2 + tC) = minimum \tag{8.2}$$

obtains is the optimum point of production. Weber provided a locational rule of thumb in regard to transportation costs called the *material coefficient, M,* which is calculated as follows:

$$M = \frac{(tM_1 + tM_2)}{tC} \tag{8.3}$$

A Potential International Distribution

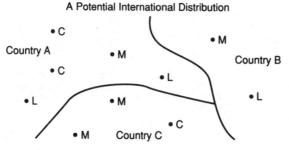

FIGURE 8.2B   A Potential International Distribution of the Factors of Production in Weber's Model

If $M = 1$, then transport charges of raw materials and the finished product are equivalent and nothing can be gained by having the location of production closer to the raw material sites or the site of consumption. However, if $M > 1$, then production is said to have a *material orientation* and is more efficient closer to a raw material site than to the market. If $M < 1$, then production has a *market orientation* and is more efficient closer to the market than to any source of raw materials. The location of the market as a "factor" of production is considered in some detail in the next section.

As mentioned above, labor costs also are considered in Weber's model, but secondarily. Labor costs were not considered simultaneously with the costs of transportation, but as a factor that might draw production away from a site considered optimal with respect to its minimum costs of transportation. For labor, Weber formulated a *labor coefficient, L,* which is calculated thusly:

$$L = \frac{W}{(tM_1 + tM_2 + tC)} \tag{8.4}$$

where W is the cost of labor. If $L = 1$, then labor and transport costs are balanced in such a way that any move toward a site where cheaper labor is available would only increase transport costs. Like the material coefficient, if $L > 1$, then production costs could be lower at a site of an input, in this case labor. However, this determination ultimately rests on the price of labor in relation to the price of transportation. Actually, the critical rule on labor orientation in production should be taken in regard to the decrease in average labor costs, $-\Delta \overline{WQ}$, relative to the increase in average transport costs, $-\Delta \overline{TQ}$, associated with production. Average costs, rather than marginal costs, are of interest because cheap labor is site-specific. It cannot be transported, under the Weber model, so it has no spatially marginal cost in the same way nonubiquitous raw materials and finished products do. If a cheap labor site could make $-\Delta \overline{WQ}/-\Delta \overline{TQ} > 1$, then production should move to that site, otherwise any savings on labor would be overwhelmed by increases in transportation charges.

Weber considered agglomeration economies and savings from cheap labor in the same way, as secondary to transportation costs. Smith (1971) extended Weber's least-cost principles to incorporate such items as government incentives, variations in managerial skill, and consideration of dynamic characteristics in geographically variable costs. The dynamic nature of the geography of costs is very important in affecting some FDI. The long-term trend is a decrease in costs of doing business over long distances. These costs are no different in their locational limitations on firms than the more particular and specific costs of transportation that are the focus of the Weber model. As Dicken's (1986) "enabling technologies" reduce the costs associated with distance (Section 8.5), other costs can be minimized through locational strategies in ways that previously could not have been effective. Due to improved technology, the costs of bringing products to market have generally decreased, as have the costs of procuring raw materials and many other inputs. Hirsch (1989) gave the example of the relatively new link between Europe and Hong Kong. Until recently, both the design and production of so-called designer clothes for the European market took place in Europe. Now, because of the rapidity of international data transmission, this clothing is designed in Europe but manufactured in low-cost Hong Kong. Any changes in specifications of the garments can be transmitted in real time, so despite their physical separation, the designer and sewers are in close business proximity.

Reduction of these costs has led to increase in investment by MNCs at places some distance from more traditional locations of production. Peripheral countries have experienced increases in inward direct investment because their labor costs remain relatively low even as their labor productivity increases. In addition, the Weber model can be taken to work in reverse. Real wages in the Core are increasing at a time when all other costs are decreasing, resulting in the Core's experience of decline in certain types of production, especially that which is labor-intensive. In addition to decreasing distribution and procurement costs, special government incentives allow MNCs to take advantage of cheap labor in Periphery countries, as in the Mexican maquiladoras (South, 1990), in ways not possible before the development of special export processing zones (Chapter 10). Even oil exploration, which must be a material-oriented operation, now has its location determined frequently by preferential tax rates as its other costs become more uniform around the world (Solomon, 1989). In addition to low real wage rates and tax incentives, it is not uncommon for peripheral countries to have less costly regulations concerning environmental degradation (Leonard and Duerksen, 1980). Not all of this type of geographical variation in costs affects location decisions with respect to Core or Periphery only. Recently, high costs of labor, high corporate tax rates, and expensive government regulation of environmental degradation have all been cited as factors in the decline of FDI in Germany in favor of other, lower-cost countries within the EC (*Economist*, 1992). Tax rates, of course, will have to be equalized across the EC if it is to be a true single market. Continuing integration should bring about equalization of exchange rates. The fact that environmental standards vary from country to country is a reflection of the inability of governments to take environmental quality seriously. Hydrological and atmospheric circulation patterns do not recognize political boundaries, nor can environmental regulations if they are to be effective.

If a cheap labor site, or the site of any low-cost factor of production, is located in a different country than other favorable factors of production or the market then there is a potential for FDI. This rationale for FDI within the Weberian framework was developed by Isard (1956) and is portrayed in Figure 8.2B. In this case, the sources of the two raw materials required for production are each in a different country than the market, so the potential for FDI exists from an initial set of conditions. Historically, foreign stocks of raw materials were a major reason for FDI to take place. Many early large MNCs were natural resource companies with interests in developing foreign supplies of petroleum or ferrous and nonferrous ores. FDI in Africa remains significantly driven by raw material requirements of MNCs with headquarters in the Core (Agodo, 1978).

The result of the international distribution of raw materials and the market as portrayed in Figure 8.2B is trade within an MNC, if the distribution leads to FDI.

Raw materials, for example, can be mined by one subsidiary of an MNC in one country and refined by another subsidiary in another country. Due to technological advance, this type of intra-firm trade can become quite sophisticated. For example, the case previously cited concerns the import into Hong Kong of clothing designs, which are a service import. In turn, Hong Kong exports finished clothing to Europe. While the import of the service is technically part of international trade, it is unlikely to be measured or even observed for purposes of customs or the exporting or importing country's current account. This type of trade, although not easily measured, is probably increasing at a rapid rate and frequently takes place within the MNC.

The uneven international distribution of productive factors is the basis for the factor endowment theory of international trade (Chapter 9). That theory also can be considered as a least-cost theory of the location of production (Ohlin, 1933). Recall the production function described in Chapter 3:

$$Q = (K, L) \tag{3.1}$$

where Q is quantity of output, K is the capital input, and L is the labor input. Recall further that production of a good may be relatively intensive in one of the factors; for example, relatively more capital than labor may be employed to produce the good. Production can be divided into groups based on factor intensity. Some goods may be labor intensive, some may be capital intensive, and, to add a third production factor, some may be intensive in the use of natural resources.

At the same time that different industries have different factor intensities, different regions or countries of the world have different factor endowments. Obviously, natural resources are not uniformly distributed over the Earth's surface. Some countries have large reserves of petroleum, others have large reserves of hydroelectric potential, or forests, and so on. Many countries—for example, Japan—have virtually no mineral resources at all. Labor endowments, too, are geographically distributed in an uneven way, and relative labor endowment can be viewed as a correlate of population density. Finally, capital endowments are variable in their distribution, with the variablity generally associated with the Core-Periphery characteristic of the global economy. Core countries, almost by definition, are well-endowed with capital, and peripheral countries are capital-deficient.

Given that a relatively large endowment of a factor in a country means that the factor's price will be relatively low, international specialization of production takes place based on the international economic geography of factor costs. Also note that factor endowment theory assumes perfectly competitive product markets, which allows the least-cost locations of production to be their optimal locations with respect to profit maximization. Importantly, least-cost locations cannot be used comprehensively until international markets are integrated under free trade.

From a least-cost perspective, it seems that foreign trade and FDI are not just substitutes, they are the same thing. For many analytical purposes, the fact that trade is taking place within an MNC or between two different enterprises makes no difference. However, Kojima (1990) has developed a model which shows that FDI based on international differences in factor endowments actually creates trade and is not just a substitute for trade, and induces increased efficiency in both the home and host countries of FDI.

Briefly, Kojima's model takes entreprenurial skill, including technological facility, as a factor of production that is highly mobile. A country well-endowed with entreprenurial skill, however, is unlikely to be well-endowed with the full range of factors of production. In turn, like other factors of production, entreprenurial skill will be in short supply in some countries that are well-endowed with other factors. FDI flows from those countries with high endowments of entreprenurial skill to those countries with shortages of the factor. The application of foreign entreprenurial skill increases the output of the FDI host country, which now is able to export its new surplus to the FDI home country, albeit within the MNC. Resources in the FDI home country can also be used more efficiently because some goods previously produced inefficiently in the home country are now imported. Resources that had been poorly used can be reallocated to the home country's sectors of international comparative advantage. Kojima's FDI model is a model of trade that extends basic factor endowment theory to trade within the MNC. Dunning (1988) has criticized Kojima's model on just this count by noting that factor endowment theory no longer seems particularly relevant to the majority of international trade, including that within the MNC.

Cost minimization also has been used with respect to the timing of FDI. Buckley and Casson (1981), for example, developed a model of FDI timing based on the different costs associated with exporting, licensing the sale of a product in a a foreign market, and FDI. Based largely on the achievement of economies of scale, their model indicates that FDI is a response to a large foreign market. Contractor (1984) found that licensing did decrease in favor of FDI in more lucrative markets, but the alternative of exporting was not considered in his study. This kind of model casts the decision on the method of serving a foreign market in the same mold as the firm's decision to "make, lease, or buy" a piece of capital equipment.

Hirsch (1976) has developed simple rules of cost comparison that can be used by a firm to decide whether to export to a foreign market or begin production there. Let P_A and P_B be the production cost in countries A and B, respectively. Let M be the export-marketing cost differential, taken as the export marketing cost less the domestic marketing cost. Let C be the cost-of-control differential, taken as the cost of controlling foreign operations less the cost of controlling domestic operations. Finally, let K be the value of some intangible type of firm-specific knowledge, not unlike Kojima's entreprenurial skill (see Section 8.4). The cost of K is the cost of replenishing required investment to keep it from becoming obsolete. The firm should export from country A to country B if

$$P_A + M < P_B + K \text{ and } P_A + M < P_B + C \qquad (8.5)$$

that is, if the cost of production at home (P_A) plus the additional cost of serving the foreign market (M) is less than the cost of producing in the foreign market (P_B) plus the use of the special knowledge (K) and less than the cost of producing in the foreign market and the additional cost of controlling the foreign operation (C). The firm should invest in the foreign market if

$$P_A + C < P_B + K \text{ and } P_A + C < P_A + M \tag{8.6}$$

that is, if the cost of producing at home plus the additional cost of controlling foreign operations is less than the cost of producing in the foreign market plus the use of the special knowledge and less than the cost of producing in the home country and the additional cost of serving the foreign market. Notice that as C decreases, as would be expected as enabling technologies improve, then the firm is steered more and more toward FDI as a means of serving a foreign market. Essentially, C represents a type of transaction cost. Like any other transaction cost, its decrease can be expected to bring about an increase in the number of transactions, other things being equal. The transport costs of the Weber model serve the same role and can be considered in the same way. The Hirsch model represents a type of conceptual updating of Weber's model, in both its characterization of critical costs and its international domain.

The comparative-cost approach to FDI usually concerns the location of production, but it can also be considered with respect to the location of investment. In the case of investment, the FDI decision can be taken as a function of a firm's discount rate in evaluating projects (see the appendix). The lower a firm's discount rate, the more profitable any long-term investment is likely to be. Also, if two firms evaluate the same project, the one with the lower discount rate is more likely to find it attractive. With respect to FDI, then, if a lower discount rate prevails in one country compared to another, the country with the lower discount rate can be expected to be an FDI source, and the country with the higher discount rate can be expected to be a destination for FDI. Interestingly, discount rates are usually strongly linked to interest rates, which are mainly functions of financial capital's real supply. Countries well-endowed with financial capital can be expected to have lower interest rates and, therefore, lower prevailing discount rates. In turn, FDI becomes a mechanism toward the equalization of interest rates and supplies of financial capital as FDI flows from capital-abundant sources to capital-deficient destinations.

Graham and Krugman (1989) have not found any evidence to support this *cost of capital model* of FDI, although their examination includes only the recent experience of the United States. They found that FDI in the United States has been increasing systematically over time in apparent disregard of interest rate differentials between the United States and its leading sources of FDI, especially the United Kingdom. Further, Bavishi and Ricks (1981) found that MNCs frequently finance their direct investments in the destination country, which indicates that a lower cost of capital in their headquarters' country was not a basis for the investment decision.

Thus far, the least-cost basis for FDI has been described mainly with respect to minimizing the cost of factors of production such as labor and raw materials. As previously noted, however, Weber's model incorporated the condition that a producer could be market-oriented so that its lowest-cost location could be at or near the market. This condition holds especially if ubiquitous factors of production are used, meaning production costs are geographically uniform. There are geographical variations in costs within the Core, but they are not as great as variations between Core and Periphery. Given that most FDI is intra-Core, it seems that FDI is mostly market-oriented when considered at the national scale. Presence in the American market, for example, is usually the most important location factor cited by foreign-based MNCs operating in the United States (Ajami and Ricks, 1981; Harrington et al., 1986; Schoenberger, 1985; Tong and Walter, 1980). Frequently, FDI in the service sector is a result of the seller of a service attempting to maintain a client that is operating in a foreign country. Many international banks have opened foreign offices to serve foreign subsidiaries of domestic clients (Cho, 1985; Nigh, et al., 1986). For some financial services, such as auditing, governments have restricted this kind of international piggybacking (Bavishi and Wyman, 1983).

The attraction of the market as a production location follows the rule of cost minimization under the Weber model when transport costs are minimized. Harris (1954) wrote the *aggregate travel model,* which defines the optimum location as the place, *i*, where conditions occur that minimize

$$A_i = \sum_{j=1}^{n} Q_j T_{ij} \qquad (8.7)$$

where *A* is the aggregate travel required to serve the markets defined by Q_j, and *T* is a transportation charge. The relation of Harris's to Hirsch's (1976) model is derived by allowing *T* to be expanded to a "cost of control" charge, which can include transport and other costs as well. Because the model is multiplicative, this specification conforms to models such as Buckley's and Casson's (1981) that concern the empirical reality of large markets inducing FDI, as opposed to exports or license agreements. As *Q* becomes large, $Q_j T_{ij}$ must also become large even if average values of T_{ij} are low. Because the least-cost criterion requires A_i be minimized, a large market typically requires that $i = \max j$; that is, the cost-minimizing solution requires production at larger points of consumption. In an international context especially, where costs of serving foreign markets at long distances can be high, a market-oriented product is most likely to be produced at the major markets instead of in just one country.

8.3 MARKET IMPERFECTIONS

The market orientation of FDI does not necessarily develop from attempts to minimize costs in perfectly competitive markets. In fact, a market orientation is more likely to arise from attempts to maximize revenues in imperfectly competitive markets (Webber, 1972). Imperfect markets arise from a number of sources, not least of which is geographical separation of producer and consumer, and the associated costs. In international markets, significant intervention by governments has frequently separated markets as well, and provided a basis for FDI to take place as a direct substitute for exporting. Capital controls, essentially trade restrictions on the flow of finance, have been cited as the basis for the expansion of American banks into Europe (Brimmer and Dahl, 1975). FDI can be used as a hedge against the risk of future trade restrictions. An important reason for establishment of production in the United States by Japanese firms (Chang, 1989; Chernotsky, 1989) was anticipation of stricter limits on import of their products by the U.S. government.

The use of FDI by MNCs in the interest of risk reduction was also suggested by Hartman (1979). His model indicated that MNCs could use their international ownership positions to achieve financial gain by playing off variations in national taxation policies. This kind of geographical manipulation by MNCs is described in Chapter 10, in the context of intra-MNC trade. FDI as a method of risk reduction has also been considered from the viewpoint of contemporary portfolio theory. As described in Chapter 6, portfolio risk is measured as the variation in returns to the aggregated assets of a portfolio. In the case of FDI, the productive assets of an MNC are taken as the portfolio, and their geographical diversification is considered as a method of risk reduction for the MNC. While not a primary motive for FDI, it has been suggested that geographical diversification can provide the same sort of benefits to MNCs that it can to individual investors (Rugman, 1975; Hanink, 1985; Madura and Whyte, 1990).

Actually, reducing the portfolio risk of a corporation's productive assets can take place in three ways: product diversification, export diversification, and multinational diversification (Miller and Pras, 1980). Product diversification can provide stability to a corporation's earnings stream by offsetting demand cycles for individual products. Export diversification does the same thing geographically by using different geographical markets rather than different product markets. Multinational diversification accomplishes the same sort of stability as export diversification, with the added benefit of providing different political and economic environments for production as well as markets. There is some evidence that multinational diversification involving FDI is the most effective method of corporate portfolio risk reduction (Wolf, 1977; Miller and Pras, 1980). Further, Shaked (1986) has found that the probability of failure of an MNC is less than the probability of failure of an equivalent domestic corporation. He also notes that MNCs were better capitalized, which could explain their relative success. Similarly, because product diversification, export diversification, and multinational diversification are not mutually exclusive, much of the evidence for MNC benefits derived from geographical diversification through FDI is not clear-cut (Davidson and McFetridge, 1984; Hisey and Caves, 1985).

The potential benefits of geographical diversification of FDI by MNCs are based on segmentation of markets. Such diversification effects disappear in a world with no variations in factor costs, market preferences, or government policies. However, even if national markets were completely open and free of restrictions, and factor costs were everywhere the same, then geographical markets would be different and, therefore, imperfect as long as there are economies of scale. In addition, whether distance between producer and consumer generates additional costs due to transport charges, other costs of servicing a market over a long distance, or a low level of sales due to unfamiliarity, the separation of geographical markets guarantees at least the potential for geographically differentiated markets.

Almost any good produced has particular characteristics, either real or imagined, that qualitatively differentiate it from its direct competitors at the level of consumption. A general good—breakfast cereal for example—can be differentiated into various products such as corn flakes, wheat flakes, and so on. At a finer level, the corn flakes can be differentiated by brand name, or producer. Corn flakes are inherently quite similar from brand to brand, so producers advertise heavily to convince consumers of the superiority of their product. The superiority may be the result of the product's taste, lower price, or because it appears to be consumed by a popular movie star. The point of differentiating the product is to make consumers have special preferences for one brand over the others, so that one brand is not considered a perfect substitute for any other.

The primary starting point for development of contemporary models of international trade is the theory of differentiated markets. As described in Chapter 9, this theory provides an explanatory base for much of contemporary international trade among the economies of the Core. In addition, it can be used to describe market-oriented FDI, especially because such FDI is heavily intra-Core. The link between market-oriented trade and investment can be illustrated in the context of central place theory (Chapter 4). Recall that the central place models of Christaller (1933) and Lösch (1954) use the concepts of market threshold, or minimum operating scale, and range, which is related to the distance decay of demand functions, to build geographical economies. In their models, the number of products offered at a place increase with the place's size in response to increasing thresholds. High-order, high-threshold places export their high-order goods to low-order, low-threshold places that do not provide sufficient local demand for the production of high-threshold products. The exports are all down a place-size hierarchy and travel relatively short distances because transport charges lead to goods being purchased from the nearest higher-order place where they are available. Each higher-order place in the basic central place models enjoys a spatial monopoly consisting of itself and certain shares of proximal lower-order places, depending upon the spatial configuration of the region in question.

The spatial monopolies of basic central place theory are derived largely from implicitly simplistic consumer preferences that negate any demand in one place for products produced at places of equal or lower order. However, when types of preferences that conform to differentiated markets are considered, trade among places of the same order is expected to occur simply because they have domestic demand schedules that are quite similar, and their markets overlap. Either small market overlaps, or large overlaps among small markets, may be adequately served by exports alone. However, as the overlap increases, or the volume of the overlapping markets increases, a competitive position may require production within the foreign market. In fact, local production would allow the foreign producer to match more closely domestic demand in the foreign market (to more minimally differentiate its product from the majority's taste) and not just supply that market's smaller segment that prefers the import. FDI may be too costly in terms of possible market gains if the majority market in smaller countries is not large, or if market overlaps are small. Norman (1986) has developed a model of FDI in differentiated markets that also predicts a decline of exports in favor of FDI due to competition by foreign producers.

Differentiated market theory also predicts cross-FDI with respect to two large markets. When two markets are large and have considerable overlap, each can be expected to be both a source and destination of FDI between the countries. As described, the markets are effectively similar, and if FDI is appropriate from the viewpoint of a producer in one of the countries, it also will be appropriate from the viewpoint of a producer in the other country. Revenue maximization in a two-country case would yield a locational pattern similar to that calculated by Hotelling (1929) for duopolists in a linear market, except in this case the market is segmented. Hotelling found that the members of a duopoly would cluster together in the center of the market, thereby minimally differentiating by location their otherwise same products. The central location of the duopolists was in spatial equilibrium because movement by either member in either direction would cause that member to lose market share. Again, FDI in international markets allows a more minimal differentiation from majority domestic tastes, and a larger share of the domestic market, than may be achieved by exporting.

Cross-FDI of the sort described above may be expected under a variety of conditions. One of these is related to the analysis of *oligopolistic competition* in international markets. Oligopolies are industries dominated by only a few producers that, in this context, compete over international markets. Like the duopolists considered by Hotelling, oligopolists compete for market share. Frequently, market share considerations are given priority over profit maximization as a goal of the MNC. Hymer (1959) was the first to consider oligopolistic market effects in the international economy, and noted that much of FDI could not be explained by neoclassical models that assume profit maximization. When MNCs temper their goal of profit maximization with efforts to maintain market share, a form of risk-reducing behavior is induced that seems to account for actual patterns of FDI. One of these patterns is cross-investment, which is an unlikely result under a pure neoclassical model. Knickerbocker (1973) noted a *follow the leader* behavior among MNCs in oligopolistic industries, which has also been characterized as an "exchange of threat" (Graham 1978). Basically, FDI by an MNC of one country is considered a disequilibrating move for the oligopoly by its other members. They are required to make a similar investment to restore the balance of market shares. The exchange-of-threat case involves reciprocal FDI, in which a bilateral exchange of FDI takes place between two rival producers' countries. Encarnation (1989) has found that cross-FDI is increasing between Japanese and American firms in just such a rivalistic way. In a more general way, Ryans and Howard (1988) have found a dominant reaction by American MNCs to increasing foreign competition in the United States is to expand more vigorously in foreign markets. These interactions among the largest MNCs in an industry do have a tendency to reduce the differentiation in their products, and many smaller MNCs have been able to compete effectively by maintaining a high degree of product differentiation by what is called *niche marketing* in the international economy (Mascarenhas, 1986).

In addition to an oligopolistic reaction to hold market share, the similarity in the geographical pattern of FDI by MNCs in the same industry may be the result of a type of locational risk reduction. Davidson (1980) found that the geographical realm of the MNC increased significantly with its experience in the international economy. Younger MNCs concentrated their FDI in nearby similar markets, but expanded their locational patterns as they aged. In an interesting parallel, several analyses of the locational preferences of foreign-headquartered MNCs in the United States have also uncovered a type of experience effect in their geography (McConnell, 1980; Glickman and Woodward, 1988; and Bagchi-Sen and Wheeler, 1989). Their locations mirrored those of their American counterparts at first, but after some time in the United States, the longer-established MNCs and more-recent arrivals began to fashion what appear to be more specific locational strategies (see Section 8.6).

The existence of transaction costs is one reason that markets are imperfectly competitive. The costs of distance, for example, are transaction costs that limit factor mobility and create a tendency for the agglomeration of production. When populations and producers are concentrated, the transaction costs of distance are minimized. Minimization of transaction costs is also a reason that firms and corporations exist as collections of economic activities. Coase (1937) developed his theory of the firm around consolidation of activity as a means of reducing transaction costs in markets. He described four types of transaction costs: (1) brokerage costs associated with determining the appropriate price, (2) scheduling costs of integrating production, (3) contract costs of agreements between parties, and (4) exchange costs, such as sales taxes, on transactions. Coase stated that the existence of firms allows these types of costs to be reduced or eliminated. The transaction costs are associated with external markets or exchange between unrelated interests. If the exchanges take place within the firm, in internal markets, the costs do not accrue. However, once firms internalize transactions, it becomes difficult to externalize them with any confidence as to their value.

The *theory of the firm* has been extended with respect to the international economy as the *internalization theory* of the MNC (Rugman, 1980; Calvet, 1981). Kindleberger (1969) used Coase's work to explain the development of the MNC. He argued that technological expertise, in particular, is very difficult to price in a foreign market. A corporation can better maximize the value of its expertise by using the technology itself rather than selling it or renting it through a license to another corporation. MNCs develop, therefore, because internal markets for a corporation's expertise are used during geographical expansion rather than external markets. Hennart (1986), in an analysis of early FDI in tin mining, found that the internalization of superior technology is too limited a concept to explain MNC formation. He found a more general ability to reduce transaction costs that favored European over Chinese tin producers in Malaysia between 1860 and 1920. Other analyses of service sector MNCs seem to bear out this more general approach (Dunning and

Norman, 1983; Boddewyn et al., 1986), because managerial expertise and not technological superiority is at work in these cases. These results conform to Hymer's (1959) argument that FDI takes place in order to gain returns on any monopolistic advantages held by a corporation. The monopolistic advantage could be in technology, but also in any category of superior knowledge such as marketing or other form of special management ability. Buckley (1988) has noted that while internalization theory is promising with respect to analyzing the MNC, it is very difficult to examine empirically because of the complexity of MNC operations.

8.4 SYNTHETIC MODELS

The complexity of the MNC and FDI has led to the development of models that synthesize a number of theories of the firm, production, and investment. One of these models, the product life-cycle model developed by Vernon (1966), is also considered as a model of international trade in Chapter 9. Over a product's life, its design, production, and market characteristics change in such a way that its factor intensity changes. As its factor intensity changes, it will be produced most efficiently in a region that has the appropriate factor abundance. The FDI implications are clear if an MNC maintains its production of the product throughout its life cycle. Early in the cycle, it would be produced by the MNC in one country, but later in the cycle it would be produced in another. The model concerns trade and investment in manufactured products. It does not apply to FDI in raw material extraction (Mullor-Sebastian, 1983), nor does it seem to apply to service sector FDI.

The product life-cycle model suggests four general stages in the life of production and distribution of a good (Figure 8.3). The initial stage is one of product development, during which sales of the good grow at an increasing rate. The second stage consists of refining the production process as the rate of increase in sales begins to

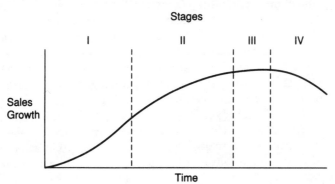

FIGURE 8.3   The Product Life Cycle in International Investment and Trade

decline. The third stage is one of maturity in both production and sales. The production function of the good is standardized, and sales volumes are large but no longer increasing. The last stage of the cycle is one of declining sales, with use of the product diminishing in the face of better alternatives.

In the initial stage of a product's life, its production function is technology- or knowledge-intensive. In the second stage, it is intensive in skilled labor, and in the third, intensive in routine labor. The fourth stage of production is capital-intensive, with the routine labor input replaced by machinery. Because the factor intensities vary by stage of life cycle, comparative advantage must vary geographically with stage of life cycle, too. In the first stage, the good should be exported from countries relatively well endowed with technology. Countries with relatively large endowments of skilled labor should export the good during the second stage, and countries with relatively large general labor endowments should export the good during the third stage. The good should be exported from countries with sufficiently large capital endowments during the fourth stage. Core economies, with their relatively large endowments of technology, skilled labor (human capital), and capital should be the exporters during all but the the third stage. During the third, labor-intensive, stage of production, the primary source of exports should be the Periphery.

The product life-cycle model of FDI synthesizes the internalization theory of the MNC and industrial location theory. Vernon (1966) distinguished the trade effect of the product life cycle from its FDI effect by arguing that foreign production would not take place unless the firm held some monopolistic advantage. Such an advantage would be required because it would be the only source of competitive cost saving to a firm operating in a foreign country. The fact that a country is a least-cost location for production of a product at any stage of the product's life cycle should be apparent to any potential producer. If the lowest-cost place of production is in a foreign country, then that country's producers should be more competitive than any outside entrant if knowledge is uniformly held. If the outside entrant, the MNC, has some special and unique knowledge, then the knowledge itself is a type of internal factor of production. External factors, or those factors widely available, determine places of production. Internal factors determine whether production is conducted by an MNC.

In a revision of his earlier work, Vernon (1979) questioned whether the development of MNCs has limited the applicability of the product life-cycle model to the analysis of FDI. He suggested that MNCs are now in a position to develop production locations in a once-and-for-all sense because of their global networks. Therefore, the sequential nature of production locations is less likely than when MNCs had less geographical spread. Further, the increasing homogeneity of markets seemed to obviate any locational switching within the Core; for instance, from the United States to a location in Western Europe. However, he did not extend his limitation to the poorer countries, and Auty (1984) found evidence of a product life-cycle basis for petrochemical investment switching from Core locations to locations in the Periphery. This kind of locational shift in investment has implications for economic development (Section 8.7).

In a comprehensive approach, Dunning (1977) has developed the *eclectic model* of FDI which synthesizes location theory and the theory of the firm in the same manner as the product life-cycle model, but does not concern international trade. The eclectic model contains three conditions that must be satisfied for a firm to take up FDI (Dunning, 1988, pp. 45–46):

1. *It possesses net ownership-specific advantages vis-a-vis firms of other nationalities in serving particular markets. These ownership advantages largely take the form of the possession of intangible assets, and/or of coordinating or risk-reducing advantages which are, at least for a period of time, exclusive or specific to the firm possessing them.*

2. *Assuming condition one is satisfied, it must be more beneficial to the enterprise possessing these advantages to use them (or their output) itself rather than to sell or lease them to foreign firms; this it does through existing value-added chains or the involvement of new ones. These advantages are called internalization advantages.*

3. *Assuming conditions one and two are satisfied, it must be in the global interests of the enterprise to utilize these advantages in conjunction with at least some factor inputs (including natural resources) outside its home country; otherwise foreign markets would be served entirely by exports and domestic markets by domestic production. These advantages are termed the locational advantages of countries.*

The eclectic model is quite general and is not limited in its implications to manufacturing. Gray and Gray (1981) and Cho (1985) have found it applicable to the service sector in their studies of multinational banking. Unfortunately, its specification in the form of contingencies makes empirical testing difficult (Dunning, 1979). Perhaps its best use is as a representation of the complex combined nature of FDI and the MNC.

8.5   INTERNATIONAL PATTERNS OF FOREIGN DIRECT INVESTMENT

While international portfolio investment has a long history, FDI in significant amounts is a relatively new prospect. The 1920s was the first decade in which FDI became a vital part of the international economy (Organisation for Economic Cooperation and Development [OECD], 1981). FDI continued to grow in the 1930s, despite the global depression. Its growth at that time helps to underscore its difference from portfolio investment, which was much more adversely affected. During the 1920s and 1930s, the United States was the dominant source of FDI, with the United Kingdom running second. Together the two countries comprised the sources of the great majority of FDI around the world. This pattern was maintained in the immediate post-World War II period and through the 1950s as well. In general, both

American and British FDI had two dominant characteristics (OECD, 1981). The first was a concentration of FDI in the primary sector in the Periphery. The second was a concentration of FDI in the Core that involved production of export replacements. As exemplified by textiles in the case of the United Kingdom and autos in the case of the United States, manufacturers in both countries have favored producing in foreign markets rather than exporting from their own countries (the United States and the United Kingdom prefer FDI to trade).

Patterns of FDI began to change in the late 1960s and 1970s in three ways. First, the locational characteristics that typified American and British FDI early on changed as FDI began to be placed more heavily in the Periphery for the purpose of lowering production costs. FDI in the Core also increased during this period of general growth in the international economy, which was facilitated by decreasing capital controls. Another important change was the increased activity of both Germany and Japan as sources of FDI around the world. Other large sources of FDI, especially in the United States, were France, the Netherlands, and Switzerland. Finally, the importance of the primary sector in FDI decreased significantly as otherwise peripheral producer countries, especially members of OPEC, began to take more control of both production and refining of petroleum. Even if the change in the international oil business had not taken place during the 1970s, the primary sector's share of global FDI would have decreased in the face of the rapid growth in manufacturing FDI and in services as well. Growth in service sector FDI was particularly encouraged as international capital controls decreased and financial services became more international (OECD, 1981).

Dicken (1986) has written of the "enabling technologies" that allowed the fairly rapid growth of FDI over the last 20 years. These technologies include improvements in transport and communications. Over time, and despite the petroleum price increases in the 1970s, the cost of transportation has decreased. Materials used in manufactured goods have become lighter, as plastic has replaced metal, for example. Also the products themselves are lighter, as in the case of transistors replacing vacuum tubes. The decrease in weight coupled with increase in container size and speed of shipment have brought about large reductions in transport costs, and these reductions allow other factors in the location of production to become more important (Section 8.3). Recent advances in communications technology, particularly the development of telecommunications, have greatly enhanced control of production or distribution in one country from offices in another country. The advance in communications technology is related to Dicken's second enabling "technology," the contemporary multilocational corporation. These organizations have developed in several forms over time, each of which lends itself to particular approaches to the international economy.

The geographical pattern of sources of FDI in 1990 was predictable in a global economy differentiated by Core and Periphery (Figure 8.1A). Obviously, significant capital-source countries must be those well-endowed with financial capital. Only 17 countries were sources of FDI in amounts greater than U.S. $1 billion in 1990, led by Italy which was the source of over $59 billion (International Monetary Fund, 1991). The United Kingdom was the source of the second largest amount, over $48 billion.

France, at nearly $35 billion, and the United States, at over $33 billion, were the other countries serving as origins for over U.S. $30 billion in 1990.

The pattern of destinations of large amounts of FDI is more complex than the geographical pattern of sources (Figure 8.1B). The Core is the dominant regional destination, but countries of the Periphery were also included among the leading destinations of FDI in 1990. Italy was the leading destination of FDI in 1990, as well as the leading origin. According to the International Monetary Fund (1991), Italy's net position in FDI was zero. The United States ($37 billion), the United Kingdom ($33 billion), Spain ($13 billion), and France (more than $12.7 billion) were the other destinations of FDI in amounts greater than $10 billion. Countries in the Periphery that were destinations of over $1 billion in 1990 were China (about $3.5 billion), Malaysia ($2.9 billion), Mexico ($2.6 billion), Thailand ($2.4 billion), Argentina ($2.0 billion), and Brazil (nearly $1.3 billion).

The peripheral countries, however, were generally exceptions. Globally, the correlation between incoming and outgoing FDI in 1990 was 0.769, which indicates that countries received proportionally about as much FDI as they sent. The flow of FDI in 1990 was predominately within the Core, the same geographical pattern as that of portfolio investment. The intra-Core flow is further illustrated in an examination of average values of FDI within the World Bank Income Groups (Table 8.1). The average flows in 1990, given as transactions, were about U.S. $3.5 billion of outgoing FDI and just under $2.8 billion of incoming FDI. The average country, therefore, was a net positive source of direct investment capital around the world. The average countries of all but the high income group, however, had much lower flows of FDI in both directions and significantly higher amounts of incoming rather than outgoing FDI. The high income countries, on average, were sources of almost $12.5 billion in FDI and destinations of just over $9.4 billion. Again, as expected, the rich countries were the net sources of FDI in 1990.

The same pattern is evident in an examination of stocks of FDI in 1990 (Table 8.1B). The transaction data concerns flows for one year, but the stocks are accumulations, the sums of all FDI. Unfortunately, data on FDI stocks are fairly thin when compared to the data on transactions. In fact, no stock data were recorded for any of the low income countries in 1990. The average country in the middle income groups was a net repository of FDI stocks. Stock values of FDI were much greater in the high income countries, on average, and their net positions showed them to be sources of about $9 billion in FDI stocks. Again, it seems that most financial capital is held within the capital sources and does not seem to flow well between Core and Periphery. The World Bank (1991A), however, has found that FDI is being used more often now as a replacement for debt financing, especially in the Periphery where the problem of debt is most severe. The flows between Core and Periphery and the effects of FDI in economic development are considered in more detail in Section 8.7.

Like the other forms of international finance, lending and portfolio investment, FDI is important to the international economy, but its value is much less than the value of merchandise trade. Even after five years (1985–1989) of growth at a rate three times that of trade in goods (United Nations Center on Transnational Corpora-

TABLE 8.1   Mean Foreign Direct Investment by World Bank Income Group, 1990*

A. Transactions

Income Group	Outgoing	Incoming
All	3,482.9	2,771.5
Low	38.0	291.4
Low Middle	12.1	414.4
High Middle	174.7	625.6
High	12,517.5	9,402.9

B. Stocks

Income Group	Outgoing	Incoming
All	79,911.2	74,508.4
Low	nr	nr
Low Middle	266.0	2,510.0
High Middle	3,685.0	5,986.0
High	115,181.1	106,286.9

* In $U.S. 1,000,000. "nr" means none reported.
Source of original data: International Monetary Fund. 1991. *Balance of Payments Statistics Yearbook 1991*, vol. 42 (Washington: International Monetary Fund).

tions, 1991), FDI transactions in 1990 were about $280 billion, only 7% of the value of merchandise trade. The relative importance of FDI and trade varies, of course, from country to country. The trade and direct investment flows of the countries listed in Table 8.2, however, do underscore the general consistency of the flows' relative importance. Although the proportions vary, each case listed has significantly greater flows in trade than in direct investment.

American transactions in FDI were net negative (incoming − outgoing) in 1990. (Recall from Chapter 4 that in the capital account of the balance of payments, incoming FDI is carried as a debit and outgoing FDI is listed as a credit.) In fact, America's net position in FDI stocks had been decreasing steadily since 1972 (Graham and Krugman, 1989). Much of the decline in the net American position was due to increasing FDI in the United States rather than any decline in American FDI abroad. The growth of FDI in the United States was fastest in the 1970s and seems to have taken place more slowly in the 1980s as portfolio investment increased. Arpan and Ricks (1981) found that the rapid influx of FDI in the United States was due to several factors, including the general growth of MNCs around the world and their interest in competing in American markets.

TABLE 8.2   Values of Foreign Direct Investment and Merchandise Trade of Selected Countries, 1990*

Income Group	Foreign Direct Investment		Merchandise Trade	
	Outgoing	Incoming	Exports	Imports
Australia	1,751	7,086	35,973	39,740
West Germany	22,520	1,430	397,912	341,248
Japan	48,050	1,760	286,768	231,223
Republic of Korea	820	715	64,837	69,585
Thailand	140	2,376	23,002	33,129
Nigeria	0	588	13,671	5,688
France	34,778	12,733	209,491	232,525
United Kingdom	21,497	33,392	185,891	224,914
United States	33,440	37,190	371,466	515,635

* In $U.S. 1,000,000.

Source: International Monetary Fund. 1991. *Balance of Payments Statistics Yearbook 1991*, vol. 42 (Washington: International Monetary Fund).

American patterns seem to correspond to global patterns of Core and Periphery distributions of FDI. Stocks of FDI, as calculated on a historical cost basis (United States Department of Commerce, 1991), are allocated in a typical way across the World Bank Income Groups (Table 8.3). Due to accounting differences, these numbers are not directly comparable to those reported by the IMF. They do show, however, that both outgoing and incoming FDI in 1990 flowed mainly within the Core. As in the international case, American FDI was highly correlated between source and destination; the correlation between outgoing and incoming FDI was 0.747 in 1990. During the 1980s the concentration of American FDI in the Core increased, on average, by a larger amount than in any of the other income groups. The relative increment of incoming FDI from the average high income country was not as dominant, but Core interests, on average, had stocks of FDI in the United States more than 35 times the value of the average country in the second-place high middle income group. Importantly, by 1990 the average high income country held greater stocks of FDI in the United States than American interests held in it (United States Department of Commerce, 1991).

The United Kingdom was the single largest source of FDI in the United States in 1990, with stocks of over $108 billion. Japan was in second place. Other countries that held over $5 billion in FDI stocks in the United States in 1990 were the Netherlands, Canada, West Germany, Switzerland, France, Australia, and Sweden. In 1990, American interests held stocks of FDI of over $10 billion in 10 countries. The largest stock was in Canada, at almost $68 billion; the list included the United Kingdom, West Germany, Switzerland, Japan, and Netherlands, France, Australia, Italy, and Brazil (the only non-Core country on the list).

TABLE 8.3   Mean American
Foreign Direct Investment by World
Bank Income Group, 1990*

Income Group	Outgoing	Incoming
All	3,804	4,876
Low	191	38
Low Middle	798	42
High Middle	2,046	443
High	13,251	15,738

* In $U.S. 1,000,000.

Source of original data: United States Department
of Commerce. 1991. *Survey of Current Business*
71/8. (Washington: U.S. Government Printing
Office).

Data on the sectoral composition of global FDI are not available for comparison, but the data on the sectoral composition of American FDI are interesting in their own right. As might be expected given the sectoral composition of the American economy, both FDI in the United States and American FDI abroad had their smallest shares in the primary sector, intermediate shares in the secondary sector, and largest shares in the tertiary sector in 1990 (Table 8.4). The nominal proportions, however, do not correspond all that closely to the sectoral employment or national income shares of the American economy. The primary sector is overrepresented in both outgoing and incoming FDI, but that can be attributed to the importance of the petroleum industry in the international economy, and the fact that the largest oil companies have long been MNCs.

The more interesting disparity is between the shares of FDI, especially incoming, in the secondary and tertiary sectors. The share of FDI seems disproportionately large in the secondary sector and, concomitantly, disproportionately small in the tertiary sector. The apparent overstock of investment on both sides of the secondary sector implies two important things. First, foreign manufacturers seem to think that they can do better than American manufacturers within the United States; at the same time, it appears that American manufacturers think that they can do better outside the United States than within it. Second, the amount of FDI held by foreign interests in the United States indicates that export and FDI are not simple substitutes. If they were, it would be expected that the secondary sector would have an understock of FDI as manufacturers produced at home or in a low-cost country for export to the American market. The substitutability of trade for FDI is also called into question by the understock of FDI in services in the United States. Although tertiary sector FDI in the United States had been growing since the mid-1970s (Bagchi-Sen and Wheeler, 1989), it declined proportionately between 1987 and 1990 compared to manufacturing (United States Department of Commerce, 1991). There is much less trade in services than in

**TABLE 8.4   Sectoral Allocations
of American Foreign Direct
Investment, 1990***

Sectors	Outgoing	Incoming
Primary	65,490	49,448
Secondary	168,220	159,998
Tertiary	187,784	194,289
TOTAL	421,494	403,735

* In $U.S. 1,000,000.

Source of original data: United States Department
of Commerce. 1991. *Survey of Current Business*
71/8. (Washington: U.S. Government Printing
Office).

merchandise, even though the tertiary, or service, sector is much larger than the secondary, or manufacturing, sector in the United States. The disparity could be accounted for by a large stock of tertiary sector FDI in the United States, but the opposite seems to hold. It appears that, due to a combination of market forces and government regulation, services remain close in aggregate to the "home good" of economic theory.

So far, the homogeneity of international patterns of FDI has been stressed, especially with respect to the general distributions across Core and Periphery. As Green (1990, p. 53) has stated, "The core-periphery model is a reflection of the distribution of corporations." This statement refers primarily to the concentration of corporate headquarters in Core regions and their branch operations in the Periphery. There are, however, important distinctions within this general geography, resulting from variations in the types and sizes of enterprises pursued by individual MNCs (Stopford and Wells, 1972; Egelhoff, 1980). There also appears to be a regional bias to the geographical patterns of FDI when national sources are considered.

In its analysis of recent geographical patterns of FDI, the United Nations Center on Transnational Corporations (1991) found the typical pattern of intra-Core and Core-to-Periphery investment. Data for 1988 show significant stocks of FDI held in the United States by EC interests, and vice versa. Smaller but still significant cross-holdings existed between the United States and Japan, and Japan and the EC; again, the bulk of FDI is within the Core. In addition to the intra-Core holdings, each primary source—the United States, EC, and Japan—also had significant geographical clusters of FDI in the Periphery. American FDI was in South America, the EC's was in Eastern Europe, and Japan's was in East Asia. Each of the clusters was dominated by its major source of FDI, and with the exception of European FDI in Brazil, regional overlap among the sources was rare.

The FDI clusters in the Periphery have an obvious geographical basis, but there is an additional factor in their composition. The peripheral clusters that formed in the case of American and EC FDI were developed as low-cost platforms for export to Core economies as well as markets in their own right. Until recently, however, market penetration was not a dominant rationale for Japanese FDI. The sourcing strategies of Japanese MNCs typically have been different than their European and American counterparts (Kogut, 1984; Kotabe and Omura, 1989). Rather than produce in foreign markets, the Japanese more often tried to achieve economies of scale in centralized production in Japan. This type of export strategy led to low proportions of manufacturing FDI unless the manufacturing was tied to cheap sources of raw materials (Dicken, 1986; Kojima, 1990). Recent Japanese FDI has been more market-oriented. For example, large investment in automotive production has been made in both England and the United States recently. The investment, however, was driven in large part by anticipated barriers to auto imports from Japan in both the EC and the United States.

Although its value is small in proportion to the global total (Table 8.1), FDI originating in the Periphery has been increasing. Among the non-oil-exporting peripheral countries, Brazil, the Philippines, and the Republic of Korea became sources of fairly large volumes of FDI during the last half of the 1970s (Committee for Economic Development, 1987). Korean MNCs do not appear to have followed any type of Japanese model in their FDI allocations. The initial investments of the large Korean MNCs, or *chaebol* (see Chapter 11), were made regionally, but in the interest of lowering production costs rather than procuring raw materials. A majority of early FDI was located in Indonesia and Thailand (Kumar and Kim, 1984). While cost reduction remains the primary motive for Korean FDI, the development of American export markets by Korean MNCs suggests that Korean manufacturing investment in the United States is likely in the near future (Chao, 1989).

8.6 INTRANATIONAL PATTERNS OF FOREIGN DIRECT INVESTMENT

FDI flows from Core to Periphery are increasingly targeted toward improving market accessibility. Traditionally, however, FDI following this general geographic flow was conducted in the interest of either gaining direct access to primary products, especially industrial raw materials, or, more recently, lowering production costs by the use of the Periphery's large supply of cheap labor. The attraction of markets is stronger than the attraction of cost minimization, so intra-Core FDI is much greater than FDI flowing from Core to Periphery. Because of different motives for FDI between Core and Periphery, the location of FDI within these regions presents different patterns as well.

As described in Section 8.3, MNCs have tended to "follow the leader" in their Core country location strategies. That is, their initial locations are typically within one of the leading industrial agglomerations of the foreign country (McConnell,

1980). Murphy (1992) has found a similar pattern of initial investment by Western European concerns in Eastern Europe. Large cities and other traditionally industrial regions in Czechoslovakia, Hungary, and Poland are the sites of most FDI. Over time, however, MNCs apparently become more confident of their ability to operate independently, and the geographical concentration of FDI begins to diminish as new investment locations are chosen using more precise criteria (Glickman and Woodward, 1988). Large-scale manufacturing FDI by the Japanese in the United States is relatively new, and appears to be distributed in about the same pattern as American manufacturing in general (Chang, 1989). This has been true of the general pattern of FDI by Japanese auto producers in the United States. Their investments have been concentrated regionally within the midwestern "automobile alley" that has been the traditional center of American automobile production. Within the region, however, more rural sites have been selected by Japanese producers in the interest of accessibility to more "flexible" labor supplies (Mair et al., 1988). General Motors followed this locational strategy in siting its Saturn plant in rural Tennessee. The Japanese have also selected sites of nontraditional automotive labor for their car production in the United Kingdom (Jones and North, 1991). Within certain sectors, however, Japanese investment has led to more comprehensive changes in manufacturing geography. For example, Florida and Kenney (1992) have described the Japenese-led westward shift of the American steel industry that occurred during the second half of the 1980s.

Japanese investment patterns are not always typical of FDI within the United States. Just as at the global scale, different sources of FDI have different locational preferences within broader regional aggregations. O'hUallachain and Reid (1992) found similarities as well as important differences in FDI locational patterns when sources of investment were considered. For example, their analysis confirmed the general pattern of decentralization of FDI in the United States over time, but found that this process was marked largely by Canadian and Japanese investment. At the same time general deconcentration was occurring, both European and Latin American FDI in the United States was becoming more spatially concentrated. A regional bias for FDI locations also was found to exist. Japanese FDI was greatest on the West Coast, and European investment was found to be most concentrated on the East Coast. Latin American FDI had its greatest levels in the Southern states, and Canadian investment was found to have its largest proportion along the U.S.-Canadian border. The use of border locations of FDI by smaller Canadian investors is a common locational strategy (Harrington et al., 1986). Much of this type of FDI is related to servicing exports and is located near ports of entry.

Border concentrations of FDI also are common in peripheral countries, but not for the same reason that they exist in Core economies such as the United States. A large proportion of FDI in the Periphery is located in *export processing zones (EPZs)* which have been developed by governments in the interest of generating demand for labor. The *maquiladora zone* of Mexico, which runs the length of that country's border with the United States, has been granted special status by the Mexican government with respect to production for export to the United States (South, 1990). Similar arrangements exist in other Latin American countries, although on smaller scales

(Grosse and Aramburu, 1991). Due to segmentation in labor markets, the EPZs offer cheap labor on a real basis, and their border/coastal positions help minimize transportation costs of their exports. EPZs are common around the world and have become significant centers of manufacturing in Malaysia (Thrift and Taylor, 1989), and in the People's Republic of China on its coast between Hong Kong and Shanghai (Leung, 1990; Fan, 1992).

Incomes are significantly higher in EPZs than in other parts of their nations' economies, but the impact of EPZs on their national economies usually is not large. For the most part, MNCs that use these enclaves use them in virtual isolation. Linkages with other parts of the MNC are international, so spatial spillovers outside the EPZ to the rest of the host economy are unusual. Without such linkages, dispersal of economic benefits are unlikely (Yannopoulos and Dunning, 1976; O'hUallachain, 1984). Ironically, segregation from the national economies in which they are located is a primary ingredient of the success of EPZs.

The World Bank (1992) has found that permitting 100% foreign ownership of enterprises, full repatriation of profits, and imports of inputs and capital equipment without customs duties or other restrictions are important factors of EPZ success. They are also factors that limit the size of any export multiplier (see Chapter 4) in an economy because internal linkages are avoided. For practical purposes, much of the service sector of an EPZ is located in another country. The most segregated EPZs are not too different in economic effect from the mining enclaves developed in the Periphery during the colonial era. Raw materials were extracted without processing from peripheral sites. Instead of raw materials, the effective export of many EPZs is cheap labor (Suarez-Villa, 1984). Unfortunately, the export of factors rarely is found to provide long-term economic benefits.

8.7 FOREIGN DIRECT INVESTMENT AND ECONOMIC DEVELOPMENT

EPZs are not well-integrated with the rest of their national economies, but at the international scale they serve to integrate those economies with the rest of the world. If integration is a process that eventually yields development, then the integrating role of EPZs may be their most important contribution to economic development in the Periphery. It has been suggested that MNCs play the leading role in integrating the Core and Periphery by their globalization of production (World Bank, 1991A). Output from EPZs and other locations in the Periphery is coordinated with that of other sources in sophisticated networks that require high degrees of coordination. MNCs have been suggested as the most effective means of overcoming barriers between countries based on culture or distance (Travis and Crum, 1984), and their abilities to integrate markets have been described as integral to the process of economic development in the Periphery (van Dam, 1979; Mentzner and Samli, 1981). By any measure, MNCs provide links between countries that would not likely exist in their absence, and many of these links are between rich and poor countries. Whether the linkages are beneficial to peripheral countries, however, is not a clear-cut case.

The effects of FDI can be divided into two classes. One class contains flow effects; the other contains the domestic effects of FDI and the MNC. One supposed benefit to an economy consists of the contributions made by MNCs to a poorer country's balance of payments (Committee for Economic Development, 1987). For example, even a poorly integrated EPZ does bring in foreign payments which can, in turn, be used to pay for imports. Another supposed benefit of FDI and the presence of MNCs in an economy is facilitation of trade (Graham and Krugman, 1989). Trade is beneficial to any economy (see Chapter 9), so the facilitating role of MNCs is beneficial as well. The internal markets of MNCs decrease transaction costs and allow transfers of products and knowledge, or innovations, despite the lack of well-defined external markets. Recall that MNCs have been suggested as a useful mode of technology transfer from rich to poor countries in their internal diffusion of innovations (Chapter 4). In a related sense, product life cycle is also diffused in a type of externally based modernization of domestic industry (Krugman, 1979). The establishment of standardized production processes in peripheral regions by MNCs sets the stage for development of more advanced forms of production, either by domestic enterprises or by the MNCs themselves.

Each argument supporting the benefits brought by FDI to an economy's international flows has been countered by arguments that the net effect of FDI is negative (Corbridge, 1986; Jenkins, 1987). For example, the case can be made that MNCs cause deterioration of a host country's balance of payments over the longer run as they repatriate profits to their headquarters' country. In addition, they do not increase the flow of trade but simply replace domestic interests. Further, the diffusion of knowledge within an MNC is rarely beneficial to a host country on the Periphery for several reasons, including its limited rate of diffusion beyond the Core, and problems with its adoption when it is diffused to the Periphery (see Chapter 4). The potential for both the market and technology diffusions embodied in an MNC's product life-cycle geography have also been questioned (Storper, 1985; Schoenberger, 1988). The oligopolistic nature of many MNCs indicates that cost competition of the sort that would drive much of the product life-cycle's geography is not that important at the international scale. Further, when cost minimization is the competitive strategy, production in the Periphery is confined to EPZs and other enclaves from which positive spillovers are limited (Hansen, 1988).

The positive domestic impacts of FDI include the ability of MNCs to more efficiently use existing domestic factors (Hogendoorn and Brown, 1979; Jenkins, 1987). For example, the existence of the EPZs is based on the ability of foreign corporations to employ domestic labor more effectively than domestic enterprises. In addition, FDI, in and of itself, is a positive increment to a country's stock of productive capital. Of the basic types of investment, direct and portfolio, direct investment provides the greatest increment to capital resources on the Periphery. In 1990, on average, net portfolio investment in the low income and low middle Income countries was negative (Table 8.5). Direct investment flows, on the other hand, had average characteristics that would be beneficial to economic development on the Periphery, at least with respect to the location of capital formation. The High Income countries, on average, had direct investment net outflows while the average country in each of the other income groups was a net recipient of FDI.

As in the case of flows, there also are arguments that the domestic impacts of FDI and MNCs are actually negative. With respect to more efficient resource utilization by MNCs, the argument is made that MNCs simply crowd out domestically generated employment. Again, the MNCs are not supplementing existing activity, but simply replacing it. With respect to investment inflows, it has been suggested that FDI is a form of recolonization of the Periphery by interests of the Core (Corbridge, 1986; Jenkins, 1987). National sovereignty, according to this line of thinking, is being exchanged for the illusory benefits of FDI. In addition, the cultural clashes engendered by large-scale capital flows from Core to Periphery can be causes of severe social disruptions as traditional systems are forcibly westernized (Alexander and Swinth, 1987).

Despite the arguments that FDI, in effect, drains resources, and that MNCs are antagonistic toward the political and developmental processes of poorer countries, the recent trend is toward encouragement of direct investment by governments of the Periphery (International Montary Fund, 1986). Tax rates on foreign investors and government restrictions on investment sectors and equity proportions have been decreasing in Africa, Asia, and Latin America (Moran, 1992). Certainly, some of this encouragement is due to the unavailability of loans in the wake of the debt crisis, but much of it is due to changing patterns of negotiation and interaction between MNCs and national governments of the Periphery (Afriyie, 1992).

TABLE 8.5   Mean Net Foreign
Investment by World Bank
Income Group, 1990*

Income Group	Direct Investment	Portfolio Investment
All	−431.8	−71.3
Low	166.0	−8.2
Low Middle	334.7	−25.6
High Middle	417.8	557.1
High	−2,991.3	−685.1

* In $U.S. 1,000,000.

Source of original data: International Monetary Fund. 1992. International Financial Statistics Yearbook 1992, vol. 42 (Washington: International Monetary Fund).

In the 1950s and 1960s, the most visible interaction between national governments and MNCs was nationalization of foreign-owned interests (Williams, 1975). Nationalization and other forms of expropriation of MNC operations had decreased considerably by the late 1970s (Minor, 1990), but the general relationship remained adversarial and restrictive (Das, 1981; Salehizadeh, 1983). By the 1980s, however, integration of MNCs and their host countries was being significantly enhanced by the increasing establishment of joint ventures, with either private or official domestic interests forming partnerships with MNCs. Initially, such partnerships were required by governments (Franko, 1989), but now they are often sought out by MNCs because local partners frequently enjoy special treatment not available to foreign corporations, and they have better knowledge of local markets.

Politics aside (if only!), FDI from Core sources is a vital but relatively small part of the mix of factors that can lead to economic development in the Periphery. Its contribution to total investment in any economy is typically limited (Table 8.6). In 1990, the low middle income countries received direct investment from foreign sources that averaged 5.5% of total investment, but the low income countries received the equivalent of only 3% of total investment. Only a few countries had incoming FDI over 5% of their total investment in 1990 (Figure 8.4). After Singapore, Australia, and the European countries are considered, the list is reduced to about twenty countries around the world. In 1990, only five of the countries with high proportions of FDI were African. Unlike the situation in Latin America, FDI in Africa is not replacing lending as a form of financial linkage between Core and Periphery. It seems that FDI, as well as foreign lending, is being reduced in Africa (Coughlin, 1990).

TABLE 8.6   Mean Net Foreign Direct Investment as a Proportion of GDP and of Total Investment by World Bank Income Group, 1990

Income Group	Net Foreign Direct Investment as a Proportion of:	
	GDP	Investment
All	0.7%	3.0%
Low	0.6%	2.9%
Low Middle	1.2%	5.5%
High Middle	0.6%	2.7%
High	0.03%	0.2%

Source of original data: International Monetary Fund. 1992. *International Financial Statistics Yearbook 1992,* vol. 42 (Washington: International Monetary Fund).

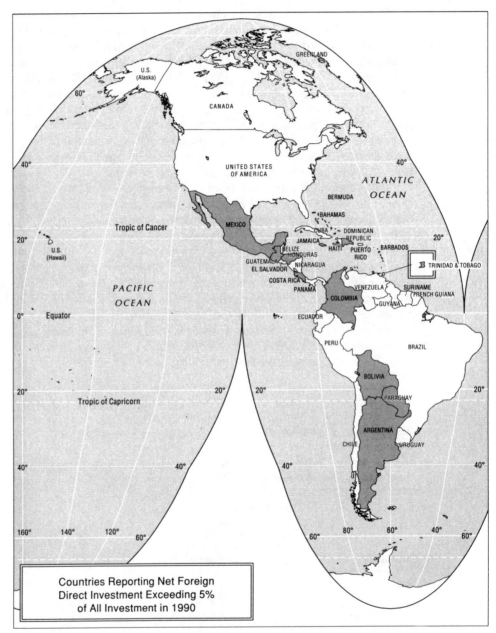

FIGURE 8.4   Countries Reporting Net Foreign Direct Investment Exceeding 5% of All Investment in 1990

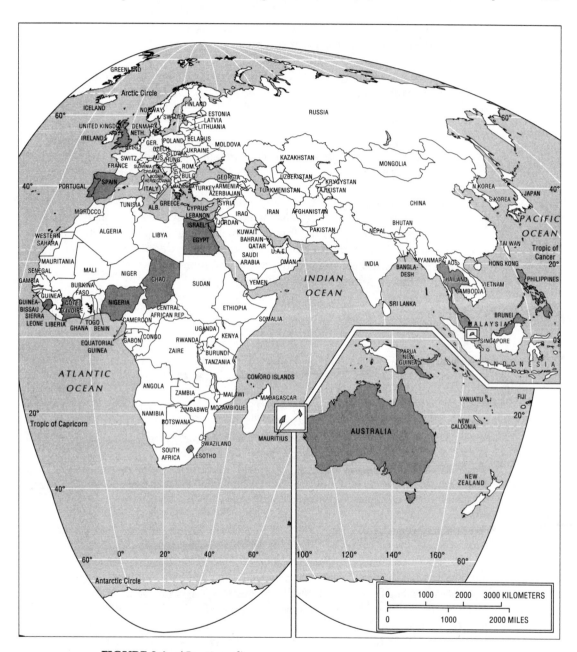

FIGURE 8.4   *(Continued)*

Writing some time ago, Ffrench-Davis and Arancibia (1972, pp. 384–5) described some important lessons that still hold:

a) *The amount of foreign capital that Latin America requires to begin its path to development inevitably leads to the impossibility of relying on this alternative. A substantial increase in the domestic savings rate . . . seems to be the main task for any underdeveloped country.*

b) *Foreign capital should only be considered as the complement to the domestic effort. . . . direct investment (can be) taken as the means of access to technological and management knowledge and to external markets. . . .*

These points are not dissimilar from the findings of the World Bank (1991B), which indicated that foreign investment aided an economy most when it could be deployed within a domestic economy that allowed microeconomic competition, enjoyed macroeconomic stability, and invested heavily in human capital. The international flow of finance is important to economic growth and development, but the most important conditions for growth seem to be established within an economy.

REFERENCES

Afriyie, K. 1991. "Enhancing FDI and Value-Added Production in Developing Economies: Governments, MNEs, and Development Agencies." *The International Trade Journal* 7: 85–110.

Agodo, O. 1978. "The Determinants of U.S. Private Manufacturing Investments in Africa." *Journal of International Business Studies* 9/3: 95–107.

Ajami, R. and D. Ricks. 1981. "Motives of Non-American Firms Investing in the United States." *Journal of International Business Studies* 12/3: 25–34.

Alexander, A. and R. Swinth. 1987. *A Value Framework for Assessing the Social Impacts of Multinational Corporations.* South Carolina Essays in International Business, no. 7 (Columbia, South Carolina: Center for International Business Studies, The University of South Carolina).

Arpan, J., E. Flowers, and D. Ricks. 1981. "Foreign Direct Investment in the United States: The State of Knowledge in Research." *Journal of International Business Studies* 12/2: 25–34.

Auty, R. 1984. "The Product Life-Cycle and the Location of the Global Petrochemical Industry after the Second Oil Shock." *Economic Geography* 60: 325–338.

Bagchi-Sen, S., and J. Wheeler. 1989. "A Spatial and Temporal Model of Foreign Direct Investment in the United States." *Economic Geography* 65: 113–129.

Bavishi, V., and D. Ricks. 1981. *Foreign Investment Analysis by the World's Multinational Corporations.* Working Paper in International Business, DOR E-81-04 (Columbia: Division of Research, College of Business Administration, The University of South Carolina).

Bavishi, V., and H. Wyman. 1983. *Who Audits the World: Trends in the Worldwide Accounting Profession* (Storrs, Connecticut: Center for Transnational Accounting and Financial Research, School of Business Administration, University of Connecticut).

Boddewyn, J., M. Halbrich, and A. Perry. 1986. "Service Multinationals: Conceptualization, Measurement and Theory." *Journal of International Business Studies* 17: 41–57.

Brimmer, A., and F. Dahl. 1975. "Growth of American International Banking: Implications for Public Policy." *Journal of Finance* 30: 341–363.

Buckley, P. 1988. "The Limits of Explanation: Testing the Internalization Theory of the Multinational Enterprise." *Journal of International Business Studies* 19: 181–193.

Buckley, P., and M. Casson. 1981. "The Optimal Timing of a Foreign Direct Investment." *The Economic Journal* 91: 75–87..

Calvet, A. 1981. "A Synthesis of Foreign Direct Investment Theories and Theories of the Multinational Firm." *Journal of International Business Studies* 12/1: 43–59.

Chang, K. 1989. "Japan's Direct Manufacturing Investment in the United States." *The Professional Geographer* 41: 314–328.

Chao, P. 1989. "Export and Reverse Investment: Strategic Implications for Newly Industrialized Countries." *Journal of International Business Studies* 20: 75–91.

Chernotsky, H. 1989. "Trade Adjustment and Foreign Direct Investment: Japan in the United States." In *Pacific Dynamics: The International Politics of Industrial Change*, S. Haggard and C. Moon, eds. (Boulder: Westview Press).

Cho, K. 1985. *Multinational Banks: Their Identities and Determinants* (Ann Arbor: UMI Research Press).

Christaller, W. 1933. *Die zentralen Orte in Suddeutschland* (Jena: Gustav Fischer). Translated from the German by C. Baskin, 1966, as *Central Places in Southern Germany* (Englewood Cliffs, New Jersey: Prentice-Hall).

Coase, R. 1937. "The Nature of the Firm." *Economica* 4: 386–405.

Committee for Economic Development. 1987. *Finance and Third World Economic Growth* (New York: Committee for Economic Development).

Contractor, F. 1984. "Choosing Between Direct Investment and Licensing: Theoretical Considerations and Empirical Tests." *Journal of International Business Studies* 15/3: 167–188.

Corbridge, S. 1986. *Capitalist World Development: A Critique of Radical Development Geography* (Totawa, New Jersey: Rowman and Littlefield).

Coughlin, P. 1990. "Kenya: Moving to the Next Phase?" In *Manufacturing Africa: Performance & Prospects of Seven Countries in Sub-Saharan Africa*, R. Riddell, ed. (Portsmouth, England: Heinemann).

Das, R. 1981. "Impact of Host Government Regulations on MNC Operation: Learning from Third World Countries." *Columbia Journal of World Business* 16/1: 85–90.

Davidson, W. 1980. "The Location of Foreign Direct Investment Activity: Country Characteristics and Experience Effects." *Journal of International Business Studies* 11/2: 9–21.

Davidson, W., and D. McFetridge. 1984. "Recent Directions in International Strategies: Production Rationalization or Portfolio Adjustment?" *Columbia Journal of World Business* 19/2: 95–101.

Dicken, P. 1986. *Global Shift: Industrial Change in a Turbulent World* (London: Harper & Row).

Dunning, J. 1977. "Trade, Location of Economic Activity and the Multinational Enterprise: A Search for an Eclectic Approach." in *The International Allocation of Economic Activity*, B. Ohlin, P. Hesselborn, and P. Wiskman, eds. (London: Macmillan).

———. 1979. "Explaining Changing Patterns of International Production: In Defence of the Eclectic Theory." *Oxford Bulletin of Economics and Statistics* 41: 269–295.

———. 1988. "The Theory of International Production." *The International Trade Journal* 3: 21–66.

Dunning, J., and G. Norman. 1983. "The Theory of the Multinational Enterprise: An Application to Multinational Office Location." *Environment and Planning A* 15: 675–692.

Economist. 1992. "Vorsprung durch Panik." February 15, pp. 53–54.

Egelhoff, W. 1980. "Structure and Strategy in Multinational Corporations: A Reexamination of the Stopford and Wells Model." *Academy of Management Proceedings* 40: 231–235.

Encarnation, D. 1989. "American-Japanese Cross Investment: A Second Front of Economic Rivalry." In *Pacific Dynamics: The International Politics of Industrial Change.*

Fan, C. 1992. "Foreign Trade and Regional Development in China." *Geographical Analysis* 24: 240–256.

Ffrench-Davis, R., and S. Arancibia. 1972. "Notes on Foreign Capital and Latin America." In *International Economics and Development,* L. Di Marco, ed. (New York: Academic Press).

Florida, R., and M. Kenney. 1992. "Restructuring in Place: Japanese Investment, Production Organization, and the Geography of Steel." *Economic Geography* 68: 146–173.

Franko, L. 1989. "Use of Minority and 50-50 Joint Ventures by United States Multinationals during the 1970s: The Interaction of Host Country Policies and Corporate Strategies." *Journal of International Business Studies* 20: 19–40.

Glickman, N., and D. Woodward. 1988. "The Location of Foreign Direct Investment in the United States: Patterns and Determinants." *International Regional Science Review* 11: 137–154.

Graham, E. 1978. "Transatlantic Investment by Multinational Firms: A Rivalistic Phenomenon?" *Journal of Post-Keynesian Economics* 1: 82–99.

Graham, E., and P. Krugman. 1989. *Foreign Direct Investment in the United States* (Washington: Institute for International Economics).

Gray, J., and H. Gray. 1981. "The Multinational Bank: A Financial MNC?" *Journal of Banking and Finance* 5: 33–63.

Green, M. 1990. *Mergers and Acquisitions: Geographical Perspectives* (New York: Routledge).

Grosse, R., and D. Aramburu. 1990. "A Bargaining View of Government/MNE Relations: The Latin American Case." *The International Trade Journal* 6: 209–238.

Hanink, D. 1985. "A Mean-Variance Model of MNF Location Strategy." *Journal of International Business Studies* 16: 165–170.

Hansen, N. 1988. "Regional Consequences of Structural Changes in the National and International Division of Labor." *International Regional Science Review* 11: 121–136.

Harrington, J., K. Burns, and M. Cheung. 1986. "Market-Oriented Foreign Investment and Regional Development: Canadian Companies in Western New York." *Economic Geography* 62: 155–166.

Harris, C. 1954. "The Market as a Factor in the Localization of Industry in the United States." *Annals of the Association of American Geographers* 44: 315–348.

Hartman, D. 1979. "Foreign Investment and Finance with Risk." *Quarterly Journal of Economics* 93: 214–232.

Hennart, J.-F. 1986. "Internalization in Practice: Early Foreign Direct Investments in Malaysian Tin Mining." *Journal of International Business Studies* 17: 131–141.

Hirsch, S. 1976. "An International Trade and Investment Theory of the Firm." *Oxford Economic Papers* 28: 258–270.

———. 1989. "Services and Service Intensity in International Trade." *Weltwirtschaftliches Archiv* 125: 45–60.

Hisey, K., and R. Caves. 1985. "Diversification Strategy and Choice of Country: Diversifying Acquisitions Abroad by U.S. Multinationals,1978–1980." *Journal of International Business Studies* 16: 51–64.

Hogendoorn, J., and W. Brown. 1979. *The New International Economics* (Reading, Massachusetts: Addison-Wesley).

Hotelling, H. 1929. "Stability in Competition." *The Economic Journal* 39: 52–79.

Hymer, S. 1959. *The International Operations of National Firms: A Study of Direct Foreign Investment.* Ph.D. dissertation, Massachusetts Institute of Technology (Cambridge, Massachusetts: MIT Press).

International Monetary Fund. 1986. *International Capital Markets: Developments and Prospects* (Washington: International Monetary Fund).

———. 1991. *Balance of Payments Statistics Yearbook,* part 1 (Washington: International Monetary Fund).

———. 1992. *International Financial Statistics Yearbook 1992,* vol. 42 (Washington: International Monetary Fund).

Isard, W. 1956. *Location and Space Economy* (Cambridge, Massachusetts: MIT Press).

Jenkins, R. 1987. *Transnational Corporations and Uneven Development: The Internationalization of Capital and the Third World* (New York: Methuen).

Jones, P., and J. North. 1991. "Japanese Motor Industry Transplants: The West European Dimension." *Economic Geography* 67: 105–123.

Kindleberger, C. 1969. *American Business Abroad* (New Haven, Connecticut: Yale University Press).

Knickerbocker, F. 1973. *Oligopolistic Reaction and Multinational Enterprise* (Boston: Harvard Business School).

Kogut, B. 1984. "Normative Observations on the International Value-Added Chain and Strategic Groups." *Journal of International Business Studies* 15/2: 151–167.

Kojima, K. 1990. *Japanese Direct Investment Abroad* (Tokyo: International Christian University).

Kotabe, M., and G. Omura. 1989. "Sourcing Strategies of European and Japanese Multinationals: A Comparison." *Journal of International Business Studies* 20: 113–130.

Krugman, P. 1979. "A Model of Innovation, Technology Transfer, and the World Distribution of Income." *Journal of Political Economy* 87: 253–266.

Kumar, K., and K. Kim. 1984. "The Korean Manufacturing Multinationals." *Journal of International Business Studies* 20/1: 45–61.

Leonard, H., and C. Duerkson. 1980. "Environmental Regulations and the Location of Industry: An International Perspective." *Columbia Journal of World Business* 15/2:.52–68.

Leung, C. 1990. "Locational Characteristics of Foreign Equity Joint Venture Investment in China." *The Professional Geographer* 42: 403–421.

Lösch, D. 1954, 2d rev. ed. *The Economics of Location.* Translated from the German by W. Woglom with W. Stolper (New Haven, Connecticut: Yale University Press).

Madura, J., and A. Whyte. 1990. "Diversification Benefits of Direct Foreign Investment." *Management International Review* 30/1: 73–85.

Mair, A., R. Florida, and M. Kenney. 1988. "The New Geography of Automobile Production: Japanese Transplants in North America." *Economic Geography* 64: 352–373.

Mascarenhas, B. 1986. "International Strategies of Non-Dominant Firms." *Journal of International Business Studies* 17: 1–25.

McConnell, J. 1980. "Foreign Direct Investment in the United States." *Annals of the Association of American Geographers* 70: 259–270.

Mentzer, J., and A. Samli. 1981. "A Model for Marketing in Economic Development." *Columbia Journal of World Business* 16/3: 91–101.

Miller, J., and B. Pras. 1980. "The Effects of Multinational and Export Diversification on the Profit Stability of U.S. Corporations." *Southern Economic Journal* 46: 792–805.

Minor, M. 1990. *Changes in Developing Country Regimes for Foreign Direct Investment: The Raw Materials Sector, 1968–1985.* South Carolina Essays in International Business, no. 7 (Columbia, South Carolina: Center for International Business Studies, The University of South Carolina).

Moran, T. 1992. "Strategic Trade Theory and the Use of Performance Requirements to Negotiate with Multinational Corporations in the Third World: Exploring a 'New' Political Economy of North-South Relations in Trade and Foreign Investment." *The International Trade Journal* 7: 45–84.

Mullor-Sebastian, A. 1983. "The Product Life-Cycle Theory: Empirical Evidence." *Journal of International Business Studies* 14/3: 95–105.

Murphy, A. 1992. "Western Investment in East-Central Europe: Emerging Patterns and Implications for State Stability." *The Professional Geographer* 44: 249–259.

Nigh, D., K. Cho, and S. Krishnan. 1986. "The Role of Location-Related Factors in U.S. Banking Abroad: An Empirical Examination." *Journal of International Business Studies* 17: 59–72.

Norman, G. 1986. "Market Strategy with Variable Entry Threats." In *Spatial Pricing and Differentiated Markets,* G. Norman, ed. (London, England: Pion).

Ohlin, B. 1933. *Interregional and International Trade* (Cambridge: Harvard University Press).

O' hUallachain, B. 1984. "Linkages and Direct Foreign Investment in the United States." *Economic Geography* 60: 238–253.

O' hUallachain, B. and N. Reid. 1992. "Source Country Differences in the Spatial Distribution of Foreign Direct Investment in the United States." *The Professional Geographer* 44: 272–285.

Organisation for Economic Cooperation and Development, 1981. *International Investment and Multinational Enterprises: Recent International Direct Investment Trends* (Paris: Organisation for Economic Cooperation and Development).

Rugman, A. 1975. "Foreign Operations and the Stability of U.S. Corporate Earnings: Risk Reduction by International Diversification." *Journal of Finance* 30: 233–234.

Rugman, A. 1980. "A New Theory of the Multinational Enterprise: Internationalization Versus Internalization." *The Columbia Journal of World Business* 15/1: 23–29.

Ryans, J., and D. Howard. 1988. "The Response of U.S. Multinational Corporations to Increased Competition for International Markets." *The International Trade Journal* 3: 67–80.

Salehizadeh, M. 1983. *Regulations of Foreign Direct Investment by Host Countries.* South Carolina Essays in International Business, no. 4 (Columbia, South Carolina: Center for International Business Studies, The University of South Carolina).

Schoenberger, E. 1985. "Foreign Manufacturing Investment in the United States: Competitive Strategies and International Location." *Economic Geography* 61: 241–259.

_____ . 1988. "Multinational Corporations and the New International Division of Labor: A Critical Appraisal." *International Regional Science Review* 11: 105–120.

Shaked, I. 1986. "Are Multinational Corporations Safer?" *Journal of International Business Studies* 17: 83–106.

Smith, D. 1971. *Industrial Location: An Economic Geographical Analysis* (New York: John Wiley & Sons).

Solomon, B. 1989. "The Search for Oil: Factors Influencing U.S. Investment in Foreign Petroleum Exploration and Development." *The Professional Geographer* 41: 39–50.

South, R. 1990. "Transnational 'Maquiladora' Location." *Annals of the Association of American Geographers* 80: 549–570.

Stopford, J., and L. Wells. 1972. *Managing the Multinational Enterprise* (New York: Basic Books).

Storper, M. 1985. "Oligopoly and the Product Cycle: Essentialism in Economic Geography." *Economic Geography* 61: 260–282.

Suarez-Villa, L. 1984. "Industrial Export Enclaves and Manufacturing Change." *Papers of the Regional Science Association* 54: 89–111.

Thrift, N., and M. Taylor. 1989. "Battleships and Cruisers: The New Geography of Multinational Corporations." In *Horizons in Human Geography*, D. Gregory and R. Walford, eds. (Totawa, New Jersey: Barnes & Noble).

Tong, H.-M., and C. Walter. 1980. "An Empirical Study of Plant Location Decisions of Foreign Manufacturing Investors in the United States." *Columbia Journal of World Business* 15/1: 66–73.

United Nations Center on Transnational Corporations. 1991. *World Investment Report 1991* (New York: United Nations).

United States Department of Commerce. 1991. *Survey of Current Business* 71/8 (Washington, DC: U.S. Government Printing Office).

Travis, L., and R. Crum. 1984. "Performance-Based Strategies for MNC Portfolio Balancing." *Columbia Journal Of World Business* 19/2: 85–94.

van Dam, A. 1979. "The Corporate Role in a North-South Dialogue." *Management International Review* 19/4: 7–12.

Vernon, R. 1966. "International Investment and International Trade in the Product Cycle." *Quarterly Journal of Economics* 90: 190–207.

Vernon, R. 1979. "The Product Cycle Hypothesis in a New International Environment." *Oxford Bulletin of Economics and Statistics* 41: 255–267.

Webber, M. 1972. *The Impact of Uncertainty on Location* (Cambridge, Massachusetts: MIT Press).

Weber, A. 1909. *Uber den Standort der Industrien*. Translated from the German by C. Friedrich, 1929, as *Alfred Weber's Theory of the Location of Industries* (Chicago, Illinois: University of Chicago Press).

Williams, M. 1975. "The Extent and Significance of the Nationalization of Foreign Owned Assets in Developing Countries, 1956–1972." *Oxford Economic Papers* 27: 260–273.

Wolf, B. 1977. "Industrial Diversification and Internationalization: Some Empirical Evidence." *The Journal of Industrial Economics* 26: 177–191.

World Bank. 1991A. *Global Economic Prospects and the Developing Countries* (Washington: World Bank).

———. 1991B. *World Development Report 1991* (New York: Oxford University Press).

———. 1992. *Export Processing Zones* (New York: Oxford University Press).

Yannopoulos, G., and J. Dunning. 1976. "Multinational Enterprises and Regional Development: An Exploratory Paper." *Regional Studies* 10: 389–399.

PART III

INTERNATIONAL TRADE

*P*ART III OF THE BOOK CONSISTS OF three chapters on the subject of international trade. Chapter 9, "International Trade Theory," begins with a review of comparative advantage as the basis for trade, and continues with a discussion of the dominant trade theory of our time, which is the factor endowment theory of Heckscher and Ohlin. This review of factor endowment theory is developed within the context of the production function. The presentation then turns to recent extensions to factor endowment theory, and the recent advances in international trade theory that rely on the concept of product differentiation and consumer preference to explain the product and geographical structures of trade.

In their basic forms, all the trade models described in Chapter 9 concern some simple benefits of free trade. In the factor endowment model, for example, producers benefit from trade because production becomes more efficient, and consumers benefit because prices decrease. In the product differentiation models, including the hierarchical market model, free trade allows increased benefits for consumers due to their ability to purchase greater or better varieties of goods than can be produced domestically.

Unfortunately, the benefits of free trade that come about so quickly in theory are slower to be realized in reality. Differences in economic and population size eliminate much of the competitive reaction of price equalization among countries. In addition, large differences in average incomes, factor endowments, scale economies, or technology among countries means that large quantities of noncompetitive goods enter into international trade. The actual spatial interaction system of international trade, as opposed to its theoretical characteristics, means that large, rich countries are more likely to benefit from trade than small, poor countries. As a response to the actual and potential imbalance in international trade, virtually all the world's countries practice some controls of their trade flows, either individually or in regional coalitions, or both. In addition, multinational corporations exercise their own trade controls through corporate practices.

Contrasts between the theory and reality of international trade are drawn in Chapter 10, "Managed Trade." The chapter begins with a discussion of the traditional barriers to trade, such as tariffs and quotas, and the array of nontariff barriers employed by individual countries. Then the chapter provides a description of two major international trade treaties, the General Agreement on Tariffs and Trade, and the Multifiber Arrangement. The chapter also includes an examination of interregional trade agreements among countries, with particular emphasis on continuing European integration, and the recent trade preference agreements between Canada and the United States. The last part of Chapter 10 concerns the special type of managed trade that takes place within the multinational corporation.

Chapter 11, "Economic Development and International Trade," emphasizes the geography of international trade. The first part of the chapter concerns the relationship between international trade and a country's economic growth and development. The chapter continues with an assessment of the importance of the structure of trade, both the aggregate split between trade in merchandise and trade in services and the more disaggregate structure of merchandise trade alone. The geographical structure of trade is then taken up, and potential processes of altering the intertwined product and geographical structures of trade are examined.

CHAPTER 9

· · ·

International Trade Theory

· · ·

9.1 INTRODUCTION

International trade theory addresses three fundamental questions in the international economy. The first question is "why?" and concerns the reason(s) that trade takes place. The second question is "what?" and concerns the array of goods that are entered into international trade. The third question is "where?" and concerns the geography of international trade. As described below, the first question is answered in the context of the second and third questions. Goods traded, or the *commodity structure* of trade, and the spatial flow of the goods, or *geographical structure* of trade, both result ideally from the potential increase of actual and perceived benefits to trading partners. The first major area of discussion in this chapter is trade's commodity structure and contains a review of classical and neoclassical trade theory as developed in economics. This body of theory largely takes supply conditions as defining the basis for determining the commodity structure of trade. The role of international differences in demand is focused upon in the second major area of discussion in the chapter, and this focus leads to the theory of trade's geographical structure.

As in all subsystems of spatial interaction in the international economy, trade flows are affected by place characteristics, or a country's domestic economy, and in turn the place characteristics are affected by the flows, which characterize a country's place in the geographical pattern of international trade. Because of the interaction between place and flow, virtually all trade theory has implications for the location of production as well as the flow of goods produced. The implications for the flow of goods are stressed in this chapter, while the implications for the location of production were stressed in Chapter 8.

9.2 COMPARATIVE ADVANTAGE AS THE BASIS OF TRADE

In *The Wealth of Nations,* Adam Smith suggested that the benefits of international trade resulted from the ability of countries to specialize their production; that the tailor and the shoemaker, for example, produced more clothing and more shoes because they specialized in the production of just one good. If each made both clothing and shoes, their volume of production would decrease and their goods would become more costly. Smith argued that just as the shoemaker and tailor made better uses of their particular talents by producing a specialized good, countries could benefit by producing only those goods for which they have particular talents. In turn, they can import goods not produced domestically in exchange for goods not produced by their partners in foreign trade.

The full development of this line of thinking was made by David Ricardo in *The Principles of Political Economy and Taxation,* published in 1817. The basis for trade described by Ricardo is called the *law of comparative advantage.* It describes, in essence, the merger of two independent national economies into one integrated economy in which the benefits of specialization in production are achieved through trade. The benefits of trade are measured through the improvement in a country's terms of trade by moving from a fully domestic to a fully international economy.

To understand the law of comparative advantage, consider the initial conditions of production of the same two commodities, pretzels and beer, in two countries, France and Germany, as described in Table 9.1A. For ease of exposition, assume (wrongfully) that the consumers of both countries have the same tastes for pretzels and beer, but that production costs, measured in the same unit, differ for each of the two goods. A cursory examination of the initial conditions seems to indicate that France could not benefit from trade with Germany. France produces pretzels at half their cost in Germany, and France produces beer at three-fourths of Germany's cost. Why should France trade with Germany? Ricardo showed that the absolute cost of production was misleading as a basis for trade. Instead it is the relative, or comparative, costs of production that determine if trade will benefit two countries.

The relative cost of pretzels to beer in France is 10/30 or .333 (Table 9.1B). That is, the production of one unit of pretzels requires 1/3 the productive resources required to produce beer. Conversely, the production of one unit of beer in France costs three times the production of one unit of pretzels. In Germany, however, the relative costs of production differ. There, pretzels require 20/40, or 1/2 the productive resources required to produce beer, and it follows that beer is twice as costly to produce as pretzels. Based on these relative costs, France has a comparative advantage in the production of pretzels because its cost of pretzels is .333(beer), while the cost of pretzels in Germany is .5(beer). Germany has a comparative advantage in the production of beer because its cost is 2(pretzels), while the cost of beer in France is 3(pretzels). On a comparative basis, France is the lower-cost producer of pretzels and Germany is the lower-cost producer of beer. But how do these comparative costs translate into international trade? The answer to this question is found by examining the barter terms of trade.

TABLE 9.1   An Example of Trade Based on Comparative Advantage: Two Countries and Two Commodities

A. Initial Conditions

	Production Costs	
	Pretzels	Beer
France	10	30
Germany	20	40

B. Domestic Comparative Costs and Barter Terms of Trade

	Comparative Costs		Barter Terms of Trade	
	Pretzels/Beer	Beer/Pretzels	Pretzels/Beer	Beer/Pretzels
France	10/30	30/10	3/1	1/3
	(0.333)	(3.000)	(3.000)	(0.333)
Germany	20/40	40/20	2/1	1/2
	(0.500)	(2.000)	(2.000)	(0.500)

C. Pre-Trade Production and Consumption

	Commodity			
	Production		Consumption	
	Pretzels	Beer	Pretzels	Beer
France	600	200	600	200
Germany	300	150	300	150

D. Possible Production and Consumption with Trade

	Commodity			
	Production		Consumption	
	Pretzels	Beer	Pretzels	Beer
Country X	900	100	600	225
Country Y	0	300	300	175

The *barter terms of trade* are defined as the ratio of imports to exports. Obviously, the higher the value of the barter terms, the more favorable is the exchange, because more goods are being bought (imported) for a smaller amount of goods being sold (exported). An increase in the barter terms of trade indicates a decrease in prices paid. The barter terms of trade can be applied in a domestic as well as a foreign context. Based completely on relative domestic prices, the purchase of 1 unit of pretzels in France requires the payment of 1/3 unit of beer so that the barter terms are 1/.333 or 3 (Table 9.1B). The purchase of 1 unit of pretzels in Germany requires the payment of 1/2 unit of beer so that the barter terms are 1/.5 or 2. Given the differences in barter terms of trade, someone wishing to buy pretzels by payment in beer would always prefer to buy pretzels from France, where it is cheaper. (The assumption here, of course, is that all pretzels and all beer taste the same; i.e., all commodities are undifferentiated). The purchase of 1 unit of beer in France requires the payment of 3 units of pretzels, defining barter terms of trade of 1/3 or .333. The purchase of 1 unit of beer in Germany costs 2 units of pretzels, for barter terms of trade equalling 1/2 or .5. In this case, someone wishing to buy beer by payment in pretzels would always prefer to purchase it in Germany. The same argument can be made with reference to opportunity costs, and with the same result.

Based on comparative costs of production, producers would prefer to produce pretzels in France and beer in Germany. Based on comparative costs of consumption, consumers would prefer to purchase pretzels in France and beer in Germany. The latter relationship provides the basis for trade because consumers in Germany are better off consuming pretzels produced in France and consumers in France are better off consuming beer produced in Germany.

What pattern of trade would develop from the conditions described? The answer is based on two conditions. First are the initial, pre-trade production and consumption characteristics of the two countries. Assume, for example, that both countries have 12,000 units of productive resources, and constant returns to scale of production. In France, *production possibilities* are any linear combination within the extremes of 1200 units of pretzels (@ 10 productive resources) or 400 units of beer (@ 30 productive resources). In Germany, the production possibilities are within the limits of 600 units of pretzels (@ 20 productive resources) or 300 units of beer (@ 40 productive resources). It is likely that both commodities will be produced in both countries before trade (they must be if both are consumed!), and one potential pattern of production and consumption is given in Table 9.1C. Based on the law of comparative advantage, a pattern of trade would arise in which one, and preferably both, of the countries will be better off than before trade.

Based strictly on comparative costs, both countries could completely specialize in the commodities in which they have the comparative advantage in production. In this case, however, consumption of beer would have to fall in the aggregate because maximum production of this commodity in Germany is 300 units and total pre-trade consumption is 350 units (Table 9.1C). This indicates that complete specialization in both countries would not take place, with, for example, 1/2 of France's production of pretzels being trade for 1/2 of Germany's production of beer.

The second condition determining the pattern of trade is the domestic barter terms of trade. These values define floor and ceiling prices in international trade. For example, the terms of trade with respect to imports of beer/exports of pretzels cannot be under .333 or above .500. If the terms of trade fell below, then France would be better off with its pre-trade system; if the terms of trade went above, then Germany would be better off with its pre-trade system. The terms of foreign trade must always be within the range of the two countries' pre-trade domestic terms of trade.

One potential pattern of production, trade, and consumption that makes both countries better off with respect to the conditions of pre-trade consumption and pricing is given in Table 9.1D. Germany specializes completely in the production of beer, but France also produces that commodity, albeit at 1/2 its previous level. The pattern of trade is the exchange of 125 units of beer produced in Germany for 300 units of pretzels produced in France. The terms of trade, beer/pretzels, are .417, as compared to France's pre-trade .333, and the terms of trade, pretzels/beer, are 2.4, as compared to Germany's pre-trade terms at 2. Both countries are better off with respect to price. In addition, this pattern of trade increases consumption with no increase in production costs. France's consumption of beer increases with trade from 200 to 225 units, and Germany's consumption of beer increases from 150 to 175 units.

9.3   FACTOR ENDOWMENTS AS THE BASIS FOR COMPARATIVE ADVANTAGE

As described, the law of comparative advantage can be invoked to produce benefits from trade. However, no comparative advantage exists if relative costs are identical between two countries. For example, if production costs of commodities 1 and 2 in country X are 10 and 30, respectively, and 100 and 300 in country Y, comparative advantage does not apply. Despite the large differences in absolute costs, the cost ratios are exactly the same between the two countries. Again, relative costs are the key to comparative advantage. Two Scandinavian economists, Heckscher (1919) and Ohlin (1933), have extended Ricardo's work on comparative advantage to include the source of differences in relative costs between countries. Their extension is referred to in particular as the Heckscher-Ohlin theory of trade, and in general as *factor endowment theory* (Hazari, 1978; Gomes, 1990). (See Chapter 8 for the implications of factor endowment theory for foreign direct investment).

Factor endowment theory states that comparative advantage arises in those countries where an industry's factor intensity corresponds to the country's greatest factor endowment. Under factor endowment theory, efficient geographical patterns of production can be achieved when factor-intensive production functions are matched with appropriate factor endowments. The efficiently produced goods of one country are traded for the efficiently produced goods of another. Increased production efficiency creates domestic surpluses that are traded for the surpluses of other goods produced in other countries.

By way of example, return to the schedule of production costs of pretzels and beer in France and Germany. Let the production function of pretzels be identical across the two countries, and assume the same for beer. Let pretzels be labor intensive in production and beer be capital intensive so that

$$\frac{\Delta Q_P}{\Delta L, K} > \frac{\Delta Q_P}{\Delta K, L} \quad \text{and} \quad \frac{\Delta Q_B}{\Delta L, K} < \frac{\Delta Q_B}{\Delta K, L} \tag{9.1}$$

where Q_P and Q_B are outputs of pretzels and beer, and Δ indicates a positive increment. As listed in Table 9.1B, the relative costs of producing pretzels are lower in France and the relative costs of producing beer are lower in Germany, so we may assume

$$\frac{pL_F}{pK_F} < 1 \quad \text{and} \quad \frac{pK_G}{pL_G} < 1 \qquad (9.2)$$

that is, the price of labor, pL, is low relative to the price of capital, pK, in France, F, and the price of capital is low compared to the price of labor in Germany, G. Given a market price for factors determined by their relative abundance, it must be that

$$\frac{qL_F}{qK_F} > \frac{qL_G}{qK_G} \qquad (9.3)$$

where qL and qK are quantities of labor and capital. Note that relative, and not absolute, factor endowments determine the relative factor prices. Given a fixed budget of expenditures on factors across both countries,

$$Q_{PF} > Q_{PG} \text{ and } Q_{BF} < Q_{BG} \qquad (9.4)$$

Production of labor-intensive pretzels is more efficient in France, and production of capital-intensive beer is more efficient in Germany. The relative surplus of pretzels produced in France can be traded to Germany for its relative surplus of beer.

As described, the factor endowment extension to the theory of comparative advantage makes an explicit one-to-one link between relative factor prices, relative output, and relative commodity prices. Factor endowments determine relative factor prices and, in turn, relative factor prices determine relative commodity costs. Once production and trade are organized along these principles the system should be self-maintaining. An increase in any factor's endowment, for example, could be expected to increase all production, but in constant relative proportions. The *Rybczynski theorem* (1955), however, shows that as long as factor costs remain fixed, an influx of any single factor causes an increase in the output only of that industry that uses the factor intensively, and a corresponding decrease in the output of the other industry. For example, suppose capital is drawn to France because of its relatively high price in that country. As the supply of capital increases in France, it should be drawn into the production of beer because of that industry's capital intensity, causing output of beer to increase. The increase in beer's output, however, cannot take place simply through additions of capital. The capital increases must be met by an increase in the labor factor as well. The additional labor to match the increase in capital used in the production of beer can be drawn only from the production of pretzels. Therefore, as output of beer increases in France, output of pretzels must decrease due to a shortage of labor, its intensively used factor.

Unless we are talking about a small country in a large international marketplace, the assumption of fixed factor costs cannot be maintained. In fact, both Ohlin (1933) and Samuelson (1948) have shown that factor prices tend to equalize under conditions of free trade. In the two-country example being presented, any influx of capital to France would have to be drawn from Germany. As the relative supply of capital to labor decreases in Germany, it increases in France. As the relative supplies change, so must the relative prices in a process called *factor price equalization*. If any factor is mobile, both factor prices must converge because the relevant prices are the relative prices of the factors. In turn, if relative prices converge between countries, comparative advantage must disappear, and with it the basis for trade. In fact, any good or factor that is mobile can be expected to have a single international price. The barter terms of international trade described as in the case of France exporting pretzels to and importing beer from Germany, must become the domestic terms of trade in both countries in trade equilibrium. If more beneficial terms of trade were available domestically in either country, then the balance of trade would alter until the international terms became the best. Domestic terms cannot be worse than the international terms, on the other hand, or no domestic trade would take place. Basically, any country's export represents a declining supply of a country's relative surplus production, and any country's import represents an increasing supply of a country's relative shortfall in production. Exporting, therefore, causes domestic prices to increase, and importing causes them to fall until, theoretically, the price of each commodity is everywhere the same. Again, this result is called the *law of one price*.

The convergence of all prices represents an equilibrium condition of equalized prices across all commodities and all factors in an international economy with no constraints to trade or factor migration. Any diversion from equal prices indicates an imbalance in supply and demand that can soon be eliminated by the flow of a good or a factor. However, there are several critical barriers to actual international trade that prevent the law of one price from being completely enforced. Individual government policies, and policies established among coalitions of countries such as in the European Community, are often designed to deflect the flow of commodities and factors from their equilibrium paths. Many of these policies, such as the use of tariffs and quotas, are discussed in the next chapter. Even if there was no government interest in the international economy's domestic effects, however, distance between points of supply and demand would effect price differences between places. Unless transportation costs are nonexistent, the barter terms of international trade used in the comparative advantage example we have cited can never be realized, nor can factor prices equalize across countries. The cost of transporting either commodities or factors is like a tax that must be considered in determining their final prices, and is just as inevitable. However, the existence of transportation costs does not void the notion of a trade equilibrium in general, just an equilibrium at equal prices.

9.4 SCALE OF PRODUCTION AND TECHNOLOGY

Factor endowment theory states that comparative advantage is based ultimately on uneven factor endowments determining differing factor prices among countries. Over time, factor prices tend to become closer across countries, however, so the growth of international trade can be expected to take place at a slower rate than the growth of world income. In reality, the growth of trade has been taking place at a faster rate than the growth of world income. Much of this growth undoubtedly is due to real decreases in transport costs and liberalization of trade policies (see Chapter 10), but some of it results from special cases of factor endowment theory. The first of these special cases concerns the role of economies of scale in international trade, and the second concerns technology. The common bond between both these cases is that the role of the domestic market in fashioning a country's comparative advantage is much more pronounced than in conventional factor endowment theory.

Factor endowment theory in general, and the Rybczynski theorem in particular, assume a competitive international economy. Individual countries are considered to be small enough that they are price takers in international markets. However, price taking is not a consistent attribute of all countries in international markets because the domestic markets of some countries are large enough to bring about economies of scale in some of their production (see Chapter 4). Production of some goods subject to economies of scale may be limited in their geography to only those countries that have sufficiently large domestic markets. Such goods are called noncompetitive because they cannot be produced in all countries (Gray, 1986). In a sense, a large domestic market can become a necessary factor of production that is not available in some countries. Unlike the uneven but always positive distribution of factors assumed in factor endowment theory, economies of scale can be viewed as an "all-or-nothing" proposition. Economies of scale are impossible to achieve below some critical size of domestic market. For certain goods, countries with sufficiently large domestic markets may be few enough in number to be able to control pricing in international markets. Countries able to achieve economies of scale domestically have a considerable edge in international trade because their favorably low absolute costs replace the usual relative costs in determining the terms of trade.

Technological superiority, like economies of scale, can be considered as a factor of production with a limited, all-or-nothing, geographical distribution. The *product life cycle* was introduced by Vernon (1966) and Wells (1968) as a type of dynamic comparative advantage model of international trade as well as investment (see Chapter 8). With respect to the international economy, the product life cycle has implications for a more dynamic interpretation of the law of comparative advantage, because it implies a dynamic production function over the life of a good (Nelson and Norman, 1977).

Vernon (1966) used the product life cycle's relationship to trade as an explanatory framework for the success of U.S. exports during the 1950s and 1960s, and Hoy and Shaw (1981) used it for an explanation of America's declining exports in the late 1970s. The United States, argued Vernon, was the technological pioneer of the post–World War II era. Because of its technological dominance, it had comparative advantage in the development of a wide array of both producer and consumer products. In addition, its domestic economy was large enough to provide economies of scale even at early stages of a product's domestic market penetration. Many of the goods exported from the United States were noncompetitive; they simply could not be produced in other countries. At the time, the United States could easily afford to import a large volume of competitive goods because its export of noncompetitive goods earned so much. More recently, however, due to the spread of technological expertise to other Core countries and even some Peripheral countries, technologically intensive goods are now more competitive. The United States can no longer import at its earlier rate because it no longer introduces new products to world markets as fast as it did before.

As an interesting counterpart to product life-cycle theory, Magee and Robins (1978) have described a *raw material cycle*. The raw material cycle has a reverse geography, in many instances, from the geography of exports in the product life cycle. In the raw material cycle, initial exports of commodities tend to be from peripheral regions, which are the initial exporters either because of some comparative advantage in the production of raw materials, or because the raw materials are noncompetitive goods. As demand for the raw materials increases, however, technological improvements take place in Core economies which allow the production of substitute commodities or the development of alternative sources of supply. During this stage, exports of the raw material from the Periphery slow down, just as exports from the Core slow down in the third stage of the product life cycle. Rather than a changing production function over the life of a product, the raw material cycle describes a changing commodity employed for a consistent use.

Product life-cycle theory is not applicable to all products (Taylor, 1986), but it does provide some insight into one of the primary problems with the factor endowment theory of international trade. If a production function can be dynamic, then the fixed industrywide production function of factor endowment theory is questionable. In fact, the inconstancy of a good's production function from country to country has been recognized for some time. *Factor intensity reversals* occur when a commodity's production is intensive in one factor in one country, but intensive in another factor in another country. For example, textile production is labor intensive in The People's Republic of China, but capital intensive in the United States. Factor intensity reversals are related to very wide price gaps, or large relative price differences, in the factors of production (Hazari, 1978). In reality, all but the first stage of the product life cycle is fixed in its factor (technology) intensity in the contemporary economy (Vernon, 1979). As in the case of textiles, and a large number of other goods, capital and labor can be widely substituted for one another. In effect, the production function is altered with regard to factor endowment, with the result that the same general commodity may be exported by a larger number of countries than would be expected under pure factor endowment theory.

In most instances, empirical evidence supporting factor endowment theory is difficult to find. A well-known empirical regularity in international trade is called the *Leontieff paradox*. Leontieff (1956) found that the United States exported labor-intensive goods and imported capital-intensive goods. The finding was paradoxical because, at the time, the United States generally was considered the country to be most heavily endowed with capital and, by a price determination, poorly endowed with labor. The Leontieff paradox apparently holds for a large number of countries, with trade patterns seemingly running counter to factor endowments and relative factor prices. Several studies have pointed to the inability of Leontieff's empirical model to capture the true factor content of trade (e.g., Leamer, 1980). Recently, Salvatore and Barazesh (1990) have been able to eliminate Leontieff's paradox from American trade, but only by removing those goods found to be natural-resource intensive in their production. Obviously, if production functions of the same good are inconsistent from country to country, if factor intensity reversals are possible, then empirical testing of factor endowment theory becomes quite difficult. When noncompetitive goods derived through economies of scale or technological superiority are also considered, it seems that empirical testing of pure factor endowment theory may be a fruitless exercise for all but a very limited number of goods. Despite problems of empirical verification, factor endowment theory remains an important context for the analysis of international trade.

9.5 PRODUCT DIFFERENTIATION AND THE PRODUCT STRUCTURE OF INTERNATIONAL TRADE

Alternative models of international trade recently have been developed in response to trade realities that are not handled easily by factor endowment theory alone. In addition to Leontieff's paradox, two important realities of contemporary trade are that (1) most of it takes place between industrialized, Core- economy countries; and (2) much of it is intraindustrial, with many countries exporting and importing the same good (Deardorf, 1984; Helpman, 1987). These realities of trade are in contradiction to factor endowment theory because trade is taking place between countries with similar rather than dissimilar factor (capital) endowments, and because intraindustry trade implies a complete breakdown of any practical realization of comparative advantage as a basis for trade.

Because of these theoretically discordant realities of international trade, the question of who trades with whom is being asked increasingly by students of international trade. As the trade question switches from "what" to "with whom," the focus of many new models of international trade has switched from supply to demand. Market characterisics, in many ways similar to those emphasized in analysis of intraregional trade, are now being emphasized in alternative international trade models that are developed within the broader context of the theory of differentiated markets. At the same time, some characteristics of international trade recently have been found useful in refining the central place model.

The primary starting point for the development of contemporary models of international trade is the concept of product, or market, differentiation (see Chapter 8). Chamberlin (1933), in his theory of monopolistic competition, suggested that products of a given single industry are never perfect substitutes. Therefore, every firm has some monopoly power, although entry of competing firms, which are also able to differentiate their products, can eliminate the excess profits available to monopolies (Dixit and Stiglitz, 1977).

Two types of product differentiation have been defined: (1) horizontal differentiation exists if products simply are different; and (2) vertical differentiation exists if there is a common ranking of product quality among consumers. Lancaster's (1979) model of vertical product differentiation is based on the theory that consumers prefer products that embody a particular set of characteristics. The most-preferred product is that which embodies the particular set of characteristics exactly, and product preference decreases as the set of embodied characteristics increases in difference from the consumer's preferred set. Less-preferred products may be consumed, but only if the consumer is compensated for the deviation from the set of preferred characteristics. Typically, the lower price of a less-preferred product compensates for its poorer set of embodied characteristics. (Many people driving a Chevrolet might prefer to drive a BMW.) The substitution of one product for another is a function of their *elasticity of substitution* (see Section 9.7), which most often is measured in terms of a price trade-off.

Helpman and Krugman (1985, Chapter 6) termed the preferences associated with horizontal differentiation as "love of variety," and the preferences associated with vertical differentiation as "ideal variety." In the love-of-variety context, a consumer's satisfaction, or utility, increases as the variety of substitutable products increases, while in the ideal-variety context, consumer utility increases as the particular characteristics of an available product become closer to the ideal product characteristics envisioned by the consumer. Neven (1986) argued that the distinction is not important from the perspective of the producer.

Differentiated market theory does much to explain both the increasing volume of intraindustrial trade and the large volume of trade among the industrial countries that have been apparent for some time. Horizontal product differentiation was first brought to the analysis of intraindustry trade by Johnson (1967). More recently Krugman (1980), in a love-of-variety context, showed analytically that intraindustry trade is an expected result of firms expanding their markets in differentiated products. Krugman (1981) also demonstrated that intraindustry trade predominates between countries with similar factor endowments because firms must differentiate their products in order to capture larger markets. Krugman's trade model is supply oriented, and its results are based on the availability of increasing returns to scale to domestic monopolists operating in markets that have no barriers to product differentiation. Large countries export more than small countries because the larger the country, the more efficient its producers. Essentially, Krugman described a variant of the factor endowment theory of trade, but scale economies rather than factor abundances drive comparative advantages (Section 9.4). As in factor endowment theory, countries in Krugman's model would specialize their domestic production, except when transportation costs in international trade overcome the average cost reductions due to economies of scale. Markusen (1981) made a similar argument for the importance of horizontal differentiation in international market expansion when the countries involved are identical. He further argued that, unlike in a comparative advantage case, consumers can be made better off with trade between identical countries, as long as the trade is in differentiated products. Similar conclusions were drawn by Dixit and Norman (1980).

Lancaster (1980) provided an extension of his ideal-variety utility model to international trade, and uses it to provide a rationalization for intraindustrial trade and trade between countries with similar economies that contradict the expectations of comparative advantage theory. Importantly, he argued that intraindustry trade will take place within the same product class, but not within identical products, which is a tenable proposition if utility is the love-of-variety form. Helpman (1981) used an ideal-variety utility function to draw trade conclusions similar to those drawn by Lancaster (1980) and Krugman (1980), even though Helpman's model incorporated unequal factor endowments. In addition to expectations of intraindustry trade between countries with similar factor endowments, Helpman also drew the interesting proposition that trade volumes increase as the differences between intercountry GNPs decrease.

In retrospect, another type of ideal-variety approach is represented in Vernon's (1966) product life cycle and other technology-based trade theories (Hughes, 1986). These approaches look to a technology gap between countries as a rationale for trade to take place. Recall that Vernon argued, at the time he developed his theory, that the United States was the source of many new or improved products in international markets because of two characteristics: superior technology, and a large domestic market that demanded innovative, high-quality goods. As products become standardized, or nondifferentiated by technology inputs, any American advantage in exporting would be lost, so the American trade position relied largely on the continual development of new high-quality products. Flam and Helpman (1987) used a type of related vertical product differentiation to model Core-Periphery trade and explain intraindustry trade between high-technology and low-technology regions.

9.6 PRODUCT DIFFERENTIATION AND THE GEOGRAPHICAL STRUCTURE OF INTERNATIONAL TRADE

The models we have described approach international trade in differentiated products from the supply side, which is the general approach of factor endowment theory. Like factor endowment theory, the supply-side product differentiation models are more concerned with the product structure than the geography of trade. However, intraindustry trade and trade between similar countries also have been assessed with special attention to geographical patterns of demand.

The most extensive work on geographical product differentiation is contained in Linder's *Essay on Trade and Transformation* (1961). In this work, Linder states that trade should not be addressed from the supply side, as in the theory of comparative advantage, but should be viewed to a large extent as the result of interrelationships among similar markets. Trade among similar markets is a function of overlapping demands, with each good produced in a country considered as a potential export, and each good consumed in a country considered a potential import. Products are differentiated by domestic producers to suit domestic tastes. However, there exist significant market segments in each country that prefer products with qualities that differ from those preferred by the domestic majority. Such products are potential imports. At the same time, if products supplied to meet domestic demand also satisfy the tastes of minority markets in other countries then these products are potential exports. The degree of similarity in international markets is defined largely, according to Linder, by the degree of similarity in per capita incomes, because groups with similar per capita incomes should have similar demand structures. Linder's model is not general, but is restricted to trade between fairly wealthy countries and excludes raw material trade (also see Gray, 1980), which he argued must take place based on factor endowments.

A highly visible example of Linder's point is the penetration of the American market by foreign automobiles. The bulk of the American market for foreign automobiles has been, and is, smaller cars. In the intermediate post–World War II period, such cars were produced in large quantities in Western Europe, with the most notable example being the German Volkswagen. The Volkswagen initially was produced to suit the majority preferences of the domestic German market, especially for low-priced transport in a still re-covering economy, and fuel efficiency under a regime of high gasoline taxes. For the most part, American tastes at the time were dominated by preferences for large cars and, because of low fuel taxes, high-horsepower but inefficient engines. However, the Volkswagen Beetle and similarly designed Western European makes of automobiles did appeal to a large enough segment of the American market so that import penetration by those cars took place. By the time of the first oil shock of the 1970s, Japanese auto producers were in a particularly good position to gain large shares of the American market by offering inexpensive, high-quality, fuel-efficient vehicles that had been developed to suit their large Japanese domestic market, which preferred such characteristics. American producers, on the other hand, were not in a position at the time to offer a sufficiently large supply of comparable automobiles simply because most domestic production was designed to conform to domestic tastes developed during a long period of cheap fuel. In addition, foreign-market penetration by American-produced autos has always been thin because of the small demand for American-style automobiles in those markets. Because, taken individually, all foreign markets are smaller than the American market, there is some logic to the seemingly myopic behavior of American automobile producers—it at least ensures a large share of the world's largest market.

Recently, Japanese auto producers have been replacing exports to the United States with their own American production. This export replacement strategy, however, is different than the one followed by American producers early on. In the past, American automobile manufacturers produced quite different makes of automobiles in foreign countries than they produced in the United States. Despite some trend toward global uniformity in design, the American method is still mainly one of geographical diversification of production by market, while the Japanese tend to replicate domestic Japanese production in foreign markets.

The geographer Grotewold (1979) made arguments that are parallel to Linder's, but predicated upon the interregional distributions of certain types of industrial agglomerations providing the basis for trade. Two types of trade in the Grotewold model, intra-Core and inter-Core trade, are the same type of trade described by Linder. Both Linder and Grotewold are describing trade in geographically differentiated products brought about because of the existence of similar, but not identical, regional demand structures. Grotewold makes the important point that similarity of industrial sector demand among regions is at least as important as similarity of household sector demand among regions in determining the geographical pattern of trade. Both Linder and Grotewold exclude primary products from their described pattern of trade among rich countries (also see Gray, 1988). Linder does so on the grounds that trade in primary products conforms to the theory of comparative advantage. Grotewold's exclusion is based on the lack of consistent regional integration among primary-goods and capital-goods producers. This lack of integration leads to a significant Core-Periphery trade that is beyond his definition of the type of trade within and between Core regions. However, as Grotewold notes, rich countries export large quantities of primary-sector goods in addition to large quantities of manufactured goods. If market similarity is as dominant a trade factor as both Linder and Grotewold indicate, then exclusion of primary products from either model may not be necessary.

According to Linder and Grotewold, similarity of international demand structures, not dissimilarity in factor endowments, is the driving force of trade. Linder also described several trade "braking" forces. The primary deterrent to international trade, according to Linder, is distance. Distance deters trade not so much because of transportation costs, which are important, but because it limits the market horizons of producers. Producers cannot supply goods to markets with which they are unfamiliar, and distance breeds unfamiliarity in the real world. Linnemann (1966) made roughly the same argument for the impact of distance on trade flows within the framework of a gravity model. Distance induces distortions in the geographical pattern of trade, according to Linder, because it may cause countries with similar per capita incomes not to trade ". . . most intensively with each other" (Linder, 1961, p. 107). Other trade distortions can be brought about by cultural and political affinities or disaffinities. Cultural and political similarities can increase trade intensity between countries despite dissimilarity in per capita incomes, while strong differences in those characteristics can limit trade intensity between otherwise equivalent markets.

The argument that trade intensity between two countries is a positive function of the similarity in the countries' per capita incomes is essentially an argument that trade intensity is a positive function of international similarity of markets or overlapping demands. This is both a product differentiation and a product variety argument (Hanink, 1988, 1989); that is, the overlapping demands encompass not just differentiated varieties of the same good, but also the number of goods in a country's basket of imports and exports. Because of domestic market constraints, poor countries can be expected to demand a smaller array of goods than wealthy countries. While overlapping demands between rich and poor countries can exist, such demands concern only a limited number of lower-price, largely income-inelastic goods (see

Section 9.7). In this sense, the market similarity argument suggests that trade intensity between two poor countries and between a rich and poor country should be equivalent. Unfortunately, the nature of the world is that there are many more poor countries than rich ones. Large empirical samples, therefore, are biased toward poor-country trade flows for which evidence supporting Linder's thesis should not be expected. In fact, many of the negative results found in empirical tests of the Linder model may result from this sample imbalance. This is because when demand overlaps are equivalent between two poor countries and one rich country, both poor countries are more likely to be able to export to the rich country simply because of the rich country's better ability to buy. Overlapping demands among wealthy countries can cover both income-inelastic and income-elastic goods, as found recently by Hunter and Markusen (1988). The potential for trade, therefore, between two wealthy countries is much greater than the potential between a wealthy and a poor country simply because a wider array of goods is covered by overlapping demands among wealthy countries. When the Linder model is tested on empirical samples confined to rich countries, the results are invariably supportive (Balassa and Bauwens, 1988a, 1988b; Hanink, 1988, 1990).

Another demand-side model of product differentiation in international trade is provided by Armington (1969). In this model, a country's demand for imports is first determined internally and then portions of the demand are allocated to country-specific sources of supply. Much of the demand allocation is determined by product preferences based on country of production. This model accounts for nationally generic preferences for such goods as Danish furniture, French wine, and Japanese automobiles. It also can account for seemingly irrational nationalistic preferences for domestic goods that otherwise would be considered inferior. In the international marketing literature, such biases toward country of production in judging the quality of a good are referred to as "country stereotypes" (Johansson and Thorelli, 1985). Many empirical analyses indicate that the perceived merit of a product can be altered significantly by biases toward country of origin, and that such biases frequently are held in common by people of one country toward products of other countries (Bilkey and Nes, 1982).

Differentiated market theory does much to explain current structural and spatial patterns of trade. Several studies show that shares of intraindustry trade between countries are significantly affected by product differentiation (e.g., Grubel and Lloyd, 1975; Pagoulatos and Sorenson, 1975; Balassa and Bauwens, 1988a). Related analyses directly encompass the degree of product differentiation in trade (e.g., Hufbauer, 1970; Forstner, 1984). Isard (1977) suggested that product differentiation is the only reasonable explanation for the inability of the law of one price to obtain the international trade of seemingly uniform goods. Empirical evidence of the role of product differentiation in the geographical pattern of trade was provided in a study that suggests Japan's recent export success is, to an extent, a function of its ability to successfully differentiate the products in its export bundle across foreign markets (Hanink, 1987). In a related analysis (Hanink, 1989), indirect evidence was found for the kind of price-quality compensation function in international trade suggested by Lancaster's (1979) utility theory. Finally, the explanatory power of gravity model analyses of international trade (e.g., Linnemann, 1966; Bergstrand, 1985), agrees with the Helpman (1981) model of product differentiation in international trade.

9.7 ELASTICITIES OF DEMAND AND SUBSTITUTION

As indicated, the substitutability of products plays an important role in current international trade theory. The degree of substitutability between two goods is considered in the form of a trade-off, or elasticity. The term *elasticity of demand* concerns the percentage rate of change in demand for a good, in response to either the percentage rate of change in consumer incomes or the price of the good. Typically, the measure of elasticity is the partial derivative of demand with respect to income or price. For simplicity, demand elasticities also are expressed in discrete form. In the case of the income elasticity of demand, D_I,

$$D_I = \frac{\Delta Q}{\Delta I} \qquad (9.5)$$

where ΔQ is the change in demand, and ΔI is the change in income. If $D_I = 1$, then the demand response to a change in income is perfect; a unit increase in income brings about a unit increase in demand. If $D_I < 1$, then relative demand for the good decreases as incomes increase, and if $D_I > 1$, then relative demand for the good increases at a rate faster than income. In the case of price elasticities, D_P,

$$-D_P = \frac{\Delta Q}{\Delta P} \qquad (9.6)$$

The elasticity of demand with respect to price is an inverse because price changes tend to be positive, thus demand for the good tends to decline with change in price. By using the inverse in the case of price elasticity, its absolute value with respect to one $(=, >, \text{ or } <)$ is interpreted in the same way as in the case of a nominal demand elasticity.

There also are some special results concerning the value of the the elasticity coefficient for both income and price. If the elasticity coefficient is equal to zero, then demand is *perfectly price or income inelastic*. That is, changes in price or income have no bearing on the good's level of demand. Certain subsistence goods, for example, may be purchased in constant quantities regardless of their price or the consumer's income (as long as hypothetically extreme cases are ignored). In addition, the elasticity coefficients may be reversed in sign. In the case of income elasticity of demand, a negative value usually indicates an *inferior good*. The demand for inferior goods decreases after a certain income threshold is reached. Bicycles, for example, are usually considered an inferior good with respect to automobiles, at least as a primary means of transportation. At lower income levels, the elasticity of demand for bicycles may be greater than one, but as income levels advance beyond some critical threshold, bicycles are abandoned in favor of automobiles. As automobiles are substituted for bicycles, the demand for bicycles decreases and the elasticity coefficient becomes negative. A negative price elasticity indicates that demand for a good actually increases as its price increases. This response can occur, for example, if the good's quality is increasing at a faster rate than its price.

In a classic study, Houthaker and Magee (1969) applied the concepts of income and price elasticity to patterns of international trade (also see Balassa, 1979). Using aggregate trade, price, and income data for the years 1951 through 1967, they calculated the import and export demand elasticities for both income and price (Table 9.2). The export elasticities concern demand for the country's goods in other countries, while the import elasticities concern the country's demand for foreign goods. The estimates of income elasticity appear to be more reliable than the estimates of price elasticity. Note that many of the price elasticities for both exports and imports are positive, and many are close to zero. It may be that income growth during the period had a tendency to overcome the demand effects of price increases. For

TABLE 9.2   Selected Trade Elasticities Calculated by Houthaker and Magee

| | Elasticities of Demand | | | |
| | Imports | | Exports | |
Country	Income	Price	Income	Price
Australia	0.90	0.83	1.18	−0.17
Belgium	1.94	−1.02	1.83	0.42
Canada	1.20	−1.46	1.41	−0.59
Denmark	1.31	−1.66	1.69	−0.56
France	1.66	0.17	1.53	−2.27
West Germany	1.80	−0.24	2.08	1.70
Italy	2.19	−0.13	2.95	−0.03
Japan	1.23	−0.72	3.55	−0.80
Netherlands	1.89	0.23	1.88	−0.82
Norway	1.40	−0.78	1.59	0.20
Portugal	1.39	−0.53	1.41	−0.07
South Africa	1.13	1.04	0.88	−2.41
Sweden	1.42	−0.79	1.76	0.67
Switzerland	1.81	−0.84	1.47	−0.58
United Kingdom	1.66	0.22	0.86	−0.44
United States	1.51	−0.54	0.99	−1.51

Source: Houthaker, H., and S. Magee. 1969. "Income and Price Elasticities in World Trade." *Review of Economics and Statistics* 51: 111–125.

example, if incomes increase twice as fast as prices, the demand effect of the price increases may be greatly diminished or eliminated. Houthaker and Magee drew some interesting policy implications from their results. For example, the American income elasticity of demand for imports is greater than the income elasticity of demand for American goods in foreign markets. The opposite condition holds in the case of Japan. If a balance of trade is a policy initiative in the United States, then the American government would be required to inhibit growth in domestic incomes relative to growth in world incomes. In Japan, the government should encourage a faster rate of income growth than exists in the rest of the world. Obviously, the American balanced trade policy would be difficult to implement. However, the prescription for Japanese policy has been followed in effect over the past few years, albeit in conjunction with an effort to increase that country's income elasticity of import demand.

The elasticity of substitution is a compound measure that describes the rate at which one good will be substituted for another. Again, using a discrete representation, the elasticity of substitution between two goods, S_{XY}, is measured with respect to price as

$$-S_{XY} = \frac{(\Delta Q_X/\Delta Q_Y) \times (\Delta P_X/\Delta P_Y)}{(\Delta P_X/\Delta P_Y) \times (\Delta Q_X/\Delta Q_Y)} \tag{9.7}$$

which compares relative demand responses of both goods to relative price changes in the goods. (The elasticity of substitution with respect to income also can be calculated.) If the value of the coefficient is zero, the two goods are not substitutes at all. If the coefficient is equal to one, then the goods are called *perfect substitutes*. This is the type of effect described in the love-of-variety preference function described in Section 9.5. The ideal-variety preference function could exhibit the same characteristic, but only if the product's qualities are perfectly correlated with prices as assumed in the hierarchical market model of international trade.

Armington (1969) used elasticity of substitution in an analytic way to describe the preferences of consumers in one country for the goods produced in another country. In this approach, if the elasticity of substitution is zero, then the goods produced in one country are consistently perceived as superior and price differentials are ignored. Goods that seem to be preferred because of their country of production are referred to as *Armington goods*. If the elasticity of substitution is equal to one, then consumers have no preference for goods based on their country of production.

9.8 A HIERARCHICAL MARKET MODEL OF INTERNATIONAL TRADE

In his work on trade, Ohlin (1933) defined a region by homogeneity of factors over continuous space. Linder defined a region by approximate homogeneity of demand structure, but the space is noncontinuous. There is no difference between the basic tenets of intraregional trade and international trade in the Linder model. However, one characteristic of intraregional trade, hierarchical flow, is not considered in Linder's work or in most other analyses of international trade (the exceptions are described below).

In a central place system of intraregional trade there is a hierarchical order of settlements (see Chapter 4). The highest-order settlement, the one with the largest population, is the focus of trade in the region because it is there that the widest variety of goods is available. Variety of goods decreases by hierarchical steps as the population of settlements decreases by hierarchical steps. The nature of the place-production hierarchy is determined by population size alone if nominal demand functions in the hierarchy are nested, because incomes are taken as homogeneous. For example, if good A has a demand threshold of 5000 and good B has a demand threshold of 2500, then a place with a population of 5000 would provide both goods. The actual source of the place-production hierarchy has been attributed to the increasing availability of scale economies with increasing population (e.g., Nourse, 1978), which is a supply-side argument. On the demand side, Pred (1966) argues that demand for a particular good is a random probability that increases with population size. Therefore, the largest place has the widest variety of goods and the smallest place has the smallest variety. Trade in a traditional central place system flows down the hierarchy, not across it. The highest-order place, therefore, can export to all other levels in the hierarchy while the lowest-order place has no export potential in a fixed system such as Christaller's (1933). Goods not available locally must be purchased at the nearest larger center where they are available. Note that goods are not traded on price differentials but simply on the basis of availability.

Tinbergen (1968) introduced a new focus to central place theory by directing attention to the balance of payments among the places in a central place system. Obviously, if only hierarchical trade flows can occur, as in traditional central place theory, a balance of payments over places is impossible in the absence of nontrade transfers (Henderson, 1972). In a traditional central place system, lower-order places are always in trade deficit to higher-order places. Tinbergen's model of a central place system restricted trade flows among places by limiting the exports of a place to its highest-order bundle of goods. As shown by Mulligan (1981), such trade can lead to a balance of payments (trade) equilibrium.

Recently, Ahn and Nourse (1988) and Parr (1987a, 1987b) have developed central place models that not only incorporate trade flows from lower- to higher-order places, but also trade flows between places that are within the same hierarchical level. Both models rely on the existence of specialized goods to induce intralevel trade and exports up the hierarchy. Parr (1987a) argues, for example, that if the assumption of homogeneous factor endowments is relaxed, then centers of the same hierarchical level can be expected to produce and export goods that have different raw material orientations. Ahn and Nourse argue that specialized goods are the basis of interindustry trade, and without interindustry trade there would be no trade at all because producer-consumer groups would be self-sufficient.

An argument for nonhierarchical trade flows within a central place system also can be made within the context of differentiated market theory. After all, nonhierarchical trade flows and intraindustry trade represent the same thing. At the same time, hierarchical trade characteristics can be applied in the analysis of international trade. Hanink (1988) provided empirical evidence that population differences among countries is a significant factor in the geographical pattern and volume of international trade. It appears that even in the international context larger places offer a greater number and variety of tradable goods.

The work of Linder, Grotewold, and the central place theorists, among others, suggests that trade is a function of interrelationships among domestic markets. Even factor endowment theory can be viewed from this perspective when its basis in comparative advantage is considered. In the context of comparative advantage, trade is the result of the interaction of domestic factor markets across countries. In light of the work reviewed above, some basic principles of of international trade as hierarchical market interactions have been developed (Hanink, 1991).

A place-production hierarchy of the sort used in central place theory is a useful framework for establishing a hierarchical market model of international trade. First, take a set of N countries with homogeneous factor endowments and large population sizes, but with variable mean incomes, I, with nonzero variances ($I = 1, \ldots, N$). Assume the variability in income is due to variability in production functions. Assume also a positive marginal propensity to consume across countries, C. Rely on Engel's law (Chapter 3) so that

$$U_C = \Sigma_N G_N \tag{9.8}$$

where U_C is the common utility in country C, and G_N denotes consumption of the Nth good (Krugman, 1980). Let utility be limited by income, because the production of a good is a function of its mean income threshold, so that

$$Q_G = (I_G, r) \tag{9.9}$$

where Q_G denotes production of a good, I_G is the good's threshold demand, which is defined in terms of average income, and r is a random term. This is a dichotomous demand function in which Q_G is realized only if I_G obtains. Define the distribution of the countries by level of income so that I denotes the order of a country. Because I indicates sufficient market threshold, let Q_I denote that the Ith good is in demand. In such a system, place C_N contains nested markets $I_N, I_{N-1}, \ldots I_1$, and potential production of goods $Q_N, Q_{N-1}, \ldots, Q_1$ and production of Q_1, the lowest-order good, takes place in all countries. Because threshold demands determine production, goods become decreasingly competitive as their order increases, and the highest-order good is perfectly noncompetitive. Extending Equation 9.9 to trade, *potential exports* can be viewed as a function of domestic incomes and foreign markets:

$$E_{ij} = (I_i, D_j, r) \tag{9.10}$$

where E_{ij} is the potential for the export of a good from the ith country to the jth country, I is mean income, D is demand, and r, again, is a random term. Equation

9.10 implies the potential for intraindustry trade, but only if I_j is equated to D_j, which is not a necessary case if incomes have nonzero variances (see below).

Trade in a traditional system of central places does not consist of exporting and importing per se, but of consumers travelling from lower-order centers to higher-order centers to purchase higher-order goods. International trade, however, is explicit trade with mobile goods and, effectively, immobile consumers. Relying on the consumer preferences associated with love of variety, the frequency of potential exports of goods, fEQ, in the system described follows the rule

$$fEQ_1 > fEQ_2 > \ldots < fEQ_N \qquad (9.11)$$

This relationship holds because threshold demands are nested. The ordering of export frequencies described in Equation 9.11 is similar to that found to exist by Thompson (1982) in a hierarchical trade system in the Philippines. Maintaining the assumption of factor homogeneity across countries, trade in a particular good, Q_K, can take place only between countries with incomes $I \geq K$: obviously, bilateral trade markets do not exist for goods that are not domestically produced. It follows that the cumulative frequency of potential intraindustry trade partners, cfT, takes the progression

$$cfTC_1 < cfTC_2 < \ldots < cfTC_N \qquad (9.12)$$

where C_N is the highest-order country.

This relationship is the same as Krugman's (1981) result of large countries exporting more than small countries. As stated, the hierarchical model assumes equal populations but variable mean incomes, therefore mean income can translate completely to the aggregate income measure of size used by Krugman. Krugman, however, derives his conclusion from a basis of scale economies and not hierachical trade.

Obviously, potential export value is a positive function of export frequency, which in turn is a positive function of mean income. Potential import value also is a function of mean income, as long as incomes have a nonzero variance. A nonzero variance about mean incomes suggests the existence of some demand for higher-order goods that are not domestically produced due to domestic threshold limits. This is why Equation 9.10 does not always define potential intraindustry trade. However, the potential relative values of both imports and exports should follow the same progression as in the rule on cumulative trade partner frequency (Equation 9.12). This is not to say that trade accounts are balanced, only that both potential import and export values are progressive by mean income in countries. Imbalance in the trade accounts of the hierarchical model are just as likely as they are in the real world of international trade.

With regard to bilateral intraindustry trade, we can define the dominant quality of a good as a set of characteristics $\overline{Q}$, where $\overline{Q}_I = f(I)$. This relationship indicates that the quality of a dominant good produced in a country is responsive to average tastes, as defined by mean income. The degree of <u>qualitative</u> substitutability among goods of the same order may then be taken as the intersection of the two countries' preferences:

$$\overline{Q}_I \cap \overline{Q}_K = (|I - K|) \qquad (9.13)$$

where $|I - K|$ is the absolute difference in mean incomes of two countries, and both I and K are at or above threshold requirements for the good in question. Because consumption schedules are taken as functions of income (Linder, 1961; Hunter and Markusen, 1988), and domestic production is driven by domestic demand, the proximity of mean incomes defines the potential common set of goods that enter bilateral trade. This, of course, is a wholly different result than that found in strict factor endowment theory, where bilateral trade is an exchange of different, rather than common, goods. The degree to which qualitative substitutes enter into actual trade must be related to relative prices as well as relative qualities, so that prices compensate for qualitative differences. Defining $\overline{P}$ as the average price of a good, then $\overline{P} = f(I)$, which indicates that price levels are determined by levels of "average" income or demand. Then

$$|\overline{P}_I - \overline{P}_K| = (|I - K|) \qquad (9.14)$$

so that absolute price differences, like market overlaps, are functions of absolute differences in income levels.

If distance between producer and consumer is costless, then a love-of-variety utility function would imply that intraindustry trade could take place in goods that are perfect substitutes, and trade values would be maximized between countries that have identical per capita incomes. The overlap of markets can determine the structure, or product composition, of a country's trade, but if distance has no trade effect, then the geographical pattern of trade can be indeterminate.

Distance can be an important determinant of trade simply because it affects delivered prices (indirectly) through transportation costs. However, distance between geographical markets in the international economy not only brings about higher delivered prices for goods, it also limits the market horizons of producers and consumers. Again, in the Linder model, producers supply goods primarily designed to suit known domestic tastes. Producers have less information concerning distant markets, so it is unlikely that they would concentrate on producing goods for unknown, or at best uncertain, demand. It also can be argued that consumer information is limited by distance. It is likely that preferences are not formed independently of experience, so the majority tastes of the domestic market must be self-reinforcing. Better-known, domestically produced varieties of goods should have an edge in competition for domestic market shares because consumer knowledge of available varieties decreases with distance from their place of production. Essentially, as similarity in demand structures increases, the more integrated the markets of two separated regions become. Trade potential is maximal between two neighboring countries with similar demand structures, but it is not minimal between two distant countries as long as their demand structures are homogeneous. Therefore, it can be argued that only the value of trade, and not the existence (i.e., nominal frequency) of trade, should be affected by distance. Distance effectively decreases the elasticity of substitution in trade, but does not drive it to zero.

REFERENCES

Ahn, J., and H. Nourse. 1988. "Spatial Economic Interdependence in an Urban Hierarchy System." *Journal of Regional Science* 28: 421–432.

Armington, P. 1969. "A Theory of Demand for Products Distinguished by Place of Production." *IMF Staff Papers* 16: 159–178.

Balassa, B. 1979. "Export Composition and Export Performance in the Industrial Countries, 1953–71." *Review of Economics and Statistics* 61: 604–607.

Balassa, B., and L. Bauwens. 1988a. *Changing Trade Patterns in Manufactured Goods: An Econometric Investigation* (Amsterdam: North-Holland).

———. 1988b. "The Determinants of Intra-European Trade in Manufactured Goods." *European Economic Review* 32: 1421–1437.

Bergstrand, J. 1985. "The Gravity Equation in International Trade: Some Microeconomic Foundations and Empirical Evidence." *Review of Economics and Statistics* 67: 474–481.

Bilkey, W., and E. Nes. 1982. "Country-of-Origin Effects on Product Evaluations." *Journal of International Business Studies* 13: 89–99.

Chamberlin, E. 1933. *The Theory of Monopolistic Competition* (Cambridge, Massachusetts: Harvard University Press).

Christaller, W. 1933. *Die zentralen Orte in Suddeutschland* (Jena: Gustav Fischer). Translated by C. Baskin, 1966, as *Central Places in Southern Germany* (Englewood Cliffs, New Jersey: Prentice-Hall).

Deardorff, A. 1984. "Testing Trade Theories and Predicting Trade Flows." In *Handbook of International Economics,* vol. 1, R. Jones and P. Kenen, eds. (Amsterdam: Elsevier).

Dixit, A., and V. Norman. 1980. *Theory of International Trade: A Dual, General Equilibrium Approach* (Digswell Place, England: James Nisbet).

Dixit, A., and J. Stiglitz. 1977. "Monopolistic Competition and Optimum Product Diversity." *American Economic Review* 67: 297–308.

Flam, H., and E. Helpman. 1987. "Vertical Product Differentiation and North-South Trade." *American Economic Review* 77: 810–822.

Forstner, H. 1984. "The Changing Pattern of International Trade in Manufactures: A Logit Analysis." *Weltwirtschaftliches Archiv* 120: 1–17.

Gomes, L. 1990. *Neoclassical International Economics: An Historical Survey* (New York: St. Martin's Press).

Gray, H. 1980. "The Theory of International Trade among Industrial Nations." *Weltwirtschaftliches Archiv* 116: 447–470.

———. 1986. "Non-Competitive Imports and Gains from Trade." *The International Trade Journal* 1: 107–129.

———. 1988. "Intra-Industry Trade: An 'Untidy' Phenomenon." *Weltwirtschaftliches Archiv* 124: 211–219.

Grotewold, A. 1979. *The Regional Theory of World Trade* (Grove City: Ptolemy Press).

Grubel, H., and P. Lloyd. 1975. *Intra-industry Trade: The Theory and Measurement of International Trade in Differentiated Products* (New York: John Wiley & Sons).

Hanink, D. 1987. "A Comparative Analysis of the Competitive Geographical Trade Performances of the USA, FRG, and Japan: The Markets and Marketers Hypothesis." *Economic Geography* 63: 293–305.

_____ . 1988. "An Extended Linder Model of International Trade." *Economic Geography* 64: 322–334.

_____ . 1989. "A Geographical Product Differentiation Model of Trade Competition in Third Markets." *Geographical Analysis* 21: 122–133.

_____ . 1990. "Linder, Again." *Weltwirtschaftliches Archiv* 126: 257–267.

_____ . 1991. "A Hierarchical Market Model of International Trade." *Geographical Analysis* 23: 147–157.

Hazari, B. 1978. *The Pure Theory of International Trade and Distortions* (New York: John Wiley & Sons).

Heckscher, E. 1919. "The Effect of Foreign Trade on the Distribution of Income." *Economisk Tidskrift* 21. Reprinted in *Readings in the Theory of International Trade,* 1950, H. Ellis and L. Metzler, eds. (Homewood, Illinois: Richard D. Irwin).

Helpman, E. 1981. "International Trade in the Presence of Product Differentiation, Economies of Scale and Monopolistic Competition: A Chamberlin-Heckscher-Ohlin Approach." *Journal of International Economics* 11: 305–340.

_____ . 1987. "Imperfect Competition and International Trade." *European Economic Review* 31: 77–81.

Helpman, E., and P. Krugman. 1985. *Market Structure and Foreign Trade: Increasing Returns, Imperfect Competition, and the International Economy* (Cambridge, Massachusetts: MIT Press).

Henderson, J. 1972. "Hierarchy Models of City Size: An Economic Evaluation." *Journal of Regional Science* 12: 435–441.

Houthaker, H., and S. Magee. 1979. "Income and Price Elasticities in World Trade." *Review of Economics and Statistics* 51: 111–125.

Hoy, H., and J. Shaw. 1981. "The United States' Comparative Advantage and its Relationship to the Product Life Cycle Theory and the World Gross National Product Share." *Columbia Journal of World Business* 16: 40–50.

Hufbauer, G. 1970. "The Impact of National Characteristics and Technology on the Commodity Composition of Trade in Manufactured Goods." In *The Technology Factor in International Trade,* R. Vernon, ed. (New York: National Bureau of Economic Research).

Hughes, K. 1986. *Exports and Technology* (Cambridge, Massachusetts: Cambridge University Press).

Hunter, L., and J. Markusen. 1988. "Per-Capita Income as a Determinant of Trade." In *Empirical Methods for International Trade,* R. Feenstra, ed. (Cambridge, Massachusetts: MIT Press).

Isard, P. 1977. "How Far Can We Push the 'Law of One Price'?" *American Economic Review* 67: 942–948.

Johansson, J., and H. Thorelli. 1985. "International Product Positioning." *Journal of International Business Studies* 16: 57–75.

Johnson, H. 1967. "International Trade Theory and Monopolistic Competition Theory." In

Monopolistic Competition Theory: Studies in Impact, R. Kuenne, ed. (New York: John Wiley & Sons).

Krugman, P. 1980. "Scale Economies, Product Differentiation, and the Pattern of Trade." *American Economic Review* 70: 950–959.

———. 1981. "Intraindustry Specialization and the Gains from Trade." *Journal of Political Economy* 89: 959–973.

Lancaster, K. 1979. *Variety, Equity and Efficiency* (New York: Columbia University Press).

———. 1980. "Intra-Industry Trade under Perfect Monopolistic Competition." *Journal of International Economics* 10: 151–75.

Leamer, E. 1980. "The Leontieff Paradox, Reconsidered." *Journal of Political Economy* 88: 495–503.

Leontieff, W. 1956. "Factor Proportions and the Structure of American Trade: Further Theoretical and Empirical Analysis." *Review of Economics and Statistics* 38: 386–407.

Linder, S. B. 1961. *An Essay on Trade and Transformation* (New York: John Wiley & Sons).

Linnemann, H. 1966. *An Econometric Study of International Trade Flows* (Amsterdam: North-Holland).

Magee, S., and N. Robins. 1978. "The Raw Material Product Cycle." In *Mineral Resources in the Pacific Area,* L. Krause and P. Hughes, eds. (San Francisco: Federal Reserve Bank of San Francisco).

Markusen, J. 1981. "Trade and the Gains from Trade with Imperfect Competition." *Journal of International Economics* 11: 531–551.

Mulligan, G. 1981. "A Note on Hierarchical Income Flows." *Environment and Planning A* 13: 747–750.

Nelson, R., and V. Norman. 1977. "Technological Change and Factor Mix over the Product Cycle." *Journal of Development Economics* 4: 3–24.

Neven, D. 1986. "Address' Models of Differentiation." In *Spatial Pricing and Differentiated Markets,* London Papers in Regional Science, no. 16, G. Norman, ed. (London: Pion).

Nourse, H. 1978. "Equivalence of Central Place and Economic Base Theories of Urban Growth." *Journal of Urban Economics* 5: 543–49.

Ohlin, B. 1933. *Interregional and International Trade.* (Cambridge, Massachusetts: Harvard University Press).

Pagoulatos, E., and R. Sorenson. 1975. "Two-Way International Trade: An Econometric Analysis." *Weltwirtschaftliches Archiv* 111: 454–465.

Parr, J. 1987a. "The Tinbergen Analysis of an Urban System and Alternative Approaches." *Environment and Planning A* 19: 187–204.

———. 1987b. "Interaction in an Urban System: Aspects of Trade and Commuting." *Economic Geography* 63: 223–240.

Pred, A. 1966. *The Spatial Dynamics of U.S. Urban-Industrial Growth, 1800–1914* (Cambridge, Massachusetts: MIT Press).

Rybczynski, T. 1955. "Factor Endowment and Relative Commodity Prices." *Economica* 22: 336–341.

Salvatore, D., and R. Barazesh. 1990. "The Factor Content of U.S. Foreign Trade and the Heckscher-Ohlin Theory." *The International Trade Journal* 5: 149–183.

Samuelson, P. 1948. "International Trade and the Equalisation of Factor Prices." *Economic Journal* 58: 163–184.

Taylor, M. 1986. "The Product-Cycle Model: A Critique." *Environment and Planning A* 18: 751–761.

Thompson, J. 1982. "An Empirical Note on the Compatability of Central Place Models and Economic Base Theory." *Journal of Regional Science* 22: 97–103.

Tinbergen, J. 1968. "The Hierarchy Model of the Size Distribution of Centers." *Papers of the Regional Science Association* 20: 65–68.

Vernon, R. 1966. "International Investment and International Trade in the Product Cycle." *Quarterly Journal of Economics* 80: 190–207.

_____. 1979. "The Product Cycle Hypothesis in a New International Environment." *Oxford Bulletin of Economics and Statistics* 41: 255–267.

Wells, L. 1968. "A Product Life Cycle for International Trade?" *Journal of Marketing* 32: 1–6.

CHAPTER 10

. . .

Managed Trade

. . .

10.1 INTRODUCTION

In their basic forms, all the trade models described in Chapter 9 concern some simple benefits of free trade. In the factor endowment model, for example, producers benefit from trade because production becomes more efficient, and consumers benefit because prices decrease. In the product differentiation models, including the hierarchical market model, free trade allows increased benefits for consumers due to their ability to purchase greater or better varieties of goods than can be produced domestically. Unfortunately, the benefits of free trade that come about so quickly in theory are slower to be realized in reality. Differences in economic and population size eliminate much of the competitive reaction of price equalization among countries. In addition, large differences in average incomes, factor endowments, scale economies, or technology among countries means that large quantities of noncompetitive goods enter into international trade. The actual place characteristics of the spatial interaction system of international trade, as opposed to the theoretical characteristics, mean that large rich countries are more likely to benefit from trade than small poor countries.

In the wake of the Great Depression and World War II, the governments of many industrial countries began a concerted effort to liberalize their trade policies. The majority of opinion at the time was that restrictive trade policies, such as the Smoot-Hawley tariff in the United States, had exacerbated and extended the Great Depression of the 1930s. In addition, the benefits of freer trade were thought to be one method of aiding rapid reconstruction of the European economies, which had been structurally and physically ravaged by the war. At the same time Core economies were liberalizing their trade policies and pursuing freer trade, many of the world's peripheral countries, several of them newly independent, were closing trade channels. Often governments in peripheral countries were not convinced of the potential benefits of free trade derived from comparative advantage. It has been argued, for example, that the only reason Ricardo's view of trade became popular in England was because it provided a theoretical basis for the highly favorable terms of British trade. At the time, England had a comparative advantage in all goods with high values. In the postwar era it seemed that the Core economies were pressing for freer trade for the same reason that England had in the past; the maintenance of favorable terms of trade with peripheral economies. In order to break Core-Periphery trade patterns, peripheral countries relied on limiting imports.

Like many government policies, trade policy is cyclical (Chung, 1990; Melese et al., 1989). Currently, the industrial countries are recasting their trade policies toward more restrictive practices (World Bank, 1987), and moving more toward bilateral trade initiatives than global ones. Peripheral countries, on the other hand, are now taking up policies of trade liberalization and opening their formerly closed markets.

This chapter contains a survey of method of trade management. It begins with an examination of management instruments typically used by national governments, including both tariff and nontariff barriers to trade. The scale then changes to a global one with a discussion of multilateral trade agreements such as the General Agreement on Tariffs and Trade (GATT). In turn, regional trade agreements, such as that of the European Community, are discussed within the context of geographical trade discrimination. Finally, the special type of managed trade that takes place within the MNC is considered. Two important barriers to trade are not directly addressed in this chapter. One is intervening distance between potential and actual trade partners, which was discussed in Chapter 9. The other is the currency exchange rate, which was treated in a more thorough manner in Chapter 5.

10.2   TARIFFS

Tariffs are taxes due, or duties, on traded goods. Tariffs can be collected on both imports and exports, but import tariffs are much more widely used by governments to manage trade. Tariffs can be levied in two ways. *Specific tariffs* are fixed duties collected on a goods weight or volume. For example, a specific tariff on an agricultural product could be a fixed amount per ton. *Ad valorem tariffs* are like sales taxes, with the level of duty determined as a fixed proportion of the price of the good. Import tariffs have a long history, but initially their primary purpose was, to use the current phrase, "revenue enhancement." The castles on the Rhine River, for example, served as trade duty collection stations, and the revenues obtained supported the local government. Before establishment of the income tax in the United States, trade duties were a primary source of federal income and contributed more than half of the country's internal revenue as late as 1910. (In 1989, trade duties accounted for about 1.5% of American federal revenues.) Tariff revenues still account for a significant portion of government revenue in a number of countries, but the general purpose of tariff policy today is to manage trade.

Put simply, the tariff is a tax that raises prices on goods, with the effect that more money is paid to maintain a fixed level of consumption, or less is consumed if a fixed budget for the good is maintained. The general effects of tariffs (and quotas) are portrayed in Figure 10.1. This representation assumes that both demand and supply are price-elastic, so the demand function is represented by a downward sloping line and the supply function is represented by the upward sloping line. The intersection of the supply and demand functions at K defines the market-clearing equilibrium price of the good in question. However, at the world price of the good, PW, domestic supply, SW, is insufficient to match domestic demand, DW. The difference in quality consumed and quantity supplied is the amount of the good that is imported.

Assume, the government applies an import tariff to a good that raises its landed price to PT. The higher price PT induces greater domestic production of the good, and domestic supplies increase from quantity SW to quantity ST. At the same time, the higher price causes demand to decrease from quantity DW to DT. Imports are still consumed in the country, but at the lower level defined by DT-ST as compared to the pre-tariff level of DW-SW.

When any tariff is enacted, three domestic interests are affected: producers, the government, and consumers. In this example, producers' gains under the tariff are defined by the area bounded by the points PT, A, F, PW of the graph. This area can be considered as rent, or income derived from nonproductive activity. The benefit to the producers is obtained by the artificial increase in prices under the tariff. The government also gains rent under the tariff price, PT. The government's rent is defined by the area A, B, D, E, which defines the tariff's revenue. The producer and government rents are transfer payments from consumers, who suffer losses defined by the area PT, B, C, PW. Consumers, under the tariff, must either pay more to maintain consumption or consume less at pre-tariff expenditures. In a conventional analysis, the *deadweight loss* to the economy is defined by the areas of the two triangles A, E, F, and B, C, D, which are the portions of consumer loss not transferred to either producers or government. The tariff price, PT, results in a national loss of income. Recently, some analysts have suggested that the deadweight loss to the economy is even greater than that defined by the sum of the areas of the two triangles. The argument is that some of the tariff revenue will be used simply to maintain the tariff's

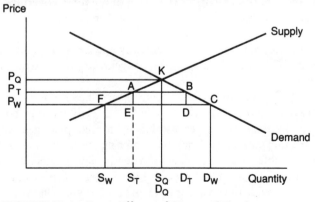

FIGURE 10.1   Some Effects of Managed Trade

collection, and that some of the producer rent will be used simply to maintain political interest in keeping the tariff. In both cases, tariff-induced rents are spent on the tariff, which is unproductive. Tariff maintenance expenditures add to the economy's deadweight loss from the tariff.

Now assume the government applies an import tariff to the good that raises its landed price to PQ. The price PQ, in this example, is the effective equilibrium price for domestic producers. Domestic supply, at SQ, and demand, at DQ, are equal, so the tariff is prohibitive. Assuming the good is completely undifferentiated, imports from foreign producers cease. In this case, producer rents are defined as the graphed area PQ, K, F, PW, and consumer losses are the area PQ, K, C, PW. Note that there are no government revenues under a prohibitive tariff because imports are nonexistent. Prohibitive tariffs have the same transfer effect as quotas, with income transferred only from consumers to producers. Nonzero quotas, however, unlike prohibitive tariffs, allow foreign producers to collect rent from the domestic economy, as described in Section 10.4 dealing with voluntary export restraints.

10.3 TARIFFS AND PROTECTIONISM

Given the relationships described in Figure 10.1, any tariff must decrease consumer welfare. Why, then, do governments employ tariffs as a policy to administer trade? Beside raising revenues, the only reason that governments have to use tariffs is to "protect" selected sectors of their domestic economies. The activity of governments in international markets is the single most important factor in distinguishing international trade from interregional trade within a country's borders. Historically, government intervention in international trade, usually in the form of some type of trade protectionism, has been part and parcel of national policy. For example, the so-called tariff of abominations is considered just as frequently in political histories of America as it is in economic histories, and the same can be said of the passage of the corn laws in the United Kingdom (Bhagwati, 1988). Most of the time, government intervention in international trade, especially limitation of imports, is a politically popular move. The benefits of free trade, even in theory, are spread over a country's entire population. In aggregate they are large, but individually may seem quite small. On the other hand, injuries from free trade tend to be concentrated and strongly felt by those directly affected.

One protectionist argument is that newly established domestic industries will be unable to gain even a domestic market foothold if directly faced by competition from longer-established foreign producers. Established foreign producers enjoy economies of scale that are unavailable to firms just entering the industry, and their edge in efficiency is impossible to overcome. A sufficiently high protective tariff denies the domestic market to foreign competitors, and the domestic firms can rely on their own captive market to provide the basis for inducing their own economies of scale. Called the "infant industry" argument for trade protection, such tariffs would be lifted once the domestic industry achieves the scale economies that are necessary to compete with established foreign producers domestically and even in international markets. This policy has been used with seeming success, for example, by the Americans and Japanese, both of which employed protective tariffs to nurture their domestic automobile industries (Hogendoorn and Brown, 1979). Many countries have extended the infant industry argument over most of their economies and employed a policy of *import substitution* as the primary method of inducing broad domestic growth in a developing country (Bruton, 1989). In addition, import substitution provides a foundation for diversifying a country's economic structure by blocking the tendency toward specialization that results from trade based on comparative advantage.

Arguments also are made for protection of declining, or "sunset," industries. In this case, foreign competition is seen as a threat to the previously established but declining domestic market of domestic producers. Foreign competition—considered to be unfair because of government subsidies to the foreign producer, unfair trading practices of the foreign producer, or even the foreign producer's undeniable edge in production efficiency—supposedly threatens the domestic economy for any of several reasons. First, and foremost, the decline of a domestic industry can lead to an increase in unemployment and a decrease in income. Pure theory calls for rapid shifts in employment from a declining sector to a growing sector, but in reality such shifts are sluggish because labor skills are not perfectly mobile in a sectoral sense, and labor is not perfectly mobile in a geographical sense. A laid-off textile worker in one region of a country is not immediately employable in the producer electronics industry in another region of the country. Other arguments for protection of a declining domestic industry center around the need to maintain certain domestic levels of production in the interest of national defense and, occasionally, national face-saving and nostalgia. Steel production in the past, and semiconductor production in the present, are examples of industries cited as critical to national interests. Currently, the Japanese insist on self-sufficiency in rice production and simply prohibit importation of raw and most processed forms of that grain.

As in the case of protective tariffs for infant industries, protective tariffs can be used to provide breathing space for established but inefficient domestic industries to regain former competitive positions. An example of this type of tariff policy is the case of Harley-Davidson motorcycles in the United States. At one time, Harley-Davidson was the heavy (500+ cubic-centimeter engine displacement) motorcycle of choice in the United States. By the early 1980s, however, Harley-Davidson was in danger of bankruptcy due to its inability to compete on either price or quality with heavy motorcycles imported from Japan. Harley-Davidson was able to convince the American government that it was unlikely to remain in business in the face of foreign competition, and the ad valorem tariff on imported heavy Japanese motorcycles was raised substantially. The increase in the tariff, however, was made with a declining schedule in which the rate would decrease to its original level after five years. The high escalation of the tariff allowed Harley-Davidson immediate relief from Japanese competition, but the declining schedule compelled Harley-Davidson to improve its production efficiency or ultimately go out of business. Harley-Davidson improved its manufacturing plant in Milwaukee and instituted other "productivity enhancements" (i.e., layoffs), and was able to strongly re-establish itself in the American market. The turnaround was faster than expected, and Harley-Davidson agreed to the reimposition of the initial tariff rate in less than the five years scheduled. A traditional industry was saved by a protective tariff of limited duration, and both chopped and full-dress "Hogs" remain vital American institutions.

Theoretically, the imposition of any tariff increases the benefits of a few at the expense of decreasing the welfare of many. In most cases, imposing a protective tariff is a political method of ameliorating a vocal special interest group. The *Stolper-Samuelson theorem* (1941) is a neoclassical factor payments corollary of the Rybczynski theorem on changes in output in international trade (Chapter 9). Stolper-Samuelson shows that in an incompletely specialized trading economy, an increase in the price of any good raises the real payment to the factor used intensively in the production of the good. An increase in the price of a labor-intensive good raises real wages paid to labor, while an increase in the price of a capital-intensive good increases real profits, as payments to the capital. Decreasing prices bring about decreasing real payments to intensively used factors. The intensively used factors are the special interests of trade protection. Higher tariffs mean higher prices and higher real payments to the relevant factors; lower tariffs mean lower prices and lower real payments. Producers of capital-intensive goods have a vested interest in high tariffs on their goods, and organizations such as labor unions have a vested interest in high tariffs on labor-intensive goods.

Governments, when resorting to tariff protection, could try to achieve a balance between benefits to the factor facing loss of real payments, and reductions in welfare to all consumers of the product. Trying to determine an accurate balance between income retained by factors and purchasing power lost by consumers is a very complicated matter that would require complete and certain knowledge of the price- and income-demand elasticities of the good in question. For example, a final price that includes a higher tariff would increase real income to some, which in turn may allow demand for an income-elastic good to remain fairly bouyant. However, the higher tariff raises the price, and if the good is price elastic in its demand as well, there would be a counter tendency for demand for the good to decrease. In cases of complete protection, a *prohibitive tariff* is placed on the good, which is designed to completely shut off foreign imports. More often, tariffs are targeted toward putting foreign prices at slightly more than, or even with, domestic prices. This type of tariff policy considers only price elasticity of demand, which tends to be a more practical approach than joint consideration of income elasticity and price elasticity. The direct aggregate income effect of a tariff typically is negligible relative to the price effect. In addition, roughly equating foreign prices to domestic prices by means of a tariff allows a government to represent its action as one taken in the interest of "fair trade" (Spich, 1986).

The United States uses *countervailing duties* to balance the competitive positions of foreign and American firms in its domestic market. Countervailing duties are tariffs designed to offset foreign price advantages that are perceived as unfair by domestic producers. Unfair foreign price competition can result from government subsidies to foreign firms that, in effect, make them lowest-cost producers (see Section 6.4). More often, however, countervailing duties are imposed to counteract foreign *dumping* of goods in the domestic market. Dumping is the practice of selling goods in a foreign market at a lower price than they are sold in the producer's domestic market. Producers dump goods for several reasons, but all are basically focused upon gaining market share in a foreign country. For this reason, dumping also is referred to as *predatory pricing*. Losses initially incurred by dumping in foreign markets can be offset by excess profits in domestic markets in the short run, and by the development of economies of scale as the foreign market share increases over a longer period.

The American government imposed countervailing duties on a large variety of imported bearings in early 1989. A charge that foreign bearings were being dumped was brought by the Torrington Company, an American producer of bearings, to the United States Commerce Department's Import Administration and its Office of Anti-Dumping Investigations. The degree of dumping is determined by the margin between a good's price in the producer's domestic market and its price in the foreign market, in this case the United States. It was determined that the price margins ranged from 9% for French bearings to 180% for Swedish bearings. That is, French producers were discounting their bearings by 9% on the American market and Swedish producers were discounting their prices by 180% in the United States as compared to their domestic prices. The countervailing duties are imposed with respect to the size of the margins. Foreign firms may maintain their pricing practices, but are required to deposit an amount equal to their value with the Department of Commerce. For example, if Swedish firms retain their 180% margin, they must deposit $18 million for every $10 million worth of bearings sold in America. If the margin is shown to have been decreased, the amount of the decrease is refunded to the depositor. If it increases, the amount of the deposit is increased. Many foreign firms have been paying such deposits for several years, because the maintenance of American market share has a greater value than the cost of the deposits.

The United States is not the only country to use counter-dumping measures. Australia and Canada, and the European Community as a single entity (see Section 10.8), also take measures against foreign goods being dumped in their markets (Stegeman, 1990). Price responses such as countervailing duties are most frequently made to ward off dumping. However, anti-dumping initiatives of a different kind have been taken toward goods imported from centrally planned economies (Brown and Koont, 1989). The use of price margins as measures of dumping severity was unfounded in such cases. Centrally planned economies have inconsistent price systems in their domestic markets that cannot be compared to their pricing of goods entered into foreign trade. Frequently, quantity restrictions, or quotas (Section 10.4), were used to limit the importation of goods that are considered to be dumped by producers from centrally planned economies.

In competitive international markets, like those assumed in factor endowment theory, tariffs are likely to have unintended negative effects that far outweigh any intended specific benefits to any particular factors of production. Countervailing duties on bearings, for example, allow "fair" trade in bearings markets and provide benefits to certain domestic producers. However, they raise general price levels of a wide array of manufactured and other products in the American economy because bearings are widely used. In addition countervailing duties and prohibitive tariffs create a tendency for inefficient use of resources by allocating factors of production to protected industries when the factors could be more efficiently employed in other industries. Again, in a competitive context, tariffs benefit a few at the expense of many. Finally, historical precedent indicates that the enactment of tariffs by one country typically is countered by retaliatory tariffs by other countries, which themselves occasion retaliation and so on. Rounds of tariff retaliation among the industrial countries have been suggested as one reason for the severity of the Great Depression.

Are there any conditions that suggest the use of tariffs could generate net benefits to an economy? Some analyses indicate that when markets are not perfectly competitive, an *optimum tariff* can be designed. An optimum tariff provides net benefits to the entire economy rather than net disbenefits. The idea of an optimum tariff originated with Bickerdike (1907) in light of work by Pigou (1906) on the use of tariffs in protecting infant industries. Optimal tariffs can be enacted when one country is large enough to become a price maker rather than price taker in the international economy. Essentially, the optimal tariff is designed as a method for a monopsonist to extract some of the *economic rent* taken from the market by a monopolist (Kenen, 1989). In this context, rent is excess profit, profit over and above marginal costs including payments to capital. Monopolists, as single producers, are able to extract rents from markets by setting prices just far enough above their true equilibrium value to maintain a large volume of trade. The upper limit of the price must be low enough not to significantly reduce sales volume due to the price elasticity of demand for the good. A monopsonist is a single buyer of a good, and therefore has some price-making power as well. In this context, the optimal tariff is one that extracts some of the monopoly's rent and places it in the treasury of the importing country with the large market. The increase of the final price of the product, tariff included, is offset by a decrease in the monopolist's price of the good which is made in order to maintain market share. Consumers are, at least, no worse off than before, and the government has increased its revenue at the expense of the foreign producer. Ultimately, the optimum tariff is a tariff that makes "the foreigner pay." Like all tariffs, however, the likely response of the producer's government is to enact a retaliatory tariff against goods from the country with the optimum tariff.

The theoretical ability to impose an optimum tariff has recently received renewed attention under the general heading of *strategic trade policy*. Recall from the last chapter that a particular focus of current theory is on trade in differentiated products. Almost all manufactured goods can be defined as differentiated in some way, if only because of their place of production. All differentiated products are monopolistic because they have no pure competition. Strategic trade policy concerns trade in these differentiated products as well as in goods that are exported by more conventional monopolists (Krugman, 1986). Typically, the argument for a strategic trade policy centers on syntheses of both the earlier thinking on optimum tariffs and the need to protect infant industries. For example, Brander and Spencer (1981), have suggested that some of the rent extracted from a foreign monopolist can be used by governments to subsidize domestic industries so that they, in turn, can extract monopoly rents from other markets. This approach to trade policy combines domestic subsidy and tariffs into a form of hybrid industrial policy targeted at certain sectors of a national economy (Cline, 1986). As summarized by Gomes (1990), strategic trade policy can be used to capitalize on spillover effects of domestic industry's research and development expenditures and production experience. These spillovers, or externalities, can provide a competitive advantage to a wide variety of domestic firms in international markets. The competitive advantage can be maintained, however, only by government efforts at ensuring the lead domestic industry's monopolistic advantage.

Ultimately, it seems that strategic policy consists of the options available to the government of the monopoly affected by the imposition of an optimum tariff. Strategic trade policy is more a policy of retaliation than initial protection. In addition, even trade policy couched in "strategic" terms seems to have the same effects as any policy of increased tariffs. In a simulation of trade in 16K RAM chips between the United States and Japan, Baldwin and Krugman (1988) found fairly standard results —that the greatest net benefits were gained by both economies when trade was free, and the benefits declined with increasing protection. Market isolation, induced by a prohibitive tariff, simply resulted in higher prices in both countries and steeply diminished consumer welfare as compared to free-trade levels.

10.4   NONTARIFF BARRIERS TO TRADE

Nontariff barriers (NTBs) to trade encompass a wide variety of methods used by governments to administer trade without direct application of tariffs (Cao, 1980; Coughlin and Wood, 1989). Laird and Yeats (1990) have defined three classes of NTBs. The first class consists of those NTBs, such as quotas, that are designed with the direct intention of distorting a product pattern or geographical pattern of trade. The second class of NTBs consists of those that have only a secondary purpose of distorting the pattern of trade; for example, legislation concerning product standards. The third class consists of government policies and procedures that have a largely unintentional trade effect, such as regional development programs intended to raise local employment levels. Deardorf and Stern (1985, 1986) have found the trade-distorting effects of NTBs to be considerably less than that of tariffs, but their use in administering trade is increasing (Bhagwati, 1988). NTBs are typically applied in a sector-specific way, with apparel, textiles, footwear, some machinery, and especially agricultural products as common targets. NTBs also are being used in a country-specific manner, with virtually all products of a country as their target.

Quotas, or quantitative import restrictions, are made by volume or value. In the first case, the volume or number of units of a good is physically limited; in the second case, a ceiling on the good's total import value is declared. Quotas have almost the same effect on trade as tariffs, with the exception that they rarely provide any government revenue. In one sense, there is no difference at all between a prohibitive tariff and a zero quota. Selling quota rights, either to domestic importers or foreign exporters, has been suggested as a means of deriving government revenue from the quota. Quotas are most often applied through a license agreement with importers of the good. The license defines the quantitative restriction, and license holders effectively are monopolists of the good in the domestic market. Like all monopolists, the license holders are able to extract monopoly rents from the market. The government could recover these monopoly rents by auctioning the licenses. Ideally, the winning bid at the auction block should be the value of the monopoly rent, with the government as auctioneer and seller of the license taking the proceeds.

In general, the use of quotas violates much of the letter and most of the intent of the multilateral trade liberalization treaty, the *General Agreement on Tariffs and Trade,* or GATT (see Section 10.6). In order to at least pay lip service to the GATT, countries negotiate "orderly marketing agreements," or *voluntary export restraints (VERS)* with foreign producers and even foreign governments. VERS avoid the issue of the direct imposition of a quota, but they have the same effect. VERS have been used in the past by the United States to curb imports of certain types of steel from the countries in the EC, Brazil, and the Republic of Korea. VERS are usually reached under a threat of stricter quotas being imposed by the importing country's government. Stockhausen (1988) has found that the initial discussion of VERS generally leads to a surge of imports of the good in question, as foreign producers raise their exports in order to build the largest possible volume base from which to negotiate.

Currently, VERS are used by the United States to limit its imports of Japanese automobiles, and the EC has negotiated VERS with Japanese auto producers that began in 1992 and will last five years. (Currently, most West European countries use tariffs and/or direct quotas to effectively close their markets to Japanese autos.) The typical effect of VERS is illustrated in a well-known study of their impact on the automobile market (Collyns and Dunaway, 1987). It was estimated that during the years 1981 through 1984, as many as 75,000 automotive jobs were saved in the United States in response to the VERS on Japanese cars. However, it was also estimated that the total loss in consumer welfare, in 1984 alone, was about $6.6 billion. The loss in welfare was allocated as $5.1 billion in gains to American producers and $1.5 billion to Japanese producers. American producers were able to raise prices because Japanese imports were restricted in number so that competition was decreased. At the same time, Japanese producers were able to raise prices because their products were in short supply. In addition, the average price of a Japanese automobile increased because the Japanese suppliers tended to import more expensive models with more options on which they earned the highest profit margins. The prices of light Japanese trucks, which were not imported under a VER, remained fairly stable during the period. Casas and Gelbard (1987) have found that tariffs are superior to quotas, and quotas superior to VERS, as methods of managing trade.

Quotas and VERS are not the only quantitative trade restrictions used by governments. One alternative to VERS is the *nonautomatic import authorization (NAIA)*. NAIAs are limitations placed on the freedom to import, through the use of import licenses. Frequently, such licenses are used as a method of applying import quotas on a discretionary basis. For example, foreign import quotas may be waived by government licenses, distributed on a case-by-case basis if a good is found to be in short domestic supply. Other NAIA programs require an importer to be able to meet certain government objectives. Some countries require that a certain portion of some goods sold domestically, or purchased by the government, have certain levels of *domestic content*. A final product may be assembled by a domestic producer, but many of its intermediate components are imports. NAIAs can be used to require a larger share of domestic components in a final product so that domestic content requirements are met.

NAIAs often are used in the attempt to balance the merchandise trade account. The issue of NAIAs for this purpose requires an import-export linkage. Firms are licensed to import foreign products only if they can guarantee a certain level of exports in general, or if the imported foreign products will be used in intermediate form in producing a good for export markets. Brazil required its foreign-owned automotive producers to export about $21 billion worth of vehicles during the second half of the 1980s, in exchange for licenses to import parts duty free. The Brazilian case is an example of a recent trend toward *countertrade requirements,* in which exporting and importing are viewed as a single transaction incorporating immediate reciprocity (Lecraw, 1989; Mirus and Yeung, 1986). Currently, NAIAs are used more frequently than VERS by EC members. Among the industrial countries, New Zealand uses NAIAs with the greatest frequency, applying them to over 25% of imports. They are not used by the American government (Coughlin and Wood, 1989).

NTBs such as quotas, VERS, and NAIAs are used with the direct intention of distorting the pattern of trade. In addition to these direct forms, NTBs arise as secondary impacts of primarily domestic-oriented policies. The two most common forms of secondary NTBs result from the imposition of product standards and comprehensive customs clearing procedures. Most countries have some sort of government-imposed standards with regard to product quality. These standards encompass a wide array of concerns, from consumer safety to technical specifications. In the United States, for example, the Consumer Product Safety Commission devises standards to which products sold in the American market must conform. As another example, new automobiles currently sold in the United States must be equipped with catalytic converters as pollution controls, and therefore must burn unleaded gasoline. Products manufactured in other countries must conform to American standards before delivery to the American market. The standards were not established with import control in mind, but their effect is to limit imports to those goods which conform to the standards. Some American producers have argued that the Japanese rely on product standards to directly restrain imports. A well-known case concerned aluminum baseball bats, which at one time were prohibited from sale in Japan as unsafe. Japan, of course, is the leading market for baseball products outside of the Americas, so American producers were eager to gain entrance. Considerable negotiations convinced the Japanese to relax their bat standards, which led to the importation of American metal bats. Now, both "pings" and "cracks" can be heard on their diamonds.

Customs documentation and other entry procedures are ideally established with attention to general border and revenue control. However, ease of entry is of interest to foreign concerns seeking access to a domestic market. Transaction costs associated with cumbersome documentation requirements, long waiting periods at border transit points, and other processing delays drive up prices of delivered goods. Differential product standards and customs procedures frequently are effective NTBs and not just nuisances. The comprehensive EC '92 initiatives (see Section 10.8) originated from concerns that variability in national product standards and entry procedures would prevent establishment of a single market within the EC despite the absence of tariff and direct NRB restrictions among members.

10.5 EXPORT MANAGEMENT

Governments promote export of their country's products as well as limit imports. A common form of export management is a production subsidy, although such subsidies are not always intended to have direct effects on the pattern of trade. In a study of Western European practices, Ford and Suyker (1990) found that direct grants, tax concessions, low-interest loans, and direct equity participation are the most commonly used instruments of government subsidy to industry. Two of the purposes of government subsidies—support for industrial R&D, and regional development—are only indirectly linked in most cases to managed trade. However, the other three purposes for industrial subsidies cited by Ford and Suyker—support for new industries, support for declining industries, and export promotion—are provided with trade in mind. Subsidies in support of new and/or declining industry are simply alternatives to tariff and other NTB protection, while export promotion has an obvious purpose.

The economic rationale for industrial subsidies rests on the imperfect competition in international markets. The most commonly cited cause of imperfect competition in these cases is the importance of economies of scale and the related high costs of entry into the market (Grossman, 1990). As we have described, if economies of scale are important in an industry it is difficult for new firms to undertake production on a competitive basis. Huge front-end investments are required, which may not be attractive in financial markets because they lead to heavy short-term losses and uncertain long-term gains. In addition, if the product is technology- or knowledge-intensive, local sources of these factors may be undeveloped. Because governments are better able to afford delayed returns on investment and have broader economic and noneconomic goals than private investors, industrial subsidies are viewed as sound policy. Government subsidies to producers not only improve the potential for exports but limit the potential for imports as well, and many subsidy programs are designed with this dual objective.

A well-known case concerns the competition between Boeing, an American airframe manufacturer, and Airbus Industrie, a consortium of Western European producers. Large-scale passenger airframe production is an industry in which both economies of scale and technology-intensity are critical. Boeing, which has been in the business a long time, held a superior international competitive position and a virtual monopoly in the marketplace with its 767 model. Airbus Industrie developed a competitive model in its A300 and entered the market with production subsidies estimated by the American government at $10 billion, although this figure is denied by the Europeans. Using a simulation analysis, as in their examination of American and Japanese trade in 16K RAM chips, Baldwin and Krugman (1987) found that both Americans and Europeans incurred losses because of subsidies to Airbus Industrie. Airlines and their passengers in third markets were made better off, however, because the competition led to lower aircraft prices. Essentially, industrial subsidies have the same effect on trade as tariffs, and like tariffs they can lead to retaliation by countersubsidy (Phaup and Auten, 1988).

In addition to production subsidies, Airbus Industrie was recently provided a direct export-promotion subsidy of over $2 billion by the German government. The export-promotion subsidy took the form of a guarantee against any exchange rate losses incurred by Airbus Industrie in any non-EC market. Financial subsidies are a common means of export promotion. In addition to guaranteeing exchange rates, governments also guarantee prices by providing insurance against nonpayment, and guarantee rates of return by allowing tax credits on export production and even insurance against unanticipated increases in costs. Additionally, foreign purchases of domestic products are subsidized by favorable interest rates on loans underwritten by government export-import banks. The disparity between the higher rates charged by the American export-import bank and the lower rate charged by European export-import banks on agricultural exports to third markets has been a contentious issue between the United States and the EC for years.

By European standards, American export promotion of particular goods is virtually nonexistent. American export policy tends to follow two directions. One direction is toward the elimination of real or perceived trade barriers to American goods in foreign markets. This policy is represented primarily in the *Super 301* provision of 1988's Omnibus Trade and Competitiveness Act. The Act signalled a marked shift in American policy from free toward managed trade. The Super 301 provision, now elapsed, required the U.S. trade representative to provide a list of countries that appear to be unfairly or unduly restricting the sales of American goods in their domestic markets. In the first Super 301 report, 34 countries were cited and made a priority for intensive bilateral trade negotiations. Under the Super 301 provisions, failure of a targeted country to sufficiently open its markets to American goods requires the implementation of a retaliatory closing of the American market. Japan headed the initial list, and the two governments reached a sweeping settlement intended to open Japanese markets to American manufactured and agricultural products. In addition to removing some NTBs, the Japanese agreed to make "structural adjustments" intended to raise their level of domestic demand for American goods in general. The adjustments included decontrolling retail distribution in Japan and discouraging high rates of personal savings.

The primary direction of American export promotion is to enable smaller companies to market their products internationally. The International Trade Administration of the Department of Commerce provides a series of programs to assist smaller firms. The Foreign Buyer Program arranges exhibits of American products in foreign countries and the attendance of suitable foreign customers. The Trade Missions and Matchmakers programs use embassy staff to arrange local contacts and advertising and provide language interpreters. The Export Contact List and Agent/Distributor Services provide information and establish local links that facilitate product distribution in foreign countries. The International Trade Administration also provides foreign market research and analysis through its Comparison Shopping Service and *World Trade Data Reports*. These programs and services are designed to help reduce exporting costs that may otherwise preclude small firms from marketing their products in foreign countries. Individual American states provide similar services, but on a more limited scale. A primary purpose of these programs is to encourage smaller firms to enter foreign markets, but the benefits of these types of programs usually accrue to firms that are already exporting. Several studies have suggested that a smaller firm's decision to export is largely a function of management attitude, and if managers are not export-oriented then government programs are frequently ignored (McConnell, 1979; Le Heron, 1980; Dichtl et al., 1990).

Many countries encourage trade in general, and exports in particular, by establishing *foreign trade zones (FTZs),* which provide directly visible links between the local and international economies. FTZs are local regions in which goods can be imported free of duty. Ideally, the duty-free imports are intermediate products that are combined in finished goods that will be exported. The imports are duty free because they are considered to be goods in transit, and not actually landed in a country's domestic market (also see Section 10.9). FTZs have a long history. The Hanseatic League consisted of cities involved in trade on the North and Baltic Seas in the Middle Ages. Sections of these cities were effective FTZs for goods in transit among Hanseatic League members.

More recently, the Irish government established a duty-free retail zone at Shannon International Airport in the early 1950s, when Shannon was an important node in trans-Atlantic air travel. (Duty-free shopping facilities for embarking passengers is quite common at international airports today.) In 1959, the duty-free zone was extended to commercial goods for re-export, and since that time FTZs have been established in about 80 different countries. Many of the major ports in Western Europe, including Southampton in England and Hamburg in Germany, have FTZs. American FTZs range in size from single warehouses to the entire length of the border between Mexico and the United States. Although their primary purpose is to increase exports, most FTZs in the United States result in a net increase in imports (Tansuhaj and Gentry, 1987; Alavi and Thompson, 1988). This increase in net imports results from the use of NTZs as holding tanks for inventory of foreign parts used in production. As long as the goods remain in the FTZ, they are not subject to inventory taxes.

Exports are not always promoted by governments. Sometimes they are discouraged and even prohibited. Controls range from export licensing to full embargo. Usually export controls are enacted as substitutes for military action and are economic means of achieving political goals. Export controls are imposed both unilaterally, as in the case of the American grain embargo of the Soviet Union in the late

1970s, and multilaterally, as in the cases of OPEC's oil embargo in 1978 and the UN sanctions on trade with Iraq in late 1990. Since the end of World War II, the country most frequently imposing export sanctions has been the United States while the country most frequently sanctioned has been the Soviet Union (Nollen, 1987).

One unilateral action taken by the United States against the Soviet Union was the embargo of export and re-export of American-origin gas and oil pipeline equipment. The intent was to undermine the ability of the Soviets to earn foreign exchange by sales of oil and gas in Western Europe, as punishment for the Soviet invasion of Afghanistan. The embargo was an innovative one because of its extension to re-exports, which meant that foreign subsidiaries of American MNCs were required to breach existing contracts with the Soviet Union. Technically, the foreign subsidiaries are beyond legal control of the American government. The embargo was ineffective because producers from other countries were able to supply the embargoed equipment. The Soviets remained in Afghanistan for some time, and American companies lost about $2.3 billion (Nollen, 1987). Grotewold (1987) has argued that the consistent failure of American trade sanctions against the Soviet Union resulted from relatively low importance of the United States as a Soviet trade partner. The low level of integration of the American and Soviet economies allowed the Soviets to easily find sources of many goods otherwise imported from the United States. The grain embargo failed, for example, because the Soviets had no trouble finding other sources.

In the case of some products, however, the United States was joined by most other suppliers in controlling exports to the Soviet Union and its former Warsaw Pact allies in Eastern Europe, and countries with communist governments in other parts of the world. Countries belonging to NATO (except Iceland) and Japan and Australia operated the Coordinating Committee for Multilateral Export Controls (COCOM). COCOM maintained export rules among its members which strictly limited the export of goods which had even limited indirect military applications to the Warsaw Pact countries. In 1987, COCOM rules were violated by Toshiba Machine of Japan, and Kongsberg Vappenfabrik of Norway, when they sold certain technologically sophisticated machine tools to the Soviet Union that could be used in the manufacture of silent submarine propellers. Both companies were indicted for violating their country's export laws, and certain Toshiba products were barred from American markets.

Cheating in one form or another is a common result of economic sanctions on both the import and export side. Economic sanctions, urged but not required, by the UN on the Republic of South Africa have been fairly ineffective. The trade sanctions were only marginally effective because they were not widely adopted, and because they were consistently evaded. South African coal, for example, was used in prohibited European markets after it was blended in Rotterdam with coal produced in other countries. South African textile exports were simply mislabeled as originating in other countries. The flow of exports to South Africa followed the same sort of path, and many goods prohibited for sale to South Africa by the American and many European governments were purchased instead from other countries.

Even the "frontline" countries that border South Africa and the other countries in the region have found it difficult to enforce sanctions. The economies of Angola,

Botswana, Zimbabwe, Mozambique, and even Zambia, Zaire, and Tanzania are simply too integrated with the South African economy. South African products are frequently imported by these countries through third countries because South African sources are willing to supply credit. In turn, many projects in these countries are financed from South Africa, which is far and away the region's largest source of capital.

The dismantling of apartheid in South Africa was the goal of the UN-endorsed sanctions, but progress toward that end can be attributed only partially to the sanctions and more to domestic changes in South African politics. The UN and the United States as much as admitted the relative ineffectiveness of sanctions recently, when trade prohibitions were abandoned in favor of deadly force as the method of driving Iraq from Kuwait.

10.6 MULTILATERAL TRADE AGREEMENTS: THE GATT

The *General Agreement on Tariffs and Trade (GATT)* is an international trade treaty with close to 100 signatories, or "members." The initial impetus to the GATT came at the Bretton Woods conference of 1944, but only as a side issue in the reinvigoration of the world's economy in the aftermath of the Great Depression and World War II. The GATT that exists today actually results directly from the failure to establish an International Trade Organization (ITO) as a special agency of the UN. The United States moved the establishment of the ITO in the UN in 1946, and a charter for the agency was written in Havana in 1947 (Fraser, 1987). However, ratifications of the charter by UN members were slow to take place, and even the United States failed to ratify. The GATT actually was sort of a prototype ITO that was provisionally accepted by eight countries in 1948: Australia, Belgium, Canada, France, Luxembourg, the Netherlands, the United Kingdom, and the United States. It has served as an alternative to the ITO since that time.

The original and continuing purpose of the GATT is to improve the prospects of world trade and economic development. A primary method of improving the prospects of trade is by providing *transparency* of trade regulations. Transparency, in this case, means that all barriers to trade are recognizable and straightforward. Almost all of the NTBs described above are in violation of the spirit, if not the letter, of the GATT. The GATT states that restrictions on trade may only take the form of duties, taxes, or other charges, and that quotas, import and export licenses, and any other quantitative restrictions may not be used. In addition, subsidies that affect trade must be made known to other countries, and even state-owned enterprises must not be given preferred treatment with regard to trade.

In addition to transparency, the GATT also prohibits geographical discrimination in trade by its inclusion of regulations concerning the general applicability of *most-favored nation (MFN)* treatment among its members. In a bilateral context,

MFN is the most favorable treatment with respect to trade that one country can give another. If all countries are accorded MFN treatment it means that all countries are treated, with respect to trade, in exactly the same way. Tariff levies cannot discriminate in favor of one country over another, and geographically discriminatory quantitative restrictions are specifically prohibited.

In addition to transparency and general MNF treatment, the last special concern of the GATT is reciprocity. The reciprocity in the GATT is one-sided, however, and only requires that tariffs be lowered on any country's imports if that country's exports experience a decline in tariffs in another country. Retaliatory tariff increases are prohibited. Even countervailing duties imposed to offset dumping are discouraged in the GATT. The purpose of reciprocity in the GATT is to provide a basis for continual decreases in tariffs.

The GATT, like the Pope, has no armed divisions, so the treaty is virtually unenforceable. It also has a series of clauses that, when invoked, can be used to violate the principles of transparency, MFN treatment, and reciprocity singly or in full combination. Jackson (1989) noted that the clauses are necessary if the GATT is to conform to the national laws of most countries. The so-called escape clause concerns the safeguard of a country's balance of payments. Either an increase in tariffs or the imposition of import quotas may be used if a country's balance of payments is threatened by ongoing patterns of trade. Imports of a good that cause harm to domestic producers may be removed from GATT rules as well, under the safeguards clause. Quantitative restrictions may be used if their purpose is to ensure maintenance of domestic product standards, or to ensure compliance with customs procedures. Customs unions and free-trade areas are not prohibited by the GATT as long as their formation is derived from a lowering of trade barriers among members and not an increase in trade barriers to nonmembers (see Section 10.8). The GATT also takes into account differences in level of development among members, and countries with low standards of living are able to selectively enforce most provisions. In addition, most poor countries are eligible to receive preferential treatment in their trade with rich countries.

Including its inception, the GATT has undergone eight rounds of negotiations, which have been named for either the people who instigated the negotiations or the places where the negotiations began. The two most important rounds that have been fully completed are the Kennedy round of 1964–1967, and the Tokyo round of 1973–1979. (Note the duration of the negotiations. Several people have remarked that GATT stands for "general agreement to talk and talk.")

The interests of the developing countries were a primary focus of the Kennedy round of GATT negotiations, and the round included measures toward increasing poor countries' export markets over time. Developed countries were encouraged to arrange financing of export expansion in poor countries and to generally make positive efforts toward the development of poorer countries. Exports of primary products and so-called tropical products are now particularly encouraged under the GATT. Many primary-product exporters are reliant on a very limited range of exports (Lewis, 1989), and such export concentrations frequently yield very unstable earnings in international trade (see Chapter 11). Distinctions between imports of raw primary products and primary products in finished form have been reduced, and efforts have been made to stabilize their prices. In addition, most trade barriers have been removed by richer countries to encourage higher levels of consumption of primary products as a method of ensuring stable world prices.

The Kennedy round widened the GATT rules concerning trade preferences for developing countries and eventually led to the *Generalized System of Preferences (GSP)*. Under the GSP, rich countries are able to provide significant trade preferences to poorer countries, and the poorer countries are able to accept the preferences without reciprocity. The GSP concerns both poorer countries in general and trade in some of their particular products, especially manufactured goods. Each industrial country following the GSP is able to grant its preferences to a selected group of poorer countries. The GSP is, in some respects, an outgrowth of the British Commonwealth system of preferences. As such, it has been suggested as a form of neocolonialism, especially because GSP treatment is usually tied to political pressure (Jackson, 1989). In addition to the GSP, a special treaty called the Multifiber Arrangement was established under GATT auspices in 1973. Its affect on trade in textiles and apparel between rich and poor countries is examined in Chapter 11.

The Tokyo round of GATT negotiations focused on the reduction of NTBs (Deardorf and Stern, 1986). In particular it dealt with technical barriers to trade, government procurement policies, customs procedures, and the imposition of anti-dumping duties. It also focused on the use of temporary safeguards enacted by rich countries to limit imports from developing countries, despite the GSP (Koekkoek, 1987). Ironically, the GSP was undermined by the general tariff reductions of the Tokyo round, which made products from poorer countries less competitive in international markets (MacPhee, 1987).

The current round of GATT negotiations, ongoing at the time of this writing, is called the Uruguay round. In addition to the usual negotiations on tariff reductions and continuing use of NTBs (Czinkota and Talbot, 1986), the round is raising important issues of trade in intellectual property, services, and agriculture (Hufbauer, 1989). Unlike earlier GATT rounds, the current one may result in more trade restrictions than fewer. Many analysts are concerned, and some are hopeful, that multilateral trade agreements will be replaced by a series of bilateral ones in an era of increasingly managed trade.

Intellectual property issues primarily concern trade in pirated and counterfeit goods. Products such as computer software, for example, have their primary value in their embodiment of a way of thinking. Their value-added rises from their content of an intangible factor. Pharmaceutical drugs and some other chemicals frequently derive their value in the same way. The design of such items is difficult but their reproduction is easy. Patent, copyright, and trademark holders feel that they receive insufficient economic return on their special expertise because of abuses of intellectual property rights in international markets. Interests in poorer countries are concerned that highly restrictive GATT regulations on trade in intellectual property will make the costs of certain items, considered to be critical to health, welfare, and economic development, prohibitive.

One of the problems associated with trade in intellectual property is that it is a relatively new and growing item in international trade. The same problem concerns trade in services. Management of service trade cannot always be accomplished by usual methods. Services, for the most part, are intangible items. Quotas and other quantitative restrictions would be difficult to apply, unless they are strict prohibitions. The United States put services on the table at the Uruguay round and was especially concerned with limiting enactment of any barriers to their trade. Initially, the American proposal was simply to put services into the basic GATT framework of transparency and reciprocity. Developing countries feel, however, that service trade needs to be strictly regulated and should be left outside the GATT framework. Interestingly, the American position was about to be accepted under the GATT in late 1990, but the Americans pulled an about-face and withdrew the proposal to liberalize service trade. Apparently, American financial service interests had become apprehensive of their ability to compete domestically against Japanese and West European sellers of financial services.

According to Hufbauer (1989), the negotiations on agriculture are pivotal to the success of the Uruguay round. Agricultural trade is the most restricted of any commodity or merchandise group, and many of the restrictions are not transparent. There are three major interests in international agricultural trade: the United States, the EC, and the Cairns Group. The Cairns Group, named after the Australian town in which it was organized, consists of Argentina, Australia, Brazil, Canada, Chile, Colombia, Fiji, Hungary, Indonesia, Malaysia, New Zealand, the Philippines, Thailand, and Uruguay. The Cairns Group and the Americans feel that the EC's Common Agricultural Policy of subsidies and price supports unfairly limits international trade in agriculture. The EC counters that all parties employ similar subsidies. Initially, the United States and the Cairns Group suggested, in different proposals, the eventual elimination of all agricultural subsidies. The EC has suggested some short-term subsidy freezes, and the removal of some quotas on a limited variety of agricultural products. As of this writing, the negotiations concerning both services and agriculture are at a stalemate.

10.7 COMMODITY TRADE AGREEMENTS

Because of declining terms of trade and unstable prices, primary-products producers have organized frequently in the interest of controlling both supplies and prices in international markets. During this century, well over 50 international commodity trade organizations have been established. These organizations have been used in attempts to control trade in natural rubber, copper, wheat, tea, sugar, coffee, and cocoa, among other commodities, but the most influential of these cartels has been OPEC (see Epilogue). The cartels employ two basic and related methods to control supply and price. One is the use of export quotas as a method of controlling physical quantities of the commodity in the market. The other is *valorization* of the commodity, or price-fixing, above commonly competitive prices. Efforts at valorization, obviously, are supported by limitations on supply.

The degree of success of any of the international commodity cartels is open to question. Typically, they have yielded income gains to their members, but only over the short run. No cartel has ever been able to completely control a commodity's supply. Certain producers do not join the cartel, alternative sources for the commodity are developed, and even substitute products are synthesized in the face of high prices (Magee, 1980). Because cartel membership is voluntary, individual members each must be satisfied with the results or their incentive to remain in the cartel can be lost. Frequently, commodity cartel members cheat, if only temporarily, by exporting beyond their quota or arranging transactions at lower than established prices.

OPEC, in its effort to control international trade in petroleum, has experienced the full range of problems in cartel maintenance and the added problem of political disagreements among its members. OPEC was established at a conference in Baghdad in 1960, called in response to a reduction in posted oil prices by the leading multinational oil companies. The conferees were Iran, Iraq, Kuwait, Saudi Arabia, and Venezuela, and these countries and Qatar formalized the establishment of OPEC in 1961. Since that time, the membership has grown and now includes Algeria, Ecuador, Gabon, Indonesia, Libya, Nigeria, and the United Arab Emirates.

OPEC's major effect on world oil markets was first realized in 1973, when a subset of its membership called the Organization of Arab Petroleum Exporting Countries (OAPEC) reduced or fully embargoed oil deliveries to certain industrial countries. The purpose of the embargo was to pressure western countries, especially the United States, to take an impartial approach to issues in the Middle East that revolved around Arab-Israeli conflicts. The price increases in petroleum at that time and later in the decade resulted in international recession and a vast redistribution in income away from petroleum consumers toward petroleum exporters. By 1987, however, OPEC's influence on international trade in petroleum had waned considerably, and since that time there has been serious speculation about its demise.

The decline of OPEC's ability to control oil supplies and prices fits generally with the pattern of decline typical across commodity cartels. The rapid increase in petroleum prices induced rapid increases in alternative petroleum supplies. Major producers such as the United Kingdom, Norway, and Mexico, were able to offset supply limitations supported by OPEC. The United States experienced a surge in oil production and expansion of its geography to Alaska. OPEC held a 48% share of world oil production in 1979, but only 37% in 1989. In addition to the increase in supply, concerted efforts were made for the first time in the industrial countries to improve efficiency in energy use, and the marginal return to energy inputs was increased in both producer and consumer sectors. Alternative sources of supply and improved efficiency worked in tandem to counteract the quantitative restrictions and valorization of OPEC oil, and by late 1990 the real price of oil was at its lowest level in 40 years at $17 per barrel, about $1 less than OPEC's posted price.

The fact that oil prices were below the posted price in 1990 meant that all the OPEC countries were cheating on the agreement. The cheating had begun much earlier as a response to the decline in oil prices that had lasted about seven years. Targeted rates of oil revenues could be maintained only if supplies exceeding quotas were put on the international market. In addition, as quotas were raised, price competition within OPEC developed as individual countries attempted to maintain market share. During the 1980s, the interests of OPEC's members became less homogeneous and three camps emerged within the cartel. One camp consists of members outside the Persian Gulf. Venezuela and Nigeria, for example, have been concerned with the overriding emphasis that the Gulf countries place on Middle Eastern politics in oil supply decisions. The Gulf states of Saudi Arabia, Iran, Iraq, Kuwait, and the United Arab Emirates have tended to combine in controlling OPEC procedures. Within the Gulf states, however, a split has developed between Iraq and Iran and the other three countries. Iraq and Iran want OPEC to be more aggressive in its pricing because oil exports are their chief sources of foreign exchange and financing reconstruction in the wake of their war. Kuwait and the others, however, are as much reliant on their foreign investments as their oil exports for income. They urge lower prices and larger supplies of petroleum as measures of encouraging the western industrial growth in which they now have a vested interest.

In late 1990 the intra-Gulf dispute came to a head, as the Iraquis accused Kuwait of cheating on its export quota and undercutting posted prices in the market. Iraq was urging a price of $21 a barrel, but the Kuwaitis wanted to stabilize the market at the existing price of $17. In August, Iraq invaded Kuwait and declared it an integral part of its country. It is unlikely that OPEC will be able to function as it has, or that its membership will remain intact, in the aftermath of the larger war that began in January of 1991 and ended quickly with Iraq's expulsion from Kuwait.

10.8 REGIONAL TRADE AGREEMENTS

The decline of the GATT may give way not only to increased bilateral trade agreements but also to increased reliance on regional trade agreements. In addition to the EC 92 initiatives, which were intended to increase trade liberalization within the EC and solidify current intraregional patterns, the United States and Canada have recently signed a free-trade agreement, and several North African countries have now started on the path toward economic integration. All three of these regional agreements, and others, are types of *geographically discriminatory trade arrangements (GDTAs)*, which are allowed under the GATT (Hamilton and Whalley, 1985). Tinbergen (1954) wrote that GDTAs could be achieved by either negative or positive actions. On the negative side, a GDTA is achieved by removing current barriers to trade and obstacles toward increasing liberalization of trade policy. On the positive side, a GDTA is achieved by development of new policies and institutions that enable a freer flow of exchange among the member countries. In reality, the development of a GDTA requires both positive and negative measures.

There are four basic types of GDTAs (Balassa, 1961). One is a *free-trade union,* in which the member countries remove barriers to trade among themselves, but reserve the right to maintain individual trade policies toward countries outside the union. A second type is the *customs union,* which is like the free-trade union with respect to internal policy but also requires common policies toward nonmember countries. A third type of GDTA is the *common market,* which is similar to a customs union but carries a common policy of free flows of factors of production as well as goods among its member countries. A fourth type is the *economic union,* a common market extended to unification of fiscal and monetary policies among its member countries. El-Agraa (1989) has added a fifth type of GDTA, which encompasses *complete political integration* and entails the sovereignty of a completely central authority. This last type of GDTA is actually one of unification of any member countries. El-Agraa points out that the first four types of GDTAs should not be considered to be evolutionary stages toward the last. Further, any of the first three types could be realized on a sectorally specific basis and not necessarily applied to a country's full economy.

GDTAs have grown since the 1950s, but not all GDTA effects are beneficial to their member countries or to world trade in general. Viner (1950) divided GDTA effects into two classes: *trade creation* and *trade diversion.* Trade creation is effected by a GDTA when a decrease in trade barriers among members allows either an increase in the volume of existing trade or the addition of products entered into trade. A decrease in tariffs is analogous to a decrease in transportation costs among GDTA countries. Prices of landed goods become generally lower with tariff repeal, and any good with a negative price elasticity of demand will experience an increase in consumption. In addition, the repeal of any prohibitive tariffs will allow goods previously consumed only from domestic supply to enter into trade. Trade diversion takes place if a formerly higher-cost supplier becomes the lowest-cost supplier due to tariff reductions. The diversion of trade is away from lower-cost producers outside the GDTA and toward a producer within the GDTA. Trade diversion is most likely in a customs union because all the members maintain a common external tariff.

An additional effect of GDTAs may be *trade deflection,* which is most likely to occur under a free-trade union that does not carry a common external tariff. If all members except one of a free-trade union carry high external tariffs on a particular good, interests in the single low-tariff member can simply import the product for re-export to the other member countries. The low-tariff member simply acts as a wholesaler of a good that otherwise would be of limited demand in the other countries of the GDTA. (MNCs use a type of trade deflection as a marketing strategy. See Section 10.9). Ideally, the purpose of GDTAs is trade creation and the derivation of greater benefits to the GDTA as a single entity. A GDTA even can lead to a redistribution of income from richer to poorer members (Fluckiger, 1987). Wonnacott and Wonnacott (1981), however, have made the realistic assertion that most GDTAs arise from national self-interest in penetrating the import markets of other members.

Several ingredients for a trade-creating GDTA have been suggested (Gunter, 1989). Trade creation is most likely to occur if the GDTA has many members; if trade accounts for a relatively small proportion of members' production; if a relatively high proportion of trade exists among members as compared to proportions of trade between members and nonmembers; if there is a low common external tariff; and if there are wide differences among members in their costs of producing tradable goods. Existing patterns of production and trade may be the most critical factors in forming a successful, trade-creating GDTA with well-spread benefits (Hanink and Cromley, 1993). Grotewold (1982) has suggested that the failure of the Latin American Free Trade Association in 1980 resulted from the inability of Brazil, its dominant member, to alter its trade pattern from one directd away from Latin America to one within Latin America. Simulation analyses of hypothetical GDTAs conducted by Hamilton and Whalley (1985) tend to confirm the importance of the role of existing trade patterns in yielding benefits from GDTAs.

Both active and relatively inactive versions of the first three types of GDTAs are in operation (Table 10.1), and there is some effort taking place to create the fourth type within the EC. The fifth type has been attempted a number of times, with the longest-lasting established in the United States when its Constitution replaced the earlier Articles of Confederation. Currently, the European Community (EC) and the

TABLE 10.1 Full Members of Selected Geographically Discriminatory Trade Arrangements

Arab Maghreb Union (AMU): Algeria, Libya, Mauritania, Morocco, Tunisia

Association of South-East Asian Nations (ASEAN): Brunei, Indonesia, Malaysia, Philippines, Singapore, Thailand

Caribbean Community (CARICOM): Antigua and Barbuda, Bahamas, Barbados, Belize, Dominica, Grenada, Guyana, Jamaica, Montserrat, St. Kits and Nevis, St. Lucia, St. Vincent and the Grenadines, Trinidad and Tobago

Central American Common Market (SIECA): Costa Rica, El Salvador, Guatemala, Honduras, Nicaragua

*Council for Mutual Economic Assistance (CMEA or COMECON): Bulgaria, Cuba, Czechoslovakia, Hungary, Mongolia, Poland, Romania, U.S.S.R., Vietnam

Economic Community of Central African States (CEEAC): Burundi, Cameroon, Central African Republic, Chad, Congo, Equatorial Guinea, Gabon, Rwanda, Sao Tome and Principe, Zaire

European Community (EC): Belgium, Denmark, France, Germany, Greece, Ireland, Italy, Luxembourg, Netherlands, Portugal, Spain, United Kingdom

European Free Trade Association (EFTA): Austria, Finland, Iceland, Norway, Sweden, Switzerland

Latin America Integration Association (ALADI): Argentina, Bolivia, Brazil, Chile, Colombia, Ecuador, Mexico, Paraguay, Peru, Uruguay, Venezuela

Preferential Trade Area (PTA): Angola, Botswana, Comoros, Djibouti, Ethiopia, Kenya, Lesotho, Malawi, Mauritius, Mozambique, Swaziland, Tanzania, Uganda, Zambia, Zimbabwe

Southern African Customs Union (SACU): Botswana, Lesotho, Republic of South Africa, Swaziland

West African Economic Community (CEAO): Benin, Burkina Faso, Cote d'Ivoire, Mali, Niger, Senegal

* The CMEA was effectively dismantled on January 1, 1991.

free-trade agreement of Canada and the United States can be taken as representing the extremes of GDTAs in operation.

Within the typology of GDTAs, the EC is a common market undergoing a transition toward an economic union. The EC actually began as a sectorally specific GDTA. In 1951, Belgium, France, Italy, Luxembourg, the Netherlands, and West Germany signed the Treaty of Paris establishing the *European Coal and Steel Community (ECSC)*. The purpose of the ECSC was to coordinate coal and steel production among its members in order to accelerate the rebuilding of the European economies devastated by World War II. The establishment of the ECSC was a remarkable political achievement because it included the former Axis countries of Germany and Italy. NATO also included such a combination, but it did not require close economic cooperation. The success of the ECSC led to the wider *European Economic Community (EEC)*, established among the same members by the Treaty of Rome in 1957. In addition, the Treaty of Rome established *Euratom*, which allowed for coordination of the development of peaceful applications of atomic power.

The EEC called for the broad elimination of tariffs, quantitative restrictions, and other barriers to trade among its members, and the establishment of common external tariffs. It also enabled the free movement of factors, including labor, services, and capital, within its constituents. The treaty of Rome called for the establishment of common agricultural and transportation policies. In 1973, the United Kingdom, Ireland, and Denmark joined the EEC; they were followed by Greece in 1981, and Portugal and Spain in 1986.

The EC maintains interest in economic development at both the regional scale within its members, and at the broader international scale as well. The European Regional Development Fund was established in 1975 as a method of financing remedies for the regional imbalances in employment and incomes within the Community. The Common Agricultural Policy (CAP) is used toward this purpose as well, because agricultural regions are a focus of the development program. International development is encouraged by special trade links with poorer countries, through a series of *Lomé Conventions*, initially established in Lomé, Togo, in 1975. Currently, about 70 countries in Africa, the Pacific, and the Caribbean are granted duty-free market access to the EC, as well as special financial and technical assistance. The Lomé Conventions allow for the maintenance of economic ties between the European countries and many of their former colonies around the world.

Analyses of the effectiveness of the EC have been conducted and seem to fall in two general classes. One class contains analyses of the trade effects of EC links. For example, Jacquemin and Sapir (1988) have found that standardized intermediate goods are traded mainly within the EC. On the other hand, goods that benefit from economies of scale in their production, and less-standardized consumer goods, are heavily involved in extra-EC trade. In addition, they found that government purchasing policies seem to encourage imports from outside the Community, especially imports of services. The other general class of EC analyses concerns the effects of EC enlargement and its potential effects of trade diversion and creation. Pomfret (1981), for example, assessed the impact of the EC additions of Greece, Portugal, and Spain on the extra-EC economies in the Mediterranean. His work suggested that the highest potential for trade diversion involved manufactured goods produced in Turkey and

Cyprus, and agricultural goods exported from Algeria, Israel, and Tunisia. It is probably not coincidental that both Israel and Turkey have petitioned for membership in the EC. A related analysis by Callahan (1989) studied the trade frictions between American citrus producers and EC importers brought about by the addition of Spain and Portugal to the EC. The common external tariff of the EC made Spanish and Portuguese citrus products more competitive than American citrus products in the EC, resulting in a steep decline of American exports to Europe. The EC, under threat of retaliation, agreed to pay a large indemnity to American citrus producers in an effort to compensate for the diverted trade.

In an effort to remove NTBs within the Community and provide for increasing levels of integration and harmonization of national policies among its members, the *Single European Act* was signed in 1986. This series of initiatives, popularly referred to as the *EC '92* initiatives, is wide-ranging (Owen and Dynes, 1990). It includes establishment of uniform product standards (Greer, 1989) and provides special attention to liberalizing trade in services and capital (Eurofi, 1989). Perhaps the most important initiatives of EC '92 address steps toward establishment of a single European currency, although this element of European integration was set back by British and Italian actions in mid-1992 (see Chapter 5).

Fuller integration of the markets encompassed in the EC '92 initiatives has created significant concern both within and without Europe. Within the EC, questions have been raised about the future disposition of regional development programs (Begg, 1989). Although spending on regional development will increase, regional development policy is increasingly perceived as a form of NTB protection of declining industries that defies the intention of integration policy. In Europe, concern has been voiced over the future of the European Free Trade Association (EFTA) which has served historically as a more loosely knit GDTA alternative to the EC (Nell, 1990; Neumann, 1990). Its future may be that of a "waiting room" for potential new members of the EC, but a GDTA with only transitory members probably would be difficult to maintain. Non-European countries have expressed misgivings over both the procedures and intended results of the EC '92 initiatives. Both poorer countries and rich countries, such as the United States and Japan, are fearful that a "Fortress Europe" mentality is arising that will severely limit future prospects for trade between the EC and nonmembers. It has been suggested that the trade effects of EC '92 will be marginally positive for nonmembers (Koekkoek et al., 1990), but that the EC's other external economic policies are not at a stage in which their effects can be determined. Rich countries are primarily concerned with their potential loss of markets for both goods and services in the EC. The American government, for example, has been fairly insistent of the need for openness in the establishment of EC-wide product standards and greater relaxation of government procurement policies toward goods producers in non-EC countries (House Subcommittee on International Economic Policy and Trade, 1989).

Within the typology of GDTAs, the Canadian-American free-trade agreement represents a free-trade union. The free-trade agreement was signed in 1988 and began its first phase in 1989. The entire agreement should be in full force by the year 2000. In one respect, the American-Canadian agreement is similar to the EC '92 initiatives. Rather than calling for any fundamental adjustments, it more or less fine-tunes existing trade relationships (McCulloch, 1990). By value, about two-thirds of existing trade between Canada and the United States was duty free before the agreement, largely because of free trade in automotive products.

The general provisions of the free-trade agreement include phased-in reductions of existing tariffs on goods and specific rules prohibiting quantitative restrictions (Morici, 1989). The free-trade agreement also addresses the possibility of its use in trade deflection by prescribing domestic content requirements for goods entered into American-Canadian trade. For example, if American tariffs are lower than Canadian tariffs on a particular good, a third country's producer cannot export the goods to America for later free entry to the Canadian market. An important feature of the American-Canadian agreement is its use of *national treatment*. Simply stated, the national treatment provisions require any American firm operating in Canada to be treated by the Canadian government as if it were a Canadian firm, and Canadian firms to be treated as American firms when operating in the United States. The primary exceptions to the free-trade agreement are Canadian cultural-industries—for example, publishing—which are assured viability by trade restriction if necessary.

Perhaps the most important parts of the American-Canadian free-trade agreement deal with trade in invisibles: services and capital (Grubel, 1989; Harrington, 1989). Most business services, in particular, have been accomodated in the same way as tradable goods, especially in regard to national treatment of providers. Financial services, however, especially banking, remain more restricted because the regulatory structure of banking is so complex in the United States (Morici, 1989). Transportation services also are less affected by the agreement than other business services. Direct investment, or trade in capital, is less regulated under the free-trade agreement, and national treatment applies. Canada, however, still reserves the right to screen direct investments of over C$150 million.

The service and investment provisions of the free-trade agreement are the most forward looking because they concern items that are growing in importance in all international trade. With regard to goods, many observers feel that the agreement will not have a material effect because of the very large volume of trade between Canada and the United States that already existed. Many analyses of the potential effects of the free-trade agreement, conducted in preparation for its enactment, focused upon the Canadian economy. In general, the agreement was of more concern in Canada, where it was a significant political issue, than in the United States, where it was virtually ignored by all but a handful of members of Congress and a few special-interest groups. Most analyses suggest that the agreement benefits the Canadian economy more than the American economy, and in general the net benefits to both will be fairly thin (Rugman and Anderson, 1987; Brown and Stern, 1989).

Talks on expansion of the free-trade agreement to include Mexico were begun before the Canadian-American agreement was even completed (Macchiarola, 1990). In fact, former President Bush outlined a plan to extend the free-trade agreement not only to all of North America but to the entire Western Hemisphere. To some degree, however, the hemispheric extension can be viewed largely as a threatened response to any European trade barriers raised by the EC '92 initiatives. Even the inclusion only of Mexico in a North American free-trade agreement, while intriguing, is not easily done. Although Mexico is relatively wealthy by world standards, it is poor by the standards of the continent. Current trade between Mexico and the United States and Mexico and Canada is far short of the levels of American-Canadian trade, although trade within MNCs operating on both sides of the Mexican-American border is significant (see below). Because of the disparities in wealth between Canada and the United States on the one side and Mexico on the other, Mexico's inclusion in the free-trade agreement may require a complex overhaul of North American trade and investment patterns. Essentially, such an agreement requires a new treaty, creating a *North American Free Trade Area (NAFTA)*. It is not just a simple extension of the American-Canadian agreement.

The creation of NAFTA has generated controversy along a number of lines. Organized labor in the United States and Canada is concerned about disparity in incomes between Mexico and the other two countries and fears the loss of manufacturing employment to cheaper locations in Mexico. Environmentalists are concerned that corporations that find U.S. and Canadian environmental regulations too costly can avoid such constraints by transferring operations to Mexico. In addition, both interests are concerned that a form of neoclassical leveling will affect the Canadian and American economies, as wages will be suppressed and environmental standards relaxed in both countries in order to compete more effectively with the lower costs of Mexico (*NAFTA Digest*, 1992A; *NAFTA Digest*, 1992B).

Because of the traditionally thin links between Canada and Mexico, Canadian reaction to NAFTA is one of disinterest compared to the contention surrounding the Canada-U.S. agreement. Even considering the concerns of organized labor and environmental organizations, general opinion in the United States is one of disinterest as well. This disinterest is not prevalent, however, in the southwestern part of the United States, particularly in Texas where NAFTA's proponents are strongest. The region has strong ties to the Mexican economy and also strong cultural affinities that span the border (Hansen, 1981).

Virtually the entire length of Mexico's border with the United States was already a free-trade zone containing so-called maquiladora operations of MNCs using cheap Mexican labor in the final assembly of goods for export, primarily re-export to the United States (South, 1990). A significant volume of American imports of Mexican goods actually flows just a few miles, basically only from the Mexican side of the border to the American side. American exports to Mexico also are concentrated in origin from the Southwest, at a proportional level almost three times that of the country as a whole (Erickson and Hayward, 1991). The development of NAFTA is considered by its proponents as a vital means to improve the regional economies of both northern Mexico and the southwestern United States.

10.9 TRADE WITHIN THE MULTINATIONAL CORPORATION

Conventional trade theory and conventional methods of managing trade effectively assume that producers are confined as entities within one country and markets are confined as entities in other countries. Trade results from production in one country and consumption in another. However, the existence of multinational corporations (MNCs) complicates trade in two ways. First, MNCs, by definition, are located in more than one country. Second, MNCs operate their own subsystems of spatial interaction. Each functional unit of an MNC is potentially both a producer and a consumer, so trade over the MNC structure can be quite complex. Frequently, MNCs are called *transnational corporations* in recognition of their internal systems of spatial interaction comprised of specialized nodes and flows. In the context of transnationalism, MNCs are viewed as enterprises that transcend and frequently compete with the interests of individual countries.

Trade within MNCs, or *intrafirm trade,* has been increasing along with the spread of MNCs across the global economy. It has been estimated, for example, that about 40% of all American trade is intrafirm trade consisting of imports and exports between MNCs based in the United States and their foreign branches or subsidiaries, and imports and exports between foreign-based MNCs and their American operations (Cho, 1988). Intrafirm trade is frequently targeted as the source of the now chronic deficit in American merchandise trade (Hipple, 1990). Recent estimates have indicated that the trade balance of American interests, rather than America as a country, is positive. In this type of accounting, the local sales of a German subsidiary of an American-based MNC count as an export, and so do sales of domestic firms to foreign MNCs within the United States (*Economist,* 1990). Neither type of transaction, of course, would be carried in America's current account.

Basically, intrafirm trade is motivated by two general factors. Much of the MNCs' intrafirm trade conforms to trade predicted by international trade theory. Factor endowment theory goes a long way in explaining intrafirm trade in the MNC if a final good is defined as an aggregation of inputs comprised of intermediate products, raw materials, and technology. Comparative advantage in production of each of the inputs is unlikely to exist in any single country. The geographical extent of the MNC allows it to benefit by its ability to produce each component of a final good in that country with the relevant comparative advantage. (This matching of input production and comparative advantage by the MNC was more fully discussed in Chapter 8.) Final assembly of the good requires both imports and exports of the components across their locations of production, but all of this trade takes place within the firm in an internal system of spatial interaction called *global rationalization* (Kogut, 1984; Mascarenhas, 1984). Alternatively, one key factor of production—call it technology or know-how—has a single geographical source within the MNC. Components intensively embodying this factor are diffused through the firm from the single source to multiple receptors. Recent studies have found that more-innovative MNCs tend to rely more heavily on intrafirm trade than do less-innovative MNCs (Kotabe, 1990; Siddharthan and Kumar, 1990). Intrafirm trade in know-how extends to methods as well as manufactured goods (Terpstra and Aydin, 1981).

The impact of product differentiation in international trade also affects intrafirm trade by MNCs. Many MNCs modify otherwise standard products to the particular tastes of an individual domestic market (Kotabe and Omura, 1989). The standardized good is produced at one or a number of least-cost locations, exported-imported within the MNC, and modified at point of sale. In addition, MNCs employ a type of trade deflection by sourcing products in countries that have positive consumer stereotypes (Han and Terpstra, 1988). In some instances, products produced in one country are sent to another simply for labelling. In a sense, prestige is taken as an embodied factor of production for purposes of marketing.

Although much of intrafirm trade conforms to theory, a significant portion of the MNCs' intrafirm trade is conducted as a response to direct and indirect management of trade by national governments (Agmon and Hekman, 1989). A common purpose of intrafirm trade simply is tax avoidance (Korth, 1985). Most of the industrial countries collect income taxes, but with variable rates and types of deductions and credits. An MNC can play off one country's tax system against another's through so-called *transfer pricing,* a system of preferential pricing of intrafirm transfers. Transfer pricing allows the MNC to shift taxable income from a high-tax country to a low-tax country, or to hide taxable income altogether. In addition, so-called *tax havens,* countries that have virtually no taxes on income from particular transactions, are used to eliminate a wide range of tax liabilities. Stewart (1989) found that Ireland has many of the attributes of a tax haven, and suggests that this is a major reason for its recent rapid rates of economic growth. MNCs that located in Ireland were effectively exempt from taxes on manufacturing profits, and many of them used intrafirm transfer prices to throw all their profits to Irish sources. MacCharles (1987) has suggested that financial advantage, as opposed to fundamental economic advantage, explains many of the geographical patterns of intrafirm trade within MNCs.

Most industrial countries encourage intrafirm trade by MNCs through tariff provisions that allow low-duty or duty-free importation of goods sent abroad for processing or final assembly. In the United States, two tariff schedule items, 806.30 and 807.00, are referred to as the *Offshore Assembly Provision (OAP).* The OAP especially encourages American companies to make final assembly of goods for domestic consumption in countries with low labor costs. Tariffs are collected only on the foreign value-added of the re-entering goods, and if cheap labor is the source of the foreign value-added, then it is low. Several poorer countries have further encouraged their use as cheap labor sites in the OAP process, both for American and other producers, by establishing free-trade zones in which goods to be finished for re-export are not subject to tariffs. Poorer countries rely on the free-trade zones and OAPs to provide employment and foreign exchange earnings (Suarez-Villa, 1984; Boltuck et al., 1990). The maquiladora zone in Mexico is an example.

REFERENCES

Agmon, T., and C. Hekman, eds. 1989. *Trade Policy and Corporate Business Decisions* (New York: Oxford University Press).

Alavi, J., and H. Thompson. 1988. "Toward a Theory of Foreign Trade Zones." *The International Trade Journal* 3: 203–217.

Balassa, B. 1967. *Studies in Trade Liberalisation* (Baltimore, Maryland: Johns Hopkins University Press).

Baldwin, R., and P. Krugman. 1987. "Market Access and International Competition: A Simulation Study of 16K Random Access Memories." In *Empirical Studies in International Trade*, R. Feenstra, ed. (Cambridge, Massachusetts: MIT Press).

———. 1988. "Industrial Policy and Competition in Wide-Bodied Aircraft." In *Trade Policy Issues and Empirical Analysis*, R. Baldwin, ed. (Chicago, Illinois: University of Chicago Press).

Begg, I. 1989. "The Regional Dimension of the '1992' Proposals." *Regional Studies* 23: 368–376.

Bhagwati, J. 1988. *Protectionism* (Cambridge, Massachusetts: MIT Press).

Bickerdike, C. 1907. "Review of *Protective and Preferential Import Duties* by A.C. Pigou." *Economic Journal* 17: 99.

Boltuck, R., J. Mendez, T. Murray, and D. Rousslang. 1990. "Offshore Assembly Provisions in the U.S.: Some Possible Trade Effects of their Repeal." *Weltwirtschaftliches Archiv* 126: 709–721.

Brander, J., and B. Spencer. 1981. "Tariffs and the Extraction of Foreign Monopoly Rents under Potential Entry." *Canadian Journal of Economics* 14: 371–389.

Brown, D., and R. Stern. 1989. "Computable General Equilibrium Estimates of the Gains from U.S.-Canadian Trade Liberalisation." In *Economic Aspects of Regional Trading Arrangements*, D. Greenway, T. Hyclak, and R. Thornton, eds. (New York: New York University Press).

Brown, S., and S. Koont. 1989. "Optimal Foreign Trade Pricing in CPEs under Endogenous Uncertainty: The Case of Dumping." *The International Trade Journal* 3: 415–439.

Bruton, H. 1989. "Import Substitution." In *Handbook of Development Economics*, vol. II, H. Chenery and T. Srinivasan, eds. (Amsterdam: Elsevier).

Callahan, C. 1989. "EC Enlargement and US-EC Trade Frictions." In *Economic Aspects of Regional Trading Arrangements*.

Cao, A. 1980. "Non-Tariff Barriers to U.S. Manufactured Exports." *Columbia Journal of World Business* 15: 93–102.

Casas, F., and E. Gelbard. 1987. "Tariffs and Quotas in the Presence of Foreign Monopoly." *The International Trade Journal* 1: 289–303.

Cho, K. 1988. "Determinants of Intra-Firm Trade: A Search for a Theoretical Framework." *The International Trade Journal* 3: 167–185.

Chung, J. 1990. "The Trade Policy Cycle in the United States." *The International Trade Journal* 4: 279–291.

Cline, W. 1986. "U.S. Trade and Industrial Policy: The Experience of Textiles, Steel, and Automobiles." In *Strategic Trade Policy and the New International Economics*, P. Krugman, ed. (Cambridge, Massachusetts: MIT Press).

Collins, C., and S. Dunaway. 1987. "The Cost of Trade Restraints: The Case of Japanese Automobile Exports to the United States." *IMF Staff Papers* 35: 150–175.

Coughlin, C., and G. Wood. 1989. "An Introduction to Non-Tariff Barriers to Trade." *Review*, Federal Reserve Bank of St. Louis, 71(1): 32–46.

Czinkota, M., and A. Talbot. 1986. "GATT Regulation of Countertrade: Issues and Prospects." *The International Trade Journal* 1: 155–174.

Deardorf, A., and R. Stern. 1985. "The Structure of Tariff Protection: Effects of Foreign Tariffs and NTBs." *Review of Economics and Statistics* 67: 539–548.

_____ . 1986. *The Michigan Model of World Production and Trade* (Cambridge, Massachusetts: MIT Press).

Dichtl, E., H. Koeglmayr, and S. Mueller. 1990. "International Orientation as a Precondition for Export Success." *Journal of International Business Studies* 21: 23–38.

The Economist. 1990. "The State of the Nation State." December 22, pp. 43–46.

El-Agraa, A. 1989. *The Theory and Measurement of International Economic Integration* (New York: St. Martin's Press).

Erickson, R., and D. Hayward. 1991. "The International Flows of Industrial Exports from U.S. Regions." *Annals of the Association of American Geographers* 81: 371–390.

Eurofi. 1989. *1992-Planning for Financial Services and the Insurance Sector* (London: Butterworths).

Fluckiger, Y. 1987. "The Theory of Transfers in a Multilateral World: The Customs Union Case." *The International Trade Journal* 2: 173–192.

Ford, R., and W. Suyker. 1990. "Industrial Subsidies in the OECD Economies." *OECD Economic Studies* 15: 37–81.

Fraser, R. 1987. *The World Financial System* (Burnt Mill, England: Longman).

Geer, T. 1989. "Product Liability in the European Economic Communities: The New Situation." *Journal of International Business Studies* 20: 337–348.

Gomes, L. 1990. *Neoclassical International Economics: An Historical Survey* (New York: St. Martin's Press).

Grossman, G. 1990. "Promoting New Industrial Activities: A Survey of Recent Arguments and Evidence." *OECD Economic Studies* 14: 87–125.

Grotewold, A. 1982. "The Failure of LAFTA and the Success of the Regional Theory of World Trade." *GeoJournal* 6: 195–196.

_____ . 1987. "Nations as Economic Regions." *GeoJournal* 15: 91–96.

Grubel, H. 1989. "Issues in Free Trade in Services between Canada and the United States." In *Economic Aspects of Regional Trading Arrangements.*

Gunter, F. 1989. "Customs Union Theory: Retrospect and Prospect." In *Economic Aspects of Regional Trading Arrangements.*

Hamilton, B., and J. Whalley. 1985. "Geographically Discriminatory Trade Arrangements." *Review of Economics and Statistics* 67: 446–455.

Han, C., and V. Terpstra. 1988. "Country-of-Origin Effects for Uni-National and Bi-National Products." *Journal of International Business Studies* 19: 235–255.

Hanink, D., and R. Cromley. 1993. "Univariate Classification of Differentiated International Markets." *Environment and Planning* 25: 409–424.

Hansen, N. 1981. *The Border Economy: Regional Development in the Southwest* (Austin: University of Texas Press).

Harrington, J. 1989. "Implications of the Canada-United States Free Trade Agreement for Regional Provision of Producer Services." *Economic Geography* 65: 314–328.

Hipple, F. 1990. "Multinational Companies and the Growth of the U.S. Trade Deficit." *The International Trade Journal* 5: 217–234.

Hogendoorn, J., and W. Brown. 1979. *The New International Economics* (Reading, Massachusetts: Addison-Wesley).

House Subcommittee on International Economic Policy and Trade. 1989. *Economic Community's 1992 Economic Integration Plan* (Washington: U.S. Government Printing Office).

Hufbauer, G. 1989. *The Free Trade Debate: Background Paper* (New York: Priority Press).

Jackson, J. 1989. *The World Trading System: Law and Policy of International Economic Relations* (Cambridge, Massachusetts: MIT Press).

Jacquemin, A., and A. Sapir. 1988. "International Trade and Integration of the European Community: An Econometric Analysis." *European Economic Review* 32: 1439–1449.

Kenen, P. 1989. *The International Economy.* 2d ed. (Englewood Cliffs, New Jersey: Prentice Hall).

Koekkoek, A., A. Kuyvenhoven, and W. Molle. 1990. "Europe 1992 and the Developing Countries: An Overview." *Journal of Common Market Studies* 29: 111–131.

Koekkoek, K. 1987. "The Developing Countries in the New GATT Round: Safeguards Revisited." *The International Trade Journal* 1: 319–337.

Kogut, B. 1984. "Normative Observations on the International Value-Added Chain and Strategic Groups." *Journal of International Business Studies* 15/2: 151–167.

Korth, C. 1985. *International Business: Environment and Management.* 2d ed. (Englewood Cliffs, New Jersey: Prentice-Hall).

Kotabe, M. 1990. "The Relationship between Offshore Sourcing and Innovativeness of U.S. Multinational Firms: An Empirical Investigation." *Journal of International Business Studies* 21: 623–638.

Kotabe, M., and G. Omura. 1989. "Sourcing Strategies of European and Japanese Multinationals: A Comparison." *Journal of International Business Studies* 20: 113–130.

Krugman, P., ed. 1986. *Strategic Trade Policy and the New International Economics* (Cambridge, Massachusetts: MIT Press).

Laird, S., and A. Yeats. 1990. "Trends in Nontariff Barriers of Developed Countries, 1966–1986." *Weltwirtschaftliches Archiv* 126: 299–325.

Lecraw, D. 1989. "The Management of Countertrade: Factors Influencing Success." *Journal of International Business Studies* 20: 41–59.

Le Heron, R. 1980. "Exports and Linkage Development in Manufacturing Firms: The Example of Export Promotion in New Zealand." *Economic Geography* 56: 281–299.

Lewis, S. 1989. "Primary Exporting Countries." In *Handbook of Development Economics,* vol. II.

MacCharles, D. 1987. *Trade among Multinationals: Intra-Industry Trade and National Competitiveness* (London: Croom Helm).

Macchiarola, P. 1990. "Mexico as a Trading Partner." *Proceedings of the Academy of Political Science* 37/4: 90–109.

MacPhee, C. 1987. "Tokyo Round Tariff Reductions and the Less Developed Countries." *The International Trade Journal* 1: 371–396.

Magee, S. 1980. *International Trade* (Reading, Pennsylvania: Addison-Wesley).

Mascarenhas, B. 1984. "The Coordination of Manufacturing Interdependence in Multinational Companies." *Journal of International Business Studies* 15/3: 91–106.

McConnell, J. 1979. "The Export Decision: An Empirical Study of Firm Behavior." *Economic Geography* 55: 171–183.

McCulloch, R. 1990. "The United States-Canada Free Trade Agreement." *Proceedings of the Academy of Political Science* 37/4: 79–89.

Melese, F., W. Shugart II, and J. Henderson. 1989. "Tit-for-Tat, Tariffs, and Time: A Dynamic Model of Trade Policy." *The International Trade Journal* 4: 167–186.

Mirus, R., and B. Yeung. 1986. "Economic Incentives for Countertrade." *Journal of International Business Studies* 17: 27–39.

Morici, P. 1989. "The Canadian-U.S. Free Trade Agreement: Origins, Contents and Prospects." In *Economic Aspects of Regional Trading Arrangements*.

NAFTA Digest. 1992A. "NAFTA and Texas-Part I." 1/2: 1–4.

———. 1992B. "NAFTA and Texas-Part II." 1/2: 1–2.

Nell, P. 1990. "EFTA in the 1990s: The Search for a New Identity." *Journal of Common Market Studies* 28: 332–356.

Neumann, I. 1990. "The European Free Trade Association: The Problems of an All-European Role." *Journal of Common Market Studies* 28: 359–378.

Nollen, S. 1987. "Business Costs and Business Policy for Export Controls." *Journal of International Business Studies* 18: 1–18.

Owen, R., and M. Dynes. 1990. *The Times Guide to 1992.* 2d ed. (London: Times Books).

Phaup, E., and M. Auten. 1988. "Responses to Foreign Export Subsidies." *The International Trade Journal* 2: 287–299.

Pigou, A. 1906. *Protective and Preferential Import Duties* (London: Macmillan).

Pomfret, R. 1981. "The Impact of EEC Enlargement on Non-Member Mediterranean Countries' Exports to the EEC." *The Economic Journal* 91: 726–729.

Rugman, A., and A. Anderson. 1987. "U.S.-Canadian Trade Liberalization: A Survey." *The International Trade Journal* 1: 219–250.

Siddharthan, N., and N. Kumar. 1990. "The Determinants of Inter-Industry Variations in the Proportion of Intra-Firm Trade: The Behavior of U.S. Multinationals." *Weltwirtschaftliches Archive* 126: 581–591.

South, R. 1990. "Transnational 'Maquiladora' Location." *Annals of the Association of American Geographers* 80: 549–570.

Spich, R. "Free Trade as Ideology, Fair Trade as Goal: Problems of an Ideological Approach to U.S. Trade Policy." *The International Trade Journal* 1: 129–154.

Stegeman, K. 1990. "EC Anti-Dumping Policy: Are Price Undertakings a Legal Substitute for Illegal Price Fixing?" *Weltwirtschaftliches Archive* 126: 268–298.

Stewart, J. 1989. "Transfer Pricing: Some Empirical Evidence from Ireland." *Journal of Economic Studies* 16/3: 40–56.

Stockhausen, G. 1988. "A Model of Exporting Country Response to the Threat of a Foreign Import Quota." *The International Trade Journal* 2: 319–336.

Stolper, W., and P. Samuelson. 1941. "Protection and Real Wages." *Review of Economic Studies* 9: 58–73.

Suarez-Villa, L. 1984. "Industrial Export Enclaves and Manufacturing Change." *Papers of the Regional Science Association* 54: 89–111.

Tansuhaj, P., and J. Gentry. 1987. "Firm Differences in Perceptions of the Facilitating Role of Foreign Trade Zones in Global Marketing and Logistics." *Journal of International Business Studies* 18: 19–33.

Terpstra, V., and N. Aydin. 1981. "Marketing Know-How Transfers by Multinationals: A Case Study in Turkey." *Journal of International Business Studies* 12/3: 35–48.

Tinbergen, J. 1954. *International Economic Integration* (Amsterdam: Elsevier).

Viner, J. 1950. *The Customs Union Issue* (New York: Carnegie Endowment for International Peace).

Wonnacott, P., and R. Wonnacott. 1981. "Is Unilateral Tariff Reduction Preferable to a Customs Union? The Curious Case of the Missing Foreign Tariffs." *American Economic Review* 71: 704–714.

World Bank. 1987. *World Development Report 1987* (New York: Oxford University Press).

CHAPTER 11

· · ·

Economic Development
and Trade

· · ·

11.1   INTRODUCTION

Chapters 9 and 10 dealt with trade theory and trade management, respectively. Essentially, the benefits of trade to an economy are obtained when a country's terms of trade are favorable. Classical comparative advantage and factor endowment theories of trade, described in Chapter 9, portray a world in which rational trade yields favorable terms of trade to both bilateral partners. If this was not the case, trade would not take place. Achieving favorable terms of trade, however, is not automatic, and many of the policies of managed trade described in Chapter 10 are employed in the hope of improving terms of trade that are currently poor, or perceived as headed toward decline. Recall that some of the policies of managed trade concern trade in particular products and others concern trade with particular countries. Governments sometimes are wise, and in the case of trade they correctly understand that its product structure as well as geographical structure are pivotal in effecting its success.

This chapter addresses the role of international trade in national economic growth and development. Both the product structure and geographical structure of trade are considered as related characteristics that affect trade, and in turn, the effectiveness of trade in economic development. Currently, most world trade takes place within the set of rich countries that comprise the Core of the international economy. This pattern of trade is not surprising on the theoretical grounds of international trade in differentiated products, nor is it surprising in light of current practices of trade management. It seems that the best hope for poorer countries is to become more Corelike. Trade within the Periphery is growing, but major markets remain in the Core. Improving poor trade performance appears to require an integrated mix of domestic policy and economic adjustment that is focused on external relationships. This leads to the unhappy proposition that growth requires trade, but trade requires growth!

This chapter begins with a brief discussion of the benefits expected to accrue to an economy actively engaged in trade, then considers the national income effects of a country's terms of trade and summarizes terms of trade problems. The chapter then takes up the the trade balance effects of a country's product structure of trade. Emphasis is placed on the problem of commodity concentration in trade, and on trade in services and in textiles. The last broad topic of the chapter is the trade balance effect of a country's geographical structure of trade. Current geographical patterns are considered in the context of flows both within and across the sets of rich and poor countries.

11.2 TRADE, GROWTH, AND ECONOMIC DEVELOPMENT

The general benefits of free trade are indicated in the theory of comparative advantage. Under free trade, countries are able to consume more than under a closed system of production and exchange. World welfare is increased under free trade as production systems are rationalized toward appropriate relative costs and thereby made more efficient. Beyond the additions to both production and consumption derived from the realization of comparative advantage, additional gains from trade can be obtained from realizations of economies of scale and by technology transfers.

The expectations of economies from scale due to trade were first described by Adam Smith in his *Wealth of Nations*. Recall from Chapter 3 that Smith described economies of scale as deriving from ". . . the extent of the market." As the market increases in size, opportunities for specialization in production increase, and an increase in specialization means an increase in production efficiency. If a country is able to export its goods to foreign markets, the extent of the foreign market induces greater domestic specialization and efficiency of production.

On the other hand, gains from trade arising from technology transfer are achieved through importing. Krugman (1990), for example, describes the transfer of technology as a copycat process in which poorer countries develop domestic technologies by imitating the technology embodied in their imports from richer countries. In addition, the presence of imports in a domestic market can improve the domestic economy in two other ways. First, imports of competitive goods tend to force domestic producers to maintain high levels of production efficiency and to be more competitive in both cost and quality than if the domestic market was closed to foreign products. Second, imports of noncompetitive primary and intermediate goods, which are not available domestically, allow a country's enterprises to produce a wider variety of finished goods for both domestic consumption and export. Not unlike the truism that "it takes money to make money," in many cases "it takes imports to make exports."

Theoretically, the benefits of trade are all growth-inducing, but at the same time it is not really clear whether growth leads trade or trade leads growth. Ram (1985), for example, provided empirical evidence that exports are an important basis for economic growth, while Sato (1977) argued that export growth can take place only if led by a growing domestic economy. Lewis (1979, p. 74) has has remarked that trade is the lubricating oil to the engine of growth, which he argued is actually technological improvement. The more prevalent view, however, is that trade is the engine of growth, and this view has been held for some time.

Is trade an engine of growth? The answer to this question is not at all straightforward. Recall from the discussion of the export base and central place multipliers in Chapter 4 that trade multipliers tend to increase with size of place. In an international context, the extension would be at the level of national income; that is, as GDP increases so would any export multiplier. In addition, an export multiplier must be some function of the degree of integration between the export sector and the domestic, or service, sector. A complicating factor is that size and integration frequently are related.

The relationship between size of an economy and an export multiplier can lead to difficulty in separating the foreign from the domestic economy. Remember that a large multiplier means that a small increment of export employment induces a large increment of domestic economy employment, and a small multiplier means that export employment gains comprise most of total employment gains. Hoare (1985), in an analysis of British regional economies, found a relatively small foreign export effect. Erickson (1989), studying American regions, also found a relatively small direct contribution to employment gains from exporting. A reasonable explanation for the findings in both studies, and the one offered by both authors, is that if a country has a very large domestic economy then its export sector is relatively unimportant in its employment effect when compared to the employment effect of the domestic economy. This is an extension of the "law of the declining share of trade with respect to country size." On the other hand, their findings also conform to a large export multiplier due to size, and the resulting large gains in "domestic" employment and small gains in "export" employment.

If the degree of integration between the export and domestic sectors is great, then the importance of the export sector to the domestic economy can be overestimated in the same way that it may be underestimated in large economies. Discrimination between domestic and export effects is difficult when the two sectors are effectively one. Of course when export and domestic sectors are poorly connected, then the opposite problem, one of overestimation of export effects, can occur. Export enclaves, such as the maquiladora zone of Mexico, are virtually isolated from the rest of a country's economy. In these cases, any growth due to exports remains virtually isolated as well. National growth rates increase as functions of exports but the regional incidence of growth is highly uneven (Chapter 8).

In the engine-of-growth context, cross-sectional estimates were made of the growth "response" to exports and total trade turnover (exports plus imports) for 1990. The response coefficient is the value $\hat{b}$ calculated from the linear equation

$$lnGDP = \hat{a} + \hat{b}lnT \tag{11.1}$$

where $lnGDP$ is the natural logarithm of GDP, and lnT is the natural logarithm of trade. The income response coefficient was calculated for four values of T:

(1) merchandise exports, which includes all visible manufactured and primary goods; (2) service exports, broadly defined to include nonfactor services, transportation, travel, and the investment items of the current account (see Chapter 4); (3) the sum of merchandise and service exports; and (4) total trade turnover, which is the sum of merchandise and service exports plus imports. In all cases the income response coefficients should be taken as rough descriptive measures rather than strict analytical point values.

Worldwide, the income response coefficient is about 0.9 for all three of the export measures (Table 11.1). The basic interpretation is that for each dollar's worth of increase in exports, national income increases about 90 cents. In the case of total trade turnover, the relationship is virtually one for one. The national income response coefficients, however, vary across the World Bank income groups. The basic tendency of the income response coefficients is to increase as national incomes increase. The trends of the values are mixed within the lower income groups, but in each case the income response coefficient is always highest for the high income countries. Interestingly, the high income countries are the only ones that have a consistent national income response greater than one across all three export measures. The national income response to total trade turnover also generally increases by increasing income group, but in this case the response coefficient is consistently greater than one. Given the relatively low levels of the income responses to exporting in the lower income groups, the higher response to total trade turnover implicitly indicates that imports are as able as, if not more able than, exports to generate growth, especially at lower income levels. At the least, there seem to be constant or increasing returns to trade in general in the international economy.

Similar evidence of the benefits of trade in general, rather than just exports, to a national economy has been found elsewhere and serves as the basis for arguments for the importance of international and even unilateral trade liberalization. Bhagwati (1988), for example, has noted that trade liberalization and economic growth have been fundamentally intertwined in the post–World War II global economy and raises

TABLE 11.1 The Response of National Income to Exports and Total Trade Turnover by World Bank Income Group, 1990

Income Group	Merchandise Exports	Service Exports	All Exports	Total Trade Turnover
All	0.887	0.869	0.917	0.988
Low	0.867	0.905	0.898	1.010
Low Middle	0.857	0.823	0.986	1.025
High Middle	0.882	0.602	0.883	1.038
High	1.169	1.099	1.181	1.192

Source of original data: International Monetary Fund. 1991. *Balance of Payments Statistics Yearbook 1991* (Washington: International Monetary Fund); and World Bank. 1992. *World Development Report 1992* (New York: Oxford University Press).

concerns about the apparent increase in protectionist attitudes among the rich industrial countries. The increase in protectionism seems to be short-sighted because of the importance of imports, directly and indirectly, throughout a country's economy. An analysis of the American economy, for example, has shown that import restrictions can lead to aggregate declines in employment rates and even a decline in capitalization levels as defined in stock markets (Canto et al., 1986). A very thorough analysis of the link between trade liberalization and growth has led to the conclusion that elimination of import quotas, in particular, has led to increased economic growth in poorer countries (Papageorgiou et al., 1990). This study also emphasized the importance of establishing appropriate domestic conditions for the advancement of trade, including fiscal and monetary policies that ease international exchange.

As emphasized throughout this book, places and flows interact in any system of spatial interaction. Domestic policies can affect the flow of trade and, in turn, trade tends to enhance domestic growth. In addition to policy, of course, the goods and services entered into trade must be some function of the variety and amounts of goods and services produced and consumed in a country (recall the hierarchical trade model described in Chapter 9). The composition of trade across income groups is illustrative of the place-flow relationship in the system of trade interaction. On average, countries export and import merchandise valued at about 24% of their GDPs (Table 11.2). Service trade is a smaller proportion of their national incomes, with service exports at about 7% and service imports at about 9% of GDP. However, disaggregation to World Bank income groups again indicates fairly systematic differences in trade's proportion of GDP only with respect to merchandise. In the cases of service exports and imports, there are no systematic increases with income. In fact, service imports tend to decrease in proportion to national income as national income increases. The category of service imports, however, is the only one led by the low income group. It has the lowest share of national income in both types of exports and in merchandise imports. Conversely, the high income countries are in last place among the groups in

TABLE 11.2 Exports and Imports as a Percent of National Income by World Bank Income Group, 1990

Income Group	Mean Percent of GDP			
	Merchandise Exports	Service Exports	Merchandise Imports	Service Imports
All	24.2	7.0	28.5	9.0
Low	15.5	4.5	23.4	9.5
Low Middle	25.4	9.3	29.6	9.4
High Middle	27.0	5.0	24.3	8.8
High	32.3	8.6	36.8	8.0

Source of original data: International Monetary Fund. 1991. *Balance of Payments Statistics Yearbook 1991* (Washington: International Monetary Fund); and World Bank. 1992. *World Development Report 1992* (New York: Oxford University Press).

only the category of service imports, and have the highest proportion of income represented in both imports and exports of merchandise.

What is the discriminating factor between the poorest countries as a group and the rest of the world? It may be their relatively low levels of agricultural productivity. Recall from Chapter 3 that the low income group of countries was the only one of the World Bank groups with a productivity coefficient in agriculture less than one. In addition, it was the only income group in which agriculture held the largest sectoral share of GDP. The World Bank (1987) has suggested that the large share of the poor countries GDP in agriculture is the result of its low productivity levels. Low agricultural productivity binds a domestic economy to that sector by limiting incomes and therefore demand for manufactured goods and services. The lack of domestic demand for these items limits diversification in domestic production which, in turn, limits the supply of tradable goods and services. In this case, specialization is an apparent result of inefficiency rather than efficiency resulting from specialization.

Lewis summarizes the problem in his essay, *The Evolution of the International Economic Order* (1977, p. 76):

1. *The principal cause of the poverty of the developing countries, and of their poor factoral terms of trade, is that half their labor force (more or less) produces food at very low productivity levels. This limits the domestic market for manufactures and services, keeps the propensity to import too high, reduces taxable capacity and savings, and provides goods and services for export on unfavorable terms. To alter this is the fundamental way to change LDC/MDC relations. But this takes time.*

2. *Meanwhile, LDCs need a more rapid rate of growth of exports, to pay for needed imports and to meet their debt obligations. MDCs should make more space for the LDCs in world trade, by reducing their barriers to LDC exports of manufactures and agricultural products. This is the best and most effective way of helping the LDCs.*

Lewis's first point concerns the domestic characteristics of the poor countries (LDC stands for Less Developed Countries). His second point concerns the flows between the poor countries and the rich ones (MDC stands for More Developed Countries). Supply and demand drive the flows of trade, but the flows are filtered in their nodal effects by the terms of trade.

11.3 THE TERMS OF TRADE AND NATIONAL INCOME

Elias (1972) has provided a model of the national income effect of the terms of trade:

$$Y = D(L, K) + TT \times X(L, K) \tag{11.2}$$

where Y is national income; D is the real value, net of foreign inputs, of goods that are produced and consumed domestically; L is labor input; K is capital input; TT is the terms of trade, defined in terms of the ratio of export values to import values; and X is the real value, net of foreign inputs, of export goods. In this representation, the trade contribution to national income is defined by both the terms of trade and the level of output exported, $X(L, K)$. Therefore, national income gains from trade can be derived in several ways. Obviously, an increase in exports or an improvement in the terms of trade, holding the other constant, increases national income. A decline in exports or in the terms of trade, holding the other constant, decreases national income. However, the two sources of income growth from trade can move in opposite directions, and as long as the terms of trade improve at a faster (slower) rate than the aggregate value of exports declines (increases) then national income can increase (decrease). So national income can decline in the face of either improving or declining terms of trade.

In a recent analysis of thirty-three countries in Africa, Svedberg (1991) examined the interaction of changing terms of trade and changing export volumes in determining variations in aggregate export earnings. He found mixed results. During the period 1954–1969, all twenty-six of the thirty-three countries that experienced real growth in export earnings could attribute it to increasing export volumes while terms of trade remained flat. During the period 1970–1985, only eight countries experienced real growth in export earnings. Five could attribute their growth to increasing export volumes, and three to improving terms of trade. Further, of the eleven countries that experienced significant declines in export earnings, seven had declining export volumes and four had declining terms of trade.

Restrictive national trade policy usually results from a current or anticipated decline in a country's terms of trade. Such a decline is a problem for a national economy for two reasons: it can lead to slow growth or even declining national income, and it can lead to a deterioration in a country's current account. Several reasons have been given for declining terms of trade, most of which focus on the trade problems of poor countries (Thirlwall, 1977). The most commonly cited reason for declining terms of trade among poor countries is their tendency to export more primary products than manufactured goods (Lewis, 1989). Over time, the tendency of primary-goods prices has been to remain relatively flat as compared to the prices of manufactures. The price problem of primary goods has two sources. One is the relatively small increase, especially in richer countries, in the demand for primary products as incomes grow (Harrod, 1973). Especially with regard to food exports, Engel's law plays an important role in international trade. In addition, product substitution and improved efficiency in the use of industrial raw materials tends to retard any real increases in primary-goods prices.

Another argument for the inevitability of declining terms of trade for poorer countries is that technological progress takes place much more quickly in richer countries, and this technological progress is embodied in their exports. These exports, because they contain higher technology than the otherwise equivalent exports of poorer countries, have higher real prices. This argument is similar to the argument of Prebisch and others for import substitution (see Chapter 4). Richer countries have monopoly power in certain industries which raise barriers to entry by enterprises in poorer countries. The policy of import substitution limits foreign access to a poorer domestic market, enabling domestic enterprises to enter production (Bruton, 1989). In addition to erecting barriers to entry, industrial country monopolies are able to extract rents by higher-than-competitive pricing in poorer countries. This rent-seeking behavior ensures increasingly favorable terms of trade for the rich countries at the expense of decreasing terms of trade for poor countries.

Finally, a decline in the terms of trade for poor countries may result from the inability of poor-country economies to adjust their resources. It is more difficult to reallocate resources, either geographically or sectorally, in poor countries than in rich ones, so reactions to declining terms of trade are difficult to make. Rothschild (1985) has described the export boom that accompanies the sectoral, or structural, adjustment of a poor country's economy. Unfortunately, such structural adjustment in poor countries is difficult to make. Again, sectoral shifts in poor countries may be slowed by their low productivity in agriculture which limits expansion in other sectors. Essentially, this argument is one of the inability of neoclassical rules to pertain to poorer economies. A related problem of overspecialization in poorer countries is referred to as *immiserising growth,* or growth that brings misery. Under the theory of comparative advantage, one of the benefits of free trade is the ability of a country to specialize in its production. The specialization under trade leads to increased efficiency and output. However, if a country's economy is specialized in producing a primary product not in sufficient demand in foreign markets, output can grow as the terms of trade decrease (see Equation 11.2). Despite the growth in output, national income declines, and the country experiences immiserising growth (Bhagwati, 1958).

Lewis (1977) noted the poor barter terms of trade of poorer countries. Actual barter terms of trade are not available, but the World Bank (1992) has calculated a terms of trade index (1987 = 100) that describes the changing ratio of the average price of exported merchandise (export unit values) to the average price of imported merchandise (import unit values). While the resulting value is not a direct terms of trade measure, the tendencies it portrays are just as informative. In 1990, the reporting countries had a mean terms of trade index of 101; the median was 100. Both values indicate that the terms of trade in 1990, on average, had not changed since 1987. However, the general trend was one of decline from 1985 to 1990 in poorer countries. With respect to mean terms of trade, the decline was consistent across all but the high income group of countries, where the index was the same in 1985 as in 1990. With respect to median terms of trade, the high income countries are the only ones that experienced, on average, improved terms of trade in 1990 compared to 1985 (Table 11.3).

For most countries, however, the average value of exports decreased, or the average of imports increased, or both, during the period. Interestingly, while the low income group of countries had an average decline in terms of trade that slightly exceeded the average decline of all countries, both the low middle and high middle income groups experienced more serious declines. Some of this rapid decline is undoubtedly due to the large decline in the value of petroleum exports from these groups over the period. The decline in petroleum prices led to rapid declines in the terms of trade for the three oil-exporting, higher-income countries of Saudi Arabia,

**TABLE 11.3   Mean and Median
Merchandise Terms of Trade Index by
World Bank Income Group, 1985 and 1990***

Income Group	1985		1990	
	Mean	Median	Mean	Median
All	112	106	101	100
Low	112	108	100	100
Low Middle	114	110	101	99
High Middle	127	105	106	105
High	99	96	99	100

* 1987 = 100.

Source of original data: World Bank. 1992. *World Bank Development
Report 1992* (New York: Oxford University Press).

Kuwait, and the United Arab Emirates, which experienced declining terms of trade
throughout the 1980s. If a terms of trade index is defined as 1980 = 100, then all
three countries had terms of trade index values of 54 in 1987 (World Bank, 1989).

If trade does contribute to growth, the terms of trade tendencies described in
Table 11.3 suggest that it does so better for rich countries than for poor. Essentially, a
country's terms of trade is a function of its product structure and geographical
structure of trade. The arguments for the inevitabilty of declining terms of trade in
poor countries focus on the product composition of trade, but the geographical
structure of a country's trade is fundamentally important as well. As noted in Lewis's
second point, the economic development of poor countries is inevitably tied to their
ability to export to the world's richer countries which serve as the current regions of
demand. The importance of the direction of trade, as well as its composition, has also
been argued by the World Bank (1990). Inevitably, the product structure and geographical structure of trade tend to overlap, as indicated in the following sections.

11.4   THE GENERAL PRODUCT
STRUCTURE OF TRADE

Established theories of international trade concern merchandise trade but not trade in
services (Chapter 9). Their focus on merchandise trade is much the result of historical
inertia; rapid growth of domestic service sectors of the economy and the resulting
growth of service trade is a fairly recent proposition. Even now, merchandise trade is,
on average, about three times the value of service trade as broadly characterized

(Table 11.2). Recall from the discussion of the current account in Chapter 4 that service trade encompasses a wide variety of activities. It includes the earnings of factors, both labor and capital, as well as the nonfactor services of transportation, tourism, and communications; and royalties and payments for construction, engineering, communication, and other items, including film rentals. In 1990, the global value of nonfactor service exports was about U.S. $500 billion (International Monetary Fund, 1991), while the value of merchandise exports was about $3.2 trillion (thousand billion).

Hanink (1989) has noted the apparent obstacles to a general theory of international trade posed by trade in services. Because service trade is so broad in its constituent parts, consistent patterns over both merchandise and service trade are not readily evident. This problem can be illustrated by some simple comparisons. In 1990, for example, both Ghana and West Germany had ratios of service trade turnover to merchandise trade turnover of about 0.195 (International Monetary Fund, 1991). In the same year, Austria, Norway, Togo, and Ethiopia had ratios of about 0.41. No obvious pattern in these values discriminates between rich and poor countries. Rich countries such as Canada and Italy trade much more in merchandise than in services, but so do the poor countries of Nigeria and Honduras. The lack of a distinctive pattern is due, at least in part, to the wide variety of items traded in the service category and to the variable used, total trade turnover, which is the sum of exports and imports. For example, both Jordan and Saudi Arabia trade heavily in services, but Jordan is a net exporter, mainly of labor services, and Saudi Arabia is a net importer of both labor and nonfactor services.

An examination of per capita trade balances by World Bank income group does indicate at least one pattern of trade that is helpful in understanding its general composition (Table 11.4). In 1990, on average, the world's countries ran a negative per capita merchandise balance of trade as well as a negative per capita trade balance in services. Three groups of countries were not consistent with the global average. The high middle income group averaged a net positive per capita merchandise trade balance while each of the other income groups had average deficits. Two income groups had net surpluses in services, on average, in 1990. One was the low middle income group, with a small mean surplus. This mean surplus is derived from a limited number of countries, including Panama (transportation services) and Jordan (labor services), which ran very large service trade surpluses in 1990. In fact, the median, an alternative measure of the average service trade account, was negative for the low middle income group in 1990. With respect to both the mean and median, however, the average service trade account of a high income country was positive in 1990.

An interesting point of departure for an examination of service trade in the context of average national income is that services have been shown to have relatively lower prices in poor countries than in rich countries (Kravis et al., 1982). Several theoretical explanations have been offered for this disparity; both Balassa (1964) and Samuelson (1964) have provided the same theoretical rationale. Their explanation is based on low relative productivity of poor country labor in goods-producing sectors, but service sector parity of labor productivity between rich and poor countries. International trade in goods leads to lower wages, due to lower productivity, in the

**TABLE 11.4   Broad Sectoral Per
Capita Trade Balances by World
Bank Income Group, 1990: in $U.S.**

Income Group	Means	
	Merchandise	Services
All	−94.85	−4.55
Low	−17.95	−12.72
Low Middle	−54.91	5.52
High Middle	157.71	−172.42
High	−458.99	115.66

Source of original data: International Monetary
Fund. 1991. *Balance of Payments Statistics
Yearbook 1991* (Washington: International
Monetary Fund).

goods-producing sectors of the poor countries. In turn, the lower wages of poor
countries lead to lower prices paid for services, which are taken to be nontradable.
Alternatively, Panagariya (1988) has relied upon the existence of scale economies in
rich-country manufacturing as a basis for explaining the relatively low price of
services in poor countries. Lower average costs, due to economies of scale, in rich
countries provide the group with comparative advantage in the export of manufactures. Because of their comparative advantage, rich countries specialize in manufacturing to a degree that limits the supply of services, again nontradable items. The
relative deficit of services in rich countries makes their prices relatively high.

Bhagwati (1984) developed a model that assumes excessive supplies of poor-
country labor. The excess labor in poor countries means that their capital-to-labor
ratios are relatively lower than in rich countries. While trade induces equal prices
across goods, the prices of services, again nontradable, are lower, again due to lower
incomes. The excess labor of Bhagwhati's approach is of the same nature as the
unlimited supply of labor in Lewis's dual economy (Chapter 3), and Feldman and
Gang (1990) have explained low service prices in poor countries in that context. They
argue that government policies in many poor countries deplete financial resources in
rural areas in order to enhance them in major urban centers. The high cost of rural
credit drives farmers from rural areas to the urban centers where they enter the service
sector at very low wages. The constant stream of rural migrants ensures price stability
at low levels in the urban service sector.

Despite the fact that these explanations of low service prices in poor countries
assume that services cannot be traded, the demonstrable existence of the relatively
low prices may be part of the reason that per capita service trade deficits are low in the
low income countries. However, the fact that per capita service trade deficits exist at
all means that services are traded, and some recent efforts to build theories of service
trade have been made. Most involve extensions to factor endowment theory. In fact,

some service trade must be factor based. Trade in the factor services of capital and labor must be due in large part to relative supplies of these factors among countries. Even many nonfactor services can be treated in the general framework of factor endowment theory. For example, travel and tourism receipts must be at least partly a function of differing endowments of amenities such as beautiful scenery and pleasant weather across countries. Ocean transport revenues are more likely to be positive in coastal countries than in landlocked ones.

Jones and Ruane (1990) used a fairly standard approach in developing a model of service trade in a factor endowment context. They relied on differing technology endowments among countries to determine if a country would export a "service factor" that combines with other inputs, or a "service product" for final demand. Their approach is not really different from one that determines whether iron ore or finished steel is to be exported. Hirsch (1989) also used a modified factor endowment approach to trade in services. He used a "simultaneity" cost factor to determine whether a service could be traded. Unlike most merchandise, relative costs alone cannot determine whether a service can be traded, because service production and consumption can be viewed as simultaneous actions. (Recall from Chapter 3 the argument that services cannot be stored.) Hirsch's simultaneity cost is a transaction cost not unlike those associated with distance between partners. Just as the case where transportation costs can negate the benefits of trade based on relative factor endowments, simultaneity costs can eliminate the gains from trade in services between otherwise complementary regions.

Many services, especially the low-order personal sort, are not traded. For example, the services of a hair-cutter are unlikely to be directly traded across international boundaries except in most unusual circumstances. However, factor services are traded with high frequency as are many nonfactor business services, such as insurance. The hierarchical trade model, described in Chapter 9, can encompass trade in services as well as goods. The demand for services can be viewed as a function of average income thresholds. In turn, such threshold-defined demand can be considered in two ways, depending upon the way that a service is consumed: directly, or indirectly as an input in another good or service.

Personal services are consumed directly. Again, relying on Engel's law, as average incomes increase in a country it can be assumed that increasing demand thresholds are met for increasing orders of personal services. Low-income countries contain demand thresholds for only low-order services, but higher-income countries provide sufficient demand for high-order services. Recall from central place theory that low-order goods, and by simple extension, low-order services, have low prices. This is why service prices in general are cheaper in poor countries than in rich countries. The "average" service in a poor country is of a lower order than the "average" service in a rich country. In addition, low-order services are more likely to be competitively priced than high-order services because they are offered with greater frequency, and, because of their low thresholds, negligible barriers to entry by providers in poor countries.

Business services are consumed indirectly through their embodiment in goods and some personal services. The demand for business services, therefore, is derived from demand for goods and services directly supplied as functions of income thresholds. For example, a good may not be offered for sale unless the factory can obtain fire insurance and can hire tax accountants to allocate revenues and costs in an advantageous manner. As average incomes increase, more demand thresholds are achieved, and more business services are delivered due to increasing levels of derived demand. Because rich countries, almost by definition, contain more threshold-responding markets than poor ones, they not only produce a wider variety of goods but also a wider variety of services. In a sense, personal services may be in oversupply in poor countries because incomes in those countries do not provide adequate thresholds for a wide complement of business services. As described in Chapter 3, the proportional share of GDP in both services and manufacturing is relatively depressed in the low income group of countries.

Some circumstantial evidence for the hierarchical structure of service trade is provided by an examination of the per capita exports and imports of services by World Bank Income Group (Table 11.5). Nominally, the low income group of countries had a very small service trade deficit in 1990, but proportionally the deficit was the largest of any income group. Low Income countries exported only 54% of the amount of services they imported on a per capita basis. The low middle income group averaged exports at 104% of the per capita value of imports, and the high middle income group averaged 53%. The high income group of countries exported, on average, about 108% of their per capita service imports.

An important progression of per capita service trade, both exports and imports, is illustrated in Table 11.5. The average values of both imports and exports increase with group incomes, and there is a very large difference in average values between the low income group and the low middle income group, and again between the high middle income group and the high income group of countries. This progression of per capita exports as a proportion of per capita imports of services is expected under the

TABLE 11.5 Per Capita Service Exports and Imports by World Bank Income Group, 1990: in $U.S.

Income Group	Means	
	Exports	Imports
All	413.33	417.88
Low	15.04	27.76
Low Middle	134.44	128.92
High Middle	193.97	366.39
High	1532.49	1416.83

Source of original data: International Monetary Fund. 1991. *Balance of Payments Statistics Yearbook 1991* (Washington: International Monetary Fund).

hierarchical trade model, given the bases described above. The low income countries have insufficient average income thresholds to support provision of a wide array of services, and are especially short on business services. Most of the demand for business services must be met by imports in the low income group. Thresholds increase, obviously, with income groups, and so does domestic provision of business services. As domestic provision of services increases, then exports can increase in proportion to imports. At the high income level, trade in services is all but balanced on proportional terms, because these countries each tend to provide almost the full array of existing services. Within the high income group, most services can be expected to trade on the basis of their differentiated qualities.

Trade in services should follow the same principles as hierarchical trade in goods, but there are two important exceptions. The first is that, unlike goods, all services cannot be traded. Almost all personal services, as defined here, are nontradables largely due to the simultaneity factor described by Hirsch (1989). (This accounts for much of the difference between shares of trade in services and shares of services in GDP.) Recall that the service sector, on average, accounts for almost 50% of a country's GDP (Chapter 3). Service trade, on the other hand, is only about one-third the volume of merchandise trade. Most trade in services, therefore, is likely to take place among rich countries, because most trade in nonfactor services is limited to business services. Finally, MNCs trade services on both an intercorporate and intracorporate basis, just as they do with goods. Like their trade in technology (see Chapter 4), service trade within MNCs is limited mostly to the set of rich countries.

Trade in the factor services of capital and labor is the other important exception to the expectation of service trade conforming completely to hierarchical trade theory. Like raw material factors, labor and capital flows can be expected to follow the trade pattern described by factor endowment theory. Labor is relatively inexpensive in Mexico and Egypt relative to capital. Capital is relatively inexpensive in the United States and Kuwait. Mexico trades labor to the United States for capital; Egypt and Saudi Arabia follow the same pattern.

Currently, trade management practices tend to segregate nonfactor and factor services. Factor service trade is heavily regulated through border controls of both labor and capital movements. These controls tend to follow patterns suggested by the Stolper-Samuelson theorem described in Chapter 10, in that poor countries tend to heavily regulate capital flows and rich countries tend to heavily regulate labor flows, primarily through immigration controls. Labor influxes to rich countries can lower wage rates paid to domestic labor. Poor countries typically impose controls on both exports and imports of capital in an attempt to manage domestic capital formation. The export controls, obviously, are attempts to limit investment opportunities to the domestic market while the import controls tend to maintain domestic rates of return. Recently, there has been a general trend toward liberalization of capital flow controls in the poorer countries (Quirk et al., 1989) (see Chapter 8).

As indicated in Chapter 10, trade in services is a focus both of the Uruguay round of the GATT negotiations and the move toward a single European market under the general rubric of EC '92. Currently, the poorer countries are apprehensive of the trade management practices that may emerge from both discussions. It seems, however, that the EC '92 initiatives concern mainly business services, which are unlikely imports from peripheral regions (Nicolaides, 1990). Assessment of third-country impacts of EC '92 initiatives concerning the business services of banking, insurance, and trade in securities has been made only for rich countries (e.g., Eurofi, 1989).

11.5 THE PRODUCT STRUCTURE OF MERCHANDISE TRADE

As we have noted, the volume of merchandise trade is much larger than the volume of trade in services. Most analyses of the product structure of trade have concerned only merchandise, which includes the products of the primary sector. A common misconception of the product structure of trade is that poor countries export primary commodities and import manufactures, and rich-country trade follows the opposite pattern. The flow of manufactures from rich to poor in exchange for raw materials is the "ideal" of the colonial system, but only from the viewpoint of the colonizing power. The American Revolution was in part a reaction to British enforcement of such a trading pattern upon its American colonies. This type of pattern could be defended upon the grounds of comparative advantage, but only in a very static context. The practical purpose of a colonial pattern of trade impressed by the colonizing country is to ensure favorable terms of trade. In this context, dependency theory is accurate because the core economy increases its wealth at the expense of the peripheral colony.

If relative factor prices were forever constant, then a colonial pattern of trade would not have to be impressed upon a colony. Relative factor prices do change, and the actual product structure of trade is not one of rich countries only exporting manufactures and importing primary goods and poor countries only exporting primary products and importing manufactures. In 1990, on average, a country's merchandise exports were about 60% primary goods and 40% manufactured goods, while its merchandise imports were almost 31% primary goods and about 69% manufactured goods (Table 11.6). The import proportions vary across the World Bank income groups, ranging from about 36% primary goods and 64% manufactured goods in the low income group to about 24% primary goods and 76% manufactured goods in the high income group. The most distinctive trade difference associated with income, however, is the systematic increase in manufactured exports as a proportion of merchandise trade with level of per capita national income. The proportion of primary exports decreases consistently from low to high income groups, with a very marked decrease from the high middle to the high income group. Naturally, the reverse is true for proportions of merchandise exports in manufactures. Still, the average proportion of merchandise exports in primary products in high income countries is not negligible, at almost 25%. In turn, while the proportion

**TABLE 11.6 Merchandise Trade Composition
by World Bank Income Group, 1990**

	Mean Values			
	Primary Goods		Manufactured Goods	
Income Group	Percent of Imports	Percent of Exports	Percent of Imports	Percent of Exports
All	30.6	59.8	69.4	40.2
Low	35.6	75.6	64.4	24.4
Low Middle	31.5	71.3	68.5	28.7
High Middle	27.8	54.4	72.2	45.6
High	23.8	25.0	76.2	75.0

Source of original data: World Bank. 1992. *World Development Report 1992* (New York: Oxford University Press).

of merchandise exports in manufactures from the average low income country is small, it is still significant at more than 24%.

Although some rich countries, such as Australia and New Zealand, have significant exports of primary goods, no Core economies had extremely high shares (greater than 90%) of their exports in primary products in 1990 (Figure 11.1). The two dominant clusters of primary-good exporters are in Africa and Latin America. All countries that export a very large proportion of primary products are relatively poor, peripheral countries. Nearly all of the African countries, for example, have most of their merchandise exports in primary products. Conversely, nearly all of the countries with extremely high shares (70% or more) of their merchandise exports in manufactures are rich, Core-economy countries. There was in 1990, however, a distinctive cluster of poorer countries in South Asia that, along with China, had very large proportions of their exports in manufactures (Figure 11.2). This set of poorer countries is largely specialized in textile manufacturing for exports (see Section 11.6). With their exception, the map of exporters of manufactures looks much like a map of the world's Core economies.

Why do rich countries tend to export large shares of manufactures and poor countries tend to export large shares of primary products? In addition to trade based on relative factor endowments and costs, an alternative explanation has been provided by Myint (1971), who suggested that exports of primary products from poorer countries are a *vent for surplus.* Many primary products, such as mineral ores and petroleum, cannot be produced in any real sense. Countries that do not fully utilize such natural resources in their domestic economies can sell them as exports to achieve returns from foreign sources. Arabian oil can be viewed from this perspective. Saudi Arabia has a relatively small population and very small manufacturing base compared to its large stock of petroleum. If the Saudis did not export petroleum, it would go unused. Because Saudi Arabia can export large quantities of oil, it earns income that can be invested in diversifying its domestic economy and purchasing external sources of additional income.

Primary exports can provide a type of development platform for a country's economy, but only under particular circumstances (Auty, 1991). For example, if a country's exports are concentrated in a single primary product, prospects for significant increases in national income from its export are unlikely. Botswana, with diamonds, and Saudi Arabia, with oil, are exceptions. Bananas, sugar, and copper don't work well in this regard. According to the *staple theory of development*, Canada has been able to use primary exports as a development platform, but in a unique way. The Canadian experience was one of substitution over time of one primary product for another as international markets changed. However, Hayter and Barnes (1990) have suggested that ultimately there is a staples trap, and future Canadian growth lies in continuing diversification of its economy.

The experience of most countries with highly concentrated exports of primary products is one of continually declining terms of trade, or, at best, highly volatile export earnings. The volatility in export earnings also is experienced by countries that specialize in any export, primary product or not. Export concentrations, either in terms of products or market geography, tend to induce volatility in aggregate export earnings (Michaely, 1962; Massell, 1964; Batchelor et al., 1980). It seems that export structure, like a financial portfolio, should be diversified in order to limit fluctuations in earnings.

11.6   TRADE IN TEXTILES AND APPAREL AND THE MULTIFIBER ARRANGEMENT

A further disaggregation of the composition of merchandise exports by World Bank income group can shed some additional light on the product structure of international trade. As shown in Table 11.7, primary exports are fuel and other primary products, and manufactures in machinery and transportation equipment and in textiles and apparel are also listed. With reference to primary exports, note that the high middle income countries, a set that includes Saudi Arabia and and several other major oil producers, had higher proportions of fuel exports than exports of all other primary products in 1990. The opposite relative proportions held in the other income groups. Of particular interest here, however, is the allocation of export proportions between the two classes of manufactured goods. Low income countries, on average, exported textiles and clothing at a level about five times their level of exports of machinery and transportation equipment. The low middle income countries, on average, exported products in the two classes in about equal proportions, and the high middle income

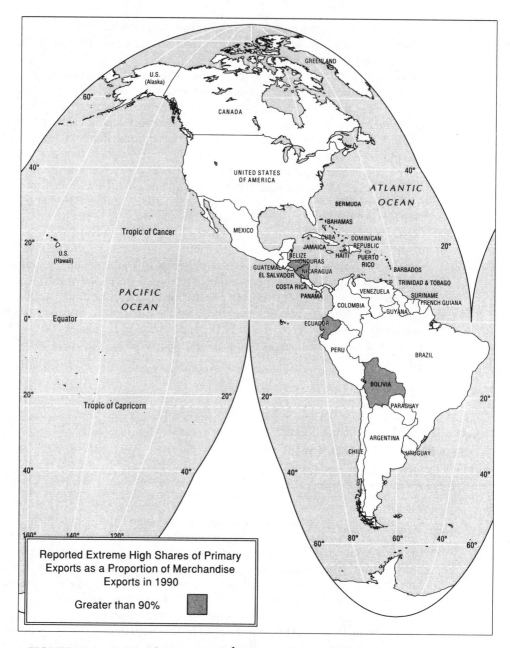

FIGURE 11.1 Reported Extreme High Shares of Primary Exports as a Proportion of Merchandise Exports in 1990

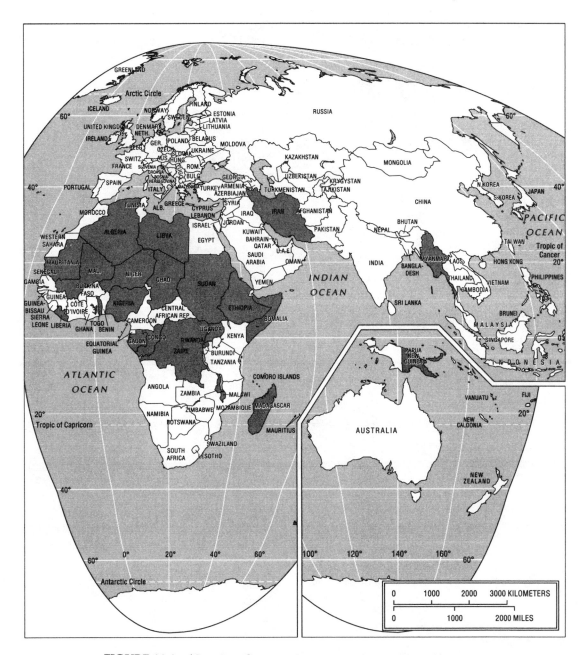

FIGURE 11.1   (Continued)

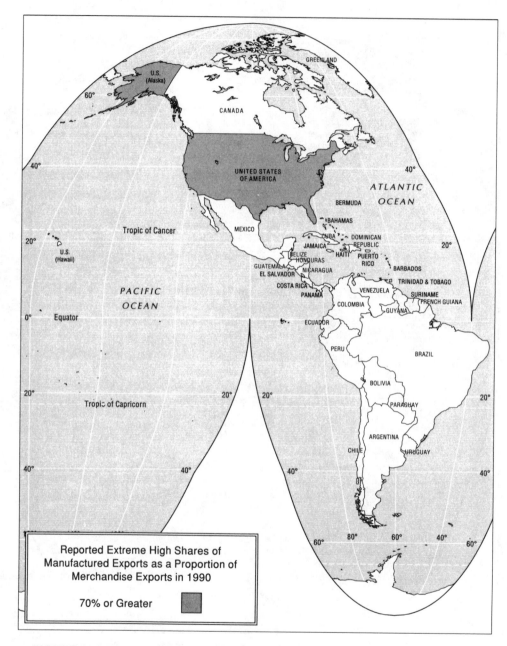

FIGURE 11.2   Reported Extreme High Shares of Manufactured Exports as a Proportion of Merchandise Exports in 1990

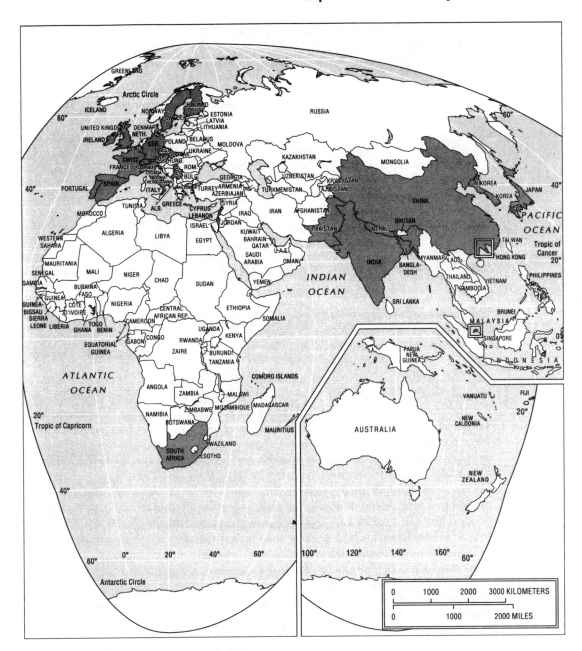

FIGURE 11.2   *(Continued)*

TABLE 11.7 Merchandise Export Composition by World Bank Income Group, 1990

| | Mean Values | | | |
| | Percent of Merchandise Exports in: | | | |
Income Group	Fuel	Other Primary	Machinery and Transportation Equipment	Textiles and Apparel
All	22.8	37.0	12.1	8.1
Low	18.2	57.4	2.0	10.3
Low Middle	28.2	43.1	8.1	8.1
High Middle	38.5	15.9	14.7	6.9
High	10.0	15.0	32.6	5.9

Source of original data: World Bank. 1992. *World Development Report 1992* (New York: Oxford University Press).

group exported machinery and transport equipment in about double its proportion of textile exports. The high income countries, however, had export shares in machinery and transport equipment more than five times their shares of textile and apparel exports.

This product structure of trade can be expected under the hierarchical market model. Textiles and apparel have very low market thresholds and, in fact, are everywhere in sufficient domestic demand for domestic production. Machinery and transport equipment is a very broad product classification, but consists of a fairly large number of high-threshold items. Poor countries export relatively small proportions of machinery because they produce relatively small amounts in their domestic markets, and poor countries export fairly large proportions of textiles and apparel because they produce these goods in large amounts. Rich countries produce large amounts of both classes of goods, but their exports of machinery are in much higher proportion than textiles and apparel for two reasons. First, export proportions of machinery are relatively high because their high demand thresholds limit the number of countries in which they are produced, and, therefore, limits competition in export markets to a few rich producers. Second, proportions of textile and apparel exports are additionally reduced because these goods are produced everywhere. Such low-order goods are the most competitive with respect to the number of supplying countries (see Appendix).

Factor endowment theory, too, can provide some explanation of the product structure of trade in manufactured goods represented in Table 11.7. However, the concept of factor intensity reversal must be drawn upon within the more general theory. Recall that factor intensity reversals can take place when differences in factor proportions are extreme (Chapter 9). Both machinery and textiles and apparel tend to be capital intensive in their production in rich countries; in fact, capital intensity seems to be a characteristic of machinery production worldwide. However, textile and apparel production can be labor intensive as well, and labor-intensive production functions are a characteristic of manufacturing in poor countries, which suffer capital deficits by definition. (The capital deficits, of course, tend to limit a poor country's attainment of domestic demand thresholds. This is one link between factor endowment theory and hierarchical market theory.) Because a factor intensity reversal is possible in the production of textiles and apparel but not in the production of machinery, the pattern of comparative advantage is rich country/machinery and poor country/textiles and apparel.

Both hierarchical market theory and factor endowment theory indicate that poor countries are better exporters of textiles and apparel than of machinery and transportation equipment. However, international trade in textiles and apparel takes place as much by institutional management as by response to fundamental markets. A majority of the world's trade in textiles and apparel is conducted under the Multifiber Arrangement (MFA), which is a type of side agreement to the GATT (World Bank, 1987). A precursor to the MFA, called the Short-Term Cotton Textile Arrangement, was first negotiated in 1961, and a revised Long-Term Arrangement was reached in 1962. The MFA came into being in 1974 as an extension of the Long-Term Arrangement to synthetic fibers. In addition, the MFA was a reaction to declining employment in industrial-country textile and apparel production and the surge of exports from smaller Asian countries. The MFA was established as a mechanism for allocating import quotas from rich to poorer countries and to control import penetration of industrial-country markets.

Under the original MFA, import penetration was guaranteed a minimum annual rate of 6% in exchange for importing-country rights to negotiate bilateral quotas that could be transferred over time and between goods. Rapid declines in the sector's employment in the EC countries between 1973 and 1978 led to a revision of the MFA that placed stricter quotas on imports and entirely shut off growth in import penetration by some goods. The MFA was revised again in 1982 and 1986, with both revisions adding additional restrictions on imports by the industrial countries. The current version of the MFA was set to expire in 1991, but talks have been extended along with the rest of the Uruguay Round of the GATT. Current negotiations seem to be leading to one of two directions. The EC has suggested that all quota restrictions be phased out over a long period. The Americans, on the other hand, have suggested that global quotas be established and bilateral quotas dropped. Global quotas would actually allow textile trade between rich countries to be removed from the usual GATT provisions that currently apply to such trade.

Despite a continuing addition of restrictions since inception of the MFA, some poor countries have been able to increase their levels of textile and apparel exports to the industrial countries. The People's Republic of China, in particular, has experienced rapid growth of this sector domestically and in its exports (Anderson and Park, 1989). One of the reasons for the success of the Chinese has been the bilateral nature of the MFA's quota system. Attempts by most industrial countries to lower Chinese textile and apparel quotas have been blocked by threatened retaliation of a closed Chinese market. Despite the fact that China is a poor country, its population makes it a potentially rich market for lower-order consumer goods produced in the industrial

TABLE 11.8 Full Members of the Organization for Economic Cooperation and Development (OECD) in 1990

*Australia	*Japan
*Austria	*Luxembourg
*Belgium	*Netherlands
*Canada	*New Zealand
*Denmark	*Norway
*Finland	Portugal
*France	*Spain
*Germany	*Sweden
Greece	*Switzerland
*Iceland	Turkey
*Ireland	*United Kingdom
*Italy	*United States

* High Income country by World Bank standards.

countries (Gillespie and Alden, 1989), and even for a wide variety of higher-order producer goods. (The Chinese market has been an object of desire for a long time. The National Association of Manufacturers was formed in the United States, in part, for the purpose of collective action to penetrate the Chinese market. The association was founded more than one hundred years ago.)

The MFA is a method for the industrial countries to overcome their lack of competitive ability in textile and apparel production in international markets (Arpan et al., 1981; Toyne et al., 1984). Typically, the plea for protection of domestic markets is made in the name of maintaining domestic employment levels, but employment characteristics of textiles and those of apparel are quite different. For example, in the United States apparel production employment is about 40% greater than textile production employment. The difference is not due to different levels of output, but to the higher productivity of textile workers. The productivity difference exists because capital-intensive textile production is the norm in industrial countries now, while apparel production is still relatively labor intensive (Hester and Barton, 1987). Import penetration ratios in textile products in the United States are only about one-third of the import penetration ratios in apparel (Hashemzadeh and Kasturi, 1989). Because of the capital intensity of textile production, it can achieve economies of scale in production and tends to be geographically concentrated (Martin and Pelzman, 1983). Consequently, labor is the primary lobbying agent for trade protection in apparel, while capital, via management, is the primary lobbying agent for protection in textile markets.

The geography of rich-country imports of textiles and apparel results from a mix of trade management and trade based on market responses. The countries belonging to the Organization for Economic Cooperation and Development (OECD) are, in general, the Core economies (Table 11.8), and, in 1990, the geographical pattern of their textile and apparel imports was basically split between sources in the Core and sources in the Periphery (Figure 11.3). The large countries of South and East Asia are able to export large amounts of textile and apparel products to the OECD countries, but the smaller countries have been limited in their market penetration by the MFA. In general, the MFA, like any other restriction to trade, has caused a decline in welfare levels of the affected countries. Recently, Trela and Whalley (1990) have estimated that the potential gains from free trade in textiles and apparel are about $23 billion dollars, with net benefits of about $8 billion to the developing countries and the rest to the United States, the EC, and Canada.

11.7   THE GEOGRAPHICAL STRUCTURE OF TRADE

The pattern of international trade in textiles and apparel suggests the ongoing relationship between market and institutional forces in the international economy. In addition, the trade pattern described indicates that the product structure and geographical structure of international trade are bound together in a complex integration. Place and product are interdependent in the international economy. Even much of the relatively low-value trade in textiles and apparel takes place on intra-Core basis, despite the fact that any real comparative advantage in these sectors seems to be in peripheral countries. Higher-value trade—for example, that in electrical machinery and electronics—is even more restricted in its geographical pattern. In 1990, only four countries not considered to have high incomes by the World Bank and not OECD members—the Republic of Korea, Mexico, Malaysia, and China—exported over $2 billion worth of these products to OECD countries in the World Bank's high income group (Figure 11.4). The dominant pattern of this trade is intraindustrial and intra-Core, and is representative of the general flow of trade in manufactured goods.

Recall from the discussion in Chapter 9 that intraindustrial and intra-Core trade are unlikely prospects under any but the loosest constructs of factor endowment theory. However, under trade theory incorporating product differentiation, such as the hierarchical market theory, intraindustry and intra-Core trade are expected. OECD trade further illustrates some of the hierarchical market properties of international production and trade (Table 11.9). On a per capita basis, the average (median) country exported about $47 worth of manufactured goods to high-income OECD countries in 1990. Included in that total were about 30¢ worth of electrical machinery and electronics, 60¢ of transportation equipment, and $8 of textiles and apparel. However, when disaggregated by World Bank income groups, average per capita export totals are consistently below the aggregate average in the two lower-income groups and consistently above the average in the two higher-income groups. The per capita export values, in addition, tend to increase consistently in the total and individual sectors from low to high income groups, as did trade in services in 1990.

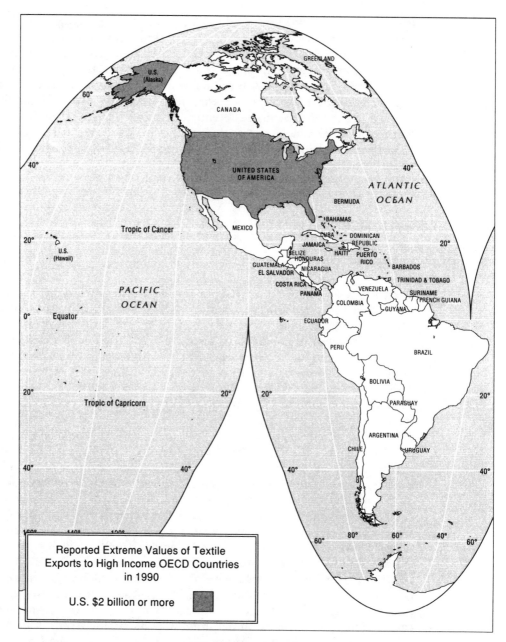

FIGURE 11.3   Reported Extreme Values of Textile Exports to High Income OECD Countries in 1990

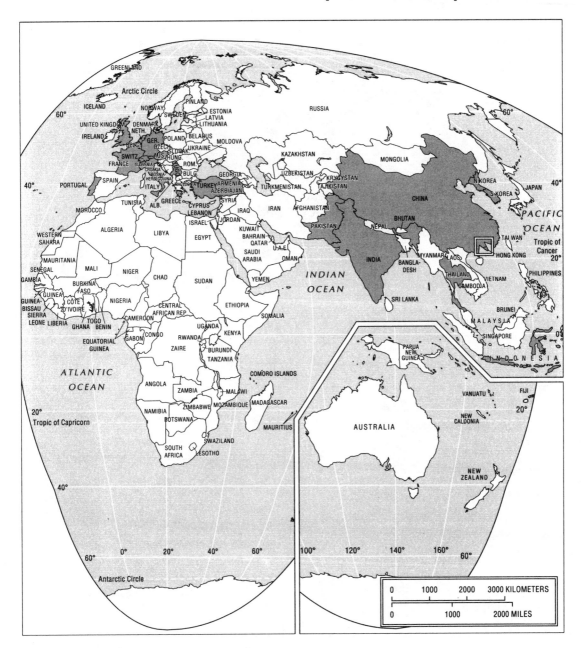

FIGURE 11.3   *(Continued)*

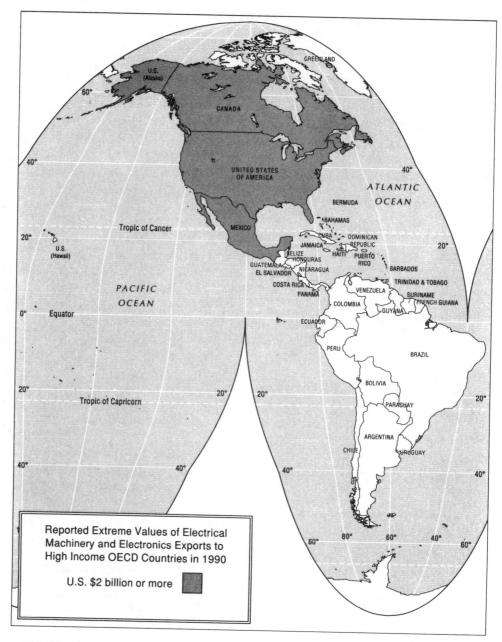

FIGURE 11.4 Reported Extreme Values of Electrical Machinery and Electronics Exports to High Income OECD Countries in 1990

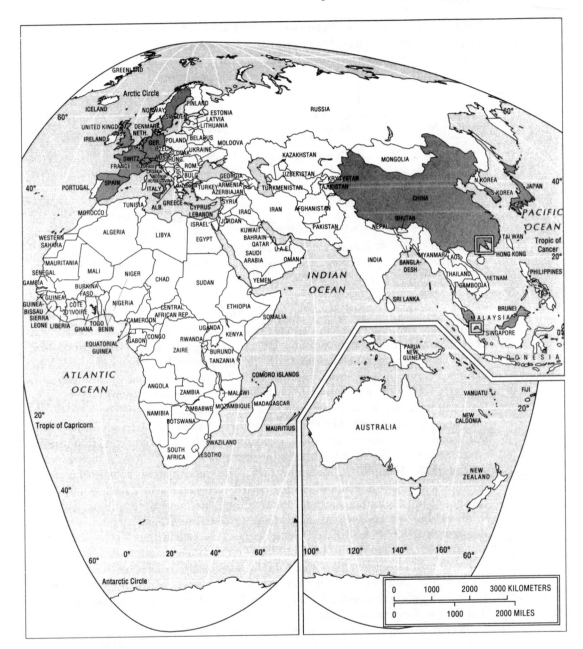

FIGURE 11.4   *(Continued)*

TABLE 11.9 Per Capita Exports of Manufactured Goods to High Income OECD Countries by World Bank Income Group, 1990*

	Median Values			
Income Group	Electrical Machinery and Electronics	Transportation Equipment	Textiles and Apparel	Total to OECD
All	0.29	0.58	8.20	47.38
Low	0.03	0.02	0.24	3.49
Low Middle	0.28	0.50	6.86	41.02
High Middle	4.97	6.81	11.42	126.54
High	243.17	205.86	147.51	2585.15

* In $U.S. Total to OECD contains sectors in addition to those listed.

Source of original data: World Bank. 1992. *World Development Report 1992* (New York: Oxford University Press).

Also as with service trade, there is a significant increase in the export values when moving from the high middle income to high income group. This is exactly as expected under the hierarchical trade model. The progression by income group from low to high is a surrogate measure of the progression in the number of overlapping markets between income group and the rich OECD countries. The greatest degree of overlap is within Core economies and this leads to the greatest intensity of trade.

Even without the MFA, per capita values of textile and apparel trade within the Core should remain high. The market thresholds in these countries are sufficient for particularly fine products that are not likely to be produced in significant quantities in poorer countries. The average price of the finer goods is high, and so is their average value in trade. Most trade contention, such as the current strain between Japan and the United States, and the most comprehensive trade agreements, such as in the EC, concern intra-Core trading patterns because those are the patterns of heaviest trade. In an analysis of the impacts of the EC '92 initiatives on peripheral countries, Koekkok et al. (1990) were hard-pressed to draw any conclusions. The concern of the initiatives is trade internal to the EC. While certain interests of other rich countries such as those in the EFTA, the United States, and Japan have been addressed, those of the Periphery have not. Rich countries trade most heavily with other rich countries, and most lightly with poor countries (Figure 11.5). The gravity model does well in its description of international trade.

Again, as suggested by Lewis in his second point (see Section 11.2), the poorer countries need to be able to increase their exports to the richer countries in order to have a real chance at economic development. Unfortunately, the current pattern of rich-country trade is a fairly persistent one. Peschel (1985), addressing the stability of international trade patterns, has suggested that spatial structures are self-reinforcing. Nodal patterns induce flow characteristics which in turn reinforce the patterns of the nodes. The stability of trade patterns is, in many cases, a result of historical inertia.

Livingstone (1976) found that export market losses to both the United Kingdom and France that resulted from the independence of their former colonies were each around 5%. Essentially, the colonial pattern of trade remained intact in the post-colonial period. Nierop and De Vos (1989) found some changes in trading blocs between1950 and 1980, but mostly due to accretion as trade expanded. For example, Japan and, to a lesser degree, some other East Asian countries became part of a bloc that encompassed both North America and the EC countries. The dominant growth of the trade bloc between 1950 and 1980, however, was a result of the strengthening of ties between the United States and the EC, primarily the United Kingdom and West Germany. Basically, a Core trading bloc was reinforced during the period.

11.8 CHANGING STRUCTURES OF INTERNATIONAL TRADE

The example of Japan and some other East Asian countries becoming integrated within the Core trading bloc indicates that while geographical patterns of trade are persistent they are not permanent. Any pattern of exchange has two fundamental bases that are not exclusive of each other. One is supply and the other is demand; change in these can alter the pattern of exchange. Changes in supply and demand in international markets can arise from several sources, either institutional, market based, or some combination of the two. Again, there are both internal, or place, and external, or flow, characteristics to consider when assessing changes in a system of spatial interaction like international trade (see appendix).

One approach to understanding changing trade structure is to examine it as a response to domestic growth. Krueger (1977) has provided a model of trade and development, in the context of factor endowment theory, which contains an explanation of "export switching" by a country as its income increases. Krueger considered a world that contains two sectors, agriculture and manufacturing, and three factors, land, labor, and capital. Labor is freely mobile between the two sectors, but land is productive only in agriculture and capital is productive only in manufacturing. Productivity, and therefore the wage rate, increases with land-to-labor ratios in agriculture and with capital-to-labor ratios in manufacturing. Initially, a country's production specialization tendency will rise from its relative endowments of capital and land, assuming the supply of labor is everywhere the same.

Krueger focused on a country's transition from complete specialization in agriculture to the point of being a net exporter of manufactured goods. For example, consider a country with no capital stock. It must be completely specialized in agriculture because there can be no production of manufactured goods. It can be expected that such a country will export food and import at least some manufactured goods. In general, any savings in the agricultural economy will translate into capital formation, which allows establishment of a manufacturing sector. In turn, the rising level of capital and establishment of manufacturing lead to increasing wage levels in the

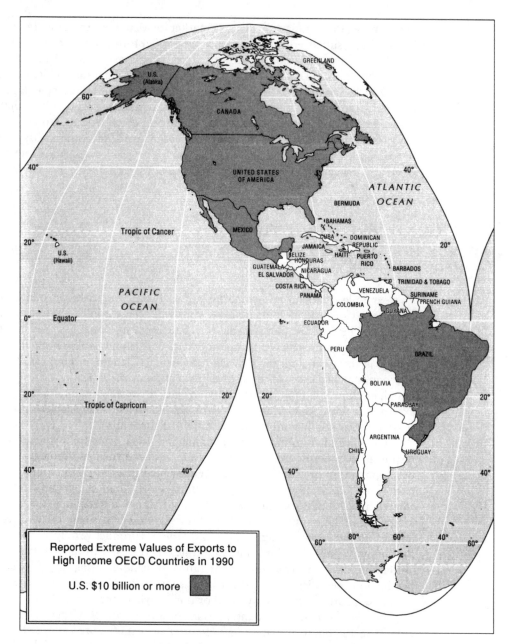

FIGURE 11.5   Reported Extreme Values of Exports to High Income OECD Countries in 1990

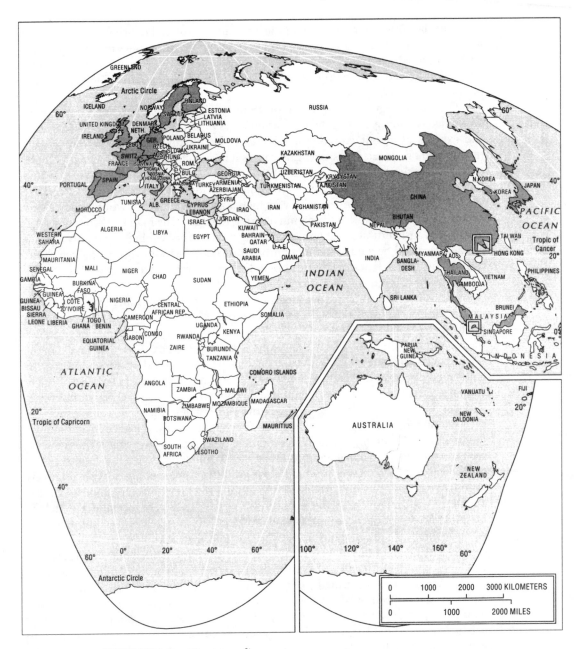

FIGURE 11.5 *(Continued)*

economy, because labor is drawn off the land and into manufacturing. Even if capital formation is relatively slow, labor mobility between sectors implies that manufacturing wages have a tendency to increase as long as agricultural wages are increasing. Krueger described economic development with limited rather than unlimited supplies of labor.

The country undergoes a transition from specialization in agriculture to a more diversified economy. As this diversification takes place, agricultural exports decrease and exports of manufactured goods increase. Eventually, the country can reach a tipping point in its sectoral shares that causes it to switch from being a net agricultural exporter to a net exporter of manufactured goods. Krueger argued that the type and speed of transition from agriculture to manufacturing is a function of initial relative endowment of land. Countries with very high land-to-labor ratios would require very high capital-to-labor ratios for manufacturing to begin. The high land-to-labor ratio means that agricultural productivity and wages would be very high, and only equivalent wages could be paid in manufacturing if capital-to-labor ratios were high there, too. If the initial land-to labor ratio is low, then manufacturing would require relatively low capital-to-labor ratios.

Because of the capital requirements needed to offset the productivity advantages in agriculture resulting from high land-to-labor ratios, efficient agricultural producers are likely to remain relatively specialized in agriculture for a long time. In addition, their manufacturing sectors, once developed, are likely to be capital intensive. On the other hand, countries with relatively inefficient agricultural sectors, due to low land-to-labor ratios, are likely to enter manufacturing more quickly because of lower capital requirements, and their manufacturing is likely to be relatively labor intensive. Krueger points to the examples of Argentina and Japan in the 1920s. Argentina was rich, but underdeveloped in the sense that its economy was specialized in agriculture. Japan was poor, but developed in its economic diversity and growing manufacturing sector. Argentina had a high land-to-labor ratio while Japan had a low land-to-labor ratio. The results of Krueger's model for trade are that countries with relatively productive primary sectors are likely to continue to export primary goods. Primary exporters with relatively inefficient primary sectors are likely to make a switch to manufactured exports more rapidly, and those exports are likely to be labor intensive.

The simultaneous relationship between income growth and export switching also can be considered in the context of the hierarchical trade model, but with respect to changing manufacturing exports rather than a switch from primary to manufactured goods. Average income growth, induced by whatever means, leads to successively higher demand thresholds and a wider variety of goods in production. Lower-order goods are not expected to be abandoned in their domestic production, but their average prices should increase. Lower-order goods also are not withdrawn from export, but their higher average price causes their foreign market to decline. The country becomes more competitive in its export of its higher-order goods because such goods have a lower frequency of production but a higher frequency of markets, in both cases measured by number of countries. The general result is that a country is expected to shift from net exports of lower-order goods and net imports of higher-order goods to net imports of lower-order goods and net exports of higher-order goods as its income increases relative to average world income.

Another line of analysis of trade structure dynamics suggests a type of trickle-down mechanism in international production and trade. Flam and Helpman (1987), for example, described a progression of exporting switches between a rich and a poor region. The model is cast in the theory of vertical, qualitative product differentiation, with the rich region producing and exporting high-price, high-quality goods while the poor region produces and exports low-cost goods of lower quality. Note that this structure of trade is as expected in the hierarchical market model, at least with respect to price. Rates of technological change are more rapid in the poor region than in the rich one. Catching up is easier than advancing the technological frontier because the rich region effectively diffuses its technology to the poor region, while rich-region technology must be self-learned. The transmission of technology allows fast catch-up rates of the quality of poor-region products relative to the products of the rich region. The qualitative characteristics of a single good equalize between the regions, but the poor region becomes the sole producer because it can offer a commonly produced good at a lower price. Rich regions must keep offering new goods as exports to poorer regions, and in turn import today what they exported yesterday.

The Flam and Helpman model is similar to the changing structure of trade under an international product cycle. In addition, it is similar to the export cycle described by Balassa (1983). The Balassa export cycle concerns shifts in comparative advantage during the process of economic development that are virtual corollaries to Rostow's stages of development (Chapter 3). Initially, a country's comparative advantage is in the primary sector. A second stage of exporting is reached as a country's comparative advantage shifts to labor-intensive manufactures, and a third stage follows in which the country's comparative advantage is in capital-intensive goods. The progression from labor-intensive to capital-intensive manufacturing is a point where the export cycle model differs from Krueger's model, which indicates that the export shift is from primary goods to either labor-intensive or capital-intensive manufactures.

Empirical evidence for the export cycle is not hard to find. Georgiou and Thoumi (1989), for example, have shown that Latin American exports to the United States began a transition from primary goods to manufactured goods during the 1980s. A frequently used empirical approach to the export cycle is to measure a country's "revealed" comparative advantage over time. Initially calculated by Balassa (1965), the general formula for *revealed comparative advantage (RCA)* is:

$$RCA_{ij} = \frac{x_{ij} \,|\, X_{it}}{x_{wj} \,|\, X_{wt}} \qquad (11.3)$$

where x_{ij} is the export by country i of product j and X_{it} is its total exports. In the denominator, the w subscript indicates world exports. (The revealed comparative advantage formula is essentially the same thing as the location quotient used to assess relative shares of sectoral employment in regional analysis.) If $RCA > 1$, then a country appears to have a comparative advantage in a product because its export is a greater share of the country's exports than in world exports as a whole. If $RCA < 1$, then the country is exporting a comparatively small share of the product.

Donges and Riedel (1977) have noted that RCA does not really measure comparative advantage at all, because observable patterns of trade are not necessarily the optimum ones that would obtain under a true system based on comparative advantage. In addition, geographical price patterns cannot be observed in RCA, and the geography of trade by price is effected by spatial patterns of comparative advantage. Another problem with the RCA index is that it tends to vary not only with true export switching but also with world price levels. Finally, as argued by Yeats (1985), the RCA index is not really comparable across sectors, but only within a sector over time, and only if world price levels are taken into account.

Despite its recognized problems, the RCA index does provide some interesting descriptive results that tend to support the concept of the export cycle. The changing export structure of Japan when measured by RCA is an example. Balassa and Noland (1989) have found that, from 1967 to 1983, Japan lost its comparative advantage in labor-intensive goods and increased its comparative advantage in human capital-intensive goods and high technology-intensive goods. Lutz (1987) has analyzed RCA values for a large number of countries. He found that RCA shifts occurred as expected, with income growth, within those poorer countries that have experienced high rates of growth in incomes over the last few years.

The export cycle model, like Flam and Helpman's two-region model, frequently is specified as encompassing an interregional substitution of exports. For example, Japan's shift to more capital-intensive export goods meant that the Republic of Korea and Singapore could inherit the export of more labor-intensive goods (Chow, 1990). In this context, the export cycle can be viewed, at least in part, as the outcome of a spatial diffusion process. Rana (1990) has examined the extent of export cycle diffusion from Japanese source to the larger Asian and Pacific region. Thus far, the spatial spread of the export cycle seems to be limited only to the so-called Newly Industrializing Countries (NICs) of the Republic of Korea, Taiwan, Hong Kong, and Singapore, all of which are in fairly close geographic and economic proximity to Japan.

Despite the simple appeal of an export cycle resulting from a spatial diffusion process, domestic economic changes must occur before a country can change its exports. A more likely explanation of regionalized export cycles, particularly as identified by the RCA index, can be based on an increase of demand in one of the region's countries. Demand-induced increases in a country's export of a particular product can boost that country's RCA for the product. Exports from countries neighboring the country of demand should increase at a faster rate than world exports simply due to proximity. A distance-based link between growth at a market and production and export structure of regions supplying that market has been shown by Peet (1969) in his analysis of changing agricultural demand in the United Kingdom and its effect on its colonial empire.

Grotewold (1990) attempted to determine future core-area growth in order to identify future regions of trade expansion. He suggested that Brazil can serve as a regional growth center for much of South America. In addition, he found that the

Republic of Korea may now be a competitive source to Japan for future growth in East Asia. Grotewold also found incipient cores of regional growth in other countries that may never come to fruition because of political limitations. Israel and South Africa, for example, face regional political constraints. In addition, Grotewold suggested that the growth of trade in Eastern Europe was constrained by administered prices. As long as the Soviet Union, in particular, maintained centralized control of its economy, Eastern Europe could not benefit from intraregional integration. External trade links were also limited for countries in Eastern Europe and the Soviet Union because their institutional procedures for international exchange were very different than those of most other countries (Kogut, 1986).

In terms of volume, exports from the Core to the Periphery indicate that Core markets are the Periphery's most important. However, during the 1970s, trade among the poorer countries began to increase at a faster rate than trade between the poor and the rich (Thomas, 1988). Trade in manufactured goods, in particular, increased rapidly at a rate of about 24% a year as compared to an annual increase of 5% in world trade as a whole. The increase in intra-Peripheral trade in manufactured goods has been especially helpful in stabilizing the export revenues of many poorer countries (Reynolds, 1979). In general, markets for manufactured goods are more stable than markets for primary goods.

Amsden (1980) has found that the best Peripheral markets for Peripheral manufacturers are in consumer durables; for example, sewing machines and so-called white goods such as refrigerators. She found that consumer durables are the major share of manufactured goods trade within Latin America, but that producer goods, or capital equipment, were still imported mainly from countries in the Core. This pattern of trade is expected under the hierarchical model. Consumer durables typically have lower domestic market thresholds than most producer goods. Consumer durables are produced in both lower-order countries of the Periphery and higher-order countries of the Core, but market overlaps within the Periphery are more extensive than market overlaps between Core and Periphery. Geographical proximity and cultural ties reinforce the intra-Peripheral market overlaps, but the biggest factor is price. Otherwise equivalent goods are lower priced in Peripheral markets than in Core markets, and most intra-Peripheral trade in manufactured goods is highly price elastic (Thomas, 1988). Because producer goods have high domestic market thresholds, their production is usually confined to the Core, and the pattern of trade remains exports from Core to Periphery.

11.9 TRADE AND ECONOMIC DEVELOPMENT: THE CASE OF THE REPUBLIC OF KOREA

The ability of a country to use trade as an engine of growth seems to depend upon a number of conditions. The country's export structure, both in terms of products and geography, must be favorable, but trade structure is ultimately derived from a combination of external relationships and domestic conditions. The former involves direct interactions with the economy but is based to a large degree upon the latter. Domestic markets and domestic factor supplies play a critical role in a country's ability to compete in international markets, and domestic policy may play just as important a role. Love (1984) has argued that domestic policy changes may be the most important factor in improving a country's competitiveness in international trade. The Republic of Korea provides a good example of a country's use of trade as an engine of growth, and of the interplay between internal and external considerations in trade and economic development.

Korea was annexed by Japan in 1910 and at the end of World War II divided into a northern zone occupied by the Soviet Union and a southern zone occupied by the United States. In 1948, the division of Korea was politically formalized with the establishment of the Republic of Korea in the South and the Democratic People's Republic, under the rule of the Communist Party, in the North. Occupying forces were withdrawn from both countries in 1949, and in 1950 the North Koreans invaded South Korea. The South Koreans were aided by a UN military command and the North Koreans by armed forces of the People's Republic of China. The war ended in a virtual stalemate and hostilities were ceased by an armistice on July 27, 1953. At the time, both governments were virtual dictatorships, with the communist Kim Il Sung in the North and the right-wing Syngman Rhee in the South. Kim is still in control of the North, as of this writing, but Rhee was succeeded by a series of military dictators in the South until 1987, when Roh Tae Woo was elected president of the Republic of Korea in a fairly free and democratic election.

At the end of the Korean War in 1953, the South Korean economy was faced with bleak prospects for economic growth. The Japanese colonial system had used the north for manufacturing because of its relatively large stock of raw materials, and the south for agricultural production. As a result, South Korea, in 1953, had virtually no capital stock to use as a basis for growth, and also was devastated by the war. However, it did have a guaranteed export market in the United States, because the American foreign policy goal of containment of both the Soviet Union and the People's Republic of China required an economically and militarily strong South Korea.

Initially, the South Korean government attempted a policy of import substitution as a means of domestic economic growth (Krueger, 1987). The government relied upon American foreign aid, more than the United States as a foreign market, to finance domestic sectors. In addition, it relied on what amounted to a virtually unlimited supply of labor drawn from agricultural underemployment for use in nascent domestic manufacturing. The policy of general import substitution, however, was ineffective in generating real income growth during the 1950s, and by 1960 South Korean growth policy began to focus on exports and took on an *outward orientation*.

The outward orientation of the Republic of Korea consisted of a mix of five policies with combined domestic and external components. First, the government encouraged the formation of a limited number of large general business enterprises that control, in concert with the government, South Korean production. Called *chaebol,* these enterprises are similar to American conglomerates. Four of these businesses are as large as any operating in the international economy: Samsung, Hyundai, Luck-Goldstar, and Dawoo had international sales of over $10 billion in 1989 (Jackson, 1990). The second related government policy was to maintain relatively low wages for Korean labor, mainly by suppression of labor unions. The emphasis on large enterprise allowed the achievement of economies of scale in production which, in tandem with low wages, allowed Korean products to compete on cost in any international market. Additionally, the government limited the location of production to only the largest centers, primarily Seoul and Pusan, in order to gain additional cost savings through agglomeration economies and to limit public investment requirements for infrastructure (Lee, 1989).

Encouragement of large-scale enterprise, maintenance of cheap labor, and restrictions on location of production are inherently domestic policies that were used to set a foundation for the external ones. The two major policies directly concerned with encouragement of exporting were exchange rate adjustments and the removal of import duties on inputs to be used by exporting sectors (Krueger, 1987; Balassa, 1989). Beginning in 1960, the exchange rate of the Korean won was managed in order to compensate for fluctuations in external markets that could limit growth of export earnings. Removal of import duties on foreign inputs allowed both the necessary flow of inputs required for the export sector and provided an appearance of openness in their own economy that served the South Koreans well in their penetration of foreign markets. The Koreans did maintain selective import substitution policies, however, in sectors such as steel (Fujita and James, 1990) that were critical to shipbuilding and to other important export sectors.

By 1967 the effects of the outward orientation of the Korean economy began to be realized and gains in real per capita income took off. Wage rate limitations were partially relaxed and savings grew, as did rates of domestic capital investment and development of indigenous technologies. In addition to the growth experienced by the national economy, as indicated by increases in aggregate measures, regional growth began as well. In the earlier years of implementation of the export-led growth policy, its impacts were localized and limited to only the country's largest cities. This, of course, was due to the restrictions placed on industrial location by the government. However, as growth took place, locational restrictions were eased and both branch plants and new main plants were established in other parts of the country. In their analysis of the electronics industry in the Republic of Korea, Suarez-Villa and Han (1990) found that significant interregional integration of the industry had occurred by the mid-1980s. While Seoul continued to be the primary center of the industry and the geographical focus of the benefits of the industry's success, major gains in employment and income also were being experienced in most other regions of the country.

Currently, it seems as if the policy of export-led growth in South Korea was successful. Obviously, significant economic growth has been achieved. Importantly, the economic gains have been spread throughout the country as interregional integration of export production has taken place. Even more importantly, the repressive political system has liberalized, with much of the liberalization due to rising standards of living (see Chapter 3). The great success of the Korean export strategy, however, will have to lead to two changes in the future, both related to changes in international markets.

In order to maintain high rates of growth in national income, South Korea will have to export to a wider number of markets and, at the same time, begin to concentrate its efforts on broader development of its domestic economy. Strong reliance on a few rich-country markets, primarily the United States and Japan, for most of its exports cannot be sustained. The American market, in particular, looks tenuous in the face of South Korea's decreasing strategic importance and the likelihood of more management of trade by the American government. Any decline in the loss of the American market, however, can be potentially offset by increasing the number of smaller foreign markets for exports, and by producing more specifically for growing domestic demand.

REFERENCES

Amsden, A. 1980. "The Industry Characteristics of Intra–Third World Trade in Manufactures." *Economic Development and Cultural Change* 29: 1–19.

Anderson, K., and Y. Park. 1989. "China and the International Relocation of World Textile and Clothing Activity." *Weltwirtschaftliches Archiv* 125: 129–148.

Arpan, J., J. de la Torre, and B. Toyne. 1981. "International Developments and the U.S. Apparel Industry." *Journal of International Business Studies* 12/3: 49–64.

Auty, R. 1991. "Third World Response to Global Processes: The Mineral Economies." *The Professional Geographer* 43: 68–76.

Balassa, B. 1964. "The Purchasing Power Parity Doctrine: A Reappraisal." *Journal of Political Economy* 72: 584–596.

———. 1965. "Trade Liberalization and 'Revealed' Comparative Advantage." *Manchester School of Economics and Social Studies* 33: 99–123.

———. 1983. *The Newly Industrializing Countries in the World Economy* (New York: Pergamon).

———. 1989. "Outward Orientation." In *Handbook of Development Economics*, vol. 2, H. Chenery and T. Srinivasan, eds. (Amsterdam: Elsevier).

Balassa, B., and M. Noland. 1989. "'Revealed' Comparative Advantage in Japan and the United States." *Journal of Economic Integration* 4(2): 8–22.

Batchelor, R., R. Major, and A. Morgan. 1980. *Industrialisation and the Basis for Trade* (Cambridge, Massachusetts: Cambridge University Press).

Bhagwati, J. 1958. "Immiserising Growth: A Geometrical Note." *Review of Economic Studies* 25: 201–205.

———. 1984. "Why are Services Cheaper in the Poor Countries?" *Economic Journal* 94: 279–286.

———. 1988. *Protectionism* (Cambridge, Massachusetts: MIT Press).

Bruton, H. 1989. "Import Substitution." in *Handbook of Development Economics,* vol. 2.

Canto, V., J. Dietrich, A. Jain, and V. Mudaliar. 1986. "The Determinants and Consequences of Across-the-Board Trade Restrictions in the U.S. Economy." *The International Trade Journal* 1: 65–87.

Chow, P. 1990. "The Revealed Comparative Advantage of the East Asian NICs." *The International Trade Journal* 5: 235–262.

Donges, J., and J. Riedel. 1977. "The Expansion of Manufactured Exports in Developing Countries: An Empirical Assessment of Supply and Demand Issues." *Weltwirtschaftliches Archiv* 113: 58–85.

Elias, V. 1972. "The Contribution of Foreign Trade to National Income." In *International Economics and Development*, L. di Marco, ed. (New York: Academic Press).

Erickson, R. 1989. "Export Performance and State Industrial Growth." *Economic Geography* 65: 280–292.

Eurofi. 1989. *1992-Planning for Financial Services and the Insurance Sector* (London: Butterworths).

Feldman, D., and I. Gang. 1990. "Financial Development and the Price of Services." *Economic Development and Cultural Change* 38: 341–352.

Flam, H., and E. Helpman. 1987. "Vertical Product Differentiation and North-South Trade." *American Economic Review* 77: 810–822.

Fujita, N., and W. James. 1990. "Export Oriented Growth of Output and Employment in Taiwan and Korea, 1973/74–1983/84." *Weltwirtschaftliches Archiv* 126: 737–753.

Georgiou, G., and F. Thoumi. 1989. "U.S.-Latin America Trade Flows: 1967–1985." *Journal of International Economic Integration* 4/2: 70–84.

Gillespie, K., and D. Alden. 1989. "Consumer Product Export Opportunities to Liberalizing LDCs: A Life-Cycle Approach." *Journal of International Business Studies* 20: 93–112.

Grotewold, A. 1990. "Searching for Core Area Growth." *GeoJournal* 22: 399–407.

Hanink, D. 1989. "Trade Theories, Scale, and Structure." *Economic Geography* 65: 267–270.

Harrod, R. 1973. *Economic Dynamics* (London: Macmillan).

Hashemzadeh, N., and P. Kasturi. 1989. "Employment Effects of International Trade in the United States." *The International Trade Journal* 4: 187–202.

Hayter, R., and T. Barnes. 1990. "Innis' Staple Theory, Exports, and Recession: British Columbia, 1981–86." *Economic Geography* 66: 156–173.

Hester, S., and D. Barton. 1987. "Textile Protectionism in the United States: An Empirical Examination." *The International Trade Journal* 2: 81–95.

Hirsch, S. 1989. "Services and Service Intensity in International Trade." *Weltwirtschaftliches Archiv* 125: 45–60.

Hoare, A. 1985. "Great Britain and her Exports: An Exploratory Regional Analysis." *Tijdschrift voor economische en sociale Geografie* 76: 9–21.

International Monetary Fund. 1991. *Balance of Payments Statistics Yearbook*, vol. 42, part 1 (Washington: International Monetary Fund).

Jackson, T. 1990. "Survey of South Korea." *Economist*, August 18.

Jones, R., and F. Ruane. 1990. "Appraising the Options for International Trade in Services." *Oxford Economic Papers* 42: 672–687.

Koekkoek, A., A. Kuyvenhoven, and W. Molle. 1990. "Europe 1992 and the Developing Countries: An Overview." *Journal of Common Market Studies* 29: 111–131.

Kogut, B. 1986. "On Designing Contracts to Guarantee Enforceability: Theory and Evidence from East-West Trade." *Journal of International Business Studies* 17: 47–61.

Kravis, I., A. Heston, and R. Summers. 1982. *World Product and Income: International Comparisons of Real Gross Product* (Baltimore, Maryland: Johns Hopkins University Press).

Krueger, A. 1977. *Growth, Distortions, and Patterns of Trade among Many Countries* (Princeton, New Jersey: International Finance Section, Department of Economics, Princeton University).

——— . 1987. "The Importance of Economic Policy in Development: Contrasts between Korea and Turkey." In *Protection and Competition in International Trade: Essays in Honor of W. M. Corden*, H. Kierzkowski, ed. (London: Basil Blackwell).

Krugman, P. 1990. *Rethinking International Trade* (Cambridge, Massachusetts: MIT Press).

Lee, H.-Y. 1989. "Growth Determinants in the Core-Periphery of Korea." *International Regional Science Review* 12: 147–163.

Lewis, S. 1989. "Primary Exporting Countries." in *Handbook of Development Economics*, vol. 2.

Lewis, W. A. 1977. *The Evolution of the International Economic Order* (Princeton, New Jersey: Princeton University Press).

Livingstone, I. 1976. "The Impact of Colonialism and Independence on Export Growth in Britain and France." *Oxford Bulletin of Economics and Statistics* 38: 211–218.

Love, J. 1984. "External Market Conditions, Competitiveness, Diversification and LDCs' Exports." *Journal of Development Economics* 16: 279–291.

Lutz, J. 1987. "Shifting Comparative Advantage, the NICs, and the Developing Countries." *The International Trade Journal* 1: 339–358.

Martin, R., and J. Pelzman. 1983. "The Regional Welfare Effects of Tariff Reductions on Textile Products." *Journal of Regional Science* 23: 323–336.

Massell, B. 1964. "Export Concentration and Fluctuations in Export Earnings: A Cross-Section Analysis." *American Economic Review* 54: 47–63.

Michaely, M. 1962. *Concentration in International Trade* (Amsterdam: North-Holland).

Myint, H. 1971. *Economic Theory and the Underdeveloped Countries* (London: Oxford University Press).

Nicolaides, P. 1990. "Responding to European Integration: Developing Countries and Services." *Journal of Common Market Studies* 20: 201–215.

Nierop, T., and S. De Vos. 1989. "Of Shrinking Empires and Changing Roles: World Trade Patterns in the Postwar Period." *Tijdschrift voor economische en sociale Geografie* 79: 343–364.

Panagariya, A. 1988. "A Theoretical Explanation of Some Stylized Facts of Economic Growth." *Quarterly Journal of Economics* 103: 509–526.

Papageorgiou, D., M. Michaely, and A. Choski. 1990. *Liberalizing Foreign Trade* (Cambridge, Massachusetts: Basil Blackwell).

Peschel, K. 1985. "Spatial Structures in International Trade: An Analysis of Long-Term Developments." *Papers of the Regional Science Association* 58: 97–111.

Peet, R. 1969. "The Spatial Expansion of Commercial Agriculture in the Nineteenth Century." *Economic Geography* 45: 283–301.

Quirk, P., M. Gilman, K. Huh, P. Leeahtam, and J. Landell-Mills. 1989. *Developments in International Exchange and Trade Systems* (Washington: International Monetary Fund).

Ram, R. 1985. "Exports and Economic Growth: Some Additional Evidence." *Economic Development and Cultural Change* 37: 415–425.

Rana, P. 1990. "Shifting Comparative Advantage among Asian and Pacific Countries." *The International Trade Journal* 4: 243–258.

Reynolds, S. 1979. "Fluctuations in Export Earnings and Economic Patterns of Asian Countries: A Comment on the Role of Intraregional Trade." *Economic Development and Cultural Change* 27: 785–790.

Rothschild, K. 1985. "Exports, Growth, and Catching-Up: Some Remarks and Crude Calculations." *Weltwirtschaftliches Archiv* 121: 304–314.

Samuelson, P. 1964. "Theoretical Notes on Trade Problems." *Review of Economics and Statistics* 46: 145–154.

Sato, K. 1977. "The Demand Function for Industrial Exports: A Cross-Country Analysis." *Review of Economics and Statistics* 59: 456–464.

Suarez-Villa, L., and P.-H. Han. 1990. "The Rise of Korea's Electronics Industry: Technological Change, Growth, and Territorial Distribution." *Economic Geography* 66: 273–292.

Svedberg, P. 1991. "The Export Performance of Sub-Saharan Africa." *Economic Development and Cultural Change* 39: 549–566.

Thirlwall, A. 1977. *Growth and Development*. 2d ed. (New York: John Wiley & Sons).

Thomas, H. 1988. *A Study of Trade among Developing Countries, 1950–1980: An Appraisal of the Emerging Pattern* (Amsterdam: North-Holland).

Toyne, B., J. Arpan, A. Barnett, D. Ricks, and T. Shimp. 1984. "The International Competitiveness of the U.S. Textile Mill Products Industry: Corporate Strategies for the Future." *Journal of International Business Studies* 12/3: 145–165.

Trela, I., and J. Whalley. 1990. "Global Effects of Developed Country Trade Restrictions on Textiles and Apparel." *The Economic Journal* 100: 1190–1205.

World Bank. 1987. *World Development Report 1987* (New York: Oxford University Press).

———. 1989. *World Development Report 1989* (New York: Oxford University Press).

———. 1990. *World Development Report 1990* (New York: Oxford University Press).

———. 1992. *World Development Report 1992* (New York: Oxford University Press).

Yeats, A. 1985. "On the Appropriate Interpretation of the Revealed Comparative Advantage Index: Implications of a Methodology Based on Industry Sector Analysis." *Weltwirtschaftliches Archiv* 121: 61–73.

EPILOGUE

· · ·

Interdependence and Integration
in the International Economy

· · ·

E.1 INTRODUCTION

As described in Chapter 1, economic geography's special perspective focuses on *spatial interaction* in an economy. Systems of spatial interaction have two primary components: places, and the flows that link them. The first part of the book described pertinent characteristics of countries as places in the international economy, and the second and third parts described two general forms of flows: flows of finance in international investment and lending, and flows of goods and services in international trade. One point emphasized in this treatment is that the process of spatial interaction is an integrating one, so spatial interaction across the world's economies is fundamental to international economic development.

This Epilogue contains summary examinations of three major events in the recent and ongoing integration of the international economy viewed from the perspective of spatial interaction. The three events are (1) the end of the convertibility of the American dollar into gold, (2) the OPEC oil embargo, and (3) the environmental summit meeting held in Rio de Janeiro. Each of these events took place because of the increasing interaction among the world's economies, and each has signalled important changes in that interaction as well. The first event signalled the end of American hegemony, or full authority, in the world's economy and was the result of the relative growth of Western Europe and Japan in the world's other rich economies. The second event signalled the real and potential impacts that decisions made in the Periphery could have on the rich economies; a sign of dependency turning to interdependency. The third event signalled growing recognition of the true interdependence of the pursuit of economic growth by rich and poor countries because of the international environmental implications of that growth.

E.2   THE END OF BRETTON WOODS AND THE FALL AND RISE OF THE U.S. DOLLAR

On August 15, 1971, U.S. president Richard Nixon announced the end of the convertibility of the American dollar into gold. Nixon's action destabilized an international currency system that had been established in late 1944 at a conference held in Bretton Woods, New Hampshire. The Bretton Woods conference had as its intention the establishment of a workable and consistent framework for postwar economic recovery and international economic relations (Foreman-Peck, 1983). As part of the effort to establish a consistent framework for economic interaction, a system of fixed international valuation of currencies was developed under the auspices of the International Monetary Fund (IMF), which was formed at the conference. Members of the newly formed IMF were required to peg, or guarantee, their currency's value in terms of gold or a certain amount of U.S. dollars. The U.S. dollar was pegged at $35.00 per ounce of gold. Currency values were not perfectly rigid, but allowed a 1% valuation band either above or below their "fixed" values. Technically, a claimant at the U.S. Treasury could expect to be required to tender between $34.65 and $35.35 for an ounce of gold. The small valuation band, however, effectively defined a system of fixed exchange rates among IMF members. For practical purposes, the Bretton Woods system made the U.S. dollar as good as, if not better, than gold. The U.S. dollar became an official international reserve asset which, like gold, could be drawn on for international transactions and, unlike gold, also had a rapidly increasing source of supply that could be relied on to finance the recovery of many of the national economies devastated during World War II. Because of the relative size of its domestic economy, and the fact that its physical capital and civilian population had survived the war intact, the United States was recognized by the Bretton Woods conference as the "engine of growth" in the postwar world economy.

In the long run, the Bretton Woods currency system was doomed by the success of the conference's overall mission of postwar economic recovery and growth. As the West European and Japanese economies became strong, the comparative size of the American economy diminished. The strength of the dollar, based on American hegemony in the international economy, declined to the point where it could no longer be supported by fiat at the Bretton Woods level. In 1950, the United States held slightly more than half of the world's total reserves. By 1960 the U.S. share of world reserves was 32%, and by 1970 the U.S. share was about 15% (*International Financial Statistics Yearbook*, 1988). The decrease in the position of the U.S. reserve holdings between 1950 and 1970 was symptomatic of and made possible the relative economic growth outside the United States during the period. In addition, it shows the rapid increase in holdings of the U.S. dollar, the primary reserve asset during the period, outside the United States. When the supply of a good is greater than demand, the price of the good can be expected to decrease, and the supply of dollars was outpacing demand. The demand for dollars declined sharply in 1970 when the U.S.

economy was in recession while the Japanese and West European economies remained robust. American interest rates decreased while foreign rates remained high, and offshore banks and other firms rapidly exchanged their dollars for other currencies in order to take advantage of greater rates of return in non-U.S. financial markets. The resulting accumulation of dollars in foreign central banks, particularly in the Federal Republic of Germany, forced the U.S. government to admit that it could no longer back the dollar in gold, at least at $35.00 per ounce.

The United States effectively killed the Bretton Woods currency system by reneging on its earlier peg of the dollar. Obviously, if the United States could no longer support claims against the system's key currency, the system could no longer exist. Initially, an attempt was made to revive the system in December of 1971 when the dollar was devalued about 8.6% and pegged at $38.00 per ounce of gold within a 2.25% (plus or minus) valuation band. However, the United States has never resumed exchanging gold for dollars, so since August 15, 1971, the value of its dollar has been determined almost completely by the appraisal of the international currency market. The value of the dollar has fluctuated widely since 1972, but one particularly interesting change in its value took place from 1980 through 1987. During that period, its lowest level on a trade-weighted basis occurred in 1980 and its highest level in 1985. By 1987, its value had dropped back below its pre-float level of early 1973.

The most apparent effect of the dollar's rapid appreciation in value during most of the 1980–1987 period was the rapid decline of the U.S. merchandise trade balance. From 1980 through 1987, the United States accumulated a merchandise trade deficit of over 800 billion dollars. Several reasons for this continuing trade deficit have been offered, including a general decline in the relative quality of American goods (Krugman and Hatsopoulos, 1987) and cyclical demand for American goods in foreign markets (Laffer, 1986; Williamson and Miller, 1987), but there is no doubt that the dollar's high value in international currency markets was a primary factor in the rapid decline of America's trade position (Feldstein, 1985). The price effects of changing currency values are inarguable on a fundamental basis. As the dollar increases in value, foreign goods become cheaper in the American market and American goods become more expensive in foreign markets. As the dollar decreases in value this price geography reverses. During the 1980–1987 period the rise and fall of the U.S. dollar had a markedly greater effect on American imports than on American exports (Table E.1). Exports did decline early in the period as the value of the dollar rose, but then remained relatively stable until 1987 when the value of the dollar dropped significantly. Imports, however, with the exception of a decrease in 1982, continued on a strong upward trajectory throughout the period, including 1987. The American merchandise trade balance during the period, therefore, was largely a function of U.S. consumption of relatively cheap foreign goods at consistently increasing levels, and not a function of declining exports to foreign markets faced with high-priced American goods.

Despite the abandonment of the Bretton Woods currency system, the dollar maintains itself as the primary currency in the international economy. The persistence of the dollar's relative importance can be attributed to several reasons, including an international pricing system under which most raw materials, including petroleum,

TABLE E.1   U.S. Dollar Exchange Rate Index, Export Index, and Import Index, 1979–1987*

Year	U.S.† Exchange Index	Export Index	Import Index
1979	100.0	100.0	100.0
1980	99.2	121.3	115.6
1981	116.8	128.4	122.9
1982	132.4	116.6	114.6
1983	142.2	110.2	121.4
1984	157.0	119.7	153.4
1985	162.5	117.1	162.6
1986	127.4	119.4	174.1
1987	110.0	137.6	190.7

* 1979 = 100.0.

† The first column is the U.S. dollar exchange rate index.

Source: Calculated from data in *International Financial Statistics Yearbook.* 1988. (New York: International Monetary Fund); and *Direction of Trade Statistics Yearbook.* 1988. (New York: International Monetary Fund).

have prices denominated in U.S. dollars, the large amount of international lending denominated in U.S. dollars, and the sheer size of the American market. Because of the U.S. dollar's continued strong role in the international economy, its fluctuation can be expected to have a strong impact on most of the world's national economies in a variety of ways, but particularly and most directly in their trade. Focusing on exports alone, as the dollar increases in value against the currency of another country, that country can be expected to increase its exports to the United States. The dollar's trade effect, however, extends beyond the bilateral relationship into third markets. Increasing dollar values make American goods less competitive in third markets, allowing foreign producers selling goods priced in cheaper currencies to increase their share of third markets at the expense of American producers. In turn, as the U.S. dollar decreases in exchange value, foreign producers' exports should decrease, not only to the United States but also to the third markets. Obviously, the exchange rate/export relationship described is a generalization, but it holds up well over a variety of individual countries.

The rise and fall of the American dollar from 1980 through 1987 can be readily interpreted from the perspective of dynamic spatial interaction. Domestic tax cuts enacted in the United States in the beginning of the Reagan administration (1981–1989) spurred rapid growth in the American economy. This growth was accompanied by high real interest rates, which were linked to the growing fiscal deficit that resulted from the tax cuts. Both the rate of growth in the United States and its high interest rates were conditions that made it an attractive destination for flows of international investment. At the time, Western European economies were in recession, and Japan's economy was experiencing low growth rates because of the recent increase in oil prices (see below), so the United States was experiencing the only strong growth among the larger national economies. Because investment in the United States is denominated in U.S. dollars, the value of the American dollar increased in currency exchange markets. In turn, the high value of the dollar encouraged rapid increases in U.S. imports, which encouraged growth in foreign countries, and helped diminish U.S. exports and other domestic production, diminishing U.S. domestic growth. While the value of the dollar began to decrease in the mid-1980s for a number of reasons, some of the decrease can be attributed to the flows of trade that altered the international economic conditions which caused the dollar to increase in value in the early part of that decade. The economic condition that initiated a flow was, in turn, altered by the flow.

E.3 THE OPEC EMBARGO
AND THE OIL PRICE SHOCKS

In November of 1973, following an Arabian embargo of oil to the Netherlands and the United States, OPEC began a seven-year series of oil price increases that led to at least two global economic recessions. Perhaps the most visible international economic events of the postwar years have been the two so-called oil shocks of 1973 and 1979. Before 1970, cheap oil was taken for granted and oil production around the world was controlled largely by a small number of multinational corporations headquartered in the industrialized countries. The first oil shock can be viewed as an extension of the Arab oil embargo related to the Arab-Israeli war of 1973, but that event was more symbolic than effective. Actually, the first oil shock came as a result of growing conflict over oil revenues between multinational oil corporations and the sovereign states, mainly in the Middle East, where oil was produced. President Qadaffi of Libya was able to force Occidental Petroleum to accept a price increase in 1970. Libyan actions impressed the Organization of Petroleum Exporting Countries (OPEC)—Libya was not a member at the time—and their prices began increasing late that year (Hogendorn and Brown, 1979). Initially, price increases were negotiated between the oil-producing countries and the oil corporations, but in 1973 OPEC began a series of unilateral price increases that resulted in the 1973 shock. The price of Saudi Arabian oil was $1.800 per barrel in 1970, $2.285 in 1971, and $2.479 in 1972; oil prices increased slowly under negotiation. However, the unilateral price increases were rapid, with Arabian oil priced at $5.036 per barrel in 1973 and $11.251 in 1974, a doubling of a doubling in a two-year period.

At the international scale, the impacts of the first oil shock were widespread and devastating to the non-oil exporters. Inflation increased drastically in industrialized and other countries, and there was a worldwide recession in 1975. The combination of high oil prices and recession, however, was enough to halt significant oil price increases by bringing about both increasing rates of production by non-OPEC countries such as Canada, the United Kingdom, and Mexico, and decreasing rates of demand in consuming countries. In the interest of increasing oil revenues, OPEC planned a series of gradual price increases to begin in 1978 and continue through 1979. The revolution in Iran, a major oil producer, in 1978 precipitated instead rapid oil price increases over the next two years. In 1978, Arabian oil had a posted price of $12.704 per barrel, in 1979 it was $24.000, and in 1980 the price rose to $32.000 a barrel. Prices increased in 1981 to $34.000 a barrel and held there through 1983. They began to decline in 1984, and by 1987 a barrel of Saudi Arabian oil had a posted price of $17.520 (*Twentieth Century Petroleum Statistics*, 1989). The international impacts of the second oil shock were the same as those of the first, inflation and recession, for most nonexporting countries, but these problems generally were less severe and of a shorter duration the second time around.

The second oil shock concerned a system of flows in the international economy involving both trade and finance. These flows altered the geography of oil production in such a way that the flows were effectively self-braking. This process can be illustrated at an international scale of analysis. However, effects of interactions in the international economy are not always realized uniformly across national economies, and this was true of the second oil shock's impact on the United States. The international oil price increases of the 1970s were reflected by increasing prices, despite controls, of American oil. American states with economies dominated by manufacturing realized declines in employment and slowed growth in personal incomes due to international and American oil price increases. States with significant oil and other fuel resources, on the other hand, experienced economic boom.

Four states where oil production plays a major economic role, Alaska, Louisiana, Oklahoma, and Texas, were particularly affected by the changing oil prices of the 1979–1987 period. Average American oil prices peaked in 1981, the first full year of decontrolled prices, and reached their low point in 1986. Real personal earnings from fuel production in Louisiana and Texas had their high and low points in those respective years. Alaskan personal earnings from fuel production also reached their highest level in 1981, but were approximately the same in 1986 (Bureau of Economic Analysis, 1989). Alaska was the only one of the four states to have greater oil production in 1986 than in 1981, so lower unit prices were offset by greater production volumes (*Twentieth Century Petroleum Statistics*, 1989). Production quantities also played a role in Oklahoma, where real personal earnings from fuel production peaked in 1984, the same year as that state's peak oil production during the period.

The oil industry is linked strongly to all other sectors of the economies of the four states. The rise and decline of petroleum prices during the period, because of the linkages, had a critical affect on per capita income levels in the four states during the period (Table E.2). With the exception of Alaska—a special case because of its small population and distance from the bulk of the American economy—per capita incomes in these states historically have lagged behind the American average. The lag was induced by their relative lack of capital-intensive manufacturing, the sector that

TABLE E.2   Average American Oil Price per Barrel, and State Per Capita Income as Percent of U.S. Per Capita Income: Alaska, Louisiana, Oklahoma, and Texas, 1979–1987

Year	Average Oil Price	State Per Capita Income as Percent of U.S. Per Capita Income			
		Alaska	Louisiana	Oklahoma	Texas
1979	$12.64	139	85	93	98
1980	21.59	139	88	95	99
1981	31.77	141	90	98	102
1982	28.52	151	89	99	102
1983	26.19	150	86	92	99
1984	25.88	138	83	89	97
1985	24.09	135	81	88	97
1986	12.51	127	77	84	93
1987	15.41	119	74	81	90

Source: *Twentieth Century Petroleum Statistics*. 1988 (Dallas, Texas: DeGloyer and MacNaughton); and Bureau of Economic Analysis, Department of Commerce, 1989. *State Personal Income: 1929–87* (Washington: U.S. Government Printing Office).

typically provides highest average incomes. However, from 1979 through 1982, per capita incomes in these states grew quickly, and in the case of Texas, surpassed the value for the United States as a whole. The decline of oil prices led to relative declines of per capita income in all four states after 1982, and by 1987 each of the states was at a relative level well below that of 1979.

E.4   THE UN CONFERENCE ON ENVIRONMENT AND DEVELOPMENT

The implications of the decisions made on oil prices in the Middle East for household incomes in Oklahoma illustrate the degree of integration that exists in the contemporary international economy. The integration described in that case results from the spatial interaction encompassed in contemporary international markets. The growing international integration of markets was extended to the international integration of broad environmental interests by the UN Conference on Environment and Development held in Rio de Janeiro June 3–14, 1992.

Popularly referred to as the *environmental summit*, the conference was not the first of its kind, but it was the first to encompass such a wide array of environmental interests at the global scale and to have virtually complete global participation.

Among the issues considered at the conference were the maintenance of biodiversity, the reduction of carbon dioxide emissions and emissions of other greenhouse gases, and principles of forest conservation. The *Rio Declaration* and *Agenda 21* were issued at the conference's end. The former contains the agreed-upon principles of equitable attainment of developmental and environmental needs in the international economy, and the latter contains detailed prescriptions for putting the principles into practice.

As recognized at the conference, international cooperation in efforts at environmental preservation and integration of policies toward the environment must take into consideration both the similarities and the differences in the environmental problems faced by countries of different income levels. Certain problems are shared by all countries. Among the list of pressing international environmental concerns considered by the U.S. Congress, for example, not one can be considered only a "national" problem (Table E.3). Some of the problems are inherently multilateral in character. Global climate change and stratospheric ozone depletion, for example, have uneven sources and incidences of ill effects, but no place on the globe is isolated on both counts. Another issue requiring multilateral treatment is preservation of the environment in Antarctica, a continent currently administered by a number of countries. Some of the problems, such as transboundary water pollution and marine

TABLE E.3 Selected Issues of International Economic Growth and Effects on Environmental Quality

1. Global climate change
2. Stratospheric ozone depletion
3. Biological diversity maintenance
4. Tropical deforestation/global forest protection
5. Preservation of the Antarctic environment
6. Marine pollution
7. Transboundary water pollution
8. Transboundary air pollution
9. International waste shipment
10. Trade and the environment

Source: Congressional Research Service. 1991. *Selected Major International Environmental Issues: A Briefing Book.* Report prepared for the Committee on Foreign Affairs, U.S. House of Representatives (Washington: U.S. Government Printing Office).

pollution such as oil spills, are more localized. Even these problems however, require at least bilateral coordination in their solution.

The differences among countries in their environmental problems are frequently functions of the differences in their incomes. A study by the World Bank (1992) found systematic relationships between wealth and certain environmental problems. The world's low-income economies tend to have low levels of sanitation and high levels of aeresol particles; the world's middle-income countries have high concentrations of sulfur dioxide in their air and problems of rapid deforestation; and the world's high-income countries have high levels of industrial and household waste and their air has high proportions of carbon dioxide. A useful generalization may be that environmental problems with sources in the Core are those associated with the wastefulness of affluence, while those with distinctive sources in the Periphery result from the problems of poverty (Barbier, 1989; Kirdar, 1992).

Even environmental problems with fairly localized sources frequently have international effects. Tropical deforestation takes place, by definition, in limited parts of the world but has global implications with respect to related atmospheric changes. The surplus of industrial waste generated in rich countries is often shipped to poorer countries, not only on barges but also borne by ocean currents. The environmental summit at Rio took place in one respect as a response to an increasing level of international economic integration that has generated such extensive economic activity that the global environment has been put at risk (Stern et al., 1992). In another respect, that same meeting may be the impetus to an increased level of spatial interaction in the international economy that can lead toward global-scale integration of economic growth and environmental sustenance.

REFERENCES

Barbier, E. 1989. *Economics, Natural-Resource Scarcity and Development: Conventional and Alternative Views* (London: Earthscan Publications).

Bureau of Economic Analysis. 1989. *State Personal Income: 1929–87* (Washington: U.S. Government Printing Office).

Congressional Research Service. 1991. *Selected Major International Environmental Issues: A Briefing Book.* Report prepared for the Committee on Foreign Affairs, U.S. House of Representatives (Washington: U.S. Government Printing Office).

Direction of Trade Statistics Yearbook (New York: International Monetary Fund, 1988).

Feldstein, M. 1985. "The View from North America." Chapter 2 in *Global Economic Imbalances,* C.F. Bergsten, ed. (Washington: Institute for International Economics).

Foreman-Peck, J. 1983. *A History of the World Economy: International Economic Relations Since 1850* (Totawa, New Jersey: Barnes & Noble).

Hogendorn, J., and W. Brown. 1979. *The New International Economics* (Reading, Massachusetts: Addison-Wesley).

*International Financial Statistics Yearbook.*1988. (New York: International Monetary Fund).

Kirdar, U. 1992. "Issues and Questions." Chapter 1 in *Change: Threat or Opportunity*, U. Kirdar, ed. (New York: United Nations Publications).

Krugman, P., and G. Hatsopoulos. 1987. "The Problem of U.S. Competitiveness in Manufacturing." *New England Economic Review* January/February:18–29.

Laffer, A. 1986. "Minding our Ps and Qs: Exchange Rates and Foreign Trade." *The International Trade Journal* 1:1–26.

Stern, P., O. Young, and D. Druckman. eds. 1992. *Global Environmental Change: Understanding the Human Dimensions* (Washington: National Academy Press).

Twentieth Century Petroleum Statistics. 1988. (Dallas, Texas: DeGloyer and MacNaughton).

Williamson, J., and M. Miller. 1987. *Targets and Indicators: A Blueprint for the International Coordination of Economic Policy* (Washington: Institute for International Economics).

World Bank. 1992. *World Development Report 1992* (New York: Oxford University Press).

Appendix

. . .

Trade and Finance
over Spatial Structure

. . .

A good part of this book has emphasized the disparities between rich and poor countries and, regardless of the elegance of neoclassical models, the persistence of these disparities over time. This appendix portrays some of the fundamental problems of equalization over space by considering flows directly in the context of spatial structure.

A.1 THE INHERENT IMBALANCE
OF SPATIAL FLOWS

The inherent imbalance in spatial exchange systems is illustrated here by three different examples. The first example is a spatial flow system in which the probability of exchange is determined solely as a function of distance decay. The second example uses a measure of fixed geographic potential to calculate exchange probabilities. The third example relies on a variable measure of geographic potentials in determining variable flow probabilities across countries. The same set of "countries" is used in all three examples. It consists of a series of five countries placed at equal unit distance intervals along a line, i.e., A_____B_____C_____D_____E. Each of the five countries is assumed to generate flows both to itself and to the other four countries in the set. Finally, the flows in all three cases refer to flows of funds.

361

In the first case, a simple distance decay function is used to define a matrix of exchange probabilities between the countries:

$$P(E_{ij}) = \frac{d_{ij}}{\sum\limits_{j=1}^{5} d_{ij}} \tag{A.1}$$

where $P(E_{ij})$ is the probability of an outward flow from the ith to the jth country, and d_{ij} is the measure of intervening distance. Note that the "outward" flows include the flow within each country when $i = j$. The exchange probabilities among the five countries calculated from Equation A.1 are listed in Table A.1A as a 5×5 matrix.

Note that the elements on the principal diagonal of the exchange probability matrix have the highest values in both their rows and columns. This is an expected result when distance decay is the sole determinant of spatial interaction because each country is closer to itself than to any other country. In addition, note that the sum of each row is 1. This latter property of the the exchange matrix allows the flow of funds among the countries to be characterized as a Markov process, which is a difference equation that takes the form (Schneider, Steeg, and Young, 1982, p. 63):

$$\mathbf{f}^{t+1} = \mathbf{f}^t \mathbf{P} \tag{A.2}$$

where $\mathbf{f}^{t+1}$ is a $1 \times n$ vector of distributions at time $t + 1$; $\mathbf{f}^t$ is a $1 \times n$ vector of the original proportional distributions, that is, $\Sigma f = 1$; and $\mathbf{P}$ is an $n \times n$ matrix of row-wise exhaustive transition probabilities, that is, $\sum\limits_{j=1}^{n} P_{ij} = 1$. (See Lee, Judge, and Zellman, 1977, for a thorough review of the applications of Markov models in econometric analyses.)

In this example, the initial distribution indicates that each country, at the initial time period, contains one-fifth of the total funds over the five countries (Table A.1B). After one round of exchange, the least central countries, A and E, have diminished proportions of funds, while the more central countries, B, C, and D, have net increases in their proportions. Similar proportional changes continue over the next two rounds, with gains in the center taking place at the expense of losses in the periphery. The third round results given in Table A.1B are equilibrium distributions that will not change in future time periods. This equilibrium actually is the convergence in the product vector, $\mathbf{f}^{t+1}$, which derives from the use of proportions in the exchange matrix $\mathbf{P}$. The values in $\mathbf{P}$ reveal the source of the unequal exchange in this system. The column sums in the exchange matrix are not unit values. Each country's column sum divided by its row sum defines that country's flow-of-funds ratio, or multiplier. The more central a country with respect to the spatial distribution, the higher the flow-of-funds multiplier. This location-multiplier relationship is similar to the relationship found between city or region size and the size of either the central place or economic base multiplier. Given the numbers at hand, C, the most centrally

TABLE A.1 Case 1: Distance Decay

A. The Exchange Probabilities

		INFLOWS					
Countries		A	B	C	D	E	Total
OUTFLOWS	A	.438	.219	.146	.109	.088	1.000
	B	.194	.386	.194	.129	.097	1.000
	C	.125	.188	.374	.188	.125	1.000
	D	.097	.129	.194	.386	.194	1.000
	E	.088	.109	.145	.219	.438	1.000
Total		.942	1.031	1.054	1.031	.942	5.000

B. The Distributions

		Initial	Round 1	Round 2	Round 3
COUNTRIES	A	.200	.188	.185	.184
	B	.200	.206	.208	.208
	C	.200	.212	.214	.216
	D	.200	.206	.208	.208
	E	.200	.188	.185	.184
Total		1.000	1.000	1.000	1.000

located country, experiences an inflow of 1.054 for every unit of outflow, while the spatially peripheral countries receive inflows at a rate of only 94% of outflows.

A measure of geographic potential is used to calculate the exchange probabilities for the second example:

$$P(E_{ij}) = \frac{A_i}{\sum_{i=1}^{5} A_j} \qquad (A.3)$$

where A_i is defined as market potential (Chapter 4). Market weights are assigned to the countries in the system—$A = 5, B = 4, C = 3, D = 2$, and $E = 1$—in such a way as to counteract the effect of distance decay that dominated the exchange probabilities in the first example. Because of the allocation, country A becomes the economic center of the flow system defined by the probabilities in Table A.2A, while the geographically peripheral status of country E is compounded by its low potential. Due to its high initial allocation (Table A.2B), country A has the highest flow-of-funds multiplier in the set of five countries while country E has the lowest. In the first example, the equilibrium distribution was essentially a function of total proximity because interaction was a simple function of distance decay. Here, in the second

TABLE A.2 Case 2: Market Potential

A. The Exchange Probabilities

		INFLOWS					
Countries		A	B	C	D	E	Total
OUTFLOWS	A	.575	.230	.115	.057	.023	1.000
	B	.280	.449	.168	.075	.028	1.000
	C	.208	.250	.375	.125	.042	1.000
	D	.190	.203	.228	.303	.076	1.000
	E	.200	.200	.200	.200	.200	1.000
Total		1.453	1.332	1.086	0.760	0.369	5.000

B. The Distributions

		Initial	Round 1	Round 2	Round 3	Round 4
COUNTRIES	A	.333	.347	.354	.356	.358
	B	.267	.286	.292	.293	.294
	C	.200	.202	.200	.199	.198
	D	.133	.118	.111	.110	.109
	E	.067	.047	.043	.042	.041
Total		1.000	1.000	1.000	1.000	1.000

example, the equilibrium distribution is a function of the initial distribution of funds, which by design were allocated to more than counteract the distances between countries. As in the first example, however, an equilibrium distribution is achieved (now by the fourth round of exchange) because the initial exchange probabilities were unaltered.

The invariance of the exchange probabilities employed in both of the first two examples is an unlikely prospect in real-world economic flows. As discussed by Fotheringham and Webber (1980), the flows in a set of spatial interactions must have an impact on the attractiveness of the nodes, so that in simple terms,

$$I_{ij}^{t+1} = (M_i + I_{ij}^t)(M_j + I_{ij}^t)(D_{ij}^{-k}) \qquad (A.4)$$

The interactions from an earlier round of interaction should be added net to the mass variables in a system of economic flows. Recall, for example, that net trade is a component of GDP, so a nonzero trade balance must either be added to or subtracted from national income derived internally. This relationship between flows and "size" is examined in the last example of unbalanced spatial flows. In this example, the probabilities of exchange are calculated as

$$P(E_{ij}) = \frac{A^*_i}{\sum\limits_{i=1}^{5} A^*_i} \qquad (A.5)$$

where the * denotes a recursive value of A_i, which is recalculated for each round of exchange. A net inflow is added to the previous round's value of A_i, while a net outflow is subtracted.

The initial set of exchange probabilities and the initial distribution of funds used in this example are the same as in the second example (Table A.2). Unlike both of the earlier examples, however, the exchange matrix is not invariant over time, but changes with each round as the geographic potential of each country changes as shown in Table A.3A. (See Kelton, 1984, for a review of related nonstationary

TABLE A.3   Case 3: Recursive Market Potential

A. The Exchange Probabilities after Round 1

| | INFLOWS | | | | | |
Countries	A	B	C	D	E	Total
A	.582	.240	.113	.049	.016	1.000
B	.283	.469	.165	.064	.019	1.000
C	.216	.268	.377	.110	.029	1.000
D	.204	.225	.238	.278	.055	1.000
E	.221	.228	.214	.188	.149	1.000
Total	1.506	1.430	1.107	0.689	0.268	5.000

(OUTFLOWS label on left for rows A–E)

B. The Distributions

	Initial	Round 1	Round 2	Round 3	Round 4
A	.333	.347	.360	.375	.389
B	.267	.286	.309	.333	.359
C	.200	.202	.201	.195	.184
D	.133	.118	.100	.079	.058
E	.067	.047	.030	.018	.010
Total	1.000	1.000	1.000	1.000	1.000

(COUNTRIES label on left for rows A–E)

Markov probabilities in economic flows.) The recursive calculation of the exchange probabilities yields consistently decreasing allocations of funds to countries C, D, and E, and increasing allocations to countries A and B. The fast equilibrium solutions of the first two examples do not appear in this example (Table A.3B), and eventually country A's allocation will approach 100%, and all the other countries' allocations, including country B's, will approach zero.

Each of the three cases described shows different characteristics of spatial exchange but they all illustrate the seemingly fundamental imbalance in spatial flows. Size and/or centrality determine the direction of flows, and even in the simplest case, flows are unbalanced because no two countries can be in the same location. Even when physical distance effects are largely obviated, as in the examples using either the basic or recursive geographic potential measure, a type of economic distance results that continues to guide the flows between center and periphery, however defined. All three cases represent the fundamental tendency for spatial economic flows to be unbalanced, but only the last case represents spatial disequilibrium. Obviously, the last case in particular is unrealistic in terms of being economically sustainable. Alterations in exchange rates, for example, could modify the pattern of disequilibria in the flows. However, the implications of the last case would be frightening, indeed, if it were not true that regions and countries can grow by internal as well as external processes.

A.2 EXPORT SWITCHING IN A SPATIAL CONTEXT

As described in Chapter 11, poor countries tend to be specialized in their exports and have poor terms of trade while rich countries tend to have more diverse export product structures and more favorable terms of trade. These relationships can be taken as a spatial problem and illustrated in the context of a simple export potential model. In addition, two other linked points are made in this appendix. One concerns the process of export switching, and the other concerns an equilibrium of exchange in a spatial system.

In the description of spatial flows given in Section A.1, the constant increase in geographic potential of the largest country was a result of only a single item entered into exchange. Obviously, a more realistic system of exchange would contain more than one good. Here, the system of spatial exchange is extended to more than one good, and while the basic premise of unequal spatial exchange is maintained, one possible equilibrium in a multi-good system is described. Use as a starting point the ending allocations of income described as the equilibrium condition of the case of simple distance decay in Section A.1 (Table A.1). Let per capita incomes be related by those proportions so that each country has the per capita income listed in Table A.4A. In addition, let each country have the same static population, so that aggregate national incomes are in the same proportion as per capita incomes.

TABLE A.4   Scaled Market Potentials, Equilibrium Shares, and Equilibrium Export Values

A. Scaled Market Potentials

Countries	Per Capita Incomes	GOODS		
		1	2	3
A	920	.184	0	0
B	1040	.208	.328	0
C	1080	.216	.344	1.000
D	1040	.208	.328	0
E	920	.184	0	0
Totals	5000	1.000	1.000	1.000

B. Possible Equilibrium Market Shares

Countries	GOODS		
	1	2	3
A	.343	0	0
B	.130	.426	0
C	.054	.148	1.000
D	.130	.426	0
E	.343	0	0
Totals	1.000	1.000	1.000

C. Equilibrium Export Values

Countries	Per Capita Incomes	GOODS			Total Exports
		1	2	3	
A	920	920	0	0	920
B	1040	349	691	0	1040
C	1080	148	239	693	1080
D	1040	349	691	0	1040
E	920	920	0	0	920
Totals	5000 =	2686 +	1621 +	693 =	5000

In the initial case, each country had the same allocation of income and, using the same fixed level listed in Table A.4A, it must have been 1000. Spatial exchange caused peripheral incomes, those in countries A and E, to decline, while core incomes, those in B, C, and D, increased. Country C, being in the center, had the greatest gains from spatial exchange and so has the greatest income now. This type of change in incomes could be the reason that different-ordered centers emerge from the homogeneous plain of central place theory, if trade among centers of the same order was allowed and took place on a love-of-variety basis. It is allowed here, under the hierarchical market model of international trade developed in Chapter 9. Assume that the per capita income threshold for domestic production of good 1 is very low, so that it will always be produced in every country. However, let the per capita income threshold of good 2 be 1001, and the per capita income threshold of good 3 be 1051. These thresholds limit the production of good 2 to countries B, C, and D, while good 3 only is produced in country C. Recall that, as in conventional central place theory, higher-order goods are in demand in lower-order places in the hierarchical market model of international trade, but are not in domestic supply.

Given these conditions, an export potential for each country for each good can be taken as

$$E_i = \sum_{j=1}^{5} \frac{I_j}{d_{ij}} \qquad (A.6)$$

where E_i is the export potential of a country, I_j is the per capita income of an export market, and d_{ij} is a measure of distance between the exporting country and the importing country. As in section A.1, a country can export to itself. The values of E_i can be scaled to sum to one, so that

$$pE_i = \frac{E_i}{\sum_{i=1}^{5} E_i} \qquad (A.7)$$

where pE_i is a country's potential share of the market for any good.

Potential market shares are listed in Table A.4A. Each country has a potential share of the market for good 1, but only countries B, C, and D have sufficient domestic market thresholds to supply good 2, and only country C can supply good 3. Country C, due to its combination of maximum income and accessibility, has the greatest potential share of every market. Countries A and E, due to their combinations of peripheral location and lowest incomes, have the smallest potential share of the market for their only export good. The listing of potential market shares in Table A.4A suggests some of the characteristics of international trade described in Chapter 11. First of all, the poorer countries in the example, like poorer countries in the real world, are limited in their export variety. Second, in addition to the commodity concentration of the poor countries, these countries are faced with poor terms of trade. Implicitly, higher-order goods have higher unit prices than lower-order goods, otherwise income thresholds would be meaningless. In this case, again as in the real world, poorer countries are exporting a good with a low unit value and importing goods with higher unit values, yielding poor terms of trade.

Despite the poor terms of trade faced by the peripheral countries in the example, an equilibrium in trade can be achieved by export switching. A characteristic of the export cycle is that richer countries abandon lower-value products in export for higher-valued ones (Balassa, 1983). Poorer countries then inherit the export products cast off by the richer countries in an export switching process. The process is top-down because the richer countries hold the initiative. For the rich country, an export switching rule could be

$$\frac{\Delta M_i}{\Delta M_j} > 0 \quad \text{if} \quad \frac{rM_i}{rM_j} > \frac{cM_i}{cM_j} \qquad (A.8)$$

where ΔM is a change in exports to a market, rM is the the unit price paid in the market, and cM is the cost of supplying the market. Obviously, the advantage of switching from one export to another must outweigh any costs incurred.

Assuming the rate of unit price increase is less than the unit cost increase in switching exports from lower- to higher-order goods, then it could be that country C would lessen its exports of goods 1 and 2 and raise its exports of good 3. In turn, countries B and D would inherit much of country A's potential share of the market for good 2. As countries B and D reallocate resources from the export of good 1 to the export of good 2, countries A and E gain market share in the lowest-order good. A possible equilibrium of potential market shares is given in Table A.4B. Country C has not completely abandoned export of any of the three goods, but has yielded market share to its competitors in the two lower-order goods. In a like manner, countries B and D have yielded market share in good 1 to countries A and E in favor of concentrating their efforts in exporting good 2.

The export values resulting from the equilibrium export market shares are given in Table A.4C. Each country exports, including to its own market, a per capita value just equal to its per capita income. The values do not imply autarky, even in countries A and E, because each country partakes in both interindustry trade and intraindustry trade, with only the exception of good 3, which is produced only in country C. This solution of equilibrium values is a stable one if the system remains closed. Countries cannot lose per capita income due to trade. However, they cannot gain income either. While the system of exchange is in equilibrium, it remains unequal.

A.3 TEMPORAL AND SPATIAL DISCOUNTING

As described in Chapter 7, part of a loan's interest rate is a function of the time value of money. Basically, the use of $100 today is conventionally taken as having a higher value than the use of $100 tomorrow, and the use of $100 tomorrow is taken as having a higher value than $100 in one week's time, and so on. A common way to measure the time value of money is to calculate the *present value* of a sum that will be held in the future. The present value of a future sum, PVS, can be calculated as:

$$PVS = \frac{S}{(1 + r)^t} \qquad (A.9)$$

where S is the sum, t is a time period, and r is an interest rate, or rate of discount.

The interplay between the interest rate and the length of time until a sum of money is received affects the present value of the sum, unless the sum is held immediately (Table A.5). Given three interest rates of 1%, 5%, and 10%, the present value of a future sum varies dramatically over just four years. After only one year, the present value of $100 varies by about $8 between the 1% rate and the 10% rate. At the end of four years, the difference is close to $28. With respect to time alone, a discount rate of 1% reduces the present value of $100 in four years to $96.10, while a discount rate of 10% makes $100 in four years time worth only $68.30 today. The values in parentheses in Table A.5 are the amounts of money needed in the future to provide $100 of present value. For example, if the discount rate is 1%, then $104.06 in four years has a present value of $100 today, but if the discount rate is 10%, then one would require $146.41 in four years to compensate the forgone use of $100 today.

Temporal discounting is well known and taken for granted. There is some evidence of a type of spatial discounting as well. Lösch (1954), for example, found that the discount rate varied between Federal Reserve Bank districts in the United States. Further, he found a consistent increase with distance in the interest rates charged on the loans of banks within Texas. One type of spatial variation in interest rates is illustrated in Table A.6A, using the same set of hypothetical countries, A-E, used in Sections A.1 and A.2. In this case, the spatial discount is due to an increase in transaction costs with distance. The transaction costs are taken to be spatially compound, so that

$$PVS = \frac{S}{(1 + r)^c} \tag{A.10}$$

where r is 5% (for purposes of this example) and c is the sum of *connectivities*, or adjacencies, used as unit distances between lending and borrowing countries. The result of the spatially compounded discounting is a steep reduction over distance in the present value of a $100 loan. As the present values decrease from $100, an offset would be required for lending to take place in a foreign country, and the offset would increase monotonically with distance.

An alternative form of spatial discount can occur as a negative function of distance from the Core. Webber (1972) has suggested that uncertainty in the economy increases with distance from the Core, so interest rates should increase as well. Lenders would require an interest premium to offset the uncertainty. Conceptually, uncertainty cannot be quantified in the same way as risk. Risks have calculable probabilities while uncertain events do not. However, risk-equivalent values of uncertainty frequently are estimated for practical purposes. Table A.6B illustrates spatial discounting that is a function of distance from the Core. Only one row is necessary in this case because all lenders, regardless of origin, face the same spatial array of discounts. Spatial discounting with respect to the Core, regardless of a loan's origin, provides an explanation of capital flight (see Chapter 7).

TABLE A.5 Temporal Discounting*

Temporally Discounted Value of $100

Time	Discount Rates		
	1%	**5%**	**10%**
Current (0)	100.00 (100.00)	100.00 (100.00)	100.00 (100.00)
In 1 year	99.01 (101.00)	95.24 (105.00)	90.91 (110.00)
In 2 years	98.03 (102.01)	90.70 (110.25)	82.64 (121.00)
In 3 years	97.06 (103.03)	86.38 (115.76)	75.13 (133.10)
In 4 years	95.15 (104.06)	78.35 (121.55)	62.09 (146.41)

* Compensation values in parentheses.

TABLE A.6 Spatial Discounting

A. Spatial Discounting as a Function of Distance from a Loan's Origin

		BORROWERS			
Countries	**A**	**B**	**C**	**D**	**E**
LENDERS A	100.00	95.24	90.70	86.38	82.27
B	95.24	100.00	95.24	90.70	86.38
C	90.70	95.24	100.00	95.24	90.70
D	86.38	90.70	95.24	100.00	95.24
E	82.27	86.38	90.70	95.24	100.00

B. Spatial Discounting as a Function of Distance from the Core

		BORROWERS			
Countries	**A**	**B**	**C**	**D**	**E**
All Lenders	90.70	95.24	100.00	95.24	90.70

Whether spatial discounting is based on distance from a loan's origin or from the Core, peripheral regions face a relative shortage of foreign lending compared to regions in the Core. If the spatial discount is a function of distance from the loan's origin, borrowers in the center of the spatial economy can offer lower average offsets to lenders than borrowers in the Periphery can offer. If the spatial discount is a function of distance from the Core, than even peripheral lenders would prefer lending to the Core rather than lending in their peripheral country. Both spatial cases provide explanations of shortages of foreign finance in peripheral countries unless governments guarantee that the loans will be repaid. Government guarantees are alternative offsets to the financial ones required by the spatial discounts.

REFERENCES

Balassa, B. 1983. *The Newly Industrializing Countries in the World Economy* (New York: Pergamon).

Fotheringham, A., and M. Webber. 1980. "Spatial Structure and the Parameters of Spatial Interaction Models." *Geographical Analysis* 12: 33–46.

Kelton, C. 1984. "Nonstationary Markov Modeling: An Application to Wage-Influenced Industrial Relocation." *International Regional Science Review* 9: 75–90.

Lee, T., G. Judge, and A. Zellner. 1977. *Estimating the Parameters of the Markov Probability Model from Aggregate Time Series Data.* 2d ed. (Amsterdam: North-Holland).

Lösch, A. 1954. *The Economics of Location.* 2d rev. ed. Translated from the German by W. Woglom with W. Stolper (New Haven, Connecticut: Yale University Press).

Schneider, D., M. Steeg, and F. Young. 1982. *Linear Algebra: A Concrete Introduction* (New York: Macmillan).

Webber, M. 1972. *Impact of Uncertainty on Location* (Cambridge, Massachusetts: MIT Press).

Author Index

Subject Index

Printed and bound in Singapore by Kin Keong Printing Co. Pte. Ltd.